Overcoming Parent–Child

Contact Problems

Overcoming Parent–Child Contact Problems

Family-Based Interventions for Resistance, Rejection, and Alienation

EDITED BY ABIGAIL M. JUDGE

ROBIN M. DEUTSCH

OXFORD
UNIVERSITY PRESS

OXFORD
UNIVERSITY PRESS

Oxford University Press is a department of the University of Oxford. It furthers
the University's objective of excellence in research, scholarship, and education
by publishing worldwide. Oxford is a registered trade mark of Oxford University
Press in the UK and certain other countries.

Published in the United States of America by Oxford University Press
198 Madison Avenue, New York, NY 10016, United States of America.

© Oxford University Press 2017

CIP data is on file at the Library of Congress
ISBN 978-0-19-023520-8

CONTENTS

Acknowledgments vii
About the Editors ix
Contributors xi

1. Introduction 1
   Leslie M. Drozd and Nicholas Bala

PART I Family-Based Interventions: Indicators, Models, and Clinical Challenges

2. Clinical Decision-Making in Parent–Child Contact Problem Cases: Tailoring the Intervention to the Family's Needs 13
   Barbara J. Fidler and Peggie Ward

3. The Current Status of Outpatient Approaches to Parent–Child Contact Problems 63
   Shely Polak and John A. Moran

4. More Than Words: The Use of Experiential Therapies in the Treatment of Families With Parent–Child Contact Problems and Parental Alienation 91
   Abigail M. Judge and Rebecca Bailey

5. The Perfect Storm: High-Conflict Family Dynamics, Complex Therapist Reactions, and Suggestions for Clinical Management 107
   Abigail M. Judge and Peggie Ward

PART II The *Overcoming Barriers* Approach

6. Overview of the *Overcoming Barriers* Approach 131
   Peggie Ward, Robin M. Deutsch, and Matthew J. Sullivan

7. Management of the Camp Experience: The Integration of the Milieu and the Clinical Team 152
   Carole Blane, M. Tyler Sullivan, Daniel M. Wolfson, and Abigail M. Judge

8. "East Group": Group Work With Favored Parents 171
Peggie Ward

9. "West Group": Group Interventions for Rejected Parents 193
Matthew J. Sullivan

10. "Common Ground": The Children's Group 211
Robin M. Deutsch, Abigail M. Judge, and Barbara J. Fidler

11. Coparenting, Parenting, and Child-Focused Family Interventions 222
Matthew J. Sullivan, Robin M. Deutsch, and Peggie Ward

12. Translating the Overcoming Barriers Approach to Outpatient Settings 243
Barbara J. Fidler, Peggie Ward, and Robin M. Deutsch

13. Program Evaluation, Training, and Dissemination 277
Michael Saini and Robin M. Deutsch

14. Conclusion 307
Janet R. Johnston

Index 325

ACKNOWLEDGMENTS

Dr. Abigail Judge would like to acknowledge the developers of Overcoming Barriers Family Camp (OBFC), Drs. Peggie Ward, Matt Sullivan, and Robin Deutsch, who so graciously welcomed me aboard their clinical team. To my mentor and coeditor, Robin Deutsch, thank you for the initial invitation to work at OBFC during my postdoctoral fellowship and for the many collaborations that have followed, especially this book.

Dr. Robin Deutsch would like to acknowledge the founders of Overcoming Barriers. To Carole Blane, Jim Mendell, Dr. Matt Sullivan, and Dr. Peggie Ward, thank you for your vision, passion, and constancy. To my coeditor, Abigail Judge, thank you for joining me in every step of this venture from simple notion to completed volume.

Although this volume describes OBFC (as well as other family-based interventions), we wish to distinguish the camp from its parent organization, Overcoming Barriers. The latter is a 501(c)(3) nonprofit organization created to promote children's healthy relationships with their parents in situations where a child is at risk of losing a relationship with a parent because of family conflict following high-conflict divorce. In addition to hosting OBFC, Overcoming Barriers facilitates professional trainings and provides resources to families.

The editors gratefully acknowledge the leadership of Overcoming Barriers and OBFC and, in particular, the clinicians and camp staff who have worked tirelessly and with great sensitivity at the program from its inception in 2008. Without the commitment of these dedicated professionals we would not have the knowledge, experience, and understanding to create this book.

Finally, to the families who, willingly or not, entrusted themselves to us and taught us how to respond to the complexities of their family situations, we express our most sincere gratitude.

Abigail M. Judge, Ph.D., is a clinical and child and family forensic psychologist. Dr. Judge maintains a private practice in Cambridge, MA, is a forensic consultant at the Law and Psychiatry Service at the Massachusetts General Hospital, and holds an academic appointment at the Harvard Medical School. Dr. Judge provides psychotherapy, consultation, forensic evaluation, expert witness testimony, and reunification intervention. Dr. Judge has implemented intensive models of family-based reunification following high-conflict divorce as a member of the clinical team at Overcoming Barriers Family Camp and an associate clinician at Transitioning Families. Dr. Judge publishes on topics at the interface of adolescent development and the legal system, including youth-produced sexual images ("sexting"), domestic minor sex trafficking, and family reunification. She coedited the book *Adolescent Sexual Behavior in the Digital Age: Considerations for Clinicians, Legal Professionals and Educators*, published by Oxford University Press in 2014, and she presents widely to schools, mental health professionals, and parent groups on related topics.

Robin M. Deutsch, Ph.D., ABPP, is a child and family forensic psychologist board certified in couples and family practice. She is director of the Center of Excellence for Children, Families and the Law at William James College, in Newton, MA, where she developed the Certificate in Child and Family Forensic Issues and the Child and Family Evaluation Service. Formerly an associate clinical professor at Harvard Medical School and for over 20 years director of training and forensic services at the Children and the Law program at Massachusetts General Hospital, she is a founding board member of Overcoming Barriers. She provides mediation, consultation, reunification intervention, expert witness testimony, and parenting coordination services, as well as training for mental health professionals, lawyers, and judges on child custody evaluation, issues related to high-conflict divorce, and parenting coordination. She has published extensively on complex issues related to child and family adjustment, including attachment, high-conflict divorce, family reunification, parenting plans, and parenting coordination. Dr. Deutsch is on the editorial board of the *Family Court Review* and is a former president of the Association of Family and Conciliation Courts (AFCC), former president of the Massachusetts chapter of AFCC, former chair of the American Psychological Association (APA) ethics committee, and a member of both the AFCC and APA committees that developed guidelines for parenting coordinators.

CONTRIBUTORS

Rebecca Bailey, Ph.D.,
Clinical Director, Transitioning
  Families, Glen Ellen, CA
Consultant, Stable Paths, Miami, FL

Nicholas Bala, J.D., LL.M.
Faculty of Law, Queen's University,
  Kingston, ON, Canada

Carole Blane, B.A., IBCLC
Program Director, Overcoming
  Barriers, Inc., New York, NY

Robin M. Deutsch, Ph.D., ABPP
Independent Practice, Wellesley, MA
William James College, Newton, MA

Leslie M. Drozd, Ph.D.
Independent Practice, Newport
  Beach, CA

Barbara J. Fidler, Ph.D., Acc.FM.
Independent Practice, Toronto,
  ON, Canada

Janet R. Johnston, Ph.D.
Emeritus Faculty, San Jose State
  University, San Jose, CA

Abigail M. Judge, Ph.D.
Independent Practice,
  Cambridge, MA
Forensic Consultant,
  Law & Psychiatry Service,
  Massachusetts General Hospital,
  Boston, MA

John A. Moran, Ph.D.
Independent Practice, Phoenix, AZ

Shely Polak, M.S.W., R.S.W., Acc.FM.
Doctoral Candidate, Factor-
  Inwentash Faculty of Social Work,
  University of Toronto, Toronto, ON,
  Canada

Michael Saini, Ph.D.
Factor-Inwentash Faculty of
  Social Work, University of Toronto,
  Toronto, ON, Canada

M. Tyler Sullivan, B.A.
Operations Director, Overcoming
  Barriers Inc.
Juris Doctor Candidate,
  Golden Gate University
  School of Law, San Francisco, CA

Matthew J. Sullivan, Ph.D.
Independent Practice, Palo Alto, CA

Peggie Ward, Ph.D.
Coparenting Assessment Center,
  Natick, MA

Daniel M. Wolfson, M.A.
Doctoral Candidate, William
  James College Psy.D. Program,
  Newton, MA

Overcoming Parent–Child
Contact Problems

Introduction

LESLIE M. DROZD AND NICHOLAS BALA ■

There is growing recognition by professionals, by parents, and in popular culture that when parents separate or divorce, or even if they have never lived together, serious problems can arise of children resisting contact with or rejecting one parent. In these situations, often referred to as "alienation" cases, the favored parent is considered responsible for undermining the child's relationship with the other parent. It is clear, however, that there is a complex spectrum of reasons for children to resist contact with a parent, ranging from, at one end, a child's adaptive response to abuse by a rejected parent to, at the other end, the malicious influence of a parent seeking to undermine a child's relationship with the other parent because of anger over the failure of the parents' romantic relationship. The latter situation can appropriately be characterized as alienation. Alienation and related problems with postseparation parent–child relationships are subjects of intense debate and controversy involving advocacy groups, researchers and writers, and, in individual cases, the professionals, parents, and even the children involved.

One issue about which there is significant consensus is that alienation cases pose serious risks to children and cause anguish to parents. It is also widely accepted that the traditional approaches of the law and the justice system have failed to deal adequately with these cases. The law and the justice system are very blunt social instruments. The ultimate legal sanctions for violation of court orders are typically limited to seizure of property to satisfy judicially found debts or imprisonment for contempt.

It is now widely agreed that justice system professionals and mental health professionals must collaborate to develop effective, child-focused responses to noncompliance with agreements or orders about parenting. One set of responses that has been developed involves reversal of custody to allow a previously rejected parent to establish a good relationship with the child, usually with intensive mental health intervention to assist the child through the often difficult transition process (Gardner, 2001; Warshak, 2010).

While there is a role for custody reversal as a response to alienation, this process is highly intrusive and generally requires suspension of contact between the

child and the favored parent, along with the threat or reality of police enforcement, contempt, and imprisonment for former spouses (or even children) who
fail to comply with court orders. In addition to being very intrusive and often very
expensive, custody reversal does not always succeed and may further traumatize
already vulnerable children. Most significantly, this process rarely results in children establishing good relationships with both parents.

This book focuses on a different range of approaches to parent–child contact
problems that involve the family justice system and mental health professionals.
These interventions engage children and both of their parents. Such family-based
interventions use psychoeducation, treatment, and various engagement strategies to improve parent–child relationships and child outcomes. While a significant portion of the book is devoted to analysis of one particular intensive family
relationship pilot project that most of the contributors were involved with, the
Overcoming Barriers (OCB) program, these authors recognize that OCB is just
one model of a family-based program and so consider it in a broader context.

The book emphasizes the value of early assessment and intervention, given that
alienating processes thrive when a child has little or no contact with a parent.
Often the best antidote to a situation where a child is resisting contact with a parent is for the child to spend time with that parent; however, a simple judicial directive or parental agreement is often inadequate to achieve that objective. Although
early intervention is clearly preferable, the contributors recognize that this is not
always achieved or even possible, and the book discusses a range of interventions
that may be undertaken over time. It is sometimes necessary to have a series of
interventions involving both of the parents and children with the objectives of
improving understanding and relationships.

While the authors of this book recognize that there is a role for custody reversal, they feel that this response should be used only in the most severe cases (and
not even all of those). Custody reversal almost inevitably requires a court order
after an embittering trial; very rarely will a favored parent consider a settlement
that involves complete reversal of custody. One of the advantages of the family-
based approach advocated in this book is that interventions of this kind can be
the basis for settlement of litigation, which is generally preferable for resolution
of family disputes to a full trial, as it is less expensive, is less intrusive, and yields
more durable results. The family relationships approaches that are the subject of
this book thus can be very useful for judges and lawyers trying to help parents
resolve high-conflict cases without a trial though they can also be appropriate for
some cases that may be resolved by a judge after a trial.

This volume has two parts. Part I provides a conceptual foundation for parent–
child contact problems, key tenets of family intervention, and common clinical
dilemmas. In Chapter 2, "Clinical Decision-Making in Parent–Child Contact
Problem Cases: Tailoring the Intervention to the Family's Needs," Barbara Fidler
and Peggie Ward provide the conceptual framework for the entire book. They
define and explain terms and concepts, and they establish the central objective
of a family-based intervention: for each child to have a healthy and functional
relationship with both parents. Such a relationship involves the child's being able

to accept and integrate both good and bad qualities of each parent, coupled with flexible thinking, the capacity for multiple perspective taking, and good communication and problem-solving skills. Not surprisingly, these abilities are indices of mature interpersonal skills and relationships.

In Chapter 3, "The Current Status of Outpatient Approaches to Parent–child Contact Problems," Shely Polak and John Moran point out that traditional outpatient therapies do not work well for addressing parent–child contact issues in separating or divorcing families. Family courts are increasingly accepting testimony about alienation and designing orders that mandate family-based interventions to save parent–child relationships from the path of destruction that some are on.

In Chapter 4, "More Than Words: The Use of Experiential Therapies in the Treatment of Families with Parent–Child Contact Problems and Parental Alienation," Abigail Judge and Rebecca Bailey consider the theoretical and clinical literature on experiential family relationship therapies. Simply put, these are therapies that get the patient and the clinician out of the office. To the extent that these experiential therapies involve play, movement, and other physical activity, they may help the parents and the children improve self- and co-regulation within families while potentially leading to reductions in emotional reactivity. Improvements may include reduced anxiety, more constructive problem-solving, enhanced self-concept, a stronger internal locus of control, feelings of personal empowerment, greater social competence, and better interpersonal communication. Some of these therapies can lead to improved reality testing and to family members' discriminating more accurately between provocative or harmful behavior and irritation, indifference, or misattunement. Reframing behavior from being seen as dangerous to being perceived as misattuned or in need of redirection may very well promote good reality testing, reduce anxiety, and thus open doors for the development of new patterns of interaction among family members.

In Chapter 5, "The Perfect Storm: High-Conflict Family Dynamics, Complex Therapist Reactions, and Suggestions for Clinical Management," Judge and Ward write about how high-conflict cases often bring out the best and the worst in families as well as in the professionals who work with them. Such cases often involve personality disorders, high parental conflict, and complex systems involvement, in what the authors call "the perfect storm." In these circumstances, clinicians, attorneys, and judges frequently become players in the family drama, so it is important for all professionals to assess whether they are being manipulated by one or both parents and actually making a bad situation worse. Because a systems-based perspective and a team approach are essential in working with families in high conflict, scrupulous attention to inter-team dynamics is critical to preventing parallel divisive dynamics among professionals.

Part II of this book articulates the OCB approach. Ward, Robin Deutsch, and Sullivan, the founders of this approach, team up to introduce it in Chapter 6, "Overview of the Overcoming Barriers Approach." The work they do with families at the Overcoming Barriers Family Camp (OBFC) involves high-conflict cases in which one parent is often characterized as toxic, dangerous, or neglectful and the other parent as alienating. Their work involves elements of both family systems therapy and cognitive–behavioral therapy. In group work they use techniques based on learning, memory, and cognitive science. The groups are sometimes homogeneous (consisting solely of favored parents, rejected parents, or children) and sometimes heterogeneous. Some work is done in dyads, some in triads, and some with the whole family or with multiple families. The clinicians at OBFC aim to capture the rapidly changing family dynamics so they can interrupt and modify rigid, entrenched patterns. Postcamp care is critical to germinating the seeds planted at OBFC. A strong aftercare plan requires clinicians willing to work in a cohesive team model to avoid polarization and splitting reflective of the family dynamic.

Individual outpatient therapies often fail in more severe alienation cases. Overcoming Barriers is one of a number of intensive family-based programs that have been developed over the past decade to address such cases. The common thread that runs through these intensive experiences is that the work is done from a family systems perspective, since each part of the family is connected to the other. In intensive work, family members experience each other in new ways. Ward, Deutsch, and Sullivan point out that the intensive outpatient programs share common elements. For example, each program sets out to (a) repair and strengthen children's healthy relationships with both parents, (b) keep children out of the middle of their parent's conflicts, (c) address children's distorted perspectives and memories regarding rejected parents, (d) help children develop critical thinking skills and apply them to the current situation, (e) develop more effective coparent and parent–child communication, (f) confront and correct black-and-white, polarized thinking that leads to rigid and inaccurate judgments, (g) help all family members develop empathy for one another, and (h) maintain the gains made through the program with an active follow-up component.

As important as the change produced at OBFC may be, it is inaccessible to many families because of cost. One possible solution to this limitation involves training regional clinicians so that they can jump-start treatment via local intensive weekend programs. Another option involves teaching local therapists to employ the principles of "active therapy" and growth through recreational activity, which aim to disengage families from long-standing conflict by creating new experiences. The Overcoming Barriers program is dedicated to generating ongoing research that promises to find other solutions that use limited resources to solve the problem of alienation that is endemic in family courts.

In Chapter 7, "Management of the Camp Experience: Integration of the Milieu and the Clinical Team," Carole Blane, Tyler Sullivan, Daniel Wolfson, and Judge describe the OBFC experience. This experience includes the milieu, which is carefully designed to provide an emotionally and physically safe environment that removes families from the normal surroundings, distractions, memories, habits, and social groups that may support their entrenched dynamics; the new milieu allows different perspectives to develop. Those perspectives in turn allow family members to move forward, to engage in positive and cooperative activities, and to garner enough motivation to overcome negative thoughts related to the presence of resistant family members. The Overcoming Barriers Family Camp provides opportunities for parents and children to practice what they learn in psychoeducational groups by connecting positively and safely in experiences with other campers and staff. These experiences allow participants to learn that they are not alone in their difficulties. Ultimately, family members are sent home with positive memories that can help sustain agreements that they made during the intensive immersion to overcome entrenched conflicts of the past.

The two chapters that follow, Chapter 8, "'East Group': Group Work with Favored Parents," and Chapter 9, "'West Group': Group Work with Rejected Parents," Ward and Sullivan, respectively, discuss the work done in the two parent groups at OBFC. Favored parents tend to see little value in what the other parent brings to the lives of their children. These parents often share many characteristics: self-preoccupation, emotional dysregulation, a high level of mistrust, manipulativeness, "parentification" of the child, enmeshment with the child, lack of stable relationships generally, and a highly conflictual relationship with the coparent. They lack understanding of their actions and empathy for their children's place in the family dynamic. They show pervasive denial of any involvement in their children's rejection of the other parent, find conflict engaging, and are unable to let go of the other parent completely. In some cases, the favored parent has a new partner and has created a new family in which the rejected parent has no place and is seen as an intruder. Such parents enter the OBFC experience having engaged in various strategies that assure their dominance at the expense of the rejected parent and the child, including denigration of the rejected parent; limiting or interfering with the rejected parent's parenting time, mail, phone, or symbolic contact with the child, and information about the child; emotional manipulation of the child; and forming an unhealthy alliance with the child. The favored parents believe that their children like them better than the rejected parent because of their (self-perceived) exquisite attunement to them and ability to listen to and react to their children's needs, which they see as contrasting sharply with the rejected parent's inability to understand those needs. Favored parents' concerns about the rejected parent may very well have some validity. The main work with favored parents involves transforming blame of the other parent for all of their parent-child problems to acceptance of some personal responsibility, understanding the harm that their behavior does to their children, working with emotional regulation, and identifying many cognitive and memory distortions that they hold and have perpetuated in their children. Favored parents often have little if any internal motivation for changing their behavior. If they are motivated at all, it is usually by external factors such as consequences for noncompliance—in particular, the threat of further legal proceedings with the possibility of financial consequences, findings of contempt, and custody reversal.

Across the way from the favored parents at OBFC, Sullivan and his colleagues work with the rejected parents in what they call the West group. These parents come to camp believing that they are good parents whose children were turned against them by the malicious other parent. The rejected parents fail to see their contribution to the problem—and they always have a contribution. Work in the West Group concentrates on refocusing the rejected parents on what they can control and how they can move forward by shifting from being a victim to being an active participant in the change process. This transition involves a shift from helplessness and projection of the responsibility for change on others to more active and adaptive coping with the most difficult situation imaginable: their own children's rejection or refusal to have contact with them. The formula by which OCB enables this change involves maximizing enjoyment while managing and minimizing negativity (avoidance, conflict, opposition, etc.) during parenting time and avoiding any processing or discussion of the difficulties in the relationship during parent–child contact, unless it involves the management of the immediate situation.

Aftercare is critical for both the favored and rejected parents in the East and West groups and their children. Important components of this work may include work with a parent coordinator, coparenting sessions, parallel parenting, ongoing education, and the continued involvement of the courts to assure accountability. The changes in perspective initiated at camp—away from blame in favored parents and victimization in rejected parents—must be nourished and further developed. Research into the long-term efficacy of this work is ongoing.

A growing body of research shows that both high conflict and poor parenting skills—both of which are common in the families seen in OCB and other intensive immersion programs—negatively affect children. Each parent's parenting can be measured along the two dimensions of *demandingness* and *responsiveness*. In these families it is not uncommon to see one enmeshed parent (i.e., a parent with high demands and high or inconsistent responsiveness), who is frequently the favored parent, and one disengaged parent (with low demandingness and low responsiveness), who is sometimes the rejected parent, or authoritarian parent (with high demandingness and low responsiveness), who is often the rejected parent. Understanding the parent–child dynamic along these dimensions is useful in determining where to intervene with the parent–child dyad, with each parent individually, and with the coparenting dyad.

In Chapter 9, "Common Ground: The Children's Group," Deutsch, Judge, and Fidler write about the work with children at OBFP. Children in families where alienation is present and where children resist or refuse contact tend to have rigid, dependent, and enmeshed perspectives of their parents. The family system is often set up to avoid challenges to these perspectives. Avoidant behavior strongly reinforces the status quo. Without new experiences to challenge old thoughts, feelings, and behaviors, the children remain stuck with cognitive distortions and antiquated problem-solving strategies. In the children's group at OBFP, new experiences are created to seed new perspectives. Psychoeducational materials are provided as scaffolding for these new perspectives. These materials are designed to improve the children's skills for coping with interparental conflict, to develop independent thoughts and feelings in the children, and to empower them to identify and solve problems. These new skills ideally lead to improved emotional regulation and cognitive processing—all of which support the goal of the child's having new experiences that can lead to a change in perspective. Ultimately the goal in this work is to expose the children to new experiences so that they can see each of their parents more realistically and can claim their own thoughts and feelings.

In Chapter 11, Sullivan, Deutsch, and Ward write about "Coparenting, Parenting, and Child-Focused Family Interventions." The work described in this chapter begins before families arrive at the program. Families are sent to OBFC with a stipulation or a court order that states that the program's goal is to reconnect the rejected parent with the children and that mandates full and complete participation in the program. Parents must know coming into the program that they are required by the court (or agreement) to affirmatively assist the children in every aspect of the camp that will allow the children to re-establish a relationship with the rejected parent. With that foundation, the clinical team gathers essential information about the history of the family system and about external factors that are relevant to the child's rejection of a parent. For the family to be deemed appropriate for OBFC, there must be a determination that despite any of these past issues, it is in the best interests of the child to have a relationship with the rejected parent. Cases involving active and current domestic violence, substance abuse, threats of abduction, child abuse, untreated or poorly managed major mental illness, or the inability to pay for services are not appropriate for OCB work.

To participate appropriately in that work, favored parents must shift from their initial stance of protecting their children from perceived threats of emotional or physical harm to a stance in which they actively encourage contact between the children and the rejected parent. As mentioned above, their motivation for this shift comes more often than not from the court mandate that they may lose custody if they do not help their children recognize that the rejected parent has much to offer and the favored parent has made some mistakes.

The rejected parent must also come ready to participate. That means taking responsibility for past behavior (expressing understanding of its negative impact), apologizing sincerely for the behavior, and making a commitment not to engage in that behavior in the future. Further, the parent must respond to the child's usually skeptical and often derisive response to the apology in a manner that recognizes that the child's rejecting responses are understandable and acceptable. The rejected parent must reassure the child that as the relationship moves forward, the child need not worry about the past behavior's reoccurring.

The children are worked with as well at this stage. The initial work involves enabling them to focus on having an open heart and an open mind while maintaining boundaries and moving at a safe pace. Common themes in this work include helping children to be heard and understood and helping them manage their anxiety as they move from avoiding to approaching the rejected parent. This is done as a step in a desensitization process, one in which they appropriately express their anger in a manner that enables it to be accurately heard without reaction. This step opens the door to a new connection while regulating emotions.

Coparenting work is critical as well. The focus is on moving parents from high-conflict engagement to parallel engagement. Coparenting work creates a foundation for reunification with the rejected parent. The eventual goal is to establish a supported parallel parenting model that is emotionally safe for both parents in aftercare by having their engagement be highly structured and supported by a competent parenting coordinator. An additional goal is to create more manageable (i.e., more safe and functional) engagement in the coparenting interaction.

The future utility of the OCB model depends on the degree to which its basics are transferable to an outpatient setting. Fidler, Ward, and Deutsch discuss this issue in Chapter 12, "Translating the *Overcoming Barriers* Approach to Outpatient Settings." The work to be done in intensive family-based programs is mislabeled by many as "family reunification," but the more accurate description is "family reintegration." The authors describe considerations and protocols for preliminary screening, clinical intake, and contracting for an outpatient program (including the legal components); identify treatment goals; and provide an overview of various tools and resources that will help the clinician implement treatment plans customized to meet the needs of each family. Treatment goals include fostering healthy child adjustment, restoring or developing adequate parenting and coparenting skills, and removal of the child from the parental conflict. Strategies for reaching these goals include decreasing the child's feelings of fear, anger, discomfort, or anxiety about the rejected parent; expanding the perspectives of the child and parents; and shifting the child's perceptions and feelings toward a less polarized view of each parent. For the parents, strategies include decreasing parental conflict, improving individual parenting skills, and improving parent alliance. Further strategies include improving the relationships and conflict management skills of coparents, healing parent–child relationships, establishing appropriate parent–child boundaries and correct alignments, decreasing parent–child conflict, improving communication and problem-solving among all family members, and enhancing empathy and compassionate relationships.

Three components of the OCB model that are applicable in an outpatient setting include an intensive, whole-family approach; use of experiential and recreational activities; and coordinated case management plus a team approach in which clinicians coordinate their efforts. Parent coordination work is often essential to maintain accountability and the coordination of the various components of the family treatment. One size does not fit all in cases of high-conflict separation and divorce involving strained parent–child relationships. The nature and severity of the contact problem inform the differentiated clinical and legal intervention response.

In Chapter 12, "Program Evaluation, Training, and Dissemination," Michael Saini and Deutsch discuss the challenges and limitations in the research literature on OCB to date. Given that each case of strained parent–child relationships results from a complex interaction of many factors and that many cases share overlapping factors, evaluating interventions to address such relationships has been and remains complicated. To test the effectiveness of these interventions, they need to be based on a coherent and comprehensive plan. The research model set forth in this book considers several outcome variables, including the satisfaction of the children and parents engaged in the interventions; the rebuilding of strained parent–child relationships and the reduction of alienating behaviors; the improvement in communication and cooperation between the parents; children's overall anxiety and depression levels; and the children's overall adjustment after attending the interventions. Although the outcomes to date are not conclusive, the evaluation set forth in this final chapter confirms that the overall purpose of OCB should be seen as planting seeds of hope and setting families on the road to repairing strained relationships, rather than fixing strained relationships within the limited time frame of the camp.

While we believe that this book makes a convincing argument for the value of family-based interventions in cases where children are resisting contact with a parent, the authors acknowledge that there is a need for further research and program development. The Overcoming Barriers Family Camp is an important project, worthy of study and discussion, but key questions remain about its long-term effects and the possibilities for replicating and sustaining its work. These questions, however, are also very relevant to all approaches to dealing with the disquieting issues around children resisting contact with a parent, and indeed a host of issues involved in postseparation parenting.

REFERENCES

Gardner, R. A. (2001). *Therapeutic interventions for children with parental alienation syndrome.* Cresskill, NJ: Creative Therapeutic.

Warshak, R. A. (2010). Family Bridges: Using insights from social science to reconnect parents and alienated children. *Family Court Review, 48,* 48–80.

PART I

Family-Based Interventions

*Indicators, Models,
and Clinical Challenges*

Clinical Decision-Making in Parent–Child Contact Problem Cases

Tailoring the Intervention to the Family's Needs

BARBARA J. FIDLER AND PEGGIE WARD ∎

1. INTRODUCTION

Although there is little dispute about the existence of parental alienation or the reality that a child can be unduly influenced by one parent to reject the other, controversy exists in the legal and social science literature and popular media on how best to identify, assess, and respond to children resisting contact with a parent after separation or divorce.[1]

As with many issues in family law (e.g., joint legal custody, shared parenting time, overnight visits for children under 4 years old), there are polarized, strongly gendered narratives about parent–child contact problems. While each of these gendered narratives has some validity, both have significant limitations, and neither is especially helpful as a guide for improving the lives of children or their parents (Fidler, Bala, & Saini, 2013). In reality, cases of parent–child contact problems are complex and multidetermined. Courts and family law professionals need to move beyond polarized and simplistic analyses that not only fail to capture the richness and subtlety of these cases but also mirror the inflexible, "all or nothing" thinking of alienated children and their parents.

The presence of alienation does not necessarily entail the absence of child maltreatment or intimate-partner violence, or vice versa; professionals looking at parent–child contact issues do not need to consider an either/or proposition.[2] There are abused or neglected children exposed to intimate-partner violence or compromised parenting who justifiably resist contact, *and* there are alienated children whose resistance of a parent is disproportionate to the child's actual experiences with that parent and the parental separation.

Both the nature and severity of the parent–child contact problem will inform appropriate and differentiated legal and clinical responses. Legal and mental health practitioners are not immune to cognitive biases, such as the bias blind spot (being able to identify bias in others while considering oneself immune (Neal & Brodsky, 2016) or scholar-advocacy bias (using research to support advocacy) (Emery et al., 2016). Other common cognitive biases are confirmatory, recency, repetition, source, or wishful thinking bias.[3] Practitioners are advised to consider relevant multiple hypotheses about the cause of the problem as they assess each family's circumstances and dynamics. Possible hypotheses include the following:

- One parent is exhibiting parental alienating behaviors.
- One parent has exhibited a pattern of coercive or controlling violence.
- There was no pattern of violence between the parents, but one or both of them engaged in separation-instigated violence when they separated.
- Even as one parent demonstrates alienating behavior, the other parent has engaged in behavior that, while not abusive, is contributing to child's resistance of that parent.
- The child is not alienated but has a realistic basis to resist a parent because of that parent's pattern of violence, child abuse or neglect, absence, or marked insensitivity to the child's needs.
- The preferred parent is not exhibiting malicious alienating behavior but rather is overprotective, and the child's resistance to the other parent is related to a role reversal and enmeshed dynamic with the preferred parent.

In this chapter, we

- identify the continuum of parent–child contact problems in divorcing families;
- summarize key principles and components of managing first queries, preliminary screening, and clinical intake;
- discuss the tailoring of interventions to the nature and severity of the parent–child contact problem; and
- list intervention options for different types and severities of parent–child contact problems.

2. DIFFERENTIATION OF PARENT–CHILD CONTACT PROBLEMS

Since the initial contributions of Richard Gardner (1998) our conceptualization of parent–child contact problems has evolved and become more nuanced. A child may resist or reject a parent to varying degrees and for many reasons or a combination of reasons.

Joan Kelly and Janet Johnston (2001) describe a systems-based, multifactor model that they and their colleagues have developed to explain why some children resist contact or reject a parent and remain aligned with the other parent (Figure 2.1). They identify seven interacting factors that create a "perfect storm" for a continuum of parent–child contact problems, not just alienation:

1. The alienating behavior and motivation of the aligned parent.
2. The rejected parent's inept parenting and counterrejecting behavior (before or after the rejection).
3. Domestic violence or abuse and child abuse or neglect.
4. Chronic litigation, which typically includes "tribal warfare" involving aligned personal sources (extended family, friends, new partners, and educational, mental health, or legal professionals).
5. Sibling dynamics and pressures.
6. A vulnerable child (temperament style, dependent, anxious, fearful, emotionally troubled, and with poor coping and reality testing).
7. Developmental factors (e.g., age-appropriate separation anxiety or response to conflict consistent with the cognitive development of children aged 8–15 years).

While all alienation cases involve high conflict, including lack of or ineffective coparenting communication, not all high-conflict cases involve alienation or

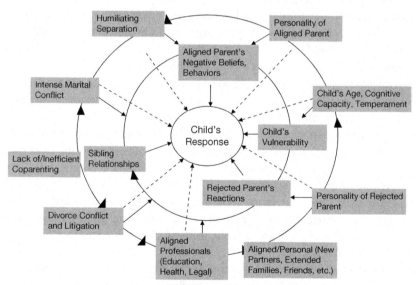

Figure 2.1 A Reformulated Model of Parent–Child Contact Problems.
Adapted from Kelly, J., & Johnston, J. (2001). The alienated child: A reformulation of parental alienation syndrome. *Family Court Review, 39*, 249–266, with permission of John Wiley and Sons.

parent–child contact problems. In addition, although it is common for separating parents to exhibit parental alienating behaviors to some extent, not all children exposed to parental conflict, bad-mouthing, or undermining will respond by resisting or rejecting a parent (Johnston, 1993; Johnston, Walters, & Olesen, 2005b).

Parent–child contact problems can be conceptualized on a continuum: affinity, alignment,[4] realistic or justified rejection (realistic estrangement), and unjustified rejection (alienation). Each type of contact problem can vary in intensity from mild to moderate to severe.

2.1. Affinity and Alignment

A child, while maintaining contact with both parents, may have an *affinity* toward one parent because of the age of the child, temperament style, gender identification, familiarity, having spent more time with that parent, or shared interests. For example, a younger child may experience normal separation anxiety from or a preference for the opposite-gender parent, while an older child may prefer the same-gender parent. The less favored parent may then blame the favored parent for alienating, say, the 3-year-old child who is exhibiting developmentally expected separation anxiety, while the favored parent may blame the other parent for poor or even abusive parenting and advocate on behalf of the child's right to refuse contact. In this situation of what may be a mild contact problem, early identification and parent education may prevent problems from escalating. For a teenager, normal adolescent rebellion may involve playing one parent off against the other or preferring the parent who makes fewer demands or offers more material goods. Such ebbs and flows of preferences (affinity) and gender identification occur in divorced and nondivorced families alike; they are normal and developmentally expected, not the result of alienation processes.

An *alignment* occurs when the child has an alliance with one parent. This alliance may develop before, during, or after separation, in response to the other parent's absence or minimal involvement in parenting, inexperience, insensitivity, or other poor parenting, even if these shortcomings do not reach the level of abuse or neglect. Alignments may also develop for divorce-specific reasons, as when a child becomes angry or upset with a parent who leaves the family, starts a new relationship, or causes the parent left behind to feel betrayed, depressed, or angry. The child's upset or moral indignation at the departed parent's behavior and subsequent resistance to seeing that parent may be an understandable reaction to the separation, at least initially. In these circumstances, the child copes with the parental separation and loyalty conflict by identifying and siding with the "left parent" who feels hurt and abandoned. Also, children may form alignments in response to new or ongoing parental conflicts, such as one parent's desire to relocate or the parents' disagreements over child or spousal support or property.

As children mature cognitively, they move from egocentric, concrete reasoning to the having the capacity to consider different perspectives simultaneously.

Younger children tend to embrace the perspective of the parent they are with at the time, with the result that they sometimes display shifting allegiances. With maturation, children acquire the capacity for reflexive thought ("I know that you know that I know") and are able to gradually retain more than one perspective at a time.

Children 9–11 years old are particularly vulnerable to getting caught in their parents' conflicts, are prone to take sides, and are at greater risk than younger children for becoming alienated. To cope with persistent and contradictory information, distress, and confusion, the latency-age child may move from shifting allegiances with each change in care to an alignment with one parent, sometimes accompanied by either resistance or refusal to spend time with the other parent. The child who does this may resort to polarized thinking, tending to perceive the situation in all-or-nothing terms: One parent is all (or mostly) good, while the other is all (or mostly) bad. Without early intervention and correction, this "reasoning" can become fixed and grow to have a life of its own, even after the negative influence of the aligned parent has abated (if it ever does).

As with affinity, alignment does not involve complete rejection of a parent but results in resistance or reluctance to have contact. The transition from one home to the other may be difficult for the child. However, the child often settles down soon after the transition, though the parents may misinterpret their child's behavioral difficulties during transitions and incorrectly blame the other parent for them. In high-conflict separations, both affinity and alignment are risk factors for alienation. In the absence of appropriate legal or clinical interventions, either one can escalate or develop into alienation, sometimes quickly.

2.2. Justified Rejection (Realistic Estrangement)

In justified rejection, the rejected parent may have been abusive or violent with the other parent (with causes that may include substance or alcohol abuse, untreated mental illness, or personality disorder), been abusive or neglectful with the child, been physically or emotionally absent in the child's life, or exhibited significantly inept parenting. The child's resistance to contact in these circumstances is justified *primarily*, though not always exclusively, by the rejected parent's actions. The resistance is an adaptive mechanism for coping with the conflict or trauma.

In cases of justified rejection, the preferred parent genuinely believes contact with the other parent is likely to be harmful to the child. While protective parents' concerns may be justified, and their restrictive gatekeeping[5] may even appear to undermine the child's relationship with the other parent, the child's reaction to the rejected parent is relatively independent of and occurs irrespective of the preferred parent's attitudes and behavior. What differentiates justified rejection from alienation is the lack of a previous relationship (or an underdeveloped relationship) or the presence of violent, truly abusive behavior toward the child, significantly compromised parenting, or both.

As is often observed in child protection cases, children exposed to intimate-partner violence or child abuse or neglect do not necessarily exhibit resistance or rejection and instead want contact with the offending parent. Unlike alienated children, these children may exhibit symptoms of anxiety, depression, trauma, or post-traumatic stress disorder (PTSD) rather than a disproportionate or unjustified reaction to their actual experience with a parent, as occurs in alienation cases.

Adding to the complexity of justified rejection, in some instances the favored parent's reactions, while protective and not malicious or intentionally alienating, may be disproportionate to the circumstances and counterproductive (Drozd & Olesen, 2004). In protecting the child, the favored parent projects her or his own experiences of distress or anger about the other parent onto the child. The parent's reactions to the child's experiences may involve distortions or even paranoia, resulting in compromised, possibly emotionally harmful parenting despite the intention to protect the child (Friedlander & Walters, 2010; Johnston, Roseby, & Kuehnle, 2009; Johnston et al., 2005b).

2.3. Alienation

A child who resists or rejects a parent because of alienation is exhibiting an unjustified response resulting from a complex interplay of the many factors depicted in Figure 2.1. The alienated child as defined by Kelly and Johnston (2001) is "a child who freely and persistently expresses unreasonable negative feelings and beliefs (such as anger, hatred, rejection, and/or fear) toward a parent that are disproportionate to their actual experience of that parent" (p. 251). Warshak (2006) expands the definition, noting that alienation is a "disturbance in which children, usually in the context of sharing a parent's negative attitudes, suffer unreasonable aversion to a person or persons with whom they formerly enjoyed normal relationships or with whom they would normally develop affectionate relationships" (p. 306). Appendix 2.B lists typical behaviors exhibited by an alienated child, the favored parent, and the rejected parent.

In alienation cases, the child's resistance or rejection is *primarily*, though rarely exclusively, the result of the alienating parent's conduct, conscious or unconscious, subtle or obvious, direct or indirect. Without the parental alienating behaviors exhibited by the favored parent, siblings, or extended family, the child would not have resisted or rejected the parent to the same extent. Darnall (1998) identifies three types of alienating parents with mild, moderate, and severe cases:

1. *Naive alienators* are passive about the relationship with the other parent and occasionally say or do something to alienate or reinforce alienation.
2. *Active alienators* cope with their hurt and anger by intermittently exhibiting alienating behaviors triggered by emotional vulnerability or poor impulse control; however, they know what they are doing is wrong.
3. *Obsessed alienators,* feeling narcissistically wounded, persistently want to hurt the other parent by destroying that parent's relationship with the child; they perceive their behavior as justified and rarely show empathy, self-control, or insight.

The favored parent, to varying degrees, may feel genuinely concerned for the child's emotional or physical safety and intentionally protective; however, the favored parent's concerns are unfounded, and there is no real risk to the child from the other parent. In the more severe cases, the favored parent may have a personality disorder or mental illness marked by disordered thinking or paranoia, such that their protective behavior is genuinely motivated but misguided. The favored parent, often the mother, as a result of her own earlier experiences, may be predisposed to certain vulnerabilities and be unable to sufficiently distinguish a perceived from an actual risk to the child. Unable to differentiate her own needs and experiences from her child's, she projects her own fears and anxieties onto the child. Although this parent may be vulnerable and have a genuine belief that the child is at risk, this can be an alienation case and may pose a significant risk to the child.

In other cases—notably, severe alienation—the alienating parent, feeling above the law and acting with malice, deliberately fabricates or knowingly makes unfounded abuse allegations to intentionally discourage, interfere with, or prevent the child's contact with the other parent. The alienating behaviors can also be more subtle or indirect. Personality disorders, mental illness or vengeance are likely contributors to the alienating parent's irrational thinking or knowingly fabricated allegations (Johnston & Campbell, 1988; Johnston, Walters, & Olesen, 2005c; Miller, 2013).

Sometimes the alienating parent is also a perpetrator of intimate-partner violence or maltreatment, and the child, through a process of identification with the aggressor, becomes alienated without justification from the victimized and now rejected parent, typically the mother (Johnston et al., 2005b). In these cases, the parental alienating behaviors and strategies are part of an abusive pattern and may result from mental illness, including substance or alcohol abuse or a personality disorder. Some domestic violence activists, who generally reject the reality or concept of alienation, maintain that behavior exhibited by the father is not alienating per se but rather is manipulation and control evident in an abusive pattern of coercive controlling violence (Meier, 2009).

In some cases, the child may develop an anxious and phobia-like response. As with phobias in general, the continued avoidance of the anxiety-provoking circumstances (parental conflict, loyalty bind) or feared object (the rejected parent), known as "anticipatory anxiety," reinforces the child's avoidance and rejection. The child's resistance or refusal also is reinforced by the preferred parent's approval and extra attention. A mutually escalating cycle of fear and anxiety develops between the child and the favored parent: the more upset the child is, the more protective and concerned the parent is, which in turn escalates the child's reactions, and so on. Separated high-conflict parents often have no direct contact and rely on secondhand information, including from their child, to form opinions about each other. Learning theory, supported by research, indicates that correction (extinction) of the avoidance is extremely difficult and requires exposure and systematic desensitization to the avoided circumstance or feared object, as will be discussed further in Chapters 9 and 12.

In alienation, the favored parent does not support the child's relationship with the rejected parent. The favored parent does not encourage the child to see or accept both the good and not so good in the other parent. Nor does the favored parent require the child to sort out difficulties with the other parent. This behavior typically differs from the favored parent's expectations when the child complains about a friend, teacher, coach, or another family member, even the favored parent. Favored parents do not sufficiently appreciate that avoidance or severing ties is an unhealthy approach to relationship problems. This disconnect in the favored parent's expectations gives the child the distinct impression that the child's relationship with the rejected parent is less important than relationships with other individuals. Moreover, the favored parent exploits the rejected parent's shortcomings and purports to leave the decision about whether to have contact up to the child, thereby sending a strong message that the relationship is unimportant. Interestingly, it is not uncommon for the favored parent who is seemingly noncommittal or lenient when it comes to the child's seeing the other parent to assert firm expectations with the child in other respects, such as doing homework, being polite with relatives and neighbors, doing chores, and so on.

Good parenting includes not only listening and validating a child's feelings but also helping the child appreciate other people's perspectives, resolving (not avoiding) conflicts, setting and following through with reasonable age-appropriate expectations, and modeling compassion, empathy, and forgiveness. These practices are not part of the favored parent's repertoire with the rejected parent.

2.4. Mixed or Hybrid Cases

Defining a mixed or hybrid case poses significant challenges for practitioners when assessing and then identifying the most appropriate intervention in a parent–child contact case. Some practitioners maintain that most cases are hybrids, while pure cases (those that include only parental alienating behavior by the favored parent or only intimate-partner violence or maltreatment by the rejected parent) are far less common (Friedlander & Walters, 2010; Garber, 2014). Empirical data on the question, however, are lacking. Even if hybrid cases are more prevalent than pure cases, practitioners must exercise caution about making assumptions or falling prey to confirmatory bias based on this generalization (Martindale, 2005). Miller (2013) notes that group data may be relied on for hypothesis generation but not for hypothesis confirmation.

Another problem with the mixed or hybrid category is that it is too often applied indiscriminately as a catch-all. This practice muddies the water for proper identification and appropriate intervention, particularly in moderate and severe cases of alienation, where some legal and clinical practitioners may resist making the hard calls (Miller, 2013).

Notwithstanding the lack of clarity and consensus about definition and prevalence, most practitioners agree that both pure and hybrid cases exist. As we elaborate further on, with mild and many moderate cases, interventions may be similar for alienation and justified rejection cases. However, in more severe cases, different legal and clinical interventions will be necessary, depending on whether the contact problem results primarily from an alienation or a justified rejection dynamic.

It is easier to identify what a mixed case is not than what it is. Mixed cases do not include affinity due to a normal developmental preference or shared interests, nor do they include the child's having an underdeveloped relationship with a parent because of that parent's absence or marked lack of involvement. Research and anecdotal reports indicate that enmeshment, boundary diffusion (role reversal), and overinvolved parenting are common in alienation cases (Friedlander & Walters, 2010; Garber, 2011; Johnston et al., 2009). In high-conflict cases, these parent–child relationship dynamics are a "red flag"—an early risk factor. Accordingly, cases involving enmeshed, overinvolved parenting are not mixed or hybrid in the same way that cases involving alienation and justified rejection may be (Fidler, Bala, & Saini, 2013). Bona fide hybrid cases will have elements of alienation and justified rejection; the degree to which these elements are mixed may vary. Like pure cases of alignment, alienation, and justified rejection, hybrid cases may manifest with varying degrees of severity.

The rejected parent's behavior can exacerbate the child's resistance or rejection. When assessing and correctly identifying a mixed case (or any parent–child contact problem), it is important to distinguish between the rejected parent's causal and reactive inappropriate or counterproductive behavior. The child may have previously enjoyed a good relationship with the parent, accommodating for any shortfalls in the parent's personality or parenting. The rejected parent may even have parented well or within acceptable limits before the contact problem began. However, in some cases, the child's reaction to previously accepted parenting limitations worsens after separation, when the other parent is not there to support the parent or buffer the child's reaction, resulting in the child's discomfort with or resistance to the now rejected parent. In other cases, the child may develop an embellished or distorted view of what he or she previously saw as a modest and known parenting flaw. And in many cases, the parent's reaction to the child's provocative behavior and rejection exacerbates the existing alienation process (Johnston et al., 2009; Warshak, 2010a).

Poor or abusive parenting, even if reactive, cannot be condoned; the negative impact on the child's feelings and relationship with the parent exhibiting that behavior is the same whether the precipitating incident or problematic parenting is causal or reactive. Still, extreme behaviors, including aggression and rudeness, exhibited by an alienated child who feels inappropriately empowered and entitled are likely to provoke or "throw off" even the most patient and caring of parents, who may have a "fight, flight, or freeze" reaction to the distress and loss they are experiencing. Careful assessment is necessary to differentiate the dispositional and situational nature of the rejected parent's emotional and behavioral reactions (Miller, 2013).

Each case must be evaluated on its own merits. When attempting to differentiate alienation from justified rejection, it is important to recognize that lapses in good parenting are commonplace; there are no perfect parents. Incidents of poor parenting by the rejected parent may occur in some, maybe even most (but not necessarily all), cases of alienation. However, poor parenting by a rejected parent in an alienation case, even when reactive to the alienation, does *not* rise to the level of neglect, emotional or physical abuse, or significantly compromised parenting. When it does rise to that level, the identification should not be alienation or even a hybrid case, but rather justified rejection. As noted above, it is primarily, though not exclusively, the disproportionate reaction of the child in combination with the parental alienating behavior that makes the contact problem alienation.

When making these sometimes fine distinctions, a key factor to consider is how the favored parent responds or does not respond to inevitable instances of poor parenting by the rejected parent. In alienation, choosing not to quell or provide an alternate more positive explanation for the child to consider, the favored parent puts a spin on the rejected parent's flaws, exaggerating and repeating them. "Legends" develop about the rejected parent, and the child is influenced to believe that parent is unworthy and in some cases dangerous, even abusive. Identifying a case as mixed or hybrid does not absolve the favored parent or minimize that parent's role in the parent–child contact problem. Intervention will necessarily involve both parents, just as it will in cases identified as either alienation or realistic estrangement.

3. THE CLINICAL DIFFERENTIATION PROCESS

3.1. Overview

Differentiating the nature and severity of the parent–child contact problem is necessary for identifying the interventions likely to be most suitable for the family's needs. High-conflict cases involving allegations of abuse and alienation require practitioners who have considerable clinical experience and specialized training, often working in consultation with their peers. In this section we summarize the clinical differentiation process, beginning with protocols for the initial referral query, preliminary screening, and subsequent clinical intake and followed by the matching process—tailoring the intervention to the nature and severity of the contact problem.

Education and/or therapy[6] are likely to be appropriate options for mild and some moderate parent-child contact problem cases regardless of the nature of the resistance while the status quo custodial arrangements continue (Johnston, Roseby & Kuehnle, 2009; Johnston, Walters & Friedlander, 2001), most of these cases benefiting from judicial case management. Families on the more difficult end of the moderate spectrum or who have moved into the severe arena require more intensive interventions. These might include use of a coordinated team with significant specialized training as well as clinical and judicial case management. A multiday "intensive 'jump-start' intervention" may help the family restructure alignments and repair the parent–child contact problem. Aftercare follow-up therapy using the outpatient model discussed in Chapter 12 is almost always necessary after an intensive intervention. The most severe cases, however, may require an interim or permanent change in custody arrangements, coupled with an interruption of contact with the alienating parent and an educational or therapeutic intervention (or both) to assist with the custody transition (Johnston & Goldman, 2010; Kelly & Johnston, 2001; Warshak, 2010a). Another option in the most severe cases is to give up on efforts to reunite the parent and child or repair their relationship and suspend the enforcement of court orders for parenting time that is not occurring (possibly putting some mechanisms in place for future contact).

Once the initial screening has occurred or after the more in-depth clinical intake, a case may be accepted for treatment or referred onward; not all cases must be or ought to be accepted. The clinician may choose to refer one or both parents to another, more experienced clinician for a custody evaluation, legal advice, or both; alternatively, the clinician may make a mandatory child protection report.

In some cases presenting with considerable complexity, including involvement of multiple agencies and previous unsuccessful therapeutic efforts, the clinician, wise to the risks of repeating failed interventions, may choose to recommend a brief, focused family consultation with the clinician, after which he or she will provide the parents and lawyers (if any) with recommendations about intervention options best suited to the family's needs. This procedure is not a custody evaluation or even a thorough clinical assessment. The clinician obtains considerable information derived from intake questionnaires, meetings with the parents (separately and, if possible, together) and the children and gathers key information from collateral sources (e.g., a guardian ad litem, custody evaluator, child protection agency, or a previous or current therapist). This clinical "look and see" consultation, which occurs prior to accepting the case for treatment, may be the most prudent and sensible approach in cases where either the parents and lawyers are unsure which intervention is most appropriate or in complex cases where therapy may have been attempted unsuccessfully. The longer the contact problem persists, the worse it becomes and the harder it is to remedy. Consequently, it is prudent to be cautious when accepting referrals for family reunification therapy, given the high rate of treatment failures in moderate and severe cases that only serve to exacerbate the contact problem and in turn cause delays in identifying more appropriate legal or clinical interventions.

3.2. Managing Initial Referral Queries: Preliminary Screening

Referrals for intervention in cases of parent–child contact problems may come from many sources. They often come from one parent, and occasionally from both parents. Referrals may also come from mental health professionals, one or both parents' lawyers, the child's lawyer, a guardian ad litem, a custody evaluator, the court, a mediator, or a parenting coordinator. The protocol for managing initial queries will vary depending on the referral source and the practitioner's approach. Regardless, setting an adequate and appropriate structure and boundaries from the initial query to preserve neutrality is imperative. Careful documentation of all substantive contacts is an essential risk management practice.

It is not uncommon for those making an initial query to be unclear or uncertain about the service they need or are asking for. Often, "reintegration" or "reunification" counseling or therapy[7] is requested. Sometimes the resisted parent is asking for individual therapy for him- or herself or the child or for parent–child therapy; sometimes the favored parent, unreceptive to his or her own involvement, is asking for therapy for the child or for the child and the resisted parent. In addition to conducting a preliminary screening, it is equally important for the clinician to provide at this stage general information about available services, location, fees, and requirements for moving to the next phase of the process. The clinician may prefer to send the referring source written information about available services (e.g., evaluations, parenting coordination, and outpatient therapy vs. weekend "intensives") or refer the source to a website for more information. The many intervention options for families with a parent–child contact problem include mediation, custody evaluation, parenting coordination, mental health consultation, expert testimony, coparenting counseling, individual child or adult therapy, and family (reunification) therapy. Referring sources will benefit from understanding the range of options and that not all cases will be suitable for whole-family therapy interventions.

At this early stage, contact with the referring source must be brief, with the clinician obtaining basic preliminary information (see the checklist in Box 2.1). It is essential to preserve neutrality and minimize perceptions of bias to the greatest extent possible. Accordingly, it is inadvisable to obtain one parent's full story at this stage. The preliminary screening may occur by telephone, or the clinician may choose to have the parents complete a brief screening form, which the clinician makes clear differs from a more thorough clinical intake process (involving, for example, questionnaires and direct contact). When the parents have lawyers, it is preferable to conduct the preliminary screening in a joint phone call (or meeting), including the child's lawyer if there is one. In other cases, a brief call may occur with one parent, and the therapist will ask the calling parent to invite the other parent to make a similar initial call. It is ill advised for the therapist to make the first contact with a parent who has not initiated contact. If one parent is unwilling to participate, the intervention options will be limited (e.g., individual parent counseling or expert or mental health consultation).

During the preliminary screening, the therapist canvases the available list of the clinical and educational reports and legal documentation to determine which of these will be most relevant for review. Copies of any existing court orders or agreements must be reviewed to verify the legal rights of each parent to make major child-related decisions, of which therapy is one (i.e., legal decision-making, joint or sole) to ensure compliance with requirements related to consent for treatment (Garber, 2013).

Often, one parent, the court, or a lawyer will request individual counseling for a child or conjoint therapy for the child and the rejected parent (Bow, Gould, & Flens, 2009). Neither option is likely to be sufficient in most cases of parent–child contact

Box 2.1

Preliminary Screening Information to Obtain During First Queries

- Parents' names, addresses (living in same home or separately), contact information, ages, marital status, and languages spoken
- Others living in same home (new partners, other children, grandparents, etc.)
- Lawyers' names and contact information, if any
- Child(ren)'s name(s), gender(s), age(s), grade(s), and special needs
- Service sought (e.g., therapy and for whom, consultation, mediation, or custody evaluation)
- Status of litigation, if any
- Status of legal custody (responsibility for major child-related decisions, including therapy), access (parenting time), and parenting plan
- Age of onset, duration, and reasons for resistance or rejection
- Allegations of intimate partner violence (all types), police involvement, restraining orders, or outstanding criminal charges
- Involvement of child protection agency (dates)
- Allegations of substance or alcohol abuse
- Current and previous therapists: parent , child and/or family
- Previous attempts at reintegration or reunification therapy (by whom, when, and duration)
- Hospitalizations
- Existence of relevant reports (e.g., psychoeducational, psychiatric, psychological testing, or supervised access)
- Presence of child custody evaluation (name of evaluator or assessor, dates)
- Are both parents willing to stipulate that it is in the child's best interests to have a good relationship with both parents, or is there a dispute about what is in the child's best interests?[a]
- If one parent is calling, does the other parent also consent to services? Is the caller willing to invite the other parent to contact the clinician?

[a] If one or both parents cannot provide this stipulation, then the therapy cannot proceed because there is a dispute about what is in the child's best interests. There may need to be a finding from the court or recommendations from a custody evaluator as to what is in the child's best interests before the therapy can begin.

---

problems; limiting treatment to one part of the family system to the exclusion of the other is unlikely to remedy the problem and may even exacerbate it (Johnston et al., 2001). Even when a referral is accepted for child therapy, best practice calls for involving both parents to obtain developmental histories and other relevant information. Depending on the circumstances, a therapist may eventually propose the involvement of one or both parents in what was initially thought to be child therapy.

Dealing with initial queries for services can be extremely time-consuming. From the first query, consideration must be given to billing practices for services. Clinicians may elect to conduct a brief screening on the telephone and not bill for services if the case is not accepted for therapy, or they may choose to establish a protocol for payment for all services rendered from the initial referral. Regardless of the clinician's policy, clarity at the outset is an important risk management practice.

The protocols chosen for both the preliminary screening and the subsequent and more thorough clinical intake will vary based on the family circumstances and the practitioner's style and approach. Like a triage process, the preliminary screening is more of a query into identifying information, key factors, and obvious rule-outs, while the clinical intake explores each of the relevant areas in more depth. Despite the variability in protocols, it is imperative to establish a systematic method that can be adjusted as appropriate based on the family circumstances.

3.3. Clinical Intake

By this stage, the clinician may have a good sense the case will be accepted for clinical intervention. However, it is possible that even after the preliminary screening the clinician will not know with certainty if the case is suitable, because sufficient information about the nature or severity of the contact problem is lacking. The more thorough clinical intake may indicate that the case should not proceed; some cases may be suitable for education or therapy (or both), while other cases may not. Although important information will be gathered during intake, it is important to recognize that it is not a truth-seeking exercise, investigation, or custody evaluation. Clinicians will be bound by mandatory child abuse reporting laws.

3.3.1. WHO IS INVOLVED IN THE CLINICAL INTAKE?
Building on information obtained during the preliminary screening, information is typically obtained, when available, from the parents' lawyers, the child's lawyer, the guardian ad litem, each parent, and stepparents or new partners. Obtaining information from certain collateral sources (e.g., a custody evaluator, a previous or current therapist, or a child protection agency) is critical and will require the consent of both parents. Explaining the process, reviewing the objectives, and obtaining consent or assent from children typically occur after the clinician has accepted the referral, though some therapists may choose to include adolescent children during the clinical intake when determining if the case is appropriate to proceed with the reintegration family therapy.

3.3.2. HOW DOES CLINICAL INTAKE OCCUR?
The clinical intake process can vary considerably. After the preliminary query or screening, which may or may not have included a brief written component, some clinicians conduct telephone interviews (with each parent separately, with both parents together, or both), while other clinicians prefer meetings. Some clinicians

require the parents to complete screening tools, semistructured clinical intake questionnaires, or both prior to the direct telephone or in-person contact. Clinicians may develop their own intake questionnaire packages based on the professional literature and resources or may rely on published tools.[8] (See Appendix 2.A for a sample intake questionnaire protocol.) Box 2.2 provides a checklist of areas of inquiry to be covered in questionnaires, on the telephone, or in meetings at this stage; these areas may overlap with preliminary screening information to some extent.

After obtaining the above-noted information during the systematic preliminary screening and clinical intake protocols, the clinician will be ready either to confirm acceptance of the case for therapy or, having determined that the case is not suitable for therapy (possibly because of the level of severity), to refer the case for other options.

Box 2.2

Clinical Intake Areas of Inquiry

- Parents' objectives for the therapy, including each parent's willingness and commitment to participate and to take responsibility for their own behavior
- Parents' accounts of individual, health, and employment history and of history of marital/couple relationship, including separation and after separation
- Parent's perceptions of the coparenting communication and conflict
- Parents' perceptions of each parent's parenting strengths and challenges
- Parents' perceptions of the problem (including when the problem began, perceptions of each child, and child's relationship with each parent)
- Parents' religious affiliations and practices
- Stepparents, new partners, or past significant partners
- Child(ren)'s developmental, medical, and psychosocial history; medical/health, educational, or special needs; and relationships with siblings
- Child protection agency involvement (reasons, dates, and location)
- Police involvement (previous and outstanding charges, peace bonds, and restraining orders)
- Allegations of intimate partner violence of all types (dangerousness, lethality, and most recent incident)
- Allegations of child abuse (physical, emotional, and sexual) and neglect; most recent incident
- Mental illness, trauma incidents, hospitalizations, prescribed medication, and diagnoses (dates and locations)
- History of and current alcohol or substance use and abuse
- Child's and parents' previous and current therapies (full details, including professional's name, contact information, dates, and who in the family participated)
- Current parenting plan (date), parenting time, legal custody, current orders (or none)

- Whether current parenting plan is being implemented as stated or ordered
- Changes to parenting plan over time, and reasons for changes
- Child's frequency and pattern of contact and quality of relationship with each parent (pre- and postseparation); if no current contact with rejected parent, last date seen, child's age at last contact, and precipitating incident prior to contact refusal
- Current legal/court status (ongoing litigation, final orders/agreements, and dates)
- Review of custody evaluation report where available/possible
- Review of relevant reports (psychoeducational, psychiatric, psychological testing, supervised access, etc.)

3.4. Tailoring the Intervention to the Nature and Severity of the Parent–Child Contact Problem

As noted above, a differential approach to problem identification, assessment, and intervention is necessary. Using a matching process, the intervention must be tailored to the nature and severity of the parent–child contact problem and to each family's unique set of circumstances. Given that delays often exacerbate the contact problem, careful consideration must be given to any previous unsuccessful legal or clinical efforts. A key question for all cases is this:

> Irrespective of the cause or nature of the parent–child contact problem (i.e., affinity, alignment, alienation, or justified rejection), is it in the child's best interests to have a good relationship with both parents? More specifically, is it best for the child to attempt to develop or repair the child's relationship with the rejected parent, correct the family alignments, and restore better individual and family functioning?

Based on a review of the social science literature, empirical research, case law, and interviews with 37 leading international experts, Fidler, Bala, and Saini (2013) articulate a differential approach for assessing and intervening with strained parent–child relationships after divorce. These authors provide a useful chart or map (Figure 4.1, pp. 94–95) that practitioners can use as a guide to best match the nature and severity of the problem when selecting clinical and educational interventions and legal remedies. The upper half of the chart identifies eight assessment dimensions; each can each be associated with three levels of severity:

1. Parental conduct; demonstrated parental alienating behaviors
2. Protection versus probability of harm
3. Impact of parental alienating behaviors on child; rigidity of child's perceptions of and behavior toward their parents
4. Frequency of parent–child contact
5. Duration of strained relationships

6. History of parents' rigidity
7. Parents' receptivity and responsiveness to suggested education or treatment (includes previous unsuccessful legal and clinical efforts to remedy the problem)
8. Compliance with court orders, parenting plans, and treatment agreements.

The lower half of the chart identifies legal remedies and educational or clinical interventions for each level of severity. This map is a working model; although not empirically tested, it is one of many useful tools practitioners can include in their clinical assessment.

Adding to the clinician's assessment tools, Appendix 2.B includes behaviors typically exhibited to varying degrees by the child, favored parent, and rejected parent in alienation cases. Many of these behaviors will be present in any case, while some may occur only in the more severe cases.

Combining information from various writings and research (e.g., Baker, 2005; Darnall, 1998; Gardner, 1998; Fidler, Bala, & Saini, 2013; Johnston et al., 2009; Kelly & Johnston, 2001; Warshak, 2001), Box 2.3 shows indicators for mild, moderate, and severe cases of alienation that will assist the practitioner in mapping the intervention to the family's needs.

Box 2.3

BEHAVIORAL MANIFESTATIONS OF ALIENATION BY LEVEL OF SEVERITY

Mild
- Usually occurs in younger children (under 8 or 9 years old).
- Some parental alienating behaviors are present (e.g., contact interference or bad-mouthing), but these are minimal, lack a consistent pattern, and likely are unwitting and not intended to prevent child's relationship with other parent.
- Preferred parent values child's relationship with other parent but occasionally displays well-intended but misguided or unnecessary protective behaviors.
- Parents are usually able to cooperate on major and day-to-day child-related decisions; parental conflict tends to be minimal, and coparenting communication is usually respectful.
- Child values relationship with both parents but displays discomfort with one parent (not extended to extended family) or may be mildly or situationally disillusioned, unhappy, or angry with one parent.
- Most but not all of Gardner's (1998) eight behaviors manifested by child are present.
- Situational and infrequent parent–child relationship strain is present (e.g., due to affinity, alignment, or expected and time-limited upset over parents' separation).

- Child shows few resisting behaviors at transitions; once preferred parent departs, child resumes comfort level with other parent.
- Parent–child contact is occurring, but with minor interruptions (e.g., lateness, missed visits, or short-lived transition difficulties in presence of preferred parent).
- Duration of any interruptions in contact is brief (e.g., not more than six months).
- Parents and child(ren) are generally flexible but may show inflexibility at times.
- Parents are generally able, with some minimal difficulty, to consistently separate their own needs and feelings from those of the child.
- Parents' statements and demonstrated behavior provide indications they are responsive to treatment or education to improve the parent–child relationship and their own parenting.
- Preferred parent can be reassured that despite their concerns about the other parent or risk to the child, it is best for the child to either develop or repair a safe and good relationship with the other parent.
- Parents are compliant with parenting plan, treatment agreement, and court orders.

Moderate

- Usually occurs in older children, commencing around 8 or 9 years old (although children as young as 4 or 5 can show early signs of becoming alienated, which fall in mild or moderate category).
- All of Gardner's (1998) eight behaviors manifested by child are present, and these are more severe than in mild alienation.
- Child may be disillusioned (unhappy about separation or new partner, angry with one parent) but not "alienated."
- Difficulties with transitions are occurring, with child insisting that she or he doesn't want to go with rejected parent.
- Child takes longer to settle in after transitions than at mild level; is initially guarded and cautious.
- Prior to transition back to favored parent, symptoms re-emerge in anticipation of returning.
- Child displays more resistance than at mild level, although reactions are mixed, confused, or inconsistent (e.g., before or during transitions or while with resisted parent).
- While some contact is occurring, it may be sporadic, infrequent, or delayed; pattern of missed opportunities for parent–child contact is evident.
- Favored parent(s) or child are generally more rigid than at mild level but show some instances of flexibility.
- Some remnants or indications of warm and loving relationship with rejected parent are present.
- Favored parent's overprotection undermines (unwittingly or intentionally) child's relationship with other parent.

- Episodic parental alienating behaviors (contact interference, bad-mouthing, undermining, exaggeration, or distortion) are more frequent than in mild cases; behaviors may be intended to alienate or may be unintentional (protective).
- Parent(s) are able, to some extent, to separate their own needs and views from those of the child.
- Favored parent can be reassured at times and to some extent, that irrespective of the cause or nature of the contact problem, it is best for the child to either repair or develop a safe and good relationship with the other parent.
- Favored parent may be willing to meet with other parent.
- Favored parent is willing to attend or is attending treatment, but sporadically or with minimal success.
- Coparenting communication may occur for specific informational transactions but is strained or nonexistent for major child-related decisions; parent communication is terse and less civil than in mild cases.
- Favored parent demonstrates periodic lapses but is generally compliant with parenting plan, treatment agreements, and court orders.
- Parent(s) inconsistently responsive to education and direction.

Severe

- Parenting by favored parent is intrusive and psychologically controlling (see Barber, Bean, & Erickson, 2002).
- Favored parent shows signs of mental illness (psychotic or psychotic-like thinking, profound emotional dysregulation, or extreme or bizarre behavior).
- Favored parent shows signs of severe personality disorders or characteristics (e.g., paranoid, antisocial, borderline, or narcissistic traits).
- Favored parent identifies actions as protecting (rights of) child despite repeated investigations or evidence demonstrating that future harm is improbable.
- Favored parent advances malicious allegations of intimate partner violence or child abuse (emotional, physical, or sexual) against the other parent, knowing these are unfounded.
- Gardner's (1998) eight behaviors manifested by child are present and are more severe than in mild or moderate cases.
- Child threatens to run away or harm self, rejected parent, or others.
- Child runs away or exhibits self-harm.
- Child acts out or behaves aggressively (toward rejected parent or others, or by destruction of property).
- Child is guarded and hypervigilant about perceived threat from rejected parent.
- Child and rejected parent have no or very infrequent contact for significant length of time (12–24 or more months); contact problem is chronic; child's resistance does not subside during any contact that does occur.

- Child and favored parent take inflexible position toward rejected parent; cannot be reassured about presence of risk; show no ability to suspend belief to even consider the possibility of another perspective.
- Favored parent or child refuses or is not a willing participant in therapy.
- Previous attempt(s) at therapy was unsuccessful.
- Favored parent shows chronic noncompliance with parenting plan, treatment agreement, and court orders.

3.4.1. Interventions for Mild and Some Moderate Cases

Early, brief individual or group parent education may prevent mild or intermittent contact resistance from escalating into more entrenched alignments or parent–child contact problems. In these cases, each parent's reaction to the child's resistance to parent contact may be misinformed and misguided. For example, in cases of affinity, the rejected parent can be educated about the child's predicament and how to best respond and not respond, while the favored parent can be reminded about the child's previously good relationship with the other parent and educated about the need to put the rejected parent's reactive behavior into context.

A multifaceted, whole-family intervention with coordinated legal, clinical, and educational components is likely to be suitable for many mild and most moderate cases, irrespective of the cause or nature of the contact problem, whether justified rejection, alienation, or a hybrid (Baker & Sauber, 2013; Freeman, Abel, Cowper-Smith, & Stein, 2004; Gardner, 1999, 2001; Johnston et al., 2001). Using a family systems framework, the therapy will include interventions with individual family members, the parents together, the family unit, and often a combination of these. (See Chapter 2 for a comprehensive list of goals for each parent, the child, parent–child dyads, and the family as a whole.) Detailed informed-consent service agreements are needed for all cases irrespective of the particular intervention. These interventions are unlike conventional therapies, given the essential role of the court for case management and the need for detailed court orders for all but the most mild of cases.

Family intervention may be on an outpatient basis when family members, in various combinations, engage in regular sessions (the single-family outpatient model). In addition, options for brief interventions include a multiday family intervention (single-family intensives) or the several-day Overcoming Barriers camp for several families. Each of these options, whether for an individual family or several families in a group, is a "whole family" intervention and requires the participation of all relevant family members (which may include, e.g., stepparents or new partners, stepsiblings, and grandparents) in various combinations (individual, parent–child dyads, coparents, entire family, etc.) as required by the therapist. A coordinated team approach is common and will be elaborated further in Chapter 12. Outpatient models may involve one or more therapists. Multiday single-family intensives typically involve at least two therapists, and often a third practitioner responsible for recreational and other activities.

Individual therapy for a child or conjoint therapy for the child and rejected parent in the absence of other interventions is contraindicated in most cases. Such therapy is unlikely to place sufficient emphasis on the significant contributions of the favored parent and other factors related to the child's relationship with the preferred parent, such as enmeshment or other role corruption, such as "parentification," "adultification," or "infantilization" (Garber, 2011). In the absence of participation of the other family members, individual child therapy often reinforces the child's cognitive distortions and problematic behavior. Further, individual therapy identifies the child as the problem or the one who is responsible for fixing the problem. Notwithstanding these concerns, in high-conflict separations where general functioning is impaired, the child and one or both parents may benefit from having their own therapists, who function in collaboration with the family therapist.

To avoid unethically taking on dual roles, the therapist must not make recommendations or determinations (arbitrate) about parenting time or legal decision-making (custody title, i.e., the parent responsible for making major child-related decisions) (Greenberg, Doi Fick, & Schnider, 2012; Sullivan & Kelly, 2001). Each parent's reaction to the child's resistance to parent contact may be misinformed and misguided. A favored parent or child who believes the therapist can determine the parenting time is likely to resist getting down to the business of repairing relationships and instead focus on lobbying the therapist to limit or stop the rejected parent's parenting time. The therapist must be able to say to the child, for example: "I know you do not want to see your mother. I'm sorry, but I can't do anything about that, because the court has ordered [or "your parents have agreed"] to the time you will be spending with each of them. I can listen to your concerns and help you and your family make your time with your mother better. You will have some choices as to how you will spend your time with your mother, so I want to hear your ideas about that."

In some cases a parenting coordinator or arbitrator may join the intervention team to assist with implementing the agreed-to or court-ordered parenting plan and minimizing parental conflict. This practitioner may function as case manager or team leader to ensure coordinated interventions among multiple professionals and prevent formation of professional alignments (Greenberg & Sullivan, 2012; Sullivan, 2004; Sullivan & Kelly, 2001). Careful attention needs to be given to systematic planning and coordination of multiple services to minimize conflict and confusion. Chapter 11 elaborates on the team and case management components of family interventions.

Psychopathology, personality disorders, poor insight, rigid defenses, attempts to present favorably and externalize blame, and noncompliance are common in high-conflict and alienation cases (Johnston et al., 2009; Johnston, Walters, & Olesen, 2005a; Miller, 2013; Siegel, Bow, & Gottlieb, 2012). Detailed and unambiguous court orders (or court orders on consent if parents are in agreement) promoting the parents' accountability, with provisions for court monitoring, provide the essential legal structural components necessary for most cases referred for reunification interventions (Fidler, Bala, & Saini, 2013; Greenberg et al., 2012; Lebow & Black, 2012; Martinson, 2010; Sullivan & Kelly, 2001).[9]

To minimize conflict and delays and maximize effective delivery of interventions, the accompanying court order should include the following terms: (1) the name(s) of the therapist(s) (or, in the absence of a specific name, requirements for minimum education, specialized training, and experience); (2) specific behavioral treatment goals, including a stipulation both parents agree it is in the child's best interests to have a healthy relationship with both parents; (3) family members required to participate; (4) limits of confidentiality; (5) procedures and extent of therapist's discretion; (6) extent of reporting to court; (7) potential sanctions for noncompliance; and (8) payment responsibilities. Intervention orders are likely to require more provisions in more severe cases than in cases of lesser severity. Compliance with court orders is more likely when the favored parent knows the court is monitoring his or her behavior. Without specified limits on confidentiality, the ability for the therapist to report to the court when necessary, and identification of potential sanctions for nonengagement as a deterrent, it is unlikely the therapy will be successful for most cases (Baker & Sauber, 2013; Fidler, Bala, & Saini, 2013). The legal or structural, educational, and therapeutic components of family therapy are discussed in Chapters 3 and 12.

Stated in broad strokes, the predominant goal of a whole-family intervention, as elaborated in Chapters 3 and 12, is to improve individual and family functioning. Such improvement includes but is not limited to correcting alignments and repairing or re-establishing the child's relationships with the resisted or rejected parent (e.g., Albertson-Kelly & Burkard, 2013; Carter, 2011; Fidler, Bala, & Saini, 2013; Friedlander & Walters, 2010; Garber, 2011; Gardner, 1999, 2001; Gottlieb, 2013; Greenberg et al., 2012; Johnston et al., 2001; Lebow & Rekhart, 2007; Walters & Friedlander, 2010). Box 2.4 lists goals for family interventions (i.e., multifaceted family therapy in outpatient settings, Overcoming Barriers camp, and single-family intensive interventions) in more detail, along with indications and contraindications for their use.

Box 2.4

GOALS, INDICATIONS, AND CONTRAINDICATIONS FOR
WHOLE-FAMILY INTERVENTIONS

Treatment Goals
- Enable child to freely relate to both parents; eliminate need to form an alliance.
- Create a "neutral middle space" (Walters & Friedlander, 2010).
- Develop, restore, and support parent–child relationships.
- Reduce use of avoidance as a way to resolve problems.
- Develop new and more effective coping strategies: effective communication, expression of feelings, conflict resolution, and tolerance for frustration and ambivalence.

- Modify cognitive distortions and black-and-white thinking; replace overly rigid views with more realistic ones.
- Teach critical thinking and multiple perspective taking.
- Teach managed emotions and moderate behavior (Eddy, 2010).
- Enhance parenting skills: Teach parent(s) about child development, behavioral management, impact of conflict on children; improve communication and conflict resolution abilities; develop family communication skills; restore appropriate coparenting and parent–child roles and boundaries.
- Enhance coparenting skills where possible; disengagement may be the preferred outcome in most but not necessarily all cases.

Indications

- Both parents show some willingness to be responsive to and compliant with therapy and court orders.
- Both parents agree to written stipulation that irrespective of the cause or reason for the parent–child contact problem (alienation, justified rejection, or elements of both), it is in the child's best interests to have a good relationship with both parents and for efforts to be made to develop, improve or repair family relationships.
- Both parents agree they are each responsible for actively participating in the therapy and the solution, even if they disagree on the extent of their respective contributions to the problem.

Contraindications

- Rejected parent is actively violent or emotionally abusive of the other parent.
- Rejected parent is actively abusive or neglectful of child.
- There is an active investigation by a child protection agency (if the court or agency has required that commencing treatment wait for outcome of investigation).
- Parental alienating behaviors or intrusive psychological parenting reach the level of emotional abuse or harm (including intimidating child to reject other parent).
- Child or favored parent holds fixed irrational beliefs about the rejected parent and the situation and has a stated desire not to change problematic behaviors and beliefs.
- Either parent has demonstrated unwillingness to fully participate in intervention, despite contrary statements to court, lawyer, therapist, or others.
- Child or favored parent has repeatedly made unsubstantiated allegations of sexual, physical, or emotional abuse (in reference to previous or new incidents) against rejected parent.
- Either parent (or child) has demonstrated, repeated disregard of or noncompliance with previous or existing court orders.
- Either parent has severe, untreated (unmedicated or unresponsive to treatment) mental illness (e.g., severe depression, bipolar disorder, psychosis, or paranoia).

- Either parent has untreated substance or alcohol abuse.
- Either parent has severe personality disorders (e.g., antisocial, paranoid, or borderline).
- There are threats made by one parent or child to the safety of other parent, child, or therapist.
- There is a risk of child abduction.
- Previous efforts at same or similar intervention have failed.
- Either parent is likely to sabotage treatment.
- Either parent has outstanding criminal charges (some therapists may choose to not commence therapy until these have been resolved).
- There are orders restraining one or both parents from participating (though in this circumstance clinicians may be able to provide therapy but not see the parents together).

3.4.2. INTERVENTIONS FOR SEVERE AND SOME MODERATE CASES OF JUSTIFIED REJECTION

In many cases of maltreatment or intimate-partner violence, a child continues to want to have contact with the offending parent; in some of these cases, however, a child may resist or reject that parent. Regardless of the child's reaction to the offending parent, these cases need to be identified as early as possible, and appropriate protection plans need to be put in place for the victimized parent or child.

In cases of justified rejection, the severity of the reasons for the contact problem will inform the most appropriate intervention, which may or may not include attempts to reintegrate the child with the rejected parent. In some cases, no parental contact may be warranted. In others, resuming contact (initially monitored or supervised) may be in the child's best interests after appropriate changes in the offending parent's behavior have been demonstrated and when the child has expressed a willingness to see the parent.

In severe justified rejection cases, when it has been determined to be in the child's best interests to attempt to repair the child's relationship with a violent, abusive, or neglectful parent, the interventions will differ from those previously discussed for cases of less severe justified rejection.

There has been a growing effort in child protection to preserve or reunify families—to keep families together and promote children living with their parents (or at least one of them). This approach requires the child protection agency to provide significant and sometimes repeated support services to one or both parents to address their significant limitations or deficiencies in parenting skills (e.g., anger control, instrumental parenting, or attunement), often related to a parent's childhood trauma, addiction, or experience with intimate partner violence. Even when the situation warrants a supervision order or placement outside the home because of the risk of abuse or neglect, the plan established by child protection agency often includes the requirement for the child and parent(s) to maintain regular supervised contact with the agency monitoring the other, sometimes mandatory interventions designed to ameliorate the parenting deficits.

Before any parent–child reintegration can occur, the unfit or abusive parent will be required to participate in individual or group treatment or rehabilitation and to demonstrate behavioral change. The child, who may exhibit symptoms of PTSD, is likely to need individual trauma-based therapy prior to any reintegration with the offending parent. Ongoing assessment by experienced practitioners is necessary to determine if and when reintegration, supported by counseling, is indicated. Any contact the child has with the offending parent needs to be supervised initially, in combination with court monitoring, case management by the child protection agency, or other professional involvement to assess whether the contact should continue and, if so, under what circumstances (i.e., frequency, duration, location, and extended or permanent supervision). Long-term supervised access in cases of justified rejection (bona fide abuse) is usually contraindicated when the offending parent has demonstrated an inability to be rehabilitated.

3.4.3. INTERVENTIONS FOR SEVERE AND SOME MODERATE CASES OF ALIENATION

In some moderate and all severe alienation cases, the parental alienating behaviors are emotionally abusive. They may result from personality disorders or mental illness (Johnston & Goldman, 2010; Miller, 2013). Education or therapy alone is unlikely to protect the child from the emotionally abusive behavior and alienation or to repair the child's relationship with the rejected parent (two related but separate goals); it may even exacerbate the problem (Clawar & Rivlin, 1991; Warshak, 2001). Delays caused by ineffective treatment will only serve to further exacerbate the problem, making it more resistant to remediation. While improvements may be observed in some severe cases during weekly outpatient multifaceted family therapy, these are unlikely to be sustained once the child returns to the orbit of the favored parent and perhaps other influences, such as those of siblings or extended family.

One option to consider in the most severe cases or when less intrusive legal or clinical remedies have failed is a temporary or permanent transfer of custody from the alienating to the rejected parent (Gardner, 1999; Warshak, 2001).[10] This last-resort remedy should never be undertaken lightly and may have inherent risks (Fidler, Bala, & Saini, 2013), just as the child remaining with the alienating parent may have inherent risks. A change in custody to the rejected parent may be warranted when this parent can adequately care for the child and demonstrate more sensitivity to and understanding of the child's psychological needs than does the favored parent. To permit the child to re-establish the previously loving relationship with the rejected parent, the change in custody is likely to require a temporary suspension of contact or supervised contact with the alienating parent. In some cases placement in a neutral location such as a boarding school, foster or group home, or with a family member may be necessary before the custody reversal can occur (Sullivan & Kelly, 2001). Psychoeducational or clinical interventions may augment these legal remedies in assisting with custodial reversal. Examples of such programs include Family Bridges (Kelly, 2010; Warshak, 2010b), Transitioning Families (Judge et al., 2016), Stable Paths (Judge & Bailey, 2015), and Family Reflections (Reay, 2015).[11]

The ultimate goal in any intervention is for the child to have a good relationship with both parents. Effective interventions require treatment of both the alienation and any comorbid conditions, including mental illness or personality disorder (Miller, 2013). It is important to recognize there is no perfect parent–child relationship. Rather, a healthy and functional relationship will include the child's ability to accept and integrate both good and bad qualities of each parent, coupled with flexible thinking, the capacity for multiple perspective taking, good communication and problem-solving skills, and so on, all of which are indices of mature interpersonal skills and relationships.

In the most severe cases, this ultimate goal is likely to require a sequential approach to intervention: first with the child and the rejected parent who has been awarded custody, followed by legal and clinical interventions to reunite the child with the previously favored parent. Similar to the sequential approach in severe cases of justified rejection (in which the child and offending parent each participate in their own therapies before reintegration), the alienating parent will need to first participate in education and individual therapy to learn about alienation, how to correct their parental alienating behaviors, and how to sufficiently support the child's relationship with the other parent before being reunited with the child. After the child is successfully reintegrated with the previously rejected parent, with a detailed and unambiguous court order for treatment, the previously favored parent will have to reconnect with the child gradually, with initial supervision and monitoring by the court, to ensure that the parent demonstrates the required sustained behavioral changes.

The short- and long-term risks involved in changing custody must be weighed against the risks of leaving the child with an emotionally disturbed, alienating parent (Fidler, Bala, & Saini, 2013; Warshak, 2001). The courts face a "stark dilemma" (Fidler & Bala, 2010): Is a change in custody likely to cause more harm than good? Do the short- or long-term benefits of placing the child with the once loved, now rejected parent outweigh the risks (e.g., of trauma or harm to self or others) of temporarily separating the child from the alienating parent? What are the likely short- and long-term detrimental effects of living in a distorted reality where the child is not free to be emotionally autonomous? Legal, mental health, and child protection professionals need to carefully consider which alternative poses the greater risk to a particular child in a particular set of family circumstances. [Child protection agencies are increasingly becoming involved in high-conflict alienation cases and in alienation cases where emotional harm or risk of emotional harm has been identified (Fidler, Bala, & Hurwitz, 2013).]

In some cases, the least detrimental long-term option is to place the child with the parent more likely to promote overall healthy psychological development and adjustment, including but not limited to a healthy relationship with the other parent. In other cases, the least detrimental option will be for the child to remain with the favored parent in the alienating environment, with no enforcement of previous orders, despite the likely severed tie with the rejecting parent. A "final" visit with the rejected parent, facilitated by a therapist or the child's lawyer, to explain to the child why the parent will not be pursuing contact for the time being is likely to be important, despite the child's reluctance.

As we have noted, a change in custody is likely to be a last resort. However, if the court waits too long to respond in this way, the intended remedy may prove ineffective (Fidler, Bala, & Saini, 2013; Warshak, 2010b). In the most severe cases, a timely judicial decision to transfer custody may be the only way to effectively address the alienation. This requires careful planning and judicial control over the transition process (Fidler, Bala, & Saini, 2013). However, even when there is severe alienation and other interventions have failed, the court may conclude that a change in custody is not appropriate and recognize that there is no effective way for a court order to ensure or even promote the re-establishment of the child's relationship with the rejected parent. In some cases, the rejected parent may lack the capacity to adequately care for the child. In other cases, it is expected that the child will "vote with his or her feet" despite the court order for a custody change.

4. SUMMARY

Parent–child contact problems may be conceptualized on a continuum that includes affinity, alignment, justified rejection, and alienation. Legal and clinical interventions must be tailored to the family's particular needs and situation, including the nature and severity of the parent–child contact problem. Careful management and screening of initial queries from parents, the court, lawyers, or other professionals are required to ensure an appropriate fit between the family and the intervention. Some cases may be suitable for family-based clinical or psychoeducational interventions (or both). Box 2.5 summarizes the interventions discussed in this chapter for less severe cases.

More severe cases of alienation and justified rejection may not be suitable for this whole-family approach. In these cases, which by definition include the presence of emotional harm or emotional abuse (Johnston et al., 2009), legal and clinical interventions are necessary, often with the involvement of the child protection agency. Such cases may require a custody change and interruption of contact with the favored parent coupled with an initial intervention with the child and the rejected parent, to be followed later by the inclusion of the favored parent where appropriate. In some cases of severe alienation, the least detrimental option may be for the child to remain with the favored parent and have no contact with the rejected parent for the time being.

Regardless of the severity of the case, psychoeducational and clinical interventions for parent–child contact problems require specialized experience and training.

BOX 2.5

SYSTEMICALLY BASED OPTIONS FOR FAMILY INTERVENTIONS IN LESS SEVERE
ALIENATION OR JUSTIFIED REJECTION CASES OR MIXED/HYBRID CASES

For Mild and Some Moderate Cases
- Psychoeducation groups for parents
- Psychoeducation or counseling for parents on individual basis
- Coparenting education or counseling for parents conjointly
- Psychoeducation groups for the child or adolescent (Pedro-Carroll, 2010)
- Individual parent mental health consultation
- Individual therapy or counseling for parent(s)
- Individual therapy for child (for early intervention in mild cases only)
- Family therapy [e.g., MultiModal Family Therapy (Friedlander & Walters, 2010; Johnston et al., 2001); child-centered conjoint therapy (Greenberg et al., 2012); family restructuring therapy (Carter, 2011); integrative family therapy (Lebow & Rekhart, 2007); structural family therapy (Gottlieb, 2013); family reunification therapy (Albertson-Kelly & Burkard, 2013); and Moving Families Forward (Jones, Hardy, & Smyth, 2015)][a]

For Other Moderate Cases
- Multiday whole-family "intensives" for a single family combined with an aftercare plan (coordinated among a team of skilled professionals who have indicated their availability to accept the particular family into treatment immediately following the intervention)[b]
- Overcoming Barriers high-conflict divorce camp for four to seven families, using a group therapy process (Sullivan, Ward, & Deutsch, 2010) combined with aftercare in place

[a] These family intervention approaches and models, which have been described in the literature, at trainings, or both, have similarities to, are informed by, and build on one another to varying degrees.
[b] Known examples include Overcoming Barriers intensives (see further elaboration in Chapter 6; www.overcomingbarriers.org), Families Moving Forward (Polak, Fidler, & Popielarczyk, 2013; www.familiesmovingforward.ca), Transitioning Families (Bailey et al., 2016; www.transitioningfamilies.com), and Stable Paths (www.stablepaths.com), a more recent program that implements the Transitioning Families model.

NOTES

1. For brevity, we use the term *divorce* to refer to actual divorce and to separation of both married and unmarried parents.
2. *Intimate-partner violence* refers to a broad range of situations involving partner abuse or violence (Centers for Disease Control, 2009; Kelly & Johnson, 2008). In the most serious cases, referred to as *coercive controlling violence*, relatively frequent

acts of physical, sexual, or emotional abuse—often involving substance abuse, personality disorder, or severe mental illness—allow a primary perpetrator (almost always male) to exert a pattern of domination, intimidation, and control over a victim, who is fearful and generally submissive and requires protection. Historically, this has been referred to as the "battering" type of domestic violence. Coercive controlling violence is differentiated from "high conflict," which may include the other types of intimate-partner violence, such as *situational couple violence* (also referred to as *conflict-instigated violence*) or *separation-instigated violence*. Situational couple violence is bilateral, having no one instigator; it occurs when an argument or conflict escalates to aggressive or physically violent behavior by one or both partners. Fear is not present, there is no pattern, and it is likely to diminish after separation. In separation-instigated violence, by contrast, there is no violence during the relationship, but there are one or more isolated incidents around the time of separation, perhaps precipitated by escalating arguments or the discovery of infidelity; as with situational couple violence, there is no ongoing pattern and no fear. Although there is some overlap between types of intimate-partner violence, and some cases cannot be neatly classified, most researchers and practitioners view it as helpful to have a typology describing the spectrum of intimate-partner violence situations. The typology provides a starting point for case assessment, as the risks and the appropriate and differentiated interventions will vary depending on the nature, intensity, and pattern of the intimate-partner violence. The negative impact of coercive controlling violence on victims and their children has been well documented (Jaffe, Wolfe, & Campbell, 2011).

3. For further elaboration on cognitive biases, risks, and clinical decision-making see Kahneman (2011), Martindale (2005), and Miller (2013).

4. Earlier writings referred to alignments as alliances (Kelly & Johnston, 2001).

5. Austin, Fieldstone, and Pruett (2012) conceptualize gatekeeping as ranging from very facilitative to very restrictive. A parent exhibiting facilitative gatekeeping is proactive in supporting child's relationship with the other parent and inclusive of the other parent, boosts the child's image of the other parent, makes ongoing efforts to communicate with the other parent, is flexible about time-sharing, and ensures that the child has opportunities to develop a relationship with the other parent. Restrictive gatekeeping may be justified when the other parent has a corroborated history of intimate-partner violence, harsh discipline of the child, child abuse, substance or alcohol abuse, a major untreated mental health disorder, or continuous and significant inappropriate parenting and coparenting behaviors that negatively affect the child. In these circumstances, limiting contact with a parent protects the child. Restrictive gatekeeping is unjustified if it arises solely from the favored parent's belief in his or her greater importance to the child, questioning the competence of other parent without foundation, needing the child, misperceiving him- or herself as marginalized, and anger at or desire to punish the other parent. In these circumstances, limiting contact reinforces inappropriate and unwarranted parental alienating behaviors.

6. Another intervention option, though beyond the scope of this chapter, is mental health consultation, which is typically provided to a parent seeking information, support, and guidance. See Hobbs-Minor and Sullivan (2008) and Simon and Stahl (2013) for further elaboration.

7. Different names have been used to describe multifaceted family therapy interventions, often referred to generically as reintegration or reunification therapy. While

reintegration of the child with the rejected parent is one important intervention goal, in this chapter and in Chapter 12 these therapies are referred to interchangeably as family therapy or family intervention.

8. Useful resources include Gardner's (1998) eight behaviors manifested by child; Table 4.1 in Fidler, Bala, and Saini (2013); Appendix 2.B of this chapter; Fidler, Bala, Birnbaum, and Kavassalis (2008); Ellis (2007); Garber's (2007) Hierarchical Decision Tree for Alienation; Drozd and Olesen's (2004) Decision Tree to Assess Alienating Parental Behaviors; and CAGE, a screening tool for substance abuse (Ewing, 1984). See Chapter 4 in Fidler, Bala, and Saini (2013) for additional assessment tools. Screening tools for intimate-partner violence include the Mediator's Assessment of Safety Issues and Concerns (MASIC; Holtzworth-Munroe, Beck, & Applegate, 2010).

9. See the Association of Family and Conciliation Courts guidelines for court-involved therapists (AFCC Task Force on Court-Involved Therapy, 2011) and issue 9(1) of the *Journal of Child Custody* (2012) for further elaboration. See Chapter 12, Appendix 12.A, for a sample treatment agreement.

10. See Warshak (2010b) and Fidler, Bala, and Saini (2013) for further elaboration of the perspectives for and against custody reversal in severe alienation cases.

11. These are known intervention programs reported in the literature; there may be others not published. Practitioners are advised to exercise due diligence when evaluating which program is the most appropriate to meet a specific family's needs. Additional information may be found at www.transitioningfamilies.com, www.warshak.com, www.stablepaths.com, and www.familyreflectionsprogram.com. See Saini, Johnston, Fidler, and Bala (2012, 2016) for reviews of published research on two of these programs.

REFERENCES

AFCC Task Force on Court-Involved Therapy. (2011). Guidelines for court-involved therapists. *Family Court Review, 49*, 564–581. Also available from http://www.afccnet.org/pdfs/Guidelines%20for%20Court%20Involved%20Therapy%20AFCC.pdf

Albertson-Kelly, J., & Burkard, B. (2013). Family reunification in a forensic setting. In A. J. L. Baker & S. R. Sauber (Eds.), *Working with alienated children and families: A clinical guidebook* (pp. 232–252). New York, NY: Routledge.

Austin, W. G., Fieldstone, L., & Pruett, M. K. (2012). *Bench book on parental gatekeeping in parenting disputes. Understanding the dynamics of gate-closing and opening behaviors for the best interest of children.* Miami, FL: Authors.

Baker, A. J. L. (2005). Parent alienation strategies: A qualitative study of adults who experienced parental alienation as a child. *American Journal of Forensic Psychology, 23*(4), 41–64.

Baker, A. M. J., & Darnall, D. (2006). Behaviors and strategies employed in parental alienation: A survey of parental experiences. *Journal of Divorce and Remarriage, 45*(1–2), 97–124.

Baker, A. J. L., & Sauber, S. R. (Eds.) (2013). *Working with alienated children and families: A clinical guidebook.* New York, NY: Routledge.

Barber, B. K., Bean, R. L., & Erickson, L. D. (2002). Expanding the study and understanding of psychological control. In B. K. Barber (Ed.), *Intrusive parenting: How psychological control affects children and adolescents* (pp. 263–289). Washington, DC: American Psychological Association.

Bow, J. N., Gould, J. W., & Flens, J. R. (2009). Examining parental alienation in child custody cases: A survey of mental health and legal professionals. *American Journal of Family Therapy, 37*(2), 127–145.

Carter, S. (2011). *Family restructuring therapy: Interventions with high conflict separations and divorces.* Scotsdale, AZ: HCI Press.

Cartwright, G. F. (2006). Beyond parental alienation syndrome: Reconciling the alienated child and the lost parent. In R. A. Gardner, S. R. Sauber & D. Lorandos (Eds.), *The international handbook of parental alienation syndrome: Conceptual, clinical and legal considerations* (pp. 286–291). Springfield, IL: Charles C Thomas, 2006.

Centers for Disease Control. (2009). *Understanding intimate partner violence. Fact sheet.* Retrieved from www.cdc.gov/violenceprevention

Clawar, S., & Rivlin, B. (1991). *Children held hostage: Dealing with programmed and brainwashed children.* New York, NY: American Bar Association Section of Family Law.

Darnall, D. (1998). *Divorce casualties: Protecting your children from parental alienation.* Lanham, MD: Taylor.

Drozd, L. M. & Olesen, N. W. (2004). Is it abuse, alienation, and/or estrangement? A decision tree. *Journal of Child Custody, 1,* 65–106.

Eddy, B. (2010). *Don't alienate the kids! Raising resilient children while avoiding high conflict divorce.* Scottsdale, AZ: High Conflict Institute Press.

Ellis, E. (2007). A stepwise approach to evaluating children for parental alienation syndrome. *Journal of Child Custody, 4*(1/2), 55–78.

Emery, R. E., Holtzworth-Munroe, A., Johnston, J. R., Pedro-Carroll, J. L., Kline Pruett, M., Saini, M., & Sandler, I. (2016). "Bending" evidence for a cause: Scholar-advocacy bias in family law. *Family Court Review, 54*(2), 134–149.

Ewing, J. A. (1984). *Detecting alcoholism: The CAGE questionnaire. JAMA 252,* 1905–1907.

Fidler, B. J., & Bala, N. (2010). Children resisting post-separation contact with a parent: Concepts, controversies and conundrums. *Family Court Review, 48,* 10–47.

Fidler, B. J., Bala, N., Birnbaum, R., & Kavassalis, K. (2008). *Challenging issues in child custody disputes. A guide for legal and mental health professionals.* Toronto: Thomson Carswell.

Fidler, B. J., Bala, N., & Hurwitz, H. (2013) *Best practice guide: Responding to emotional harm of children in high conflict separation.* Toronto: High Conflict Forum.

Fidler, B. J., Bala, N., & Saini, M.S. (2013). *Children who resist postseparation parental contact: A differential approach for legal and mental health professionals.* American Psychology–Law Society Series. New York, NY: Oxford University Press.

Freeman, R., Abel, D., Cowper-Smith, M., & Stein, L. (2004). Reconnecting children with absent parents. *Family Court Review, 42*(3), 439–459.

Friedlander, S., & Walters, M. (2010). When a child rejects a parent: Tailoring the intervention to fit the problem. *Family Court Review, 48*(1), 98–111.

Garber, B. D. (2007). Conceptualizing visitation resistance and refusal in the context of parental conflict, separation, divorce. *Family Court Review, 45*(4), 588–599.

Garber, B. D. (2011). Parental alienation and the dynamics of the enmeshed dyad: Adultification, parentification and infantilization. *Family Court Review, 49*(2), 322–335.

Garber, B. D. (2013). Providing effective, systematically informed, child-centered psychotherapists for children of divorce: Walking on thin ice. In A. J. Baker & S. R. Sauber (Eds.). *Working with alienated children and families: A clinical guidebook* (pp. 166–187). New York, NY: Routledge.

Garber, B. D. (2014). The chameleon child: Children as actors in the high conflict divorce drama. *Journal of Child Custody, 11*(1), 25–40.

Gardner, R. A. (1985). Recent trends in divorce and litigation. *Academy Forum, 29*(2), 3–7.

Gardner, R. A. (1992a). The parental alienation syndrome: A guide for mental health and legal professionals. Cresskill, NJ: Creative Therapeutics, Inc. (with updated addenda in 1994 and 1996).

Gardner, R. A. (1998). *The parental alienation syndrome* (2nd ed.). Cresskill, NJ: Creative Therapeutics.

Gardner, R. A. (1999). Family therapy of the moderate type of parental alienation syndrome. *American Journal of Family Therapy, 27*, 195–212.

Gardner, R. A. (2001). *Therapeutic interventions for children and parental alienation syndrome.* Cresskill, NJ: Creative Therapeutics.

Gottlieb, L. J. (2013). The application of structural family therapy to the treatment of parental alienation syndrome. In A. J. L. Baker & S. R. Sauber (Eds.). *Working with alienated children and families: A clinical guidebook* (pp. 209–231). New York, NY: Routledge.

Greenberg, L. R., Doi Fick, L., & Schnider, R. (2012). Keeping the developmental frame: Child-centered conjoint therapy. *Journal of Child Custody, 9*(1–2), 39–68.

Greenberg, L. R., & Sullivan, M. J. (2012). Parenting coordinator and therapist collaboration in high-conflict shared custody cases. *Journal of Child Custody, 9*(1–2), 85–107.

Hobbs-Minor, E., & Sullivan, M. (2008). Mental health consultation in child custody cases. In L. Fieldstone & C. Coates (Eds.), *Innovations in interventions with high conflict families* (pp. 159–186). Association of Family and Conciliation Courts.

Holtzworth-Munroe, A., Beck, C., & Applegate, A. G. (2010). *Mediator's Assessment of Safety Issues and Concerns (MASIC). Family Court, 48*(4), 646–662.

Jaffe, P. G., Wolfe, D. A., & Campbell, M. (2011). *Growing up with domestic violence.* Cambridge, ON: Hogrefe Publishing.

Johnston, J. R. (1993). Children of divorce who refuse visitation. In C. Depner & J. Bray (Eds.), *Nonresidential parenting: New vistas in family living* (pp. 109–135). Newbury Park, CA: Sage.

Johnston, J. R., & Campbell, L. E. (1988). *Impasses of divorce: The dynamics and resolution of family conflict.* New York, NY: Free Press.

Johnston, J. R., & Goldman, J. R. (2010). Outcomes of family counseling interventions with children who resist visitation: An addendum to Friedlander and Walters. *Family Court Review, 48*(1), 112–115.

Johnston, J., Roseby, V., & Kuehnle, K. (2009). *In the name of the child: A developmental approach to understanding and helping children of conflicted and violent divorce.* New York, NY: Springer.

Johnston, J. R., Walters, M., & Friedlander, S. (2001). Therapeutic work with alienated children and their families. *Family Court Review, 39*(3), 316–333.

Johnston, J. R., Walters, M. G., & Olesen, N. W. (2005a). Clinical ratings of parenting capacity and Rorschach protocols of custody-disputing parents: An exploratory study. *Journal of Child Custody, 2*(1/2), 159–178.

Johnston, J. R., Walters, M. G., & Olesen, N. W. (2005b). Is it alienating parenting, role reversal, or child abuse? A study of children's rejection of a parent in child custody disputes. *Journal of Emotional Abuse, 5*(4), 191–218.

Johnston, J. R., Walters, M. G., & Olesen, N. W. (2005c). The psychological functioning of alienated children in custody disputing families: An exploratory study. *American Journal of Forensic Psychology, 23*(3), 49–64.

Jones, A. G., Hardy, S. P., & Smyth, R. (2015, June). *Moving Families Forward: A program for parental alienation and high conflict.* Paper presented at the Association of Family and Conciliation Courts (AFCC) 52nd Annual Conference, New Orleans, LA. Retrieved from http://www.afccnet.org/ConferencesTraining/AFCCConferences

Judge, A. M. & Bailey, R. (2015) Clinical Protocol for Stable Paths: A *Transitioning Families* Program. Unpublished manuscript.

Judge, A. M., Bailey, R., Behrman-Lippert, J., Bailey E., Psaila, C., & Dickel, J. (2016). The Transitioning Families therapeutic reunification model in non-familial abductions. *Family Court Review, 54*(2), 232-249.

Kahneman, D. (2011). *Thinking, fast and slow.* New York, NY: Farrar, Straus and Giroux.

Kelly, J. B. (2010). Commentary on "Family Bridges: Using insights from social science to reconnect parents and alienated children" (Warshak, 2010). *Family Court Review, 48*(1), 81–90.

Kelly, J., & Johnston, J. (2001). The alienated child: A reformulation of parental alienation syndrome. *Family Court Review, 39,* 249–266.

Kelly, J. B., & Johnson, M. P. (2008). Differentiation among types of intimate partner violence: Research update and implications for interventions. *Family Court Review, 46*(3), 476–499.

Lebow, J., & Black, D. A. (2012). Considerations in court-involved therapy with parents. *Journal of Child Custody, 9*(1–2), 11–38.

Lebow, J., & Rekhart, K. N. (2007). Integrative family therapy for high-conflict divorce with disputes over child custody and visitation. *Family Process, 46,* 79–91.

Martindale, D. (2005). Confirmatory bias and confirmatory distortion. *Journal of Child Custody, 2*(1/2), 31–48.

Martinson, D. (2010). One case–one specialized judge: Why courts have an obligation to manage alienation and other high-conflict cases. *Family Court Review, 48*(1), 180–189.

Meier, J. S. (2009). A historical perspective on parental alienation syndrome and parental alienation. *Journal of Child Custody, 6,* 232–257.

Miller, S. G. (2013). Clinical reasoning and decision-making in cases of child alignment: Diagnostic and therapeutic issues. In A. J. L. Baker & S. R. Sauber (Eds.), *Working with alienated children and families: A clinical guidebook* (pp. 8–46). New York, NY: Routledge.

Neal, T., & Brodsky, S. L. (2016). Forensic psychologists' perception of bias and potential correction strategies in forensic mental health evaluations. *Psychology Public Policy and Law, 22*(1), 58–76.

Pedro-Carroll, J. (2010). *Putting children first: Proven parenting strategies for helping children thrive through divorce.* New York, NY: Avery/Penguin.

Polak, S., Fidler, B. J., & Popielarczyk, L. (2013, June). *Children resisting contact with a parent post-separation: A 3-day intensive in-home family intervention.* Paper presented at the Association of Family and Conciliation Courts (AFCC) 50th Annual Conference,

Los Angeles, CA. Retrieved from http://www.afccnet.org/ConferencesTraining/AFCCConferences

Reay, K. (2015). Family Reflections: A promising therapeutic program designed to treat severely alienated children and their family system. *American Journal of Family Therapy, 43*(2), 1–11.

Saini, M. A., Johnston, J., Fidler, B. J., & Bala, N. (2012). Empirical studies of alienation. In K. F. Kuehnle & L. M. Drozd (Eds.), *Parenting plan evaluations: Applied research for the family court* (pp. 339–441). New York, NY: Oxford University Press.

Saini, M. A., Johnston, J., Fidler, B. J., & Bala, N. (2016). Empirical studies of alienation. In L. M. Drozd, M. A. Saini, & N. Olesen (Eds.), *Parenting plan evaluations: Applied research for the family court* (2nd ed., pp. 374–430). New York, NY: Oxford University Press.

Siegel, J. C., Bow, J. N., & Gottlieb, M. C. (2012). The MMPI-2 in high conflict child custody cases. *American Journal of Forensic Psychology, 30*(3), 21–34.

Simon, R., & Stahl, P. (2013). *Forensic psychology consultation in child custody litigation: A handbook for work product review, case preparation and expert testimony.* New York, NY: American Bar Association Section of Family Law.

Sullivan, M. J. (2004). Ethical, legal and professional practice issues involved in acting as a parenting coordinator in child custody cases. *Family Court Review, 42*(3), 576–582.

Sullivan, M. J., & Kelly, J. B. (2001). Legal and psychological management of cases with an alienated child. *Family Court Review, 39*(3), 299–315.

Sullivan, M. J., Ward, P. A., & Deutsch, R. M. (2010). Overcoming Barriers Family Camp: A program for high-conflict divorced families where a child is resisting contact with a parent. *Family Court Review, 48*, 115–134.

Walters, M., & Friedlander, S. (2010). Finding a tenable middle space: Understanding the role of clinical interventions when a child refuses contact with a parent. *Journal of Child Custody, 7*, 287–328.

Warshak, R. A. (2001). Current controversies regarding parental alienation syndrome. *American Journal of Forensic Psychology, 19*(3), 29–59.

Warshak, R. A. (2006). Social science and parental alienation: Examining the disputes and the evidence. In R. A. Gardner, S. R. Sauber, & D. Lorandos (Eds.), *The international handbook of parental alienation syndrome: Conceptual, clinical and legal considerations* (pp. 352–371). Springfield, IL: Charles C Thomas.

Warshak, R. A. (2010a). *Divorce poison: How to protect your family from badmouthing and brainwashing.* New York, NY: Harper Paperbacks.

Warshak, R. A. (2010b). Family Bridges: Using insights from social science to reconnect parents and alienated children. *Family Court Review, 48*, 48–80.

APPENDIX 2.A

SAMPLE CLINICAL INTAKE QUESTIONNAIRE

Overcoming Barriers Inc.
417 Tasso Street, Palo Alto, CA 94301
overcomingbarriers@gmail.com
www.overcomingbarriers.org

INTAKE INFORMATION

GENERAL INFORMATION

Date	/ /
Referred by	
Last Name	
First Name	
Name of Child(ren)'s Other Parent	
Your Relationship to Child(ren)	
Address (incl. Zip or Postal Code)	
Email Address	
Contact Numbers	Home: Work: Cell:
Preferred Contact Method	May we call you at work?
Age	
Date of Birth	/ /
Place of Birth (City/Country)	
Significant Others/Relatives Living in the Home?	
Occupation	
Employer Name	
Employer Address	
Languages Spoken at Home	

COUNSEL INFORMATION

Firm Name	
Counsel Name	
Address (incl. Zip or Postal code)	
Contact Numbers	Phone: Fax:
Email	

COURT INFORMATION

Do you have a court order to participate in Overcoming Barriers (OCB)? If so, please list the name of the judge and the jurisdiction.	
Do you have a recommendation other than a court order to participate in OCB? If so, please list relationship with this individual and his or her contact information.	
Has there been a custody evaluation (assessment) for your family? If so, please list name and contact information for evaluator.	
Was psychological testing done as a result of the custody evaluation? If so, please list name and contact information for the psychological testing individual(s).	
Approximately how many court appearances have you had since the court process began?	

YOUR RELATIONSHIP HISTORY

Present Marital Status:	
Are you living in the same home with the children's other parent? If not, what are your current living arrangements?	

MARRIAGE/COHABITATION

Date you met	Date of marriage/ cohabitation	Date of separation	Date of divorce
/ /	/ /	/ /	/ /
Date of final separation:			/ /
Who made the decision to end the relationship?			
How were the children informed?			
Reasons for final separation:			

Please list previous marriages or common-law or serious relationships where the children have been involved:

CHILDREN

Put asterisk * by child(ren) about whom you are seeking services

Child's name	Age	Date of birth	Grade	Resides with
		/ /		
		/ /		
		/ /		
		/ /		

Children from previous or current relationships, other than above:

Child's name	Age	Date of birth	Grade	Resides with
		/ /		
		/ /		
		/ /		
		/ /		

Other persons in the home and their relationship to the children:

Are you in a new relationship?

Have any of your children been assessed through school or privately as:

Gifted?

Learning disabled?

Emotionally disturbed?

Physically handicapped?

Developmentally delayed?

Having current or chronic health needs?

DESCRIBE YOUR CHILD

Tell us about each child's temperament, likes, dislikes, strengths, and challenges:

If you have more than one child, describe (for each child):

The sibling relationship:

His/her relationship with the other parent. If there are obstacles in the way of a relationship, how would you describe them?

Does your child say anything to you about the other parent? If so, what does the child say and how do you respond?

His/her relationship with the other parent's family. If there are obstacles in those relationships, describe these. What changes do you think can be made?

If there is any other information about your child we should know, please describe (for each child).

YOUR FAMILY

Your Mother's Name	
Age	
Occupation	
Address	
Your Father's Name	
Age	
Occupation	
Address	
Has anyone in your family: Abused drugs or alcohol?	
Been in psychotherapy?	
Been hospitalized for emotional reasons?	
Received medication for emotional reasons? Been diagnosed with a mental illness that is not treated?	
Been arrested or convicted of a felony?	
Been investigated for physical or sexual child abuse?	
If yes, please provide details:	

WERE YOUR PARENTS:

Ever separated?	
If yes, when?	
Your age?	
Ever divorced?	
If yes, when?	
Your age?	
Ever remarried?	

If yes, when?	
Your age?	
Date when you moved out of your parent's home:	/ /
Your age?	
Reason for moving out?	

PERSONAL & HEALTH HISTORY

Do you have a religious affiliation?	
Is so, please identify:	
If you belong to a congregation, please indicate the frequency with which you attend services:	
Do you have a chronic or recurrent health problem or physical disability?	
If so, please explain:	
Are you currently on any prescribed medications?	
If yes, please list:	
Do you use any drugs or medications other than as prescribed?	
Has a physician ever prescribed you medication for an emotional problem?	
If so, please explain:	

Please list all mental health professionals and/or agencies with whom *you or your child(ren)* have had contact, e.g., psychiatrist, psychologist, social worker, counselors. Include full address, postal code, dates seen, and telephone and fax numbers.

Name	Title	Agency	Address	Dates Seen	Telephone	Fax

Have you ever been hospitalized?	
If yes, please provide details:	
Have you ever been under investigation by the police?	
If yes, please provide details:	
Have you or a member of your family ever been charged, arrested, and/or convicted of a crime?	
Have you or your family ever been under investigation by a child protection agency?	
Do you ever drink alcohol?	
Do you or anyone else think that your use of alcohol or drugs is a problem?	

(Note: If response to either of the above two questions is yes, please complete the form titled "Michigan Alcohol Screening Test," attached to this questionnaire.)

EDUCATION & EMPLOYMENT

Highest level of education completed	
School and degree	
Did you receive special education services?	
If yes, please elaborate:	
Did you leave any educational program prior to completion?	
If yes, please explain:	
Current occupation	
Annual income	

Detailed employment history: Please provide the following:

Job Title	Place of Work	Salary	Dates	Reason for Leaving
			/ /	
			/ /	
			/ /	
			/ /	

Hours of work:

YOUR RELATIONSHIP WITH OTHER PARENT

Describe your current relationship with your child's other parent in as much detail as you think will be helpful.
Describe your communication with the child's other parent.
Describe the level of conflict with the child's other parent.
Describe how you think your child views your relationship with his/her other parent. Has he/she witnessed arguing, fighting, physical violence?
During the relationship, have there been any incidents of physical aggression?
If yes, please provide details as well as any relevant documentation (send in):

INFORMATION REGARDING OTHER PARENT

Do you have any of the following concerns about the other parent? (indicate yes or no)

Alcohol abuse	
Drug abuse	
Emotional abuse of children	
Physical abuse of children	
Sexual abuse of children	
Sexual behaviour	
Physical health	
Criminal behavior	
Potential for violent behavior	
Potential for suicide attempt	
Child kidnapping	
If yes to any of the above, please explain:	
Is the other parent likely to express any of these concerns about you?	

If yes, please provide details:	
Does the other parent ever drink alcohol?	
If yes, please describe:	
During the relationship, important decisions were made by (indicate you, other parent, or both) about:	
Household finances	
Purchases of family property	
Children's education	
Children's healthcare	
Children's religious training	
Children's extracurricular activities	
Were you able to discuss family issues openly with one another?	

Comments on whether or not you are able to make decisions about the children cooperatively:

Have there been any incidents of verbal abuse?

In the past six months?

At any time in the relationship?

Have there been any incidents of physical abuse?

In the past six months?

At any time in the relationship?

Have charges ever been laid against you or the other parent?

Has either parent ever had a restraining order?

If there is a current restraining order, please address how this order will allow your family to attend OCB Camp:

If you answered "Yes" to <u>any</u> of the above, please provide specific details:

PARENTING SCHEDULE AND DECISION-MAKING

What is the current parenting-time schedule?	
Is there a current dispute about parenting?	
If yes, describe the nature of the dispute and indicate when it began (the approximate date):	

DOCUMENTATION

Do you have a signed/executed separation agreement?	
If so, what is the date?	/ /
Do you have a signed parenting plan?	
If so, what is the date?	/ /
Are there any court orders?	
If so, please list dates:	/ /

YOUR OBJECTIVES AND PRIMARY CONCERNS

How can the Overcoming Barriers Camp Program be of assistance to you and your family?
What needs to be different about you or the other parent to improve the situation for your child(ren)?
What needs to be different about your family to improve the situation for your child(ren)?
If there are contact difficulties between you and your child(ren), please describe in detail:
What is your greatest parenting strength?

What is your greatest parenting challenge?
What is the other parent's greatest parenting strength?
What is the other parent's greatest parenting challenge?
Provide any comments that you feel may be helpful to address/resolve the current situation:
Has any professional indicated that your child has an emotional, academic, or social problem?
If so, please elaborate:
What are your most important concerns regarding: (a) Your child(ren):
(b) Your family:
(c) Your child(ren)'s other parent:
What do you think are the most important concerns that the other parent has about you?

APPENDIX 2.B

TYPICAL BEHAVIORS AND PERCEPTIONS EXHIBITED BY THE ALIENATED CHILD, FAVORED PARENT, AND REJECTED PARENT

The following tables rely on an overview of the literature (e.g., Baker, 2005; Baker & Darnell, 2006; Cartwright, 2006; Clawar & Rivlin, 1971; Darnall, 1998; Garber, 2007, 2011, 2014; Gardner, 1985, 1992a, 1999; Johnston, Walters, & Olesen, 2005c; Kelly & Johnston, 2001; Warshak, 2001). They were initially created for Chapters 6 and 7 of Fidler, Bala, Birnbaum, and Kavassalis (2008), were then adapted for Fidler, Bala, and Saini (2013), and have been further adapted for this chapter. The behaviors listed are not differentiated by level or severity. While these behaviors are typical, not all of them will be present in every alienation case.

Alienated Child
• Shows inconsistent behavior, including indices of resistance, from one situation to another
• Demonstrates inconsistency between *statements* or *allegations* about rejected parent and *behavior* with rejected parent
• Behaves inconsistently with rejected parent (e.g., sometimes is defiant or hostile), but may behave well with other adults
• Has rigid, one-sided, "all good or all bad" opinion of each parent; idealizes one parent and devalues the other; refuses or is reticent to consider alternate views or explanations about one or both parents or the situation more generally
• Gives weak, trivial, frivolous, unelaborated, false, and irrational reasons to justify dislike, hatred, resistance, or rejection
• Revises history to eliminate or diminish any positive memories of experiences with rejected parent
• Has reactions and perceptions not justified by or disproportionate to rejected parent's behaviors
• Talks openly and without prompting about rejected parent's perceived shortcomings; may report events that child could not possibly remember (i.e., events occurring before child was 3 or 4 years old)
• Claims to be fearful but is aggressive, confrontational, even belligerent
• Calls rejected parent by first name
• Bad-mouths rejected parent's new family
• Bad-mouths or exhibits hatred of rejected parent's extended family and pets of rejected parent (hatred by association)
• Exhibits lack of guilt or ambivalence regarding cruelty or unkind behavior toward rejected parent
• Has stronger, but not necessarily healthy, psychological bond with alienating parent than with rejected parent
• Shows anger at rejected parent for perceived abandonment; blames rejected parent for divorce
• Viciously vilifies rejected parent; engages in unrelenting campaign of denigration or hatred

- When talking about rejected parent, speech is "brittle," a litany, obsessed, and artificial seeming; affect does not match words; shows no conviction; uses adult language; has a rehearsed quality
- Tells stories about one or both parents or the situation that are repetitive and lacking in detail and depth
- Uses "borrowed scenarios"—descriptions adopted from the favored parent or aligned family members
- Gives reports that mimic those of siblings rather than reflecting own experience
- Denies hope for reconciliation; does not acknowledge desire for reconciliation
- Reflexively supports favored parent in the parental conflict
- Displays "independent thinker phenomena": Claims beliefs about rejected parent are his or her own and not the alienating parent's
- Displays distorted perceptions and beliefs about rejected parent that go unchallenged by favored parent
- Expresses worry for preferred parent or desire to care for that parent; alternatively, defensively denies worry about parent
- Acts to appease, avoid rejection by, avoid withdrawal of attention by, or avoid withdrawal of love from favored parent
- Shows signs of role corruption, role reversal, or triangulation (e.g. parentification, adultification, or infantilization)
- Internalizes (e.g., has anxiety, phobic reactions, depression, or low self-esteem behavioral problems)
- Externalizes (e.g., is aggressive to people or objects or exhibits other acting out, bullying, or oppositional behavioral problems)
- May appear to function adequately in other environments (e.g., school or social) but tends to have difficulty interpersonally

---

Favored (Alienating) Parent

- Makes statements or shows behavior indicating that separation is experienced as humiliating
- Bad-mouths or denigrates other parent's qualities, parenting, or involvement with child
- Believes other parent is dangerous (harmful, angry, or mean) or sick, or portrays other parent as such
- Believes or implies that other parent never really loved or wanted the child
- Portrays self as the one who was the "real" or involved parent
- Believes other parent is not "worthy" of relationship with the child
- Acts fearful or suspicious of other parent in front of child; instills fear and rejection of other parent
- Fosters child's dependency on and need for protector in favored parent
- Portrays other parent as having abandoned the children, unloving, or uncaring
- Withdraws love and approval; makes love conditional on child's not showing love or positive feelings for other parent
- Minimizes actual and symbolic contact with other parent (e.g., removes or allows no photos or other reminders of other parent in the home)

- Insists that the child has the right to make decisions about contact; tells the child, "It's up to you"
- Refuses to talk directly to or to be in same room or close proximity with rejected parent; does not let rejected parent come to door to pick up child
- Rarely talks about other parent; uninterested in child's time with other parent after contact; gives child a cold shoulder or silent treatment or is moody after child returns, unless child expresses dissatisfaction about contact
- Refuses to hear positive comments about other parent; is quick to discount child's good times with other parent as trivial and unimportant
- Intercepts calls and messages from rejected parent
- Does not encourage child to call other parent between contacts; rationalizes that child does not ask to do so
- Tells child fun things that child missed during time with other parent
- Indulges child with material possessions and privileges
- Sets few limits on child or is rigid about routines, rules, and expectations
- Shows no concern for missed time with other parent
- Makes negative statements about other parent or situation and then denies saying them
- Reveals through body language and nonverbal communication a lack of interest in, disdain for, and disapproval of other parent
- Engages in inquisition of child after time spent with the other parent
- Discourages other parent from attending school events and activities or refuses other parent permission to do so
- Destroys or ignores telephone messages, gifts, and mail from other parent to child, or passes them on to child with disdain
- Restricts or withholds other parent's access to child-related information (e.g., about school, activities, or health)
- Distorts child's comments in ways that might justify accusations of abusive parenting or negative behavior by other parent
- Doesn't believe child has any need for relationship with other parent
- When child calls during contact with other parent and is quiet or noncommunicative, wrongly assumes child has been pressured by rejected parent or concludes child is uncomfortable with rejected parent, thereby "confirming" bad parenting, with no appreciation that child is in loyalty conflict or uncomfortable sharing positive experiences with the favored parent
- Repeatedly makes negative statements about other parent and embellishes or exaggerates negative attributes of other parent
- Neglects or avoids talking positively about other parent or child's time with other parent
- Manifests psychopathology, mental illness, personality disorder or characteristics, or substance/alcohol abuse through unfounded allegations of abuse, intimate-partner violence, or abusive or neglectful parenting
- Repeats delusional false statements to child; distorts history of other parent's participation in the child's life; claims other parent has totally changed since separation
- Projects own thoughts, feelings, and behaviors onto other parent
- Does not correct child's rude, defiant, or omnipotent behavior toward other parent (or other parent's extended family) but would never permit such behavior with others, including him- or herself

- Is convinced that other parent has harmed the child when there is no evidence
- Repeatedly makes false or fabricated allegations of sexual, physical, or emotional child abuse or intimate partner violence by other parent
- Says other parent left "us," divorced "us," and doesn't love "us"
- Overinvolves child in or confides in child about the marriage, litigation, and other adult matters
- Requires child to keep secrets from the rejected parent and to spy or report back on other parent
- Uses child to deliver verbal messages or letters to other parent
- Threatens overtly and covertly to withdraw love and affection from child unless child rejects other parent
- Manifests lack of courtesy to rejected parent directly or indirectly and to varying degrees
- Does not permit child to take certain clothing, pets, toys, etc., to contact with other parent, or to return with them
- Arranges activities that conflict with the child's scheduled parenting time with the other parent; talks to child fun or interesting activities the child missed because they were with the other parent
- Engages in "therapist shopping"
- Relocates for minor reasons and with little concern for effects on child
- Is inflexible about making occasional changes to parenting time to accommodate special events or occasions (e.g., weddings, funerals, or special birthdays)
- Changes child's last name
- Does not put other parent's name on school, extracurricular activity, and health forms
- Moves away or hides child from other parent

Rejected (Alienated) Parent

- Has lax or intermittently rigid or punitive parenting style
- Shows outrage at child's challenge to his or her authority
- Is passive or withdraws in face of conflict
- Feels helpless in response to child's dramatically changed behavior
- Is immature or self-centered in relation to child
- Puts own needs ahead of child's, similar to behavior in marriage but now reinterpreted to the extent that the parent does not see any wrongdoing
- Loses temper; exhibits angry, demanding, or intimidating character traits, but not to level of abuse
- Displays counterrejecting behavior toward child in response to child's rejection or omnipotent behavior
- Shows anxiety or mobilization in response to interpersonal or legal conflict
- Loses hope that anything or anyone can change child's new belief system about him or her
- Lacks empathic connection to child
- Continues to show critical or demanding traits present in marriage, but these become reinterpreted or minimized

- Is inept and unempathic in pursuit of child; pushes calls and letters; makes unannounced or embarrassing appearances at school or activities
- Challenges child's beliefs or attitudes and tries to convince them otherwise
- Tells child that he or she is parroting other parent
- Is dismissive of child's feelings and negative attitudes
- Attempts to induce guilt in child
- May use force to reassert parental position
- With child, vents about or blames other parent for brainwashing child; takes no responsibility for family circumstance
- Manifests characteristics of mental illness or personality disorder but not to the point of abusive or neglectful parenting

NOTE. Listed behaviors do not reach the level of abuse or warrant the child's disproportionate response or refusal of contact. If behaviors reach level of abuse, the correct identification of the contact problem is justified rejection.

3

The Current Status of Outpatient Approaches to Parent–Child Contact Problems

SHELY POLAK AND JOHN A. MORAN ∎

1. INTRODUCTION

The prevalence of children who resist or refuse contact with a parent remains unclear. Among samples of court-involved custody-disputing families, the prevalence of moderate to severe parent–child contact problems ranges from 21% to 27%, while in community samples rates are approximately 11–15% (Johnston, 1993, 2003, 2005; Johnston & Goldman, 2010; Racusin, Copans, & Mills, 1994; Wallerstein & Kelly, 1980). Despite the current ambiguity of prevalence rates, recent studies have found an increase over the past decade in the number of cases in which the issues of alienation and parent–child contact problems are raised during litigation (Bala, Hunt, & McCarney, 2010). In response to the growing recognition of parent–child contact problems, different clinical interventions, including outpatient and more intensive models, have emerged that attempt to help repair these disrupted parent–child relationships.

The problem of a child's rejecting contact with a parent gained wide recognition in the mid-1980s, through the work of late American psychiatrist Richard Gardner (1985). Since then, the subject of parent–child contact problems, including their etiology, their behavioral manifestations, and treatment approaches, has received significant attention in both the clinical and legal arenas. Some consensus about the general factors relevant to the origin of parent–child contact problems began to emerge following the publication of Kelly and Johnston's (2001) multifactorial model. That model placed the child's relationship with the parents on a continuum, at one end of which the child's relationship with both parents is positive and healthy, and at the other end of which the child is alienated from one parent and has a pathological relationship with the favored parent. Using this model, most children in both intact and separated families are believed to fall in the middle of the continuum.

Generally, empirical studies have supported the conclusion that the family dynamics that result in a child's resisting or refusing parental contact form a complex, multilevel systems problem with several factors simultaneously at play (Johnston, Walters, & Olesen, 2005b; Johnston, Roseby, & Kuehnle, 2009; Polak & Saini, 2015). These factors include poor parenting practices, a child's attachment patterns and developmental needs, the presence of a parental personality disorder, a child's distorted cognitions, a parent engaging in parental alienating behaviors, or exposure to chronic high conflict after separation in tandem with the adversarial legal system (Baker & Darnall, 2006; Childress, 2014; Fidler & Bala, 2010; Fidler, Bala, & Saini, 2013; Garber, 2004; Kelly & Johnston, 2001; Johnston, 2003; Johnston et al., 2009; Johnston, Walters, & Olesen, 2005a, 2005b; Polak & Saini, 2015).

Concurrent with the development of a coherent framework for describing and understanding the dynamics related to parent–child contact problems, family courts are increasingly accepting expert testimony about alienation (Bala et al., 2010) and designing judicial orders for interventions to intercede on behalf of the parent–child relationship.

Anecdotal evidence suggests that such interventions often include participation by the resisting child and rejected parent in weekly outpatient counseling. There is an informal professional consensus that such interventions result in little benefit and may cause the child and rejected parent to develop further resentment. The child's resentment is due to feeling forced to participate in unwanted treatment, while the rejected parent's resentment is toward the behavioral health community and the courts, given the time spent and expenses incurred for an intervention that proved to be of little value. Presumably, such treatments are not more effective because they do not intervene with other systemic factors relevant to the parent–child contact problem.

Emerging outpatient approaches differ from these interventions with respect to multiple factors, including which family members are involved, the theoretical orientation of how the problem is conceptualized and of the subsequent approach to clinical treatment, the definition of the treatment goals, the use of psychoeducational and recreational or experiential programs, and the emphasis on judicial monitoring and follow-up.

The rest of this chapter contains three major sections. In Section 2 we review factors associated with the development of parent–child contact problems within an ecological systems framework (Bronfenbrenner, 1979). Section 3 reviews the literature describing different outpatient interventions currently available for parent–child contact problems that are not justified by the rejected parent's behavior, highlighting key clinical and theoretical components of each intervention. In Section 4 we consider the more intensive interventions that are being used for cases for which outpatient treatment has been deemed insufficient.

2. RISK FACTORS ASSOCIATED WITH PARENT–CHILD CONTACT PROBLEMS

This section reviews empirical support for risk factors in the rejected parent, favored parent, interparental relationship, and child that are associated with strained parent–child relationships and the development or perpetuation of parent–child contact problems after separation (see Polak & Saini, 2015, for a comprehensive review).

2.1. Parenting Styles and Skills

In some cases, a rejected parent's own behaviors are the greatest contributor to a strained parent–child relationship or contact problem. Rejected parents often exhibit harsh, rigid, and authoritarian parenting styles. They tend to be critical and demanding, lack warmth and empathy toward the child, and make imprudent demands for the child to be independent and responsible (Darnall, 2011; Fidler & Bala, 2010; Fidler et al., 2013; Johnston & Kelly, 2004; Johnston et al., 2005a; Kelly & Johnston, 2001). Such rejected parents have little appreciation for the importance of the child's genuine thoughts, needs, and feelings; too often, they quickly conclude that the child is parroting the favored parent (Friedlander & Walters, 2010). Johnston et al. (2005a) found that rejected parents were less able to communicate effectively with their children, less involved in the children's daily activities, and experienced less pleasure, joy, or fun when relating to the children. Both rejected mothers and fathers were found to have diminished social, emotional, and psychological adjustment after divorce.

Favored parents are often involved in a dependency dynamic with their children that interferes with their ability to promote the children's independent functioning. Studies have found that preferred parents tend to be narcissistic and use more primitive defense mechanisms to manage conflict (Johnston et al., 2005a).

Once a child begins to resist a parent, both the rejected and the favored parent are confronted with challenges outside the realm of everyday parenting (Moran, Sullivan, & Sullivan, 2015). In response to the child's resistance, rejected parents must adapt their parenting style across several domains of skills: expression of affection, participation in activities with the child, communicating with the child, and managing and disciplining the child (Moran & Weinstock, 2011). If the rejected parent's style contributed to the parent–child contact problem, his or her response to the crisis of the child's resistance or rejection will likely be problematic. Rejected parents may respond reactively to the child's rejection with counterrejecting behaviors, anger, aggression, and punitive responses, or they may be passive and withdraw from parenting (Baker & Darnall, 2006; Fidler & Bala, 2010; Goldberg & Goldberg, 2013; Kelly & Johnston, 2001; Warshak, 2010). Unfortunately, such counterrejecting behaviors can reinforce allegations made by the favored parent and provide the child with realistic concerns that the favored parent can exaggerate or exploit, leading to intensified condemnation and further rejection.

2.2. Parental Alienating Behaviors

Alienating behaviors have been defined as "any constellation of behaviors, whether conscious or unconscious, that could evoke a disturbance in the relationship between a child and the other parent" (Darnall, 1998, p. 4). Baker and Darnall (2006) identified 1,300 parental alienating behaviors, which they summarized into eight groups: bad-mouthing, interfering with parenting time, interfering with mail or phone contact, interfering with symbolic contact (e.g., removing photographs), interfering with information, emotional manipulation, unhealthy alliance, and miscellaneous. Empirical evidence and clinical observations have shown that it is the favored parents who are most likely to engage in parental alienating behaviors (Baker & Darnall, 2006, 2007; Darnall, 2011; Kelly & Johnston, 2001; Fidler & Bala, 2010; Johnston et al., 2005b, 2009; Warshak, 2015).

2.3. Cognitive Level and Cognitive Distortions

Based on both clinical writing and empirical research, age appears to be an important risk factor for the development of strained parent–child relationships (Fidler et al., 2013; Johnston et al., 2009; Kelly & Johnston, 2001). A certain level of cognitive sophistication is needed to understand multiple, differing, and simultaneous perspectives with respect to the family conflict (Polak & Saini, 2015). Prior to cognitive maturation, one is likely to see a child in a high-conflict situation shift allegiances between parents or to see younger children tending to "forget" their scripts or their anger (Garber, 2014; Johnston & Roseby, 1997).

The most common age range found among children resisting contact is 9–15 years old, after sufficient cognitive maturity has been reached (Johnston et al., 2009). From a clinical standpoint, cognitive distortions are frequently present among these children. These faulty belief systems translate into rigid positions that exacerbate the parent–child conflict. Cognitive distortions commonly observed among children resisting and rejecting contact include all-or-nothing thinking (the child sees one parent as all good and the other as all bad), selective abstraction (the child focuses on one, negative detail of the rejected parent and ignores other salient features), overgeneralization (the child draws an unwarranted conclusion on the basis of one or a few isolated incidents), magnification (the child exhibits gross errors in evaluating events), and absolute, dichotomous thinking (the child polarizes all experiences into extremely negative or positive categories) (Polak, 2014). Although these cognitive biases are frequently observed in clinical practice, there is limited empirical evidence about them. At least one study on the psychological functioning of alienated children found evidence for simplistic and rigid information processing (Johnston, Walters, & Olesen, 2005c).

2.4. History of Attachment and the Parent–Child Relationship

Attachment theory, based on the works of John Bowlby (1969) and Mary Ainsworth (Ainsworth & Bell, 1970), posits that a child's healthy socio-emotional development is dependent on having an ongoing, warm, and intimate relationship with a responsive primary caregiver early in life (Ainsworth & Bell, 1970; Bowlby, 1969; Sroufe, 2000). This primary attachment relationship shapes an infant's ability to communicate and relate to the primary caregiver and eventually to other human beings (Bowlby, 1969; Schore, 2012; Schore & McIntosh, 2012).

Repeated interactions with primary caregivers form internal working models (IWMs) of one's self and the world (Bowlby, 1969; Polak, 2014). Internal working models are organized memories of past experiences, attachment needs, and expectations about the attachment figure's ability to meet those needs (Barron, 2000; Bowlby, 1982; Bretherton, 1992; Faber & Wittenborn, 2010). A child's IWM of the parent is integral to the quality of the parent–child relationship. While IWMs remain relatively stable throughout one's life, they can change as a result of subsequent life experiences and environmental factors (e.g., domestic violence, separation or divorce, and serious illness) (Sroufe, 2000). These changes may affect the quality of the parent–child attachment relationship (Lieberman, 2004).

Garber (2004) uses an attachment-based framework to help explain child alienation. He proposes that alienation may result from a child's developing a distorted IWM of the rejected parent. Garber hypothesizes that "in the extreme, one caregiver's denigrating and inaccurate messages can prompt a child to accommodate her IWM of another caregiver such that her subjective experience of security with that caregiver has little or no relationship to his or her actual sensitivity and responsiveness" (p. 61). The corrupted or distorted IWM includes inaccurate beliefs not reflective of the historical parent–child experiences. Rather, the distortion is a modification that reflects the favored parent's subjective experiences and overt or covert influences.

Since there are no specific measures to test IWMs and this construct is typically inferred based on behavior, it cannot be corroborated by empirical research. The existing research on alienation shows evidence of the use of parental alienating behaviors (Baker & Darnall, 2007; Fidler & Bala, 2010; Fidler et al., 2013) and the premature cognitive development of children that display contact problems (Johnston et al., 2009). One can deduce that this combination is a serious risk factor for the development of a distorted IWM.

It is therefore imperative for clinicians to assess the preexisting parent–child relationship and level of parental involvement prior to the physical separation. Children who had a closer attachment relationship to the favored parent before the separation may be continuing to demonstrate the same dynamics after the separation (Polak & Saini, 2015).

2.5. Personality Disorders and Parental Psychopathology

There is a substantial amount of theoretical and empirical literature on the relationship between mental disorders, including personality disorders, and compromised parenting practices (see Zahn-Waxler, Duggal, & Gruber, 2002). The professional consensus is that a mental disorder can indeed compromise parenting (Pett, Wampold, Turner, & Vaughan-Cole; 1999; Tschann, Johnston, Kline, & Wallerstein, 1990; Whiteside & Becker, 2000; Zahn-Waxler et al., 2002). This idea is substantiated by the results of a longitudinal study by Pruett, Williams, Insabella, and Little (2003) examining the association between parental psychopathology and the parent–child relationship. The participants were recruited as part of a larger court project designed to assess an intervention program designed for families in divorce proceedings or parents developing a parenting plan. The results revealed that greater parental symptomatology was associated with negative changes in the parent–child relationship. Parental symptomatology from a mental disorder may or may not be relevant to parenting skills on its own, but under the stress of parent–child contact problems, underlying behavioral health problems may be exacerbated and require an auxiliary intervention to the family reunification effort.

Higher rates of psychopathology and personality disorders have been found among alienating parents (Fidler & Bala, 2010; Gordon, Stoffey, & Bottinelli, 2008). Demby (2009) states that alienating (preferred) parents do not respond to separation with sadness or loss but instead with intense anger, sometimes leading to hatred of and a desire for revenge against the other parent. Johnston et al. (2009) report that alienating parents with personality disorders have difficulty differentiating their own needs from the needs of their children. Chapter 4 of this volume discusses the presence of maladaptive personality traits and frank personality disorders among this population in greater detail.

In the research literature, four empirical studies (Gordon et al., 2008; Johnston et al., 2005a; Lampel, 1996; Siegel & Langford, 1998) examined the psychological profiles of parents during a custody evaluation. All four studies found that on the Minnesota Multiphasic Personality Inventory, alienating parents had clinically significant higher L and K scores, which are associated with engaging in the more narcissistic and primitive defenses of denial, splitting, and projection and with clinical borderline pathology associated with reality distortions and being provocative. Findings with respect to the rejected parent were mixed. One study found no support for the idea that rejected parents contribute to the dynamics by showing primitive defenses (Gordon et al., 2008). In that study, rejected parents were found to be similar to custody-litigating parents in nonalienation cases. In contrast, Johnston and colleagues (2005a) reported finding coping deficits and difficulty modulating emotions among rejected parents.

2.6. Interparental Conflict

In a review of case law, Birnbaum and Bala (2010) reported that high interparental conflict was common to all the cases of child alienation they examined. While child alienation is found in a subset of high-conflict families, a causal link between high-conflict separation or divorce and alienation has not been established. This lack of such an association may be a consequence of the variety of definitions for what constitutes high conflict in the population of separated and divorced parents. Although the mechanism by which coparenting conflict influences child outcomes is not well understood, compromised parenting is believed to be the main pathway by which marital conflict translates into poor parent–child relationships (Krishnakumar & Buehler, 2000). Research shows that parents who are consumed by interparental conflict, both before and after separation, are less warm and empathetic and more rejecting toward their children, use harsher and more coercive discipline, and are more withdrawn from the parenting role than are separating parents who do not show such conflict (Amato & Booth, 1996; Kelly, 2012). Conflictual relationships can cause caregivers to be more irritable, emotionally drained, and less attentive and sensitive. Further, children in high-conflict families are frequently triangulated into the middle of parental disputes (Emery, 2012; Grych, 2005). It has been hypothesized that children might resist or reject contact as a way of removing themselves from such situations (Garber, 2014; Johnston et al., 2009).

Several treatment goals for the coparenting relationship are conceptually relevant to a family reunification intervention. In general, coparents need to be effective in sharing information important for the parent–child relationship, and they need to be supportive of the child's relationship with the coparent and his or her extended family (Moran & Weinstock, 2011). When one parent believes that fault for the loss of his or her relationship with their child lies with the other parent, and when that parent believes that the child is unsafe or inadequately cared for when in the coparent's care, the resulting coparenting conflict is severe and obviously distressing. In this situation, asking parents to work together to improve family relationships can seem like the least viable solution. Yet when a child is losing attachment to a parent, the favored parent can have critical information about how to repair the relationship between the child and the rejected parent. Further, it may be critical for the rejected parent to hear the favored parent's understanding of the child's resistance and the ideas that the favored parent has about how the rejected parent might best approach healing the tension in his or her relationship with the child. At the same time, it is necessary to deal with the fact that the information the favored parent has to share may consider only the flaws of the rejected parent, ignoring, minimizing, or denying her or his own contribution to the ruptured relationship.

Specific treatment goals might include developing the skills needed to manage coparenting communication and negotiating agreements on such matters as responding to the child's anxiety before and during parenting time with the rejected parent, family behavior at exchanges and public events, responding to the children's disrespectful behavior towards the rejected parent, the child's communicating with the preferred parent while with the rejected parent, how to respond if the child makes an allegation that might require mandated reporting, and the roles and guidelines for participation by stepparents and extended family in the family reunification effort.

2.7. Involvement in the Court System

Empirical research has not directly linked parent–child contact problems with a parent's involvement in the court system. However, one can extrapolate that the stress of involvement in an adversarial court process exacerbates coparenting conflict, which can trigger parental psychopathology and adversely affect the quality of parenting and the parent–child relationship (Polak & Saini, 2015). Kelly (2012) points out that the indirect negative effects of marital conflict, including litigation-related conflict, are mediated through the mother–child and father–child relationships, primarily in terms of the quality of parenting. Quality of parenting is consistently one of the best predictors of children's psychological and social adjustment (Sandler, Wheeler, & Braver, 2013).

2.8. Summary of Research on Contributing Factors

Strained parent–child relationships and parent–child contact problems are often the result of multidimensional, interconnected, and comorbid factors. This observation, supported by the empirical research described in this section, suggests that a transactional, ecological systems approach is best suited to understanding and helping correct this complex dynamic (Polak, 2014; Polak & Saini, 2015).

These complex cases require interventions that address each of the factors highlighted above that may contribute to the child's resistance or refusal toward a parent. Clinical interventions that address these factors have been integrated in most outpatient family reunification models, which we review next. It is critical that the goals of therapeutic reunification are shaped according to the underlying etiology and conceptual understanding of a child's resistance or refusal. In turn, this theoretical understanding informs the clinical skills commonly used when working with families in which parent–child contact problems are present.

3. OVERVIEW OF OUTPATIENT MODELS OF REUNIFICATION THERAPY

3.1. Definitions and Practice Standards

Reunification therapy is a recently developed therapeutic modality designed to help address parent–child contact issues in high-conflict, litigious families. The term *reintegration therapy* is used interchangeably with *reunification therapy* in this context. Clinical and educational interventions are most suitable for mild and some moderate alienation, realistic estrangement, or hybrid cases; severe cases of alienation are unlikely to respond to therapeutic interventions alone (Fidler & Bala, 2010; Friedlander & Walters, 2010, 2014; Johnston, 2005; Sullivan & Kelly, 2001; Warshak, 2010). Severe alienation typically requires intensive reunification programs, often coupled with close judicial oversight.

Despite the fact that the term *reunification therapy* is becoming more common, few detailed treatment protocols or best-practice guidelines are available to inform this type of treatment. Rather, there are varied clinical opinions and multiple approaches in use. Within the field, interventions appear to depend on the practitioner's clinical assessment and theoretical understanding of this complex issue.

There is consensus within the research literature that the reunification therapist should have specialized knowledge in the dynamics of high-conflict separated or divorced families and also competence in family therapy and cognitive–behavioral therapy. The reunification therapist should not be expected to make decisions or recommendations about custody or access, since this would mean taking on a dual role—a possible breach of ethical conduct—and would distract the therapist from maintaining focus on clinical work with the family (Darnall, 2011; Fidler & Bala, 2010).

3.2. Goals of Reunification Therapy

The goals of reunification treatment are different for the alienated child, the rejected parent, the favored parent, and the court. Table 3.1 provides an overview of the goals for the child and parents. Specifically, goals for the child may include reunifying with the rejected parent, developing an emotionally safe and trusting relationship with both parents, disentangling the child from the interparental conflict, being able to receive affection from and express affection toward both parents, and improved overall psychological health, critical thinking, and problem-solving and coping skills. Some clinicians suggest that if even direct regular contact does not resume after therapy, reconstruction of children's distorted cognitions about the family history and resolution of emotional issues that resulted from the conflict nevertheless constitutes successful reunification (DeJong & Davies, 2012). Goals for the favored and rejected parents can include developing insight into how their own individual behaviors or parenting practices have contributed to the dynamic, eliminating alienating or counterrejecting behavior (or both), decreasing the level of interparental conflict, restoring appropriate parenting, improved coparenting and parent–child roles and boundaries, improved communication patterns and conflict resolution skills, addressing distortions in perceptions and judgment, addressing divorce-related stress, and developing healthy parent–child relationships (Darnall, 2011; DeJong & Davies, 2012; Fidler et al., 2013; Friedlander & Walters, 2010; Johnston, 2005;

Table 3-1. General Goals of Family Reunification Interventions

Goals for the child	Goals for the parents
• Increase contact with rejected parent	• Eliminate alienating and counterrejecting behaviors
• Improve relationship with rejected parent	• Shift from conflicted to parallel or cooperative coparenting
• Develop healthy relationship with both parents	• Restore rejected parent's parental roles
• Minimize involvement in coparenting conflict	• Negotiate mutually supported parenting practices related to family reunification
• Reduce cognitive distortions, polarized and negative stereotypical thinking, and attitudes about rejected parent	• Reduce reliance on behavioral health and legal professionals for decision-making about family
• Improve coping and critical thinking skills	

Johnston, Walters, & Friedlander, 2001; Polak, 2014; Sullivan, Ward, & Deutsch, 2010; Warshak, 2010).

We next review several models of reunification treatment: family-based approaches, cognitive–behavioral techniques (e.g., systematic desensitization and gradual exposure), and attachment-based reunification therapy. Many of the interventions across these models have overlapping components.

3.3. Family-Based Therapeutic Approaches

In line with viewing children's resisting or refusing parental contact as a systems issue, some researchers and clinicians advocate conducting reunification therapy using a family-focused approach (Darnall, 2011; DeJong & Davies, 2012; Fidler & Bala, 2010; Friedlander & Walters, 2010, 2014; Gottlieb, 2013; Johnston et al., 2001). The aim of this approach is to shift underlying dysfunctional family dynamics that serve to maintain the contact problems. The approach involves the participation of the entire family in various combinations (i.e., individual, coparent, parent–child, and family sessions) and the inclusion of significant others or important family members (e.g., stepparents or grandparents) when necessary (Fidler et al., 2013; Friedlander & Walters, 2010; Gottlieb, 2012, 2013; Johnston et al., 2001). In this model, the reunification therapist executes appropriate releases to ensure there is an open system of communication among all family members and any outside professionals involved. Clinical interventions used in family-based therapeutic reunification include cognitive restructuring or reframing and other cognitive–behavioral techniques, parent coaching, and psychoeducation (Darnall, 2011; Fidler et al., 2013; Friedlander & Walters, 2010; Gottlieb, 2013; Johnston, 2005; Johnston et al., 2001; Sullivan & Kelly, 2001).

The family therapist meets with each of the parents in individual sessions to help improve their level of insight into how their separation, conflict, and dispute over contact has affected their child(ren). Once rapport has been established, the therapist helps each parent understand, recognize, and acknowledge how his or her behaviors have contributed to the current situation (Darnall, 2011; DeJong & Davies, 2012).

For instance, with the favored parent, individual therapy becomes the venue for expressing fears or worries and learns about the importance of limits and boundaries. The therapist encourages awareness of an inappropriate parent–child relationship and enmeshed boundaries as well as of the impact of subtle or overt alienating behaviors the therapist may gather from the feelings the parent displays in the sessions. Through a combination of cognitive restructuring and cognitive–behavioral techniques, individual therapy with the favored parent can address and differentiate valid concerns from concerns that are irrational, unsubstantiated, or distorted. Psychoeducation on the importance of children having relationships with both parents after separation, the short- and long-term benefits of effective coping skills for children, ,as well as the negative outcomes associated with chronic conflict, parentified children, and severed parent–child relationships can serve as an additional motivation for behavior modification.

Individual therapy with the rejected parent focuses on helping that parent develop awareness of how his or her behavior(s) has contributed to the family dynamic underlying the contact problem. This process includes getting the parent to admit culpability for historical incidents, harsh, rigid, or negative parenting practices, or intense emotions that have legitimately upset the child. Teaching the parent healthy and appropriate parenting skills using coaching techniques is an important aspect of the individual therapy. Coaching rejected parents on how to regulate and modulate the intensity of their emotional expression and helping them develop an effective style of expression is an essential component of therapy. Individual therapy also provides support for dealing with the intense emotions of loss, despair, rejection, shame, anger or guilt that arise from the loss of the parent–child relationship. Expressing these difficult feelings within a supportive environment can help the parent develop better coping mechanisms, thereby reducing the likelihood of that parent's responding with counterrejecting behavior. Psychoeducation on the complex dynamics associated with alienation and with children's resisting contact can help the rejected parent to develop empathy for the child and to gain a sense of control (Goldberg & Goldberg, 2013).

In meeting individually with the child, the family therapist assesses her or his views, worries, and perceptions about family roles and relationships. The therapist can use cognitive restructuring techniques (e.g., gently challenging or highlighting the child's incongruent or contradictory statements) to address distortions, develop critical-thinking skills, and differentiate the child's own experiences from those of others. Helping the child develop awareness of the existence of multiple perspectives about the same situation can help the child achieve a more realistic or rounded view of the rejected parent while potentially lessening her or his anxiety (Darnall, 2011). Further, individual sessions with the family therapist can become a place where the child can develop awareness of her or his own feelings and practice asserting her- or himself to both parents.

Coparenting sessions are used to help the parents develop a healthy working coparenting relationship. Working toward this goal entails addressing valid concerns either parent may have; discussing parenting schedules, parent–child contact, and other parenting issues; and developing healthy communication strategies. This actively disentangles the child from the situation and supports healthier parent–child boundaries while restoring the parental subsystem. For mild cases, the therapist may wish to have the parents develop a new narrative and understanding of the family history and current situation. Sharing this narrative with the child within a family therapeutic context can then serve as a cognitive restructuring clinical tool.

Dyadic work with the rejected parent and child is essential for two reasons. First, it allows the therapist to observe how the rejected parent relates to the child and assess its impact on the parent–child relationship. If the parent is engaging in inappropriate behaviors, the therapist can then guide the parent toward different behavior and hold him or her accountable for making desirable changes (Walters & Friedlander, 2010). Second, it allows the therapist to assess how the child perceives or distorts the interaction with the parent, setting the stage for the next therapeutic task, namely, correcting any such distortions.

Dyadic work with the favored parent and child is also essential for assessing parent–child boundaries and providing an opportunity for the parent to acknowledge misconceptions about the other parent and openly encourage the child's relationship with the other parent (Gottlieb, 2012, 2013). The favored parent's task is to give the child confidence that she or he can manage the difficult task of making contact with the rejected parent and to provide clear expectations that the child can and will be able to master this challenge (Deutsch, 2014).

Because individual members and family systems are resistant to change, the reunification process must remain open and transparent. To ensure that parents are each held accountable for their behavior, information about their level of cooperation should be available to the court, parenting coordinator, or attorneys. Albertson-Kelly & Burkard (2013) state that the desire for change is often absent in the favored parent and child. Since mental health professionals are limited in their ability to gain the cooperation of clients who are not motivated to make changes in their behavior, the use of the court system is an integral part of treatment: Judicial monitoring serves as external reinforcement. Dr. Leslie Drozd, a clinical psychologist and expert in alienation, states that "family systems are recalcitrant and won't change unless there is incredible accountability. . . .. [T]here has to be an external motivation before there is going to be any kind of internal motivating" (cited in Fidler et al., 2013, pp. 116–117.).

Table 3.2 summarizes the clinical literature on family-focused reintegration therapy, including the goals of therapy for the child, the rejected parent, the favored parent, and other significant individuals (e.g. new partners, extended family members, etc.) as well as potential clinical interventions to achieve these objectives.

Table 3-2. FAMILY-BASED REINTEGRATION THERAPEUTIC MODELS: TREATMENT GOALS AND CLINICAL INTERVENTIONS

	Child	Rejected parent	Favored parent	Significant individuals/coparent
Goals	• Lessen anxiety • Correct errors or fixed distortions • Improve global functioning • Develop realistic view of rejected parent rooted in actual experience • Disentangle child from parents' difficulties and ongoing conflict • Differentiate child's experience of rejected parent from aligned parent's experience • Help child develop coping skills and understand multiple perspectives • Assess and address other mental health concerns • Work through intense emotions associated with rejected parent and parental conflict	• Help parent relate to child in loving, noncoercive, and nonintrusive manner, without counterrejection • Change behavior and destructing beliefs • Help parent develop insight into his or her contribution to the problem • Get parent to acknowledge or admit real culpability, make apologies when appropriate • Address distorted or simplistic view that other parent is entirely to blame • Correct misperceptions • Provide more complex understanding of situation to help parent become more child focused and develop empathy for the child	• Get parent to allow child to have reciprocal relationship with both parents, free of interference and exposure to parental alienating behaviors. • Gain parent's cooperation and support in reunification process • Educate parent on importance of child's sustaining good continuing relationships with both parents • Address allegations and concerns about other parent and child's physical safety with therapist and rejected parent • Differentiate valid from distorted concerns • Differentiate parent's experience from realities of child's experience • Inform parent about legal consequences for not complying with court order allowing contact between child and rejected parent	• Educate significant others about their contribution to the problem • Restore coparental and parent–child roles within family • Help coparents develop new patterns of communicating with and responding to each other • Address realistic, legitimate parenting concerns • Reduce child's exposure to hostility

(continued)

Table 3-2. CONTINUED

	Child	Rejected parent	Favored parent	Significant individuals/coparent
	• Ensure child does not behave in a rude, obnoxious, or abusive manner toward rejected parent • Engage in corrective transactions between rejected parent and child as well as between all family members • Break coalitions		• Help parent set limits and respond appropriately if child's behavior is inappropriate or hurtful • Provide supportive, encouraging, and positive messages about contact with rejected parent • Redirect parent's neediness away from child and to other, appropriate sources Restore parent–child boundaries	
Clinical interventions	• Cognitive restructuring, reframing, challenging • Individual therapy sessions • New experiences with rejected parent	• Individual therapy, parent coaching, psychoeducation, coparenting sessions, parent–child sessions, family sessions	• Individual therapy, coparenting sessions, parent–child sessions, family sessions • Psychoeducation and cognitive restructuring on importance of good ongoing parent–child relationships • Active collaboration among professionals involved	• For rejected parent–child dyad: Assess inappropriate behavior by rejected parent; note discrepancies between child's stated views about contact with rejected parent and child's behavior when in rejected parent's presence

NOTE. Based on Darnall (2011), DeJong & Davies (2012), Friedlander & Walters (2010), Gottlieb (2013), Johnston, Walters, & Friedlander (2001), Walters & Friedlander (2010).

3.4. Integration of Cognitive–Behavioral Techniques

Recently, Garber (2015) analogized a child's resistance to contact and extreme polarized beliefs to presenting with a phobia-like response. Garber (2015) and Deutsch (2014) hypothesize that the child is caught in a cycle where she or he avoids the feared object (i.e., the rejected parent), and the avoidance prevents the child from having the opportunity to learn that the fear is either exaggerated or unwarranted. Pointing to meta-analytic research demonstrating the effectiveness of cognitive–behavioral therapy (CBT) for the treatment of phobic children, Garber argues for the need to break a child's phobia-like avoidance by gradually and systematically exposing the child to the rejected parent. Garber suggests that the aligned parent, rejected parent, and polarized child begin this process of systematic desensitization in their respective individual treatments with imaginal desensitization paired with relaxation techniques. That is, the child separately with his or her own therapist orders his or her particular anxieties in a fear hierarchy while also developing and practicing relaxation techniques. The goal of these sessions is to decrease subjective feelings of anxiety, to promote mastery of feeling less anxious around rejected parent, and, for the child, to develop the capacity to approach the resisted parent.

The family reunification therapist then coordinates meetings with each family member and the individual therapists to establish familiarity, credibility, and trust. Once the child and favored parent is some mastery of anxiety identification, imaginal exposure, and relaxation skills, the family therapist begins regular meetings with the child toward the expressed goal of reunification. Consistent with CBT principles of systematic desensitization, the family therapist holds these meetings in successive steps, starting with least anxiety-provoking situation on a child's fear hierarchy, with the ultimate goal of a face-to-face encounter with the rejected parent. Depending on the circumstances, exposure in these early stages may be imaginal or visual (e.g., using photographs of the rejected parent and child). Throughout this process, the family therapist maintains open and frequent communication with the parents and their therapists.

Weitzman (2013) and Walters and Friedlander (2010) described using a one-way mirror and speakerphone or Skype as safe and structured ways to rebuild a relationship with the rejected parent. In essence, these methods are also desensitization strategies to minimize a child's level of distress in response to the rejected parent and empower the child to cope with anxiety through mastery rather than avoidance.

Also informed by CBT, Baker developed the "I Don't Want to Choose" program to address children's loyalty conflicts (Baker & Andre, 2013). The goal of this psychoeducational program is to teach children alternative ways of coping with these conflicts and to enhance their resiliency in coping with other difficult postseparation challenges. The program can be implemented in a school setting by a range of professionals. It uses CBT principles such as cognitive restructuring and Socratic questioning. While it is intended to be preventative, a reintegration therapist can use aspects of the curriculum with children who present with resistant or refusing dynamics. The program focuses on helping the child develop critical-thinking skills, problem-solving skills, emotional and cognitive–behavioral problem-solving tools, and alternative ways of finding external support.

Baker's program also teaches children how to become aware of parental alienating behaviors and how to disengage from those dynamics (Baker & Andre, 2013). This process entails helping children identify parental alienating behaviors, become aware and critical of their beliefs, think about their options and choices, label their emotions, differentiate their emotions from those of others, and learn skills to disengage respectfully from the loyalty conflict. The therapist accomplishes these goals by coaching children to ask themselves questions such as "Why do I believe what I believe?," "Is there evidence to support my belief?," "What are my choices?," "What am I being pressured to do?," "What am I feeling?," and "What do I know to be true about each of my parents?"

Table 3.3 summarizes the clinical literature on reintegration therapy using cognitive–behavioral techniques.

3.5. Attachment-Based Reunification Therapy

Dr. Craig Childress has adapted an attachment-based model to family reunification therapy and the treatment of alienation. According to Childress (2014), the primary treatment foci for reunification therapy are the child's symptoms, which are considered manifestations of pathogenic parenting practices by a parent with borderline and narcissistic personality features who engages in parental alienating behaviors. In contrast to family-focused approaches, Childress argues that it is necessary for the child to be separated from the alienating parent's pathogenic parenting practices during the active phase of treatment. Childress further suggests that the child's relationship with the rejected parent should be monitored on reintroduction to the alienating parent to ensure that treatment gains are maintained and consolidated.

Childress (2014) provides a framework for attachment-based reunification therapy based on three goals and interventions:

1. Adopt a relaxed, curious, and positive therapeutic stance.
2. Reorient the child to his or her authentic experience of grief, sadness, and loss related to the divorce and to his or her desire to bond with the rejected parent.
3. Resolve the child's chronic anger.

The emotional and relationship challenges present in cases of alienation respond best when the therapist uses a relaxed and pleasant emotional tone. Childress (2014) suggests that therapists adopt a stance of curiosity about family members' behavior while also gently but consistently encouraging kindness and

Table 3-3. Cognitive–Behavioral Techniques for Use in Therapeutic Reintegration: Treatment Goals and Clinical Interventions

	Child	Rejected parent	Favored parent
Goals	• Enable child to separate from favored parent • Help child be present in reunification phase with minimal level of distress • Enable child to spend time with rejected parent with little anxiety • Teach child it is his or her right to not have to choose between parents • Teach child it is OK to love both parents. • Teach child alternative ways to cope with loyalty conflicts • Reduce psychological vulnerability associated with parental conflict • Develop child's critical-thinking skills, problem-solving skills, and emotional and cognitive–behavioral problem-solving tools	• Get parent to be able to sit down with child and therapist in calm, nondefensive manner	• Get parent to be able to talk about reunification and accompany child to reunification therapy with minimal anxiety • Get parent to support the reunification process
Clinical interventions	• Individual CBT, followed by meetings with family reunification therapist • 20 psychoeducational sessions using the "I Don't Want to Change" workbook in a peer-group setting	• Individual CBT, followed by meetings with family reunification therapist	• Individual CBT, followed by meetings with family reunification therapist

NOTE. Based on Baker & Andre (2013), Garber (2015).

compassion. The goal is to spread kindness and compassion to the family's relationships to achieve an overall calm and relaxed emotional tone.

With respect to the second of these goals, Childress (2014) suggests that that the fundamental issue in parent–child contact problems or alienation is a child's misattribution of his or her's natural grief response to the dissolution of the family, resulting in the induced loss of a formerly positive relationship with the rejected parent. According to Childress, the narcissistic and borderline features of the alienating parent prevent his or her own processing of loss, which in turn undermines the child's own capacity to grieve. The alienating parent experiences the divorce as a narcissistic injury, which activates his or her own fear of abandonment, resulting in sadness and anger to which the parent responds with resentment and vengeful wishes. The parent then transmits this reaction to the child, distorting the child's grieving process.

The essence of attachment-based reunification therapy is to help the child understand, process, and resolve the normal experience of grief and loss resulting from the family's dissolution. The therapist helps the child find his or her own authentic experiences, in contrast to those projected onto the child by the alienating parent. This process aims to help foster the child's capacity to recognize his or her own experiences, including thoughts, feelings, and perceptions.

Turning now to the matter of the child's chronic anger, Childress notes that for a child to reject a normal-range and loving parent, the child must suppress her or his attachment and intersubjectivity systems. Childress (2014) writes that "when we are angry we no longer care about the other person (attachment) and we no longer feel the other person's experience (intersubjectivity), which then allows us to do and say mean things when we are angry" (p. 8). A child's authentic feelings of grief in response to the separation or divorce are replaced with anger under the distorting influence of the other parent and the child's environment. An essential component of reunification therapy is striking a balance between challenging the child's unwarranted and unhealthy chronic anger toward the rejected parent and supporting the child's emotional authenticity by acknowledging any truth underlying the parent–child conflict. A therapist must work to help the child rely on her or his own experience for a definition of reality. The key underlying therapeutic element is helping the child to assess and challenge her or his value systems and to behave in accord with the resulting revised values. Further, Childress (2014) points to the fact that all healthy relationships contain "breach-and-repair sequences" (p. 11). All parent–child relationships encounter some level of conflict ("breaches"); however, failure to repair the breach can result in prolonged conflict and ultimately estrangement. The therapist's role is to limit the intensity and destructiveness of the interpersonal anger and help the family develop effective skills to repair breaches in a timely manner.

As noted earlier in this chapter, Garber (2004) also uses an attachment-based theory to describe how alienation and parent–child contact problems can develop. Garber suggests that reliable and valid attachment-based tools should be integrated into the psychological assessment and treatment of these dynamics

Table 3-4. Attachment-Focused Reunification Therapeutic
Models: Treatment Goals and Clinical Interventions

	Child	Rejected parent	Favored parent
Goals	• Enable child to be "authentic" (able to rely on his or her own experiences) • Help child understand, process, and resolve normal range of grief and loss resulting from family's dissolution	• Not considered	• Not considered therapeutically relevant
Clinical interventions	• Individual therapy • Psychoeducation • Parent–child sessions		

NOTE. Based on Childress (2014).

in a forensic setting. He notes, however, that evaluating his model empirically is difficult because of the lack of research on how the scaffolding of the family system influences parent–child attachment and the practical limitations on integrating attachment-based instruments and methodologies into clinical and forensic settings.

Table 3.4 summarizes the clinical literature on reintegration therapy using an attachment-based focus.

3.6. Summary of Outpatient Models of Reunification Therapy

Although limited research exists to support matching family presentations to particular interventions (see Chapter 1), the several theoretical models of outpatient reunification therapy discussed above are most likely to be effective for mild-to-moderate cases of parent–child contact problems and parental alienation (Fidler et al., 2013). Of the outpatient models reviewed, however, outcome data are available only for the family-based approach: Friedlander and Walters (2010) provided data determined by client feedback and clinical judgment. While the majority of outcomes were positive, these authors gave limited information on their methodology and their definition of "positive."

Families whose dynamics are considered moderate to severe, however, often require a more intensive approach. Over the last decade, a trend in this area of practice involves developing intensive intervention programs for families with parental alienation and other forms of child contact problems. In the next section we review these programs, including their target populations, core interventions, and goals as well as any available outcome research.

4. WHEN OUTPATIENT THERAPY IS NOT ENOUGH: INTENSIVE FAMILY REUNIFICATION INTERVENTIONS

Family Bridges: A Workshop for Troubled and Alienated Parent–Child Relationships was developed by psychologists Randy Rand, Deidre Rand, and Richard Warshak (Warshak, 2010). It is an innovative, four-consecutive-day educational and experiential residential program offered only to the rejected parent and the child. The parent–child dyad participates in the intervention after a court has determined that an interim or permanent award of custody to the rejected parent is in the child's best interests. Thus families are typically referred to Family Bridges via court order.

According to Warshak (2010), the goals of the program are to

- facilitate, repair, and strengthen children's ability to maintain healthy relationships with both parents;
- help children do what they can to avoid being in the middle of their parents' conflicts;
- strengthen children's critical-thinking skills;
- protect children from unreasonably rejecting a parent in the future;
- help children maintain balanced views and a more realistic perspective on each parent as well as themselves;
- help family members develop compassionate rather than excessively harsh or critical views of one another's actions;
- strengthen family members' ability to communicate effectively with one another and to manage conflicts in a productive manner; and
- strengthen parents' skills in nurturing their children by setting and enforcing appropriate limits and avoiding psychologically intrusive interactions.

Family Bridges was evaluated in 2008 and 2009 using a posttest design. The evaluation sample consisted of 12 families with 23 children. For 19 of the children, the follow-up information covered a span of between two and four years since completion of the workshop; the remaining 4 children had attended the workshop more recently. Warshak (2010) reports that directly following the conclusion of the program, 22 of the 23 children (96%) had restored a positive relationship with the rejected parent. Warshak does not specify any particular behaviors or outcomes that defined the restoration of a *positive* relationship but indicates this outcome was evidenced by the children's own statements, the therapist's observations, and reports from the aftercare specialist.

Among the 22 children who ended the workshop on a positive note, 4 children—3 children from one family and 1 child from another family—regressed after contact with the favored parent was restored (Warshak, 2010). In the three children from the same family, regression manifested in belligerent and physically provocative behavior, destruction of property, and repeated taunts and insults directed toward the rejected parent. The child from the other family refused contact altogether with the rejected parent. Taking these children into account brings the number of children who restored and maintained a positive relationship with the formerly rejected parent to 18 of 23 (78%). Warshak (2010) believes that for the children who did not maintain a positive relationship, the timing of the renewed contact with the favored parent was premature. However, he does not state how much time elapsed before those children resumed contact with the favored parent. (For the entire sample of favored parents, he reports that the time at which contact resumed ranged from 5 weeks to 20 months.)

Another program for intensive reunification is Transitioning Families, in Sonoma County, California, which has provided family workshops under the leadership of psychologist Rebecca Bailey since 2008. The Transitioning Families model is a family-based, solution-focused approach embedded in a highly experiential framework that includes equine and other animal-assisted therapies, cooking, and recreational activities. Transitioning Families offers workshops in cases of familial abduction in the context of parental alienation and also following custody reversal; court order or the clinical team determines which family members attend the workshops. The Transitioning Families model for abduction is described in the literature (Judge, Bailey, Behrman-Lippert, Bailey, Psalia & Dickel, 2016)), and Chapter 4 describes the experiential techniques used in its application to parental alienation. No program evaluation data for Transitioning Families are available at this time.

Another residential intervention that has recently emerged is the Family Reflections Reunification Program. Family Reflections was developed in 2013 by a family therapist and custody evaluator in British Columbia, Canada (Reay, 2015). Like Family Bridges, the program consists of a four-day retreat intended for the rejected parent and child only. Acceptance into the program is contingent on a court order for suspension of contact (direct and indirect) between the alienating parent and the child for a period of time or a reversal of custody in favor of the rejected parent. The reversal may or may not be permanent and may be contingent on the alienating parent's response to counseling (Reay, 2015). The suspension or custody reversal provides the child with time to rebuild the attachment to the rejected parent. Family Reflections takes place on a spacious property in Okanagan Valley, British Columbia, that functions as a year-round retreat for reunifying children with their rejected parents.

According to Reay (2015), the Family Reflections model integrates components of Family Bridges (Warshak, 2010; Warshak & Otis, 2010) and the Overcoming Barriers program (Sullivan et al., 2010), as well as best practices of multimedia learning. Reay (2015) highlights eight primary program goals:

- promote healthy child adjustment;
- improve the child's critical-thinking skills;
- help the child understand how and why the alienation occurred;
- help the favored parent understand how and why the alienation occurred;

- work with each family member to create more appropriate parent–parent and parent–child roles, responsibilities, and boundaries;
- strengthen each parent's ability to communicate with the other parent and resolve relevant parent–parent and parent–child conflicts;
- maintain the reunification process; and
- promote relationships between the child and both parents unless specific circumstances preclude such a relationship.

The Family Reflections Reunification Program was piloted in 2012, and Reay (2015) reports that preliminary outcome data showed a 95% success rate over 3-, 6-, 9-, and 12-month intervals. However, Reay provides little information about the research design and methodology used to obtain those results.

Two other intensive programs are the Overcoming Barriers Family Camp (OBFC), described in Chapters 6–11, and the Forging Families' Futures program, developed by Robin Deutsch and Peggie Ward in 2009 (Ward, Deutsch, & Sullivan, 2010) based on the Overcoming Barriers Family Camp approach. In both programs, clinicians and a host recreation specialist work with different combinations of members of a family over an intensive number of days (four days for OBFC and two and half days for Forging Families' Futures Program). Work with children includes helping them to understand their family (e.g., who is "in" and who is "out" and how that came to be), understand the roles family members play through role play and role switching, identify cognitive distortions, learn problem-solving skills, and become desensitized to the rejected parent, as well as giving children the opportunity to see both parents working together safely. Work with parents includes helping them to manage and understand negative thoughts and feelings, improve their communication and listening skills, understand differences between child protection and overprotection, perceive how children get into the middle of their parents' conflict, and understand how children feel about being in the middle. Coparenting work is solution focused, generating written agreements and done with the expectation that feedback will be provided to the court.

No controlled evaluation exists for any of these programs, and the outcome data that do exist are methodologically limited. Of the intensive interventions reviewed, outcome data are available for Family Bridges (Warshak, 2010), Family Reflections (Reay, 2015), and the Overcoming Barriers Family Camp (Sullivan et al., 2010). For all of the studies that produced these data, samples were small and nonrandom, no research tools were used to measure or assess outcome criteria, the reports lack information on treatment dosage and the specific treatment modalities used; and program developers themselves conducted the outcome research, a source of possible bias. In Reay's (2015) report, crucial information lacking includes the intake process, a description of the clinical sample that attended the program (e.g., child and parent ages), whether or not this sample was homogeneous (e.g., with respect to the nature of the parent–child contact problems and their intensity), and the actual clinical interventions used. The internal validity of Warshak's (2010) study is limited by (among other factors) the fact that outcomes were assessed by the rejected parent and the therapist but not the child or favored parent. In both Reay (2015) and Warshak (2010), it is unclear what observations and statements were made to aftercare specialists to determine what constituted a successful or positive outcome.

These limitations make it difficult to draw any generalizations from these studies or replicate their findings. Nonetheless, these are the only studies available that report any outcome data for intensive residential programs for families with moderate-to-severe parent–child contact problems. As such, they present an opportunity for further dialogue about how best to help such families and about the need to continue evaluating these efforts.

5. CONCLUSIONS

This chapter has reviewed the range of outpatient and intensive therapeutic modalities currently available to address parent–child contact problems, including parental alienation. Although research on these topics is growing, more rigorous research and program evaluation are desperately needed. The clinical focus of the approaches to family reunification that have been described in the literature varies depending on how the parent–child contact problem is conceptualized. Nonetheless, the interventions largely have similar treatment goals for children: decreasing anxiety associated with the rejected parent, strengthening critical-thinking skills, correcting distortions, disentangling the child from parental conflict, developing a realistic view of the rejected parent, and developing more appropriate coping skills. The approaches all anticipate that accomplishing these goals will help the child reunify with and develop a more positive relationship with the rejected parent.

While the specific goals for the favored parent and rejected parent differ markedly depending on the intervention, there is consensus on the need for the favored parent to be "on board," cooperative, and supportive of the reunification process and for the rejected parent to address and acknowledge behaviors that contributed to the dynamic underlying the contact problem. Further, there is consensus on the need for re-establishing the structural hierarchy in the family and restoring appropriate boundaries in the family system.

Despite shared goals across interventions, there are no consensus definitions of reunification and what constitutes its success. The lack of shared benchmarks and criteria for successful reunification treatment limits the ability of families, clinicians, and the judiciary to evaluate program effectiveness. An additional challenge in drawing conclusions from the available literature is the range of severity, intentionality, and other factors among families with parent–child contact problems. Without a systematic way to quantify and categorize dimensions of parent behavior and consequences for children, clinical and judicial stakeholders will struggle to match family presentations with the most effective approaches to and intensities of intervention.

REFERENCES

Ainsworth, M., & Bell, S. (1970). Attachment, exploration and separation: Illustrated by the behavior of one-year-olds in a strange situation. *Child Development, 41*(1), 49–67.

Albertson-Kelly, J., & Burkard, B. (2013). Family reunification in a forensic setting. In A. Baker & S. R. Sauber (Eds.), *Working with alienated children and families: A clinical guidebook* (pp. 232–251). New York, NY: Routledge.

Amato, P. R., & Booth, A. (1996). A prospective study of divorce and parent–child relationships. *Journal of Marriage and the Family, 58*(2), 356–365.

Baker, A., & Andre, K. (2013). Psycho-educational work with children in loyalty conflict: The "I Don't Want to Choose" program. In A. Baker & S. R. Sauber (Eds.), *Working with alienated children and families: A clinical guidebook* (pp. 149–165). New York, NY: Routledge.

Baker, A., & Darnall, D. C. (2006). Behaviours and strategies employed in parental alienation. *Journal of Divorce & Remarriage, 45*(1/2), 97–124.

Baker, A., & Darnall, D. C. (2007). A construct study of the eight symptoms of severe parental alienation syndrome. *Journal of Divorce & Remarriage, 47*(1–2), 55–75.

Bala, N., Hunt, S., & McCarney, C. (2010). Parental alienation: Canadian court cases 1989–2008. *Family Court Review, 48*(1), 164–179.

Barron, M. B. (2000). A comparison study of the normal and clinical divorce: Style of attachment, level of conflict and parent–child relationship. *Dissertation Abstracts International: Section A. Humanities & Social Sciences, 61*(8), 3350–A.

Birnbaum, R., & Bala, N. (2010). Towards a differentiation of high conflict families: An analysis of social science and Canadian case law. *Family Court Review, 48*(3), 403–416.

Bowlby, J. (1969). *A secure base: Parent–child attachment and healthy human development*. New York, NY: Basic Books.

Bowlby, J. (1982). Attachment and loss: Retrospect and prospect. *American Journal of Orthopsychiatry, 52*(4), 664–678.

Bretherton, I. (1992). The origins of attachment theory: John Bowlby and Mary Ainsworth. *Developmental Psychology, 28*(5), 759–775.

Bronfenbrenner, U. (1979). *The ecology of human development*. Cambridge, MA: Harvard University Press.

Childress, C. A. (2014). Reunification therapy: Treating "parental alienation." Retrieved March 2015 from http://drcachildress.org/asp/admin/getFile.asp?RID=83&TID=6&FN=pdf

Darnall, D. (1998). *Divorce casualties: protecting your children from parental alienation*. Dallas, TX: Taylor Publishing Co.

Darnall, D. (2011). The psychosocial treatment of parental alienation. *Child and Adolescent Psychiatric Clinics of North America, 20*, 479–494.

DeJong, M., & Davies, H. (2012). Contact refusal by children following acrimonious separation: Therapeutic approaches with children and parents. *Clinical Child Psychology and Psychiatry, 18*(2), 185–198.

Demby, S. (2009). Interparent hatred and its impact on parenting: Assessment in forensic custody evaluations. *Psychoanalytic Inquiry, 29*(6), 477–490.

Deutsch, R. M. (2014, November). *Children resisting contact with a parent: Application of intensive interventions*. Workshop presented at Association of Family and Conciliation Courts Symposium on Custody Evaluations, San Antonio, TX.

Emery, R. E. (2012). *Renegotiating family relationships: Divorce, child custody and mediation* (2nd ed.). New York, NY: Guilford Press.

Faber, A. J., & Wittenborn, A. K. (2010). The role of attachment in children's adjustment to divorce and remarriage. *Journal of Family Psychotherapy, 21*, 89–104.

Fidler, B. J., & Bala, N. (2010). Children resisting post-separation contact with a parent: Concepts, controversies, and conundrums. *Family Court Review, 48*(1), 10–47.

Fidler, B. J., Bala, N., & Saini, M. A. (2013). *Children who resist postseparation parental contact: A differential approach for legal and mental health professionals.* American Psychology–Law Society Series. New York, NY: Oxford University Press.

Friedlander, S., & Walters, M. G. (2010). When a child rejects a parent: Tailoring the intervention to fit the problem. *Family Court Review, 48*(1), 98–111.

Friedlander, S., & Walters, M. G. (2014). Interventions with children who resist or refuse post-separation contact with a parent. Workshop presented at Association of Family and Conciliation Courts California Chapter Conference, Toronto, Ontario.

Garber, B. D. (2004). Parental alienation in light of attachment theory: Consideration of the broader implication for child development, clinical practice, and forensic process. *Journal of Child Custody, 1*(4), 49–76.

Garber, B. D. (2014). The chameleon child: Children as actors in the high conflict divorce drama. *Journal of Child Custody, 11*(1), 25–40.

Garber, B. D. (2015). Cognitive–behavioral methods in high conflict divorce: Systematic desensitization adapted to parent–child reunification interventions. *Family Court Review, 53*(1), 96–112.

Gardner, R. A. (1985). Recent trends in divorce and custody litigation. *Academy Forum, 29*(2), 3–7.

Goldberg, W., & Goldberg, L. (2013). Psychotherapy with targeted parents. In A. Baker & S. R. Sauber (Eds.), *Working with alienated children and families: A clinical guidebook* (pp. 108–128). New York, NY: Routledge.

Gordon, R. M., Stoffey, R., & Bottinelli, J. (2008). MMPI-2 findings of primitive defenses in alienating parents. *American Journal of Family Therapy, 36*(2), 211–228.

Gottlieb, L. J. (2012). *The parental alienation syndrome: A family therapy and collaborative systems approach to amelioration.* Springfield, IL: Charles Thomas.

Gottlieb. L. J. (2013). The application of structural family therapy to the treatment of parental alienation syndrome. In A. Baker & S. R. Sauber (Eds.), *Working with alienated children and families: A clinical guidebook* (pp. 209–231). New York, NY: Routledge.

Grych, J. H. (2005). Interparental conflict as a risk factor for child maladjustment: Implications for the development of prevention programs. *Family Court Review, 43*(1), 97–108.

Johnston, J. R. (1993). Children of divorce who refuse visitation. In C. Depnar & J. Bray (Eds.), *Non-residential parenting: New vistas in family living* (pp. 109–135). Newbury Park, CA: Sage.

Johnston, J. R. (2003). Parental alignments and rejection: An empirical study of alienation in children of divorce. *Journal of the American Academy of Psychiatry and the Law, 31*(2), 158–170.

Johnston, J. R. (2005). Children of divorce who reject a parent and refuse visitation: Recent research and social policy implications for the alienated child. *Family Law Quarterly, 38*(4), 757–775.

Johnston, J. R., & Goldman, J. R. (2010). Outcomes of family counseling interventions with children who resist visitation: An addendum to Friedlander and Walters. *Family Court Review*, 48(1), 112–115.

Johnston, J. R., & Kelly, J. B. (2004). Rejoinder to Gardner's "Commentary on Kelly and Johnston's 'The alienated child: A reformulation of parental alienation syndrome.'" *Family Court Review*, 42(4), 622–628.

Johnston, J., & Roseby, V. (1997). *In the name of the child: A developmental approach to understanding and helping children of conflicted and violent divorce*. New York, NY: Free Press.

Johnston, J. R., Roseby, V., & Kuehnle, K. (2009). *In the name of the child: A developmental approach to understanding and helping children of conflicted and violent divorce*. New York: Springer.

Johnston, J. R., Walters, M. G. & Friedlander, S. (2001). Therapeutic work with alienated children and their families. *Family Court Review*, 39(3), 316–333.

Johnston, J. R., Walters, M., & Olesen, N. W. (2005a). Clinical ratings of parenting capacity and Rorschach protocols of custody disputing parents: An exploratory study. *Journal of Child Custody*, 2, 159–178.

Johnston, J. R., Walters, M. G., & Olesen, N. W. (2005b). Is it alienating parenting, role reversal or child abuse? An empirical study of children's rejection of a parent in child custody disputes. *Journal of Emotional Abuse*, 5(4), 191–218.

Johnston, J. R., Walters, M., & Olesen, N. W. (2005c). The psychological functioning of alienated children in custody disputing families: An exploratory study. *American Journal of Forensic Psychology*, 23, 39–64.

Judge, A. M., Bailey, R., Behrman-Lippert, J., Bailey, E., Psaila, C., & Dickel, J. (2016). The transitioning families therapeutic reunification model in nonfamilial abductions. *Family Court Review*, 54(2), 232–249.

Kelly, J. B. (2012). Risk and protective factors associated with child and adolescent adjustment following separation and divorce: Social science applications. In K. F. Kuehnle & L. M. Drozd (Eds.), *Parenting plan evaluations: Applied research for the family court* (pp. 49–84). New York, NY: Oxford University Press.

Kelly, J. B., & Johnston, J. R. (2001). The alienated child: A reformulation of parental alienation syndrome. *Family Court Review*, 39(3), 249–266.

Krishnakumar, A., & Buehler, C. (2000). Interparental conflict and parenting behaviors: A meta-analytic review. *Family Relations*, 49(1), 25–44.

Lampel, A. K. (1996). Children's alignment with parents in highly conflicted custody cases. *Family and Conciliation Courts Review*, 34(2), 229–239.

Lieberman, A. (2004). Traumatic stress and quality of attachment: Reality and internalization in disorders of infant mental health. *Infant Mental Health Jounral*, 25(4), 336–351.

Moran, J., Sullivan, T., & Sullivan, M. (2015). *Overcoming the co-parenting trap: Essential parenting skills*. Natick, MA: Overcoming Barriers.

Moran, J. A., & Weinstock, D. K. (2011). Assessing parenting skills for family court. *Journal of Child Custody*, 8(3), 166–188.

Pett, M. A., Wampold, B., Turner, C.W., & Vaughan-Cole, B. (1999). Paths of influence of divorce on preschool children's psychosocial adjustment. *Journal of Family Psychology*, 13(2), 145–164.

Polak, S. (2014). *Examining strained parent child relationships, child alienation and reintegration therapy post separation* (unpublished doctoral comprehensive paper). University of Toronto, Toronto, ON.

Polak, S., & Saini, M. (2015). Children resisting contact with a parent postseparation: Assessing this phenomenon using an ecological systems framework. *Journal of Divorce & Remarriage, 56*, 220–247.

Pruett, M. K., Williams, T. Y., Insabella, G., & Little, T. D. (2003). Family and legal indicators of child adjustment to divorce among families with young children. *Journal of Family Psychology, 17*(2), 169–180.

Racusin, R. J., Copans, S. A., & Mills, P. (1994). Characteristics of families of children who refuse post-divorce visits. *Journal of Clinical Psychology, 50*(5), 792–801.

Reay, K. M. (2015). Family Reflections: A promising therapeutic program designed to treat severely alienated children and their family system. *American Journal of Family Therapy, 43*(2), 197–207.

Saini, M., Johnston, J. R., Fidler, B. J., & Bala, N. (2012). Empirical studies of alienation. In K. F. Kuehnle & L. M. Drozd (Eds.), *Parenting plan evaluations: Applied research for the family court* (pp. 339–441). New York, NY: Oxford University Press.

Sandler, I. N., Wheeler, L. A., & Braver, S. L. (2013). Relations of parenting quality, interparental conflict, and overnights with mental health problems of children in divorcing families with high legal conflict. *Journal of Family Psychology, 27*(6), 915–924.

Schore, A. (2012). Attachment and brain development: The micro context. Paper presented at Association of Family and Conciliation Courts 49th Annual Conference, "Attachment, Brain Science and Children of Divorce: The ABCD's of Child Development for Family Law," Chicago, IL.

Schore, A., & McIntosh, J. (2012). Family law and the neuroscience of attachment part I. *Family Court Review, 49*(3), 501–512.

Siegel, J. C., & Langford, J. S. (1998). MMPI-2 validity scales and suspected parental alienation syndrome. *American Journal of Forensic Psychology, 16*(4), 5–14.

Sroufe, A. (2000). Early relationships and the development of children. *Infant Mental Health Journal, 21*(1–2), 67–74.

Sullivan, M. J., & Kelly, J. B. (2001). Legal and psychological management of cases with an alienated child. *Family Court Review, 39*(3), 299–315.

Sullivan, M. J., Ward, P. A., & Deutsch, R. M. (2010). Overcoming Barriers Family Camp: A program for high-conflict divorced families where a child is resisting contact with a parent. *Family Court Review, 48*(1), 116–135.

Tschann, J. M., Johnston, J. R., Kline, M., & Wallerstein, J. S. (1990). Conflict, loss, change and parent–child relationships: Predicting children's adjustment during divorce. *Journal of Divorce, 13*(4), 1–22.

Wallerstein, J., & Kelly, J. B. (1980). *Surviving the break-up: How children actually cope with divorce*. New York, NY: Basic Books.

Walters, M. G., & Friedlander, S. (2010). Finding a tenable middle space: Understanding the role of clinical interventions when a child refuses contact with a parent. *Journal of Child Custody, 7*, 287–328.

Ward, P., Deutsch, R. M., & Sullivan, M. (2010, June). *Group weekend retreat for alienated and estranged families: An intensive model*. Paper presented at Association of Family and Conciliation Courts 47th Annual Conference, Denver, CO.

Warshak, R. A. (2010). Family Bridges: Using insights from social science to reconnect parents and alienated children. *Family Court Review, 48*(1), 48–80.

Warshak, R. A. (2015). Poisoning parent–child relationships through the manipulation of names. *American Journal of Family Therapy, 43*(1), 4–15.

Warshak, R. A., & Otis, M. R. (2010). Helping alienated children with family bridges: Practice, research, and the pursuit of "Humbition". *Family Court Review, 48*(1), 91–97.

Weitzman, J. (2013). Reunification and the one-way mirror. In A. Baker & S. R. Sauber (Eds.), *Working with alienated children and families: A clinical guidebook* (pp. 198–208). New York: Routledge.

Whiteside, M. F., & Becker, B. (2000). Parental factors and the young child's postdivorce adjustment: A meta-analysis with implications for parenting arrangements. *Journal of Family Psychology, 14*(1), 5–26.

Zahn-Waxler, C., Duggal, S., & Gruber, R. (2002). Parental psychopathology. In M. H. Bornstein (Ed.), *Handbook of parenting: Vol. 4. Social conditions and applied parenting* (pp. 295–327). Mahwah, NJ: Lawrence Erlbaum.

4

More Than Words

*The Use of Experiential Therapies in the Treatment
of Families With Parent–Child Contact Problems
and Parental Alienation*

ABIGAIL M. JUDGE AND REBECCA BAILEY ∎

1. INTRODUCTION

Families experiencing parent–child contact problems, including parental alienation, typically enter family treatment after a trail of failed educational, clinical, and judicial interventions. This history can heighten each family member's resistance, defensiveness, and mistrust toward mental health interventions. In addition, prolonged child custody litigation can lead to an investment in blame rather than solutions and a defensive posture that can require considerable time and work to undo (Lebow & Black, 2012; Sullivan, Ward, & Deutsch, 2010; Warshak, 2010). Each of these factors contributes to a clinical situation where resistance is high, affective volatility is common, and rigid, polarized thinking prevails.

As a result, families in high conflict require innovative approaches to treatment. These approaches require clinical tools that include, but are not limited to, traditional talk-based techniques. In this chapter we propose that experiential techniques provide a robust theoretical and practical framework for such innovation. We first present a rationale for the integration of experiential techniques into family-based treatment for families with parent–child contact problems, including parental alienation. Next, we describe a number of experiential therapies (e.g., the use of nature and recreational therapy) that are employed in intensive family-based interventions for parent–child contact problems, as highlighted in the Overcoming Barriers approach. We then describe particular experiential techniques, including equine-assisted therapy and the integration of cooking and other culinary activities, developed at Transitioning Families, a program for intensive reunification intervention in California (Judge et al., 2016). To illustrate the efficacy of experiential therapies with high-conflict families, we offer brief and deidentified case examples throughout the chapter. To conclude, we discuss the integration of experiential techniques into traditional office-based treatment, where the vast majority of such families are seen. This section complements Chapter 12, on the translation of intensive intervention components to traditional outpatient therapy.

2. EXPERIENTIAL THERAPIES IN FAMILY THERAPY

Experiential psychotherapies arose from the client-centered, existential, humanistic, and Gestalt traditions. These theoretical influences led to an emphasis on enhancing patients' abilities to access and modulate emotion in the context of an affirming, supportive, empathy-based therapeutic relationship where the patient's internal resources are both assumed and valued (Gleiser, Ford, & Fosha, 2008; Greenberg, Rice, & Elliott, 1996). Experiential therapy emphasizes direct experience as the primary agent of change (Mahrer, 1983), unlike other schools of psychotherapy, where change is presumed to follow from increased insight, modification of faulty cognitions, or the practice of new behaviors (or some combination of these). Although each form of therapeutic action has a necessary place in family treatment, experiential techniques are distinguished by their emphasis on using nonverbal experience rather than verbal techniques as the primary means of modifying experience. Nonverbal experiences are theorized to reduce defensiveness and promote new learning. Experiential therapies thus aim to foster in-the-moment changes in affect, cognition, and behavior that help jump-start new learning.

2.1. The Role of Play

Experiential techniques are increasingly integrated into family therapy, particularly with patient groups who are difficult to engage (Thompson, Bender, Windsor, & Flynn, 2009). This increase may have occurred in part because experiential strategies can create more interest than verbal discussions alone for treatment-resistant populations and can offer families new opportunities for communication (Cheung, 2006). One basic experiential technique is play, including recreational games. Gil and Sobol (2005) suggested several reasons to incorporate play into the therapeutic process with families: overcoming the challenges of a family that is not verbally oriented; helping family members to be less analytical and intellectual; fostering disclosure when shame, discomfort, and distrust dominate family interactions; and promoting new relational patterns. Play is broadly defined and may be integrated into sessions in a variety of ways.

Research suggests that integrating play into family therapy increases engagement and motivation among parents and children alike (Thompson, Bender, Cardoso, & Flynn, 2011). When therapists engage with families in what researchers have called *family play*, the families may perceive therapy as fun, inclusive, and enriching of their time together. In addition, consistent with traditional family systems theory, observing interactions firsthand during play can offer a revealing glimpse into important family dynamics and roles that maintain conflict (Minuchin, 1974). Such observations include which family members lead and what strengths and difficulties the family has in problem-solving, communication, and compromise. Unlike exposure-based techniques that use role play to address interactions that have caused the family difficulty, family play activities provide a structure in which families can interact in new ways as well as feel included and respected (Gleiser et al., 2008).

As an example of family play, consider one technique we have used that is simple to incorporate into any therapeutic session. During a family session we will ask the family member who is speaking to hold an oversized ball of string or twine. When another family member speaks, the previous speaker tosses the ball to that person while holding onto an end of the string. After a while, what results is a visual depiction of communication patterns in the family. This exercise is particularly valuable when there is a high degree of triangulation in the family or when there is a lack of more direct communication within one subunit of the family (e.g., coparents). The therapist can help the family literally untangle the string as a means of highlighting areas for additional therapeutic work. For example, with one family participating in an intensive weekend intervention, it quickly became clear that the children became "entangled" in directing conversation while the coparents lacked the confidence or skills to interject. The need for the coparents to become able to hold and maintain a line of communication—both literally and metaphorically—was an image to which we returned throughout the weekend intervention. In our experience, when the therapist approaches this exercise in a playful but respectful manner, the physical illustration of tangled communication can make it easier for the family to take in the therapist's feedback and relax their defensiveness.

Recent research on the neurobiological benefits of play provides additional support for its role in family treatment. For example, Porges (2011) has observed that the reciprocity and role reversal common to many forms of play (e.g., games and physical activities with turn taking) can function as "neural exercises" that enable the coregulation of physiological states between people. This coregulation can help individuals transition efficiently from active to calm states, a critical skill for family members to acquire as part of reunification treatment. In a related line of research, recent interventions in trauma treatment use the body (e.g., movement-based activity) to target somatic regulation as a means of enhancing emotional and behavioral regulation. Not unlike the role of play, somatic interventions aim to build self-regulatory capacity by improving patients' interoceptive awareness of, attunement to, and skills for shifting physiological arousal (Warner, Spinazzola, Westcott, Gunn, & Hodgdon, 2014). The most direct access to so-called bottom-up processing (i.e., processing initiated at the sensorimotor or emotional level as opposed to processing initiated by the cortex) is achieved via direct focus on the senses as well as the body. This includes activities such as mindful awareness or meditation, physical movement, and sensorimotor therapy (Ogden, Minton, &

Pain, 2006; Siegel, 2007). To the extent that experiential therapies involving play, movement, and physical activity can improve self-and coregulation within families, they may reduce emotional reactivity and lead to more constructive problem-solving.

Therapists must take care to tailor play activities to the clinical, cultural, and demographic characteristics of the family, such as the interests of individual members (e.g., art, athletics, or animals), cultural orientation (e.g., religiosity or spirituality and individualism vs. collectivism), and personality features (e.g., openness to experience and introversion vs. extroversion).

2.2 Recreation and Nature

Family therapists may also borrow from the allied field of recreational therapy to design exercises that engage and foster new learning in families in high conflict. The American Therapeutic Recreation Association defines recreation therapy as the use of leisure activities to foster autonomy across several areas of functioning, including emotional, physical, cognitive, and social domains (ATRA Health Care Reform Task Force, 2001). The research literature on recreation therapy interventions in geriatric populations, pediatric populations, individuals with mental health disabilities, and other groups is limited but suggests that such interventions can yield improvements in psychosocial health, including decreases in depression, anxiety, stress-related symptoms, and sense of boredom and isolation (ATRA Health Care Reform Task Force, 1994; Coyle, Kinney, & Shank, 1991). This research provides an empirical foundation for the application of recreational techniques to use with families in high conflict.

As an example of recreational therapy, we have used the game "red light, green light" to give clinicians the opportunity not only to observe but also to intervene regarding parenting skills, rule expectations, collaboration, and follow-through. This game can be especially fruitful when coparents take turns as leaders and followers, with clinicians present to intervene as necessary. Process observations can be shared in the moment or at a later stage in treatment. ("Red light, green light" can also be played in the context of equine-assisted therapy, which we discuss in Section 2.3 below.)

Recreation and play can occur in an office setting, but their use in natural spaces and via interaction within natural environments may have even greater positive effects. A small but reliable evidence base supports the therapeutic benefits of natural environments and their use to promote health and prevent illness (Annerstedt & Währborg, 2011; Cason & Gillis, 1994). Such findings also underpin the creation of a therapeutic milieu, which Carole Blane, Tyler Sullivan, and colleagues discuss in Chapter 7. In family reunification treatment, especially for moderate-to-severe cases of alienation, coparents have typically last interacted only in courtrooms. In addition, there have often been long periods of no contact between the rejected parent and alienated child. Such cases require a neutral space where families can begin to reconnect. A scenic and natural surrounding provides a holding environment (Winnicott, 1965) with inherently rewarding characteristics such as vistas, fresh air, and mild temperatures, all of which can have physiologically regulating effects. For example, the Overcoming Barriers Family Camp uses a family campground (see Chapter 7), and Transitioning Families operates on a private, self-contained facility with a barn, barnyard, office space, cook's kitchen, and large outdoor space where meetings and recreational activities occur (Judge et al., 2016).

Recreational activities can be paired with the healing effects of nature. Wilderness therapy, which emerged in the 1920s to provide rehabilitation programs for adolescents engaged in high-risk behaviors, is a precedent for the use of nature in treatment (Margalit & Ben-Ari, 2014). Wilderness therapy programs involve expedition-based interventions in outdoor settings that aim to change adolescents' maladaptive behaviors via experiential learning. Such interventions are designed to enhance one's communication with peers, interpersonal abilities and skills, understanding of how one is perceived by others, and capacity to rely on oneself and staff (Clark, Marmol, Cooley, & Gathercoal, 2004; Corey & Corey, 2000; Newes & Bandoroff, 2004). Meta-analytic studies of wilderness therapy programs describe positive outcomes among adolescent participants, including enhanced self-concept and internal locus of control and improved social competence and interpersonal communication (Hans, 2000; Hattie, Marsh, Neill, & Richards, 1997).

Another form of recreational therapy is walking and hiking, with or without animals. (We discuss the therapeutic use of animals in the next section.) Walks can involve the entire family or subgroups and may serve several clinical functions. First, walks offer an opportunity for clinicians to model mindful awareness. Although many definitions of mindfulness exist, it is widely understood as a practice that facilitates a "non-elaborative, nonjudgmental, present-focused awareness" (Bishop et al., 2004; p. 232). Mindful awareness is associated with an improved capacity to regulate anxiety (Davidson et al., 2003; Harrington & Dunne, 2015). A theorized benefit of mindful awareness is improved relationships, perhaps due to an enhanced capacity to perceive nonverbal emotional signals from others (Siegel, 2007). This too could benefit high-conflict families. Additional goals of walks may be to facilitate problem-solving conversation and to provide a "time-out" in response to a problem that arose during a talk-based session. Walks with these aims typically involve one family member, or some sub-group of the family, and one clinician, who asks questions designed to foster solution-based thinking (Lebow, 2003).

In addition to the direct positive effects of exercise on anxiety and depression, research has demonstrated a promising role for aerobic exercise in enhancing fear extinction and augmenting the efficacy of exposure therapy (Powers et al., 2015). Some alienated children show a phobic response to the rejected parent, and in such cases techniques based on systematic desensitization are part of reunification treatment (Deutsch, 2014; Garber, 2015). The addition of aerobic exercise (e.g., recreational games or vigorous walking) to exposure-based techniques is therefore a promising line of intervention that clinicians should consider.

2.3. Equine-Assisted Therapy

Equine-assisted therapy (EAT) is a rapidly growing field that has been studied across a range of populations. Equine-assisted psychotherapies integrate activities with horses with a treatment program's broader theoretical framework (Klontz, Bivens, Leinart, & Klontz, 2007). A recent systematic review (Selby & Smith-Osborne, 2013) concluded that although research on the use of equines for health-related concerns was methodologically limited (e.g., there have been no randomized controlled trials), when examined in the aggregate it nonetheless offered promising evidence of the benefits of this therapeutic approach. We could locate no published evaluations of the use of EAT with families experiencing high-conflict divorce or parental alienation. We therefore set forth here a novel theoretical and clinical rationale for this application, based on the work at Transitioning Families.

Within EAT, horses are not merely companion or recreational animals but agents of therapeutic change, as they elicit a range of emotions in families that may be used as a catalyst for insight, openness, and the practice of new behavior. The Transitioning Families program assists families using horse herds. A herd is simply three or more horses that are stabled in close proximity. A herd bonds together in a manner that mimics a family unit. A simple exercise designed to highlight feelings of extreme loss involves removing one horse from the others for a brief period while the human participants are asked to simply observe silently. Removing a horse from the herd results in the horses' calling to each other in an agitated manner. This exercise has the ability to provoke a deep conversation around issues of loss. What often surfaces during this exercise is a previously unexpressed understanding of each family member's loss. In some cases, the participants have been so self-focused that they have lost empathy for the other family members. The exercise allows them to nondefensively acknowledge, often for the first time, feelings of loss in the entire family.

Practitioners of EAT carefully plan which horse should be used with which families. This choice is important for the welfare of the family as well as the animals, because certain horses respond negatively to high levels of tension, which could adversely affect their physical health (e.g., by producing colic). Also, equines can be quite unpredictable in their response to individuals, which is one reason why Transitioning Families has a clinician and horse professional working together during EAT. Family members naturally ascribe to horses human traits such as jealousy, hatred, or indifference. A horse that happens to avoid a rejected parent, for example, can provide fodder for the alienated child's campaign. These interactions may be countertherapeutic without the clinician and horse professional working in tandem.

However, even the clinical team's decision not to use a particular horse can provide a therapeutic opportunity. If a family member asks why the horse was not used, this can facilitate fruitful conversation about the negative effects of tension on physical and emotional well-being for animals and humans alike.

Horses in EAT are therefore extensions of the clinical team, whose personalities and attributes are carefully selected to foster experiential goals of reunification treatment across several levels: engagement, education, and interpersonal learning.

2.3.1. ENGAGEMENT

In cases of parental alienation, family members typically enter treatment feeling wary, angry, anxious, misperceived or mislabeled, and often resentful (Warshak, 2010). As discussed above, this often follows a history of insufficient or failed therapeutic, educational, and judicial interventions. Family members may also present with maladaptive personality traits, which may be either long-standing (e.g., personality disorders) or adaptations to protracted conflict (see Chapter 5). At the same time, it is well known that therapeutic alliance is the best predictor of positive outcome across a range of psychotherapies (Norcross, 2011), and split alliances predict worse treatment outcomes in couples and family therapy (Knobloch-Fedders, Pinsof, & Mann, 2007; Lebow, Chambers, Christensen, & Johnson, 2011). Court-involved families are very much at risk for developing split alliances because of their tendency to use primitive defenses, such as considering individuals to be all good or all bad (Doolittle & Deustch, 1999; Gordon, Stoffey, & Bottinelli, 2008; Johnston, Walters, & Olesen, 2010). Even when no personality disorders are present, rigid and polarized thinking is highly characteristic of families who are litigating child custody. This tendency is due in part to the adversarial nature of the legal system, the realm in which parents may have had the most recent interaction. Other challenges to building an alliance include parents' investment in blame and victimization, rather than solutions, and high levels of conflict between parents about who is right (Lebow, 2003; Lebow & Black, 2012).

Much like family play, horses can help establish a robust working alliance with the entire family within a relatively short time. Indeed, because equines help establish working alliances quickly, they are often employed in the treatment of populations who are less amenable to traditional office-based treatment (Selby & Smith-Osborne, 2013), a description that fits families affected by parental alienation. Specifically, equines provide opportunities for doing problem-solving tasks in a novel surrounding that enable family members to view themselves differently and to consider multiple perspectives, a key tenet of reunification (Sullivan et al., 2010; Warshak, 2010) Equine-assisted therapy is based primarily on observations rather than what is said, thereby helping to avoid common "sticking points" of traditional talk therapy with families in high conflict. Problem-solving tasks using horses can help elicit otherwise inaccessible cognitions, emotions, and behavioral patterns; clinicians may then mobilize a range of therapeutic techniques to intervene. All equine activities are followed by "processing," in which family members are encouraged to make connections between the session and their own internal states, with the therapist and horse professional helping them practice new ways of self-regulation.

Both the favored and the rejected parent enter treatment with a range of parenting challenges, many of which involve the need for improved emotional and behavioral regulation. For example, favored parents often need improved boundaries to help differentiate their feelings from those of the alienated child (Garber, 2010). Alienated children present with oppositional behaviors toward the rejecting parent that may be quite extreme (e.g., belligerence or aggression) and that few rejected parents are prepared to manage (Fidler, Bala, & Saini, 2013). Some rejected parents use rigid and authoritarian parenting styles; given the degree of estrangement, most require help relearning their children's cues. Interventions aimed at all of these parenting issues can be implemented with EAT.

As prey animals, horses are exquisitely responsive to their environment and constantly scan it for possible threats to their safety. Horses can therefore provide a reflective function for intensities in the family. Affective and behavioral dysregulation within families may be evident in horse behavior. Observing atypical horse behavior, the horse professional can explore what might be going on in the family, and the clinician may ask family members to speculate about why the horse is acting out of the norm. With one family in treatment, for example, a horse began to show highly atypical behaviors in the arena. It reared and acted aggressively, including making a biting movement toward the clinician. The clinician invited the family to speculate about what was going on. This led a young adolescent to articulate her strong anger toward her father, whom she had been vehemently rejecting. During previous therapy sessions, the adolescent had emphatically denied that she had any negative feelings toward her father and insisted that she simply disliked him. Yet despite her disavowal of anger, these emotions manifested quite organically through interaction with the horse.

Examples like this occur constantly with EAT and illustrate its potential for bringing disavowed feelings and thoughts to the surface. Once these feelings are named, there is an opportunity to foster in-the-moment and more accurate interpretations of emotional content.

2.3.2. EDUCATION AND INTERPERSONAL LEARNING

By definition, parental alienation involves problematic and entrenched alliances in the family system. For example, it is common for there to be enmeshment and role reversal between children and favored parents (Garber, 2010), including the favored parents' having difficulty distinguishing their children's feelings from their own, treating the children as confidants to their adult concerns, or using the children for emotional support or to meet their own needs (Baker & Darnall, 2006; Johnston, Walters, & Olesen, 2005a, 2005b; Kelly & Johnston, 2001). Rejected parents may present with different parenting challenges, because few of them are prepared to deal constructively with the extreme behaviors that alienated children may manifest (Fidler et al., 2013; Moran, Sullivan, & Sullivan, 2015). Parenting domains to address with rejected parents may include a harsh, rigid, or authoritarian parenting style (Kelly & Johnston, 2001), passivity or withdrawal from the other parent in times of high conflict (Baker, 2006; Gardner, 2002; Vassiliou & Cartwright, 2001), and counterrejection of the alienated child (Gardner, 1998; Kelly & Johnston, 2001; Warshak, 2003). In other cases, the rejected parent may interact with the child in a skillful and authoritative manner but his or her efforts are futile because of the child's response, the effects of third-party influence, or both. Clinicians from the Overcoming Barriers program authored a book that helps coach rejected parents for exactly this reason (Moran et al., 2015). All of these disruptions in family roles and structure maintain alienation and are highly resistant to change.

Equine-assisted therapy can help with each of these patterns by generating experiences in the "here and now" that members of the family and therapist can observe jointly. The opportunity to observe behavior in the moment provides a natural antidote to characteristics of families in high conflict that can limit traditional treatment (e.g., a focus on the past, disagreements about critical incidents, and different attributions about the same behavior). Such experiential learning gives family members the opportunity to acquire and practice nonavoidant problem-solving skills: self-regulation when emotionally flooded, devising multiple ways to approach a task, collaboration and teamwork, and asking for help, to name a few.

For example, a rejected parent may believe she approaches her child in an open, conciliatory manner. This parent's interaction with a skittish horse may provide immediate, unbiased feedback about how her behavior affects another sentient being. In turn, and with help from the clinician and horse professional, this parent may practice other ways to approach and self-regulate to foster more attuned patterns of interaction (i.e., congruence between how one feels and how one acts). In our experience, families find in-the-moment feedback from a horse less shaming than strictly talk-based therapy, particularly given the amount of labeling and judgment many families may experience in the context of litigation, custody evaluation, and the like.

Indeed, the immediacy of interpersonal learning that is possible with equines is remarkably efficient given the time-limited nature of intensive workshops. This immediacy is often evident when a family member discusses a lesson he or she learned from an equine exercise, usually in the form of crediting a particular horse for teaching him or her a new behavior. For example, one of the program's horses had startled and fled from one parent when he approached her and asked her to walk forward. He subsequently reported that the horse had taught him to modulate his tone when giving directives.

Although excellent psychoeducational models of parent education exist, it is our experience that families referred for intensive intervention can be "tired of talking" and that an overly didactic approach can increase resistance and promote overintellectualization. These are not stances that foster new learning. As already discussed, horses, as prey animals, are highly attuned to the emotions and body language of other animals, humans included. Their survival depends on an ability to interpret such actions in terms of intentions. These features make equines extremely well suited to teaching about the subtle art of communication, awareness of interpersonal boundaries, the effects of one's posture, demeanor, and affect on others, and principles of emotional contagion.

Another important feature of horses is their imposing nature; they could cause harm but do not (Nurenberg et al., 2015). Families where parental alienation exists tend to be overfocused on perceived threat, often erroneously, and are prone to misperceiving the behavior of other family members through a hostile, even paranoid lens. Such misattributions manifest in cognitive distortions among children (see Chapter 10) and, in the most extreme form, unsubstantiated or false allegations by one parent of abuse by the other parent (Johnston, Lee, Olesen & Walters, 2005; Johnston, Roseby, & Kuehnle, 2009). The opportunity for immediate feedback from a horse in EAT helps foster reality testing and helps families accurately discriminate between provocative or harmful behavior and irritation, indifference, or misattunement. Reframing behavior from dangerous to misattuned or in need of redirection promotes reality clarification, reduces anxiety in the family system, and provides an opportunity for new patterns of interacting.

Alienated children tend to be inappropriately empowered in the family system (Gardner, 2002). In EAT, children must learn to work with horses in a collaborative, nonautocratic manner to get them to perform a desired behavior. Even a simple task such as grooming a horse will require an overly empowered child to regulate his or her posture and level of autonomic arousal so that the horse does not spook or respond defensively. Clinicians may instruct or coach the child in using strategies for self-regulation (e.g., mindful breathing) that will prove useful in real-time interactions outside the barn.

The opportunity to work with an animal as imposing and potentially stubborn as a horse with the support of a clinician and horse professional provides an opportunity for immediate feedback. In our experience it is far easier for adults and children alike to accept and integrate such feedback from an animal than from yet another therapist.

2.4. Cooking, Meal Preparation, and Sharing Meals

Food preparation and sharing meals are fundamental ways that families interact, bond, and stay connected, and these interactions are typically disrupted following divorce (Brach, Camara, & Houser, 2000). Months to years may have passed since a rejected parent has shared a meal with an alienated child. Participating in activities of daily living is an essential part of children's graduated exposure to the rejected parent (Garber, 2015). If the child is going to spend parenting time with the rejected parent in any real way following the intensive intervention, they must begin with simple activities such as sharing a meal and sleeping under the same roof (Judge & Bailey, 2015). Cooking, meal preparation, and sharing meals are therefore emphasized at Transitioning Families. In our experience, enabling families to overcome these initial challenges is among the most significant interventions we make and something that is beyond the reach of traditional outpatient treatment to accomplish.

In addition, cooking is among the most powerful ways to foster safe connections, forge new memories, and evoke old memories, which are the building blocks of successful reunification. Used therapeutically, cooking takes advantage of the uniquely powerful effects of olfaction on emotional memory, colloquially referred to as the Proust phenomenon. Experimental research has confirmed that autobiographical memories evoked by odors are more emotional than memories evoked by verbal or visual cues (Herz & Schooler, 2002). This aspect of cooking is another nonverbal dimension of experiential therapies that helps foster change powerfully and also efficiently.

It is important to incorporate food that reflects the particular culture of the family into the therapeutic process. In some cases, the family is expected to cook together, which is an important experiential activity. In all cases, families are asked to eat together at a communal table. These meals often include staff members to encourage and model appropriate mealtime behavior and conversation. Very often family members have not sat together as a unit for many years. One alienated adolescent, for example, presented to an intensive intervention with assertions that he had no positive memories of his father, the parent he had rejected for several years. The chef worked with the father to prepare a recipe that he remembered cooking for the children prior to the family's highly contentious divorce. Upon smelling the family recipe that the chef and the father had prepared, the adolescent was able to recall previously disavowed positive memories. The food or cooking does not in itself heal a fractured relationship but rather provides a foundation of connection on which other interventions may build.

Food can also be used in other ways to further the goals of reunification treatment. For example, it is recommended that treatment for moderate-to-severe alienation involve instruction in critical-thinking skills, including information from the social science literature on the fallibility of memory and the ubiquity of cognitive and perceptual errors (Warshak, 2010). An exercise called "blind taste test" offers an experiential way to discuss suggestibility, which is an important but highly charged concept to address with families in high conflict. Suggestibility refers to "the degree to which the encoding, storage, retrieval, and reporting of events can be influenced by a range of internal and external factors" (Ceci & Bruck, 1995; p. 44). Such cognitive processes have been implicated in the maintenance of inappropriate parent–child alignments within high-conflict families as well as in more moderate and severe forms of parental alienation (Warshak, 2010). During reunification treatment, it is critical that family members begin to understand the importance of maintaining their own opinions when faced with input from another family member that challenges their experiences. However, discussing the importance of suggestibility to the dynamics of alienation can create defensiveness among family members because of the implication of a parent's undue influence or manipulation.

"Blind taste test" helps foster conversation about perceptual and cognitive errors in a way that families are better able to tolerate and process. In the exercise, family members are blindfolded and presented with a variety of food items to identify, with tastes ranging from easy to difficult to guess. When participants are presented with a taste that's difficult to identify, a clinician provides clues that deliberately throw them off track, even after they have come to an agreement about a particular food's identity. Following this exercise, families typically engage in a lively discussion about the power of influence and groupthink (Janis, 1982) within families.

3. APPLICATION TO OUTPATIENT SETTINGS

The majority of families seek therapy in an outpatient setting where clinicians typically lack access to animals (let alone horses), a kitchen, or even outdoor space in which to facilitate family play and other experiential techniques. Implementing aspects of experiential therapies in office-based practice therefore requires creativity and flexibility. In Chapter 12, Barbara Fidler, Peggie Ward, and Robin Deutsch describe the application of the Overcoming Barriers approach to outpatient treatment, particularly with respect to the incorporation of physical movement and recreational therapy. Integration of such techniques may pose challenges to the traditional therapeutic frame, including the length of sessions, confidentiality, billing, and insurance reimbursement. All such changes should be reflected in service agreements and addressed with families in advance of treatment.

Animal-assisted therapy in outpatient practice poses additional, unique challenges. Dogs and cats may be more accessible to most clinicians than equines. The unpredictability of all animals, however, is something that clinicians should have some experience managing (e.g., via certification of one's pet as a therapy animal) before involving an animal in treatment. At its best, animal-assisted therapy furthers therapeutic goals, but without the necessary skills it may be a distraction that family members can use to hide behind or to derail the clinical process. Maintaining the health of animals used therapeutically is another critical factor. We have observed clinicians who could not use a therapy dog because the animal became so agitated by affective tension and loud voices during a session that it would later refuse to eat.

4. CONCLUSIONS

We have set forth in this chapter a rationale for using experiential and animal-assisted therapies in the treatment of parent–child contact problems and parental alienation. The clinical challenges of engaging families affected by these problems are considerable, and the need for effective, innovative educational and therapeutic intervention is great. We suggest that experiential therapy can provide a rich theoretical framework for the integration of techniques that help to generate novel, in-the-moment experiences that involve more than words. Such experiential goals are consistent with the objectives of reunification treatment: consideration of family problems from multiple perspectives, starting to rebuild fractured interpersonal connections, and relaxation of the defensive posturing that is so common among court-involved families. The framework of experiential therapy may also dovetail theoretically with recent research in trauma treatment and mindful awareness on the importance of interventions that shift physiological states to build self-regulatory functions (Siegel, 2007; Warner et al., 2014).

At this juncture, experiential therapies and animal-assisted interventions are not mainstream aspects of most family interventions in outpatient practice, whether for parent–child contact problems or other concerns. However, evolving clinical writing and research on intensive interventions for family-based reunification (see Chapter6, including but not limited to the Overcoming Barriers approach, clearly speak to the need for a broader array of tools. Promising findings from the literature on animal-assisted therapy, recreational therapy, and physical exercise as an augmentation to behavioral therapy may be judiciously applied to family treatment for parent–child contact problems. Future writing should continue to identify promising elements that are both unique to and shared among intensive intervention programs. Many of the ideas in this chapter are based on empirical findings in areas that are related to experiential techniques (e.g., the role of exercise, mindful awareness, and the neurobiological basis of self-regulation) but that lack outcome research on their application to high-conflict families. Evaluation of these experiential components, including animal-assisted techniques, is also urgently needed to demonstrate their efficacy (see Chapter 13).

REFERENCES

Annerstedt, M., & Währborg, P. (2011). Nature-assisted therapy: Systematic review of controlled and observational studies. *Scandinavian Journal of Public Health, 39,* 371–388.

ATRA Health Care Reform Task Force. (1994). *Summary of health outcomes in recreation therapy.* American Therapeutic Recreation Association. Retrieved from www.atra-tr.org=benefitshealthoutcomes.htm

ATRA Health Care Reform Task Force. (2001). *Recreational therapy: An integral aspect of comprehensive healthcare.* American Therapeutic Recreation Association. Retrieved from www.atra- tr.org=benefitsintegral.htm

Baker, A. (2006). Patterns of parental alienation syndrome: A qualitative study of adults who were alienated from a parent as a child. *American Journal of Family Therapy, 34,* 63–78.

Baker, A., & Darnall, D. (2006). Behaviors and strategies employed in parental alienation: A survey of parental experiences. *Journal of Divorce and Remarriage, 45*(1/2), 97–124.

Bishop, S. R., Lau, M., Shapiro, S., Carlson, L., Anderson, N., Carmodym, J., & Devins, G. (2004). Mindfulness: A proposed operational definition. *Clinical Psychology: Science and Practice, 11,* 230–241.

Brach, E. L., Camara, K. A., & Houser, R. F. (2000). Patterns of dinnertime interaction in divorced and nondivorced families. *Journal of Divorce and Remarriage, 32*(3/4), 125–139.

Cason D, Gillis HL. (1994). A meta-analysis of outdoor adventure programming with adolescents. *Journal of Experiential Education, 17*(1), 40–47.

Ceci, S. J., & Bruck, M. (1995). *Jeopardy in the courtroom: A scientific analysis of children's testimony.* Washington, DC: American Psychological Association Press.

Cheung, M. (2006). *Therapeutic games and guided imagery*. Chicago, IL: Lyceum Books.

Clark, J. P., Marmol, L. M., Cooley, R., & Gathercoal, K. (2004). The effects of wilderness therapy on the clinical concerns (on Axes I, II, and IV) of troubled adolescents. *Journal of Experiential Education, 27*(2), 213–232.

Corey, M. S., & Corey, G. (2000). *Groups: Process and practice*. Pacific Grove, CA: Brooks/ Cole.

Coyle, C. P., Kinney, W. B., & Shank, J. W. (1991). A summary of benefits common to therapeutic recreation. In C. P. Coyle, W. B. Kinney, B. Riley, & J. W. Shank (Eds.), *Benefits of therapeutic recreation: A consensus view* (pp. 353–385). Philadelphia, PA: Therapeutic Recreation Program, Temple University.

Davidson, R. J., Kabat-Zinn, J., Schumacher, J., Rosenkranz, M., Muller, D., Santorelli, S. F., . . . Sheridan, J. F. (2003). Alterations in brain and immune function produced by mindfulness meditation, *Psychosomatic Medicine, 65*(4), 564–570.

Deutsch, R. M. (2014, November). *Children resisting contact with a parent: Application of intensive interventions*. Invited Presentation at AFCC Symposium on Custody Evaluations, San Antonio, TX.

Doolittle, D., & Deutsch, R. M. (1999). Children and high-conflict divorce: Theory, research and intervention. In R. M. Galatzer-Levy & L. Kraus (Eds.), *The scientific basis of child custody decisions* (pp. 425–440). New York, NY: Wiley.

Fidler, B. J., Bala, N., & Saini, M. A. (2013). *Children who resist post-separation parental contact: A differential approach for legal and mental health professionals*. New York, NY: Oxford University Press.

Garber, B. D. (2010). Parental alienation and the dynamics of the enmeshed dyad: Adultification, parentification and infantilization. *Family Court Review, 49*(2), 322–335.

Garber, B. D. (2015). Cognitive–behavioral methods in high-conflict divorce: Systematic desensitization adapted to parent–child reunification interventions. *Family Court Review, 53*(1), 96–112.

Gardner, R.A. (1998). *The parental alienation syndrome* (2nd ed.). New Jersey: Creative Therapeutics Inc.

Gardner, R.A. (2002). The empowerment of children in the development of parental alienation syndrome. *American Journal of Forensic Psychology, 20*(2), 5–29.

Gil, E., & Sobol, B. (2005). Engaging families using therapeutic play. In C. E. Bailey (Ed.), *Children in therapy: Using the family as a resource* (pp. 341–382). New York, NY: W.W. Norton.

Gleiser, K., Ford, J. D., & Fosha, D. (2008). Contrasting exposure and experiential therapies for complex posttraumatic stress disorder. *Psychotherapy: Theory, Research, Practice, Training, 45*(3), 340–360.

Gordon, R. M., Stoffey, R., & Bottinelli, J. (2008). MMPI-2 findings of primitive defenses in alienating parents, *American Journal of Family Therapy, 36*(3), 211–228.

Greenberg, L. S., Rice, L. N., & Elliott, R. K. (1996). *Facilitating emotional change: The moment-by-moment process*. New York, NY: Guilford Press.

Hans, T. A. (2000). A meta-analysis of the effects of adventure programming on locus of control. *Journal of Contemporary Psychotherapy, 30*(1), 33–60.

Harrington, A., & Dunne, J. A. (2015). When mindfulness is therapy: Ethical qualms, historical perspectives. *American Psychologist, 70*(7), 621–631.

Hattie, J., Marsh, H. W., Neill, J. T., & Richards, G. E. (1997). Adventure education and Outward Bound: Out-of-class experiences that make a lasting difference. *Review of Educational Research, 67*(1), 43–87.

Herz, R. S., & Schooler, J. W. (2002). A naturalistic study of autobiographical memories evoked by olfactory and visual cues: Testing the Proustian hypothesis. *American Journal of Psychology, 115*(1), 21–32.

Janis, I. L. (1982). *Groupthink: Psychological studies of policy decisions and fiascoes.* Boston, MA: Houghton Mifflin.

Johnston, J. R., Lee, S., Olesen, N. W., & Walters, M. G. (2005) Allegations and substantiations of abuse in custody-disputing families. *Family Court Review, 43*(2), 283–294.

Johnston, J. R., Roseby, V., & Kuehnle, K. (2009). *In the name of the child: A developmental approach to understanding and helping children of conflicted and violent divorce* (2nd ed.). New York, NY: Springer Press.

Johnston, J. R., Walters, M. G., & Olesen, N. W. (2005a). Clinical ratings of parenting capacity and Rorschach protocols of custody-disputing parents: An exploratory study. *Journal of Child Custody, 2,* 159–178.

Johnston, J. R., Walters, M. G., & Olesen, N. W. (2005b). Is it alienating parenting, role reversal or child abuse? A study of children's rejection of a parent in child custody disputes. *Journal of Emotional Abuse, 5*(4), 191–218.

Judge, A. M., & Bailey, R. (2015). *Clinical protocol for Stable Paths: A Transitioning Families program.* Unpublished manual.

Judge, A. M., Bailey, R., Behrman-Lippert, J., Bailey, E., Psaila, C., & Dickel, J. (2016). The Transitioning Families Therapeutic Reunification Model in nonfamilial abductions. *Family Court Review, 54*(2), 232–249.

Kelly, J., & Johnston, J. (2001). The alienated child: A reformulation of parental alienation syndrome. *Family Court Review, 39,* 249–266.

Klontz, B. T., Bivens, A., Leinart, D., & Klontz, T. (2007). The effectiveness of equine-assisted experiential therapy: Results of an open clinical trial. *Society and Animals, 15,* 257–267.

Knobloch-Fedders, L. M., Pinsof, W. M., & Mann, B. J. (2007). Therapeutic alliance and treatment progress in couple psychotherapy. *Journal of Marital and Family Therapy, 33*(2), 245–257.

Lebow, J. (2003). Integrative family therapy for disputes involving child custody and visitation. *Journal of Family Psychology, 17*(2), 181–192.

Lebow, J., & Black, D. A. (2012). Considerations in court-involved therapy with parents. *Journal of Child Custody, 9*(1–2), 11–38.

Lebow, J. L., Chambers, A. L., Christensen, A., & Johnson, S. M. (2011). Research on the treatment of couple distress. *Journal of Marital and Family Therapy, 38*(1), 145–168.

Mahrer, A. R. (1983). *Experiential psychotherapy: Basic practices.* Ottawa, ON: University of Ottawa Press.

Margalit, D., & Ben-Ari, A. (2014). The effect of wilderness therapy on adolescents' cognitive autonomy and self-efficacy: Results of a non-randomized trial. *Child Youth Care Forum, 43,* 181–194.

Minuchin, S. (1974). *Families and family therapy.* Cambridge, MA: Harvard University Press.

Moran, J. A., Sullivan, T., & Sullivan, M. (2015). *Overcoming the co-parenting trap: Essential parenting skills when a child resists a parent.* Overcoming Barriers.

Newes, S., & Bandoroff, S. (2004). What is adventure therapy? In S. Bandoroff & S. Newes (Eds.), *Coming of age: The evolving field of adventure therapy* (pp. 1–30). US: Association for Experimental Education.

Norcross, J. C. (Ed.) (2011). *Psychotherapy relationships that work* (2nd ed.). New York, NY: Oxford University Press.

Nurenberg, J. R., Schleifer, S. J., Shaffer, T. M., Yellin, M., Desai, P. J., Amin, R., . . . Montalvo, C. (2015). Animal-assisted therapy with chronic psychiatric inpatients: Equine-assisted psychotherapy and aggressive behavior. *Psychiatric Services, 66*(1), 80–86.

Ogden, P., Minton, K., & Pain, C. (2006). *Trauma and the body: A sensorimotor approach to psychotherapy.* New York, NY: W. W. Norton.

Porges, S. W. (2011). *The polyvagal theory: Neurophysiological foundations of emotions, attachment, communication and self-regulation.* New York, NY: W. W. Norton.

Powers, M. B., Medina, J. L., Burns, S., Kauffman, B. Y., Monfils, M., Gordon, J. G., . . . Smits, J. (2015). Exercise augmentation of exposure therapy for PTSD: Rationale and pilot efficacy data. *Cognitive Behaviour Therapy, 44*(4), 314–327.

Selby, A., & Smith-Osborne, A. (2013). A systematic review of effectiveness of complementary and adjunct therapies and interventions involving equines. *Health Psychology, 32*(4), 418–432.

Siegel, D. J. (2007). *The mindful brain: Reflection and attunement in the cultivation of well-being.* New York, NY: W. W. Norton.

Sullivan, M. J., Ward, P. A., & Deutsch, R. M. (2010). Overcoming Barriers Family Camp: A program for high-conflict divorced families where a child is resisting contact with a parent. *Family Court Review, 48,* 115–134.

Thompson, S. J., Bender, K., Cardoso, J. B., & Flynn, P. M. (2011). Experiential activities in family therapy: Perceptions of caregivers and youth. *Journal of Child and Family Studies, 20,* 560–568.

Thompson, S. J., Bender, K., Windsor, L. C., & Flynn, P. M. (2009). Keeping families engaged: The effects of home-based family therapy enhanced with experiential activities. *Social Work Research, 33*(2), 121–136.

Vassiliou, D., & Cartwright, G. (2001). The lost parents' perspective on parental alienation syndrome. *American Journal of Family Therapy, 29*(3), 181–191.

Warner, E., Spinazzola, J., Westcott, A., Gunn, C., & Hodgdon, H. (2014). The body can change the score: Empirical support for somatic regulation in the treatment of traumatized adolescents. *Journal of Child and Adolescent Trauma, 7,* 237–246.

Warshak, R. A. (2003). Bringing sense to parental alienation: A look at the disputes and the evidence. *Family Law Quarterly, 37*(2), 273–301.

Warshak, R. A. (2010). Family Bridges: Using insights from social science to reconnect parents and alienated children. *Family Court Review, 48*(1), 48–80.

Winnicott, D. W. (1965). *The maturational processes and the facilitating environment.* London, UK: Hogarth Press.

5

The Perfect Storm

*High-Conflict Family Dynamics, Complex Therapist
Reactions, and Suggestions for Clinical Management*

ABIGAIL M. JUDGE AND PEGGIE WARD ∎

1. INTRODUCTION

> In perhaps no other area of practice are legal and mental health profession-
> als so much at risk of losing their professional objectivity and becoming
> entangled with their clients, as in these high conflict family situations. . . .
> These powerful and compelling responses to the pain and suffering of
> divorcing individuals (called countertransference reactions) are impor-
> tant signals to the professional involved to regain his or her balance and
> perspective in the case.
>
> (ROSEBY & JOHNSTON, *1997, pp. 10–11*)

The observation above highlights the ways in which families experiencing high-
conflict separation or divorce provoke notoriously strong reactions in professionals. Therapist reactions can include inappropriate advocacy on behalf of patients
in the legal dispute and, at the level of professional teams, the pull on involved professionals to mirror the conflicted process of the family system through dynamics
such as polarization, rigid thinking, and inappropriate alignments (Greenberg,
Gould, Gould-Saltman, & Stahl, 2003; Sullivan & Kelly, 2001).

Many writers have described high rates of maladaptive personality characteristics such as narcissism and borderline and histrionic features, as well as frank personality disorders (PDs), among child custody–disputing parents (Baker, 2006;
Eddy, 2009; Feinberg & Greene, 1997). Johnston and Campbell (1988) reported
that 64% of their court-involved sample received a diagnosis of a PD. In addition
to frank psychopathology, custody-litigating parents present to treatment with

features that complicate formation and maintenance of a therapeutic alliance, such as high levels of defensiveness, hostility, and the tendency to blame others for their problems (Lebow & Black, 2012; for a review, see Ellis, 2000).

It is axiomatic that such traits and PDs are likely to induce strong reactions in therapists. In this chapter we suggest that it is the unique combination of personality-disordered characteristics with the dynamics of a high-conflict separation and court involvement that poses such challenges for therapists who treat families in those circumstances. Moreover, it is the combination of these three factors that gives rise to strong countertransference reactions among individual clinicians and within professional teams. We refer to this constellation—PD, high conflict, and court involvement—as the "perfect storm," and in this chapter we describe each component and then propose strategies for clinical management of the combination.

From an ethical perspective, the legal context of custody litigation heightens the importance of therapists' managing strong reactions to the perfect storm in a proactive manner (Greenberg et al., 2003). Left unexamined, therapist reactions and their enactment within teams have the potential to undermine the therapeutic and legal process, result in ethical missteps, and cause harm. In contrast, proper identification and management of high-conflict dynamics and therapist reactions may help therapists to refine clinical hypotheses, foster cohesive clinical teams, and help families disengage from conflict. Unfortunately, despite frequent references in the literature about maladaptive personality traits and disorders among custody litigants, there is surprisingly limited clinical writing about managing these dynamics in clinical practice.

Accordingly, we start with a brief review of contemporary definitions of countertransference and therapist reactions and explain our use of these terms in this chapter. Next, we review the extant empirical research on levels of psychopathology, defensiveness, and maladaptive personality characteristics among custody-litigating samples, research that is based primarily in the area of psychological assessment. This review will provide an evidence-based foundation for our discussion of the perfect storm and the range of complex countertransference reactions it can evoke. We put forth that in working with families experiencing high-conflict separation and divorce strong countertransference reactions are the rule, not the exception, and their identification and management is a critical part of intervention. This is true for beginning, intermediate, and seasoned clinicians alike. We conclude with a description of clinical best practices for management of these patterns, based on the clinical literature on managing treatment with court involvement, published practice guidelines, and our combined clinical and forensic experience.

2. DEFINITIONS OF COUNTERTRANSFERENCE AND THERAPIST REACTIONS

There are numerous definitions of countertransference, and most emphasize the emotions evoked in therapists when working with patients (Rossberg, Karterud,

Pedersen, & Friis, 2007). Freud introduced countertransference as a therapist's unconscious reactions toward patients, reactions that were presumably rooted in the therapist's own neurotic conflicts, past experiences with significant attachment figures, or both (Freud, 1910/1957; Kernberg, 1965). In Freud's original formulation, countertransference was understood as a hindrance to treatment. A different view has emerged since the 1950s, emphasizing the clinical value of therapists' emotional reactions to patients. As reviewed by Rossberg and colleagues (2007), therapist reactions are important in the therapist–patient relationship because they may provide important information about the interpersonal problems patients are struggling with. In contrast to earlier formulations, most contemporary psychodynamic perspectives view countertransference as a cocreated phenomenon based both on elements of the clinician's past and on emotions induced by the patient's behavior (Gabbard, 2004). Psychoanalytic theorists describe a clinician's emotional responses to patients, however idiosyncratic or disorienting, as potential links to a patient's internal state and therefore a source of useful clinical information (Gordon & Kirtchuk, 2008).

Attending to countertransference may be particularly important in clinical work with forensic patients, who as a group tend to "communicate by impact" (Casement, 1985) or induce strong feelings in the therapist through troubling behaviors (Aiyegbusi & Tuck, 2008). In the context of child custody disputes and parental alienation, such behaviors may include hostility, threats of litigation, a parent's repeated false allegations of abuse or intimate-partner violence, or repeated triangulation of a child in adult conflict. Although child custody-litigating parents differ from other forensic populations, a common denominator is the role of severe personality disturbance and countertransference reactions among individual therapists and professional teams (Gordon & Kirtchuk, 2008). Some clinical methodology for examining and managing these reactions is therefore a vital aspect of intervention with these families.

For the purposes of this chapter we will use the terms *therapist reactions* and *countertransference* interchangeably, but we do so with the following caveats: First, we acknowledge controversy about the role of psychoanalytic theories in forensic practice and the use of such language in child custody evaluations in particular (Martindale & Gould, 2007; Pickar, 2007). Even if psychoanalytic language is considered confusing or distracting in a legal context, these concepts still have meaning in clinical work with the families described in this book. Second, contemporary psychoanalytic definitions of countertransference include the therapist's entire reaction to a patient, not only those based in unconscious conflict or past experience. Empirical research on countertransference suggests that such reactions can indeed be measured (McIntyre & Schwartz, 1998; Najavits, 2000). Thus our use of the term countertransference refers to observable therapist behaviors that occur in response to families in high conflict. Third, we acknowledge that the most appropriate treatments for the families described in this book—namely, cognitive–behavioral techniques, psychoeducation, and integrated, solution-focused family therapy (Garber, 2015; Lebow, 2003; Lebow & Gurman, 1995)— are not primarily psychodynamic. Nevertheless, much of the clinical literature on PDs emphasizes the importance of countertransference reactions, which can relate to clinical outcome. We therefore suggest that this level of clinical analysis is germane even when the therapist is implementing a primarily behavioral intervention.

To appreciate what characteristics give rise to complex therapist reactions, we next review the empirical literature on levels of psychopathology, defensiveness, and maladaptive personality traits of custody litigants, including parental alienating behaviors. This research is based primarily in psychological assessment, including objective and projective measures.

3. PERSONALITY DISORDERS IN CUSTODY-LITIGATING SAMPLES

Clinical writing has long asserted that parents engaged in child custody disputes, especially those who engage in parental alienating behaviors, have higher rates of PDs (Baker, 2005b; Gardner, 1992; Johnston & Campbell, 1988; Johnston, Walters, & Olesen, 2005).

The revised Minnesota Multiphasic Personality Inventory (MMPI-2) is among the most widely used measures in child custody evaluations (Quinnell & Bow, 2001) and generates objective and reliable personality data about litigating parents (Pope, Butcher & Seelen, 2006). However, the MMPI-2 is subject to impression management ("faking good") and other forms of defensive reporting, which are common among custody-litigating samples (Bagby et al., 1999). Researchers have therefore recommended the use of the Lie (L) and Correction (K) scales of the MMPI-2 to evaluate potential biases when using this instrument. As noted by Johnston et al. (2005), however, this practice has not completely settled the controversy about the effect of defensive reporting on the MMPI-2 (Bagby et al., 1999; Strong, Greene, Hoppe, Johnston, & Olesen, 1999). Notwithstanding these limitations, themes have emerged in the research on child custody–litigating samples using the MMPI-2, which we will now describe.

Three empirical studies examined the psychological functioning of parents involved in child custody litigation using the MMPI-2 (Gordon, Stoffey, & Bottinelli, 2008; Lampel, 1996; Siegel & Langford, 1998). Results indicated that alienating parents had clinically significantly higher L and K scores on the MMPI-2. Such elevations are associated with individuals who engage in more narcissistic and primitive defenses of denial, splitting, and projection and with borderline psychopathology such as reality distortions and provocative behaviors (Gordon et al., 2008; Johnston et al., 2005c; Lampel, 1996; Siegel & Langford, 1998). Mothers who demonstrated parental alienating behaviors were more likely than nonalienating mothers to use denial, splitting, and projection (Siegel & Langford, 1998). Alienating parents showed more frequent use of primitive defenses (e.g., splitting and projective identification) when compared with controls based on MMPI-2 profiles (Gordon et al., 2008; Siegel & Langford, 1998). Findings with respect to rejected parents were mixed. One study found no support for the idea that rejected parents contribute to the dynamics through use of primitive defenses (Gordon et al., 2008). In that study, rejected parents were found to be similar to custody-litigating parents in nonalienation cases.

Gordon and colleagues (2008) explained how primitive, or immature, defenses operate in the context of parental alienation. Splitting occurs when the alienating or favored parent views herself or himself as all good and views the target parent as all bad. Projective identification occurs when an alienating parent denies her or his personal faults, projects them onto the target parent, and then treats the target parent in a way that induces behavior evidencing those faults. For example, an alienating parent with irrational anger may act in a way that enrages the target parent. The alienating parent or the resistant child can then claim that the target parent has an anger problem. Chronic use of primitive defenses by parents injures children by undermining their ability to form objective and independent judgments of others. Similarly, classifying an individual as all good or all bad (splitting) compromises children's capacity for healthy intimacy (R. M. Gordon et al., 2008).

Other research has examined psychological functioning of custody-disputing parents using projective tests, notably the Rorschach. Johnston and colleagues (2005) argued that the Rorschach test is more resistant to "faking good" than are more objective personality tests and self-report parenting scales, especially when the Rorschach is scored using the Comprehensive System. An exploratory study of Rorschach protocols examined personality correlates of custody-disputing parents whose parental behavior was likely to lead a child to become alienated from or rejecting of one parent after divorce (Johnston et al., 2005). Although preliminary, the results indicated that alienating coparent behavior by fathers was directly correlated with their narcissism, self-preoccupation, cognitive slippage, and rigid, authoritarian style. Alienating coparenting behavior by mothers was inversely correlated with their need for interpersonal closeness and was directly correlated with cognitive slippage. These findings are consistent with the clinical observation that parental alienating behaviors and role reversal are manifestations of narcissistic injury and disordered thinking, possibly including paranoid thinking. This can manifest in alienating parents' lack of consideration for the child's feelings and ideas and greater concern for their own (Johnston et al., 2005). In contrast with the MMPI-2 studies discussed above, Johnston et al. (2005) reported finding coping deficits among rejected parents based on Rorschach data, likely due to depression, anxiety, and difficulty modulating emotions.

4. THE PERFECT STORM: PERSONALITY DISORDERS, HIGH-CONFLICT DIVORCE, AND COMPLEX SYSTEMS INVOLVEMENT

We have discussed the prominence of personality disorders and PD traits among custody-litigating samples, including families with parent–child contact problems and parental alienation. Fortunately, there are a range of empirically based treatments for PDs that allow clinicians to work effectively with this population

(Bateman & Fonagy, 2004; Clarkin, Levy, Lenzenweger, & Kernberg, 2007; Linehan et al., 2006). All of these treatments emphasize the management of interpersonal dynamics within the therapeutic relationship; in some cases, attention to transference is a primary aspect of the treatment (Clarkin et al., 2007). This emphasis speaks to the importance of monitoring therapist reactions and using them as part of treatment when personality-disordered traits and PDs are present. Although clinical writing on managing therapist reactions to PD exists, we extend this literature by emphasizing the two additional components that contribute to the perfect storm: high-conflict family dynamics in the context of divorce or separation and involvement of the court and other third parties.

In this section we suggest that the experience of a high-conflict separation or divorce can exacerbate many PDs and change the nature of therapy. It is not only the clinical characteristics of these disorders that make clinical work with individuals or families in high conflict so challenging but also the particular ways in which those features combust when combined with the unique pressures of court involvement. That is why we call the combination of these three components the perfect storm. We will discuss each component separately before presenting strategies for clinical management of their combination.

4.1. Personality Disorders and the Therapeutic Relationship

The presence of a PD, maladaptive personality traits, or both is the first component of the perfect storm. We start with a brief review of the PDs most commonly associated with all three components.

Personality disorders are present in approximately 9.1% of the general population and have a high rate of comorbidity with other major mental health disorders (Lenzenweger, Lane, Loranger, & Kessler, 2007). According to the fifth edition of the *Diagnostic and Statistical Manual of Mental Disorders* (American Psychiatric Association, 2013), the essential features of a PD are impairments in personality functioning and the presence of pathological personality traits. Impairments may be in self functioning (i.e., identity or self-direction) or interpersonal functioning (i.e., empathy or identity). Personality disorders are organized by Clusters (A, B, and C), which are understood to share common core features. The literature suggests that negative countertransference is more likely with Clusters A and B than Cluster C (Johansen, 1983; Rossberg et al., 2007).

Cluster A personality disorders include schizoid PD, schizotypal PD, and paranoid PD. Characteristically, individuals with these disorders tend to distance themselves from others and experience extreme discomfort when interacting socially. They tend not to engage in conflict situations and are more likely to withdraw from interpersonal relationships. Such interpersonal patterns can nevertheless contribute to conflict when the individual's withdrawal exacerbates his or her partner's distress. Individuals with paranoid PD experience a nonpsychotic form of paranoia characterized by gross mistrust of others, including the belief that others intend to cause them harm. This paranoia can take the form of a generalized fear about the outside world or an encapsulated delusional system that is limited to one or more interpersonal relationships. Clinicians must differentiate between paranoid PD, delusional disorder, and a frank psychotic disorder to set realistic treatment goals and also ensure the safety of all involved. Making this distinction is particularly relevant where threats of parental abduction have been made, given the subsets of abducting parents with either frank thought disorders or paranoid delusions and of parents with heightened concern about young children having been exposed to neglectful or endangering environments by the other parent (Johnston, Girdner, & Sagatun-Edwards, 1999).

Cluster B includes antisocial, borderline, histrionic, and narcissistic PDs. Key characteristics of these disorders include emotional dysregulation, impulsive behaviors, and self-preoccupation (American Psychiatric Association, 2013). Given these core difficulties, clients with these PDs may have difficulty maintaining a stable and healthy connection with their partners or their children. Borderline PD is the most prevalent PD in Cluster B and is defined as "a pervasive pattern of instability of interpersonal relationships, self-image, affects, and marked impulsivity beginning by early adulthood and present in a variety of contexts" (American Psychiatric Association, 2013). Theoretical models of borderline PD conceive of the disorder as primarily interpersonal (Benjamin, 1996; Gunderson, 2001), which is reflected in the diagnostic criteria (e.g., a pattern of unstable and intense relationships and frantic efforts to avoid real or perceived abandonment). Recent developmental neuroscience research suggests that borderline PD follows a developmental trajectory characterized by insufficient coregulation of affect, including a long-standing difficulty feeling support and comfort from close others (Hughes, Crowell, Uyeji, & Coan, 2012). Individuals with borderline PD may alternate between overinvolvement in and withdrawal from close relationships; they often view close relationships in extremes of idealization and devaluation. Individuals with borderline PD are more likely to use the defense of splitting than are patients with other PDs (Bond, Paris, & Zweig-Frank, 1994). Research on therapist reactions using clinical vignettes and rating scales found that patients with borderline PD evoked the most anger and the least liking, empathy, and nurturance (Brody & Farber, 1996).

As reviewed by Liebman and Burnette (2013), the literature suggests that individuals with borderline PD are more likely than individuals with other Axis I and Axis II disorders to evoke negative countertransference reactions. For example, since individuals with borderline PD frequently engage in splitting (i.e., engaging with the therapist as either all good and idealized or all bad and devalued), the therapist's countertransference reactions may be similarly polarized. Such reactions include feelings of omnipotence or of helplessness, exhaustion, or rejection (Gallop, 1985; McCready, 1987). Other common countertransference reactions in clinical work with borderline PD include guilt feelings; rescue fantasies; transgression of professional boundaries; rage; helplessness and worthlessness; anxiety; and even terror (Gabbard, 1993).

Narcissistic PD, Another PD within Cluster B, is characterized by significant impairments in regulating self-esteem that result in an exaggerated self-appraisal, need for approval, and sense of entitlement. Other core features include an impaired capacity to empathize, or to recognize and identify with the feelings and needs of others. Difficulties with intimacy are also common (i.e., relationships are largely superficial and exist to regulate self-esteem). At the same time, individuals with narcissistic PD have fragile self-esteem, are prone to disparaging and devaluing others, and respond to criticism with rage or defiance. Their primary defense mechanisms are denial, splitting, and projection (Gabbard, 2004). They are also vulnerable to helplessness, low self-esteem, emptiness, and shame. While they may appear grandiose, individuals with narcissistic PD often feel extremely vulnerable.

Given the core characteristics of narcissistic PD (e.g., impairments in empathy and relationships with others), it is reasonable to conjecture that many parents with narcissistic PD will struggle to form healthy and empathic attachments to their partners or children. In the context of high-conflict separation, for example, deficits in empathy can result in a parent with narcissistic PD devaluing his or her former spouse and the spouse's role in the children's future. Johnston and Campbell (1988) observed that parents with narcissistic PD "have limited ability to recognize and respond to their children beyond their own wishes and needs" (pp. 82–83). They note as well:

> In their need to reject their former spouse, these parents do not recognize the child's attachment to the other parent. From their perspective, they and the child are one: 'I want him out of our lives'; 'She left us.' By placing value only on their own relationship with the child, they fail to acknowledge the total life of the child. They pursue their own interests with the child, more or less disregarding the other parent, thereby fragmenting the child's world. (pp. 86–87)

Narcissistic traits may also be implicated in alienation. Baker's (2005a) qualitative study described alienating parents as narcissistic and requiring excessive devotion and loyalty. Johnston and colleagues (2005) also reported narcissism among alienating fathers based on their analysis of Rorschach protocols.

Antisocial PD is also a Cluster B personality disorder. Individuals with antisocial PD derive self-esteem from personal gain, and their behavior may fail to conform to lawful or culturally normative ethical behavior. Other core features of antisocial PD include impairments in interpersonal functioning such as a lack of empathy (e.g., lack of concern for feelings, needs, or suffering of others and lack of remorse) or lack of intimacy. The diagnosis of antisocial PD requires an incapacity for mutually intimate relationships, with behavioral manifestations that can include exploitation or deceit and use of dominance or intimidation to control others (American Psychiatric Association, 2013). By definition, the lack of concern for the feelings of others, lack of remorse, and lack of intimate relationships suggest that people with antisocial PD have major difficulties in intimate relationships such as those with a spouse or children.

Regarding interactions with therapists, clinical and empirical writing indicates that individuals with antisocial PD often display manipulative behaviors, defensiveness, distrust, lack of cooperation, and noncompliance with treatment (McWilliams, 1994). They frequently show callous, cynical, and contemptuous behaviors that may pose a threat to others (Schwartz, 2000; Schwartz, Smith, & Chopko, 2007). Research suggests that patients with antisocial PD induce therapist reactions of vigilance, feeling overwhelmed, and a need for distance (Thylstrup & Hesse, 2008). The presence of antisocial PD suggests a poor prognosis for therapy, given the core deficits in empathy and a tendency to exploit others (including the therapist) for personal gain. There may also be safety concerns. Therapists should be aware that one profile of parents who abduct children in the context of custody litigation is that they present with features of antisocial PD, including narcissistic and sociopathic personality traits and a history of disrespect of authority and the law (Johnston et al., 1999).

Cluster C personality disorders include avoidant, dependent, and obsessive-compulsive PDs, all of which represent anxious and fearful personality types. Individuals with these PDs may be dependent on the other parent but do not tend to be the instigators of the conflict that led to alienation and litigation. Individuals with Cluster C characteristics or disorders may be passive in their parenting and avoidant of conflict—parenting deficits that may be common among some kinds of rejected parents (Fidler, Bala, & Saini, 2013). On the other hand, individuals with dependent or obsessive–compulsive PD may be overly involved with their children to the point of role reversal or enmeshment, as is common among favored parents (Garber, 2010). With respect to therapist reactions, research indicates that patients with Cluster C personality disorders are more likely to elicit helpful feelings than are other diagnostic groups (Thylstrup & Hesse, 2008).

4.2. High-Conflict Divorce and the Therapeutic Relationship

The second component of the perfect storm is the introduction of a high-conflict separation or divorce. Since core features of PDs include instability within relationships, difficulties regulating affect, and difficulty maintaining effective coping when faced with interpersonal crisis, a disruption like high-conflict separation will stress individuals with PDs where they are most vulnerable. As discussed earlier, when under stress, individuals with PDs show patterns of thinking (e.g., dichotomous thinking and defenses such as projection and splitting) that simplify complex interpersonal situations rather than support problem-solving. We therefore suggest that increasingly dichotomous cognitions and polarized thinking are hallmarks both of the experience of a PD and the situation of high-conflict divorce.

It is important to note that high conflict is not a unidimensional concept; there are various types and degrees of high conflict within separating families (Birnbaum & Bala, 2010). Johnston (1994) observed the need to differentiate between "normal" high conflict and pathological conflict, since the latter may signal a need for parents to have less involvement in their children's lives until the interparental conflict is reduced. Johnston therefore proposed a conceptual model based on three dimensions of conflict: the domain, tactics, and attitudinal dimensions. *Domain* refers to the type of postseparation disagreements (e.g., disagreements over ongoing financial support, property division, custody, and access to the children or differences in opinion regarding childrearing practices). *Tactics* refers to the manner in which divorcing couples try to solve disagreements (e.g., avoidance, verbal reasoning, verbal aggression, coercion, or physical aggression). Finally, the *attitudinal* dimension refers to the degree of negative emotions such as hostility that separating or divorcing parents direct toward each other, either overtly or covertly.

According to Friedman (2004), high-conflict cases are characterized by the following: high rates of litigation and relitigation, high degrees of anger and distrust, difficulties with communication between the parents about the children, intimate-partner violence issues, and alienation of a child as a result of the conduct or attitude of one parent. Conflict likely existed in the relationship prior to the separation or divorce. Furthermore, high conflict is not necessarily initiated mutually but can be driven primarily by one parent (Friedman, 2004), a distinction that may be especially useful to make in cases of parent–child contact problems, and alienation in particular (Warshak, 2000).

The experience of high-conflict separation or divorce for an already vulnerable individual, including one with a PD, can alter or dramatically shift the motivations for and goals of therapy (Greenberg et al., 2003; Perlman, 2012). Specifically, there is pressure to shift the therapeutic frame from the therapy goals to the therapist's engagement in the conflict. The therapist is likely to hear significantly more in a therapy with court involvement about external blame (usually about the other parent) as well as who is right or wrong across multiple situations. Clients may implore the therapist to validate their perspective over any other and may become sensitive to even the most gentle of challenges or redirection. The client may become more demanding, calling the therapist multiple times a week or day. The client may ask the therapist to affirm that he or she is the "better parent." If the therapist doesn't join in total support of the client's wishes, the client may devalue the therapist or threaten to leave therapy.

4.3. Child Custody Litigation, Court Involvement, and the Therapeutic Relationship

The third component of the perfect storm is child custody litigation and the involvement of the court, legal system, and potentially other systems (e.g., child protection or law enforcement). It is estimated that approximately 10% of divorcing families engage in substantial conflict within the legal system that may persist for years after separation (Grych & Fincham, 1999; Maccoby, Depner, & Mnookin, 1990). Parents involved in high-conflict divorce have ongoing concerns about the other parent's parenting, higher levels of hostility, and longer legal disputes (Maccoby et al., 1990). These cases usually involve attorneys although some litigants act pro se (i.e., represent themselves in the court action). Allegations about poor, impaired, or abusive parenting in the context of custody disputes are common, as these often create a complaint for divorce (Johnston, Roseby, & Kuehnle, 2009).

By definition, such allegations will then involve the systems charged with their investigation and adjudication (e.g., law enforcement, child protection, or the court). This development may introduce previously uninvolved third parties. Involvement with child protection agencies arises from abuse allegations, and police may become involved as a result of one or both parties alleging dangerous behavior by the other. The family is often in court on complaints for contempt or motions for other actions. Judges may order custody evaluations to determine parental strengths and weaknesses with respect to the children. Appointment of attorneys to represent children is becoming more common. Adding to the therapist's dilemma may be recommendations for additional therapists to treat certain problems, parenting coordinators to help resolve and alleviate family conflict, or special masters to decide aspects of the case. Advocates from the fields of intimate partner violence/domestic violence may also be part of the newly evolved system.

Each additional actor may impose another layer of stress on the therapeutic contract and treatment frame. Initial therapeutic goals may shift as the therapist receives multiple requests to talk with others outside the therapeutic relationship. Such requests introduce another strain on the clinical process: questions about information sharing, confidentiality, and privilege (Greenberg et al., 2003). When attorneys and courts become involved, boundaries and other aspects of informed consent initially agreed to by the therapist and client(s) lose clarity (Dwyer, 2012). Pressure to alter the therapeutic contract is intense, and there can be confusion about the therapist's potentially changed role (i.e., as the client's individual therapist versus an advocate on behalf of the client's legal case). Originally clearly defined goals, treatment plans, and client engagement may change dramatically. Another potential effect of custody litigation is a change in client motivation from using the therapy for individual change to making it a tool in the court process (Greenberg et al., 2003; Greenberg, Gould-Saltman & Gottlieb, 2008).

These changes pull most therapists into unknown and undesirable territory. In response, they may feel overwhelmed with a host of negative feelings about the client, the therapeutic process, and third-party intrusions. The therapist who began treatment with one set of expectations now faces escalation of affect, increased cognitive distortions in the client, and pulls for polarization within the treatment and from the outside. Within the perfect storm, therapists' own emotions are triggered, perhaps more intensely than during previous points in the treatment. Therapists may now struggle with how to remain supportive, empathic, and neutral and how best to navigate pulls from outside actors to step outside the therapeutic frame.

To provide an example of the perfect storm, we offer the following vignette, which is a composite sketch designed to illustrate each of the three components:

A mother with borderline PD initially sought therapy to better manage her emotions with her children. Her therapist treated her individually, with occasional conjoint meetings with the children. The client suddenly receives her husband's petition for divorce. She feels intense loss, grief, and fear of abandonment. In response, the gains she has made in therapy—improved emotion regulation and coping—are immediately compromised. She is more irritable and reactive to her children and requires more between-session support from her therapist. The divorce rapidly becomes highly litigious.

Her husband, who himself has narcissistic PD, calls the therapist and demands to know why his wife has been in treatment and why she has introduced their children to the therapist. He insists on an appointment with the therapist to explain how "wrong" the therapist has been in her work with his wife.

Around this same time, the child's guidance counselor at school calls the therapist at the mother's request. The counselor explains that the mother feels that the child is experiencing a mental health crisis and must be seen immediately. The father's attorney then calls to tell the therapist that she may not treat the child. A newly retained parenting coordinator calls the therapist to ask for information. The therapist also receives subpoenas to present to court.

Each component of the perfect storm is evident, if dramatized, in this vignette: personality-disordered characteristics, high-conflict separation, and litigation with third-party involvement. A client who sought treatment originally for help with difficulties related to her emotion regulation becomes precipitously more symptomatic as a result of an unexpected and suddenly high-conflict separation. Aggressive litigation invites in a range of new actors, who contact the therapist on behalf of their client in an ongoing legal dispute. New actors such as a parenting coordinator and individuals concerned about the child (here, the guidance counselor) strain the boundaries of the therapeutic frame. In response, the therapist may ask herself a range of questions: What has happened to the therapeutic frame? Who is the client? How can I help stabilize the client and create a therapeutic space protected from the larger systems around her? Is addressing the larger systemic issues even a therapeutic role? If so, how should I address them? What if the client continually invites the therapist into the legal dispute?

What appeared at first to be treatment of an individual with a PD has now become a variant of therapy that may no longer be familiar to the majority of clinicians. The therapist may feel anxious, inadequate, helpless, and confused as well as conflicted about role definition, ethical practice, and emergent legal dilemmas. The initial informed consent to treatment may no longer seem adequate. In the context of the perfect storm, therapy has transformed from a private, healthcare-focused situation to a more public, systems-involved, and crisis-focused one.

We suggest that each overlay of the perfect storm intensifies external pressure on the therapist to alter previously established aspects of the therapeutic frame (e.g., roles, frequency of contact, expected interactions with individuals besides the client, and questions about confidentiality and privilege). These pressures then engender emotional reactions in the therapist that may lead to ethical missteps or uncharacteristic behavior if not carefully monitored and understood.

Although we could locate no empirical studies of therapist reactions to clients experiencing high-conflict divorce, there may be common patterns of how therapists respond to elements of the perfect storm. Two possibilities are particularly notable:

> *Withdrawal from the client or premature termination.* The perfect storm may induce in the therapist feelings such as anger, frustration, and helplessness (to name just a few), and failure to effectively manage these emotions can lead the therapist to prematurely terminate the therapy and abandon the client. We distinguish this kind of termination from an ethical termination that becomes necessary when the clinical situation changes and new factors are introduced such that the therapist no longer possesses the competence to remain involved (American Psychological Association, 2010). Here the termination is due instead to the therapist's becoming overwhelmed by his or her own unprocessed or poorly managed emotional reactions to the case and failing to seek consultation.
>
> *Overinvolvement or rescuing.* This reaction may be seen as the opposite of withdrawal. It may take different forms, such as inappropriate advocacy (e.g., writing letters to the court on behalf of the client's legal position), rescuing behaviors, or joining, overidentifying, and merging with the client's emotional crisis.

There are likely variations in these responses, and in some situations, combined reactions may occur. For example, termination may follow a period of overinvolvement. Given the likelihood of strong therapist reactions, it is essential that clinicians think preventively about their practice in cases of high-conflict separation. We therefore next discuss clinical best practices for managing complex therapist reactions.

5. STRATEGIES AND BEST PRACTICES FOR MANAGING THE PERFECT STORM

Relative to the psychological literature on child custody evaluation, there has been little attention devoted to the role of the treating clinician in cases of high-conflict divorce (Greenberg & Gould, 2001). The specialty guidelines for forensic psychologists (American Psychological Association, 2011) emphasize professional standards for forensic evaluation and expert witness testimony rather than for psychotherapy with a legal nexus. To address this gap, the Association of Family and Conciliation Courts (AFCC) generated guidelines for best practices for court-involved therapists and other professionals involved in child dependency and family court litigation (AFCC, 2010; Fidnick & Deutsch, 2012). The guidelines were designed for use in combination with the ethical standards of one's profession, and they articulate several principles relevant to the management of therapist reactions.

5.1. Effects of Legal Context on Client Behavior and Therapeutic Process

First and foremost, the AFCC guidelines recommend that clinicians appreciate the effects that custody litigation has on the therapeutic process. This knowledge should inform basic elements of treatment, such as informed consent, billing, and family members' authorization to share treatment information, as well as more complicated aspects of the clinical process. For example, one guideline states that the court-involved therapist should "understand that the information provided by the client during the course of treatment is based upon the client's experience and perspective, which may sometimes be distorted or lacking balance or comprehensiveness" (AFCC, 2010, p. 27).

That guideline comports with our review of the literature on personality traits and disorders among litigating samples (e.g., rigid, polarized thinking and primitive defenses). Primitive defenses or cognitive distortion (whichever language a clinician prefers) has the effect of simplifying complex emotional experience and thinking. A goal of intervention overall is to foster more critical and expansive thinking among children and parents alike (see Chapter 10 and the ability to see family conflict from multiple perspectives. The parallel expectation is for clinicians to actively consider alterative hypotheses regarding information received from clients and maintain professional objectivity in the face of powerful interpersonal pulls (AFCC, 2010). Indeed, considering multiple hypotheses about client behavior, as well as about the behavior of the client's ex-partner and children, is a hallmark of forensic thinking as applied to clinical work with court involvement (Greenberg & Gould, 2001; Olesen & Drozd, 2012).

5.2. Maintaining a Therapeutic Alliance

A strong therapeutic alliance is the most robust predictor of a good outcome across a range of treatment outcome studies (Norcross, 2011). Forming a therapeutic alliance with each member of a family in high conflict is among the most challenging aspects of treatment. The model of integrative family therapy (Lebow, 2003, 2005) was developed for court-involved parents and highlights this aspect of treatment. Lebow and Black (2012) describe the importance of avoiding split alliances, something to which families in high conflict will be uniquely sensitive. An additional challenge to building an alliance is being able to confront problematic behavior while maintaining the therapeutic relationship.

Challenges to the alliance may be particularly strong when allegations of intimate-partner violence or abuse have been made but there has been no investigation or finding concerning the allegations. Olesen and Drozd (2012) emphasize the importance of the therapist's being empathic and understanding while also maintaining some neutrality and the capacity to consider multiple hypotheses in such situations. They write:

> Therapists can demonstrate empathy and understanding by providing and demonstrating knowledge of the effects of trauma.... Sensitive discussions between the therapist and the client about the tension between providing support and providing advocacy can create a foundation for effective therapy. A therapist who has a very good understanding of the dynamics of intimate partner violence can convey support. When the client can feel confident that the therapist really understands the situation and the dynamics, often she is better able to tolerate the therapist's lack of strong advocacy in (or about) the legal system. (Olesen & Drozd, 2012, p. 78)

Essential characteristics for therapists working with families affected by the perfect storm include understanding the systemic family context, even when working as an individual therapist; maintaining a balanced perspective on the patient's problems and needs; exploring multiple hypotheses; and, in the case of child therapists, supporting the child's independent perceptions and needs (Greenberg et al., 2003).

5.3. Self-Examination and Peer Consultation

The importance of therapists' self-examination and the role of peer consultation cannot be overstated. The principle of consultation is embedded in most professional ethics codes (American Psychological Association, 2010) and is emphasized in all expert writing about best practices in court-involved therapy (AFCC, 2010; Greenberg et al., 2003, 2008; Olesen & Drozd, 2012). Experimental evidence has shown that a therapist's awareness of his or her emotions can foster more effective management of reactions (Najavits, 2000). Given the polarization and strong countertransference pulls that define the perfect storm, however, therapists may struggle to identify their emotions and also be vulnerable to significant blind spots vis-à-vis their clients. Regularly scheduled consultation, whether with an individual expert or with a group of peers who provide court-involved treatment, can ensure a protected space in which therapist reactions can be identified and strategies for their effective management discussed.

5.4. Managing Countertransference Among Professional Teams

Therapeutic interventions for parent–child contact problems, especially those involving alienation, typically involve more than one professional. Attention to the team's structure and functioning is critical in these interventions, given the frequency of clients' polarities, distortions, and attempts to divide professionals (Sullivan & Kelly, 2001). Sullivan and Kelly (2001) describe key considerations for effective team management, including sample court orders that specify ways to manage confidentiality, communication, and linkage to the authority of the court. The appropriate management of therapist reactions and countertransference within professional teams is an additional domain to consider.

At Overcoming Barriers Family Camp, clinical staff meetings occur throughout the day. These provide an opportunity for clinicians not only to share observations and plan interventions but also to debrief and engage in reality checking about strong countertransference reactions and to seek support with them. Since groups for the rejected and favored parents are separate at the camp, group leaders may feel particularly aligned with the perspective of "their" group of parents. Similarly, the child clinicians may feel unduly protective of a child who stridently rejects contact with a parent even as the goal during the children's group is to maintain neutrality and flexible thinking, combined with appropriate concern and empathy for the child (see Chapter 10). Such countertransference reactions occur even though the clinical team is very familiar with the circumstances that led each family to camp. It is therefore likely that such reactions will be even more powerful among clinicians who see families outside an intensive setting or without the benefit of a team.

In addition to clinical meetings throughout each day of camp, an all-staff debriefing session happens on the final night of camp, after families have left the program. This session lasts several hours and is the first time the entire staff sits together to reflect on the week's events. This debriefing has unfailingly included discussion of the emotional experience of working so closely with extreme and often toxic interpersonal behaviors and dysregulated affect. For example, one clinician may feel the group has turned against him, noting that he is the only one who continues to feel compassionate about a client for whom the rest of the staff has felt only anger. On further reflection and with the protected space for debriefing, most clinicians can acknowledge a mixture of emotions that they felt reluctant to express earlier, given the force of clients' angry feelings. On other occasions, clinicians may find themselves protecting a vulnerable yet manipulative parent. The full continuum of therapist reactions comes to the fore when one clinician is willing to acknowledge openly that she felt angry and used. Both clinicians and nonclinical milieu staff all experience powerful reactions to families, highlighting the universality of countertransference reactions regardless of experience level or professional background.

Obviously, the majority of families do not receive treatment at an intensive program like Overcoming Barriers. Several lessons from the camp nevertheless translate to routine outpatient practice. As Sullivan and Kelly (2001) and others recommend, regular team meetings for all mental health professionals involved in a parent–child contact case are essential to facilitate information sharing, support a shared case formulation, restore systemic thinking, and ensure that treatment is as cost-effective as possible. Designating a "team leader" who can serve a case management function but also oversee countertransference among the team may be helpful. This individual could be a parenting coordinator or family therapist but ideally will be a professional with a thorough and systemic understanding of the family.

6. SUMMARY

Strong countertransference reactions are inherent to therapeutic practice with families in high conflict. An evolving empirical literature describes high rates of problematic personality characteristics and frank personality disorders among custody-litigating samples. This evidence base allowed us to survey features of PDs most likely to manifest in individual and family treatment with this population as well as offer practice recommendations for their clinical management. We also described the complexities and potential shifts in client motivation that accompany the addition of third parties and team members in the context of litigation. We encourage the clinician to consider the limits of her of his particular lens and relationship when working with only one part of the system (e.g., individual, couples, or family). Adopting a systems perspective when conducting individual treatment with these families is imperative (Greenberg et al., 2003), and regular communication among team members, whether remotely and in person, helps integrate their varying perspectives.

We urge clinicians to cultivate a sense of curiosity about which patterns or types of therapist reactions may be most likely to affect them and suggest that they neither can nor should assume they are personally impervious to such influences. Clinicians may be more likely to experience certain patterns based not only on therapist-specific factors (e.g., training, years of experience, or personal history) but also on the context and role in which they know the patient (e.g., as an individual or a family therapist). Given that a systems-based perspective and team approach are essential in working with families in high conflict, scrupulous attention to interteam dynamics is critical to preventing dynamics that parallel those of the clients from developing among the professionals.

REFERENCES

Aiyegbusi, A., & Tuck, G. (2008). Caring amid victims and perpetrators: Trauma and forensic mental health nursing. In J. Gordon & G. Kirtchuck (Eds.), *Psychic assaults and frightened clinicians: Countertransference in forensic settings* (pp. 11–26). London, UK: Karnac.

American Psychiatric Association (2013). *Diagnostic and statistical manual of mental disorders* (5th ed.). Washington, DC: American Psychiatric Association.

American Psychological Association (2010). *Ethical principles of psychologists and code of conduct.* Retrieved from http://www.apa.org/ethics/code/index.aspx

American Psychological Association. (2011). *Specialty guidelines for forensic psychologists*. Retrieved from http://www.apa.org/practice/guidelines/forensic-psycholgy.aspx

Association of Family and Conciliation Courts. (2010). *Guidelines for court-involved therapy*. Retrieved from http://www.afccnet.org/Portals/0/PublicDocuments/CEFCP/Guidelines%20for%20Court%20Involved%20Therapy%20AFCC.pdf

Bagby, R. M., Nicholson, R.A., Buis, T., Radovanovic, H. & Fidler, B.J. (1999). Defensive reporting on the MMPI-2 in family custody and access evaluations. *Psychological Assessment, 11*, 1, 24–28.

Baker, A. J. (2005a). The cult of parenthood: A qualitative study of parental alienation. *Cultic Studies Review, 41*(1), 1–29.

Baker, A. J. L. (2005b). Parent alienation strategies: A qualitative study of adults who experienced parental alienation as a child. *American Journal of Forensic Psychology, 23*(4), 41 63.

Baker, A. (2006). Patterns of parental alienation syndrome: A qualitative study of adults who were alienated from a parent as a child. *American Journal of Family Therapy, 34*, 63–78.

Bateman, A. W., & Fonagy, P. (2004). *Mentalization-based therapy for borderline personality disorder: A practical guide*. New York, NY: Oxford University Press.

Benjamin, L. S. (1996). *Interpersonal diagnosis and treatment of personality disorders*. New York, NY: Guilford Press.

Birnbaum, R., & Bala, N. (2010). Toward the differentiation of high-conflict families: An analysis of social science research and Canadian case law. *Family Court Review, 48*(3), 403–416.

Bond, M. P., Paris, J., & Zweig-Frank, H. (1994). Defense styles and borderline personality disorder. *Journal of Personality Disorders, 8*, 28–31.

Brody, E., & Farber, B. (1996). The effects of therapist experience and patient diagnosis on countertransference. *Psychotherapy, 33*, 372–380.

Casement, P. (1985). *On learning from the patient*. London: Brunner-Routledge.

Clarkin, J. F., Levy, K. N., Lenzenweger, M. F., & Kernberg, O. F. (2007). Evaluating three treatments for borderline personality disorder: A multiwave study. *American Journal of Psychiatry, 164*(6), 922–928.

Dwyer, S.A. (2012). Informed consent in court-involved therapy. *Journal of Child Custody, 9*(1–2), 108–125.

Eddy, B. (2009). *New ways for families in separation and divorce: Professional guidebook for judicial officers, lawyers and therapists*. Scottsdale, AZ: High Conflict Institute.

Ellis, E. M. (2000). Psychopathology of parents locked in postdivorce disputes over custody and access issues. In E. M. Ellis (Ed.), *Divorce wars: Interventions with families in conflict* (pp. 235–266). Washington, DC: American Psychological Association.

Feinberg, R., & Greene, J. T. (1997). The intractable client: Guidelines for working with personality disorders in family law. *Family and Conciliation Courts Review, 35*(3), 351–365.

Fidler, B. J., Bala, N., & Saini, M. A. (2013). *Children who resist post-separation parental contact: A differential approach for legal and mental health professionals*. New York, NY: Oxford University Press.

Fidnick, L., & Deutsch, R. M. (2012). Introduction to the AFCC Guidelines for court-involved therapy. *Journal of Child Custody, 9*, 5–10.

Freud, S. (1957). The future prospects of psychoanalytic therapy. In J. Strachey (Ed. & Trans.), *The standard edition of the complete psychological works of Sigmund Freud* (Vol. 11, pp. 139–151). London, UK: Hogarth Press. (Original work published 1910.)

Friedman, M. (2004). The so-called high conflict couple: A closer look. *American Journal of Family Therapy, 32*, 101–117.

Gabbard, G. O. (1993). An overview of countertransference with borderline patients. *Journal of Psychotherapy Practice and Research, 2*(1), 7–18.

Gabbard, G. O. (2004). *Long-term psychodynamic psychotherapy: A basic text.* Washington, DC: American Psychiatric Association.

Gallop, R. (1985). The patient is splitting. Everyone knows and nothing changes. *Journal of Psychosocial Nursing, 23*, 6–10.

Garber, B. D. (2010). Parental alienation and the dynamics of the enmeshed parent–child dyad: Adultification, parentification, and infantilization. *Family Court Review, 49*(2), 322–335.

Garber, B. D. (2015). Cognitive–behavioral methods in high-conflict divorce: Systematic desensitization adapted to parent–child reunification interventions. *Family Court Review, 53*(1), 96–112.

Gardner, R. A. (1992). *The parental alienation syndrome: A guide for mental health and legal professionals.* Cresskill, NJ: Creative Therapeutics.

Gordon, J., & Kirtchuk G. (Eds.) (2008). *Psychic assaults and frightened clinicians: Countertransference in forensic settings.* London, UK: Karnac.

Gordon, R. M., Stoffey, R., & Bottinelli, J. (2008). MMPI-2 findings of primitive defenses in alienating parents. *American Journal of Family Therapy, 36*(3), 211–228.

Greenberg, Lyn R. and Gould, Jonathan W. (2001). The treating expert: A hybrid role with firm boundaries. *Professional Psychology, Research and Practice, 32*(5), 469–478.

Greenberg, L. R., Gould, J. W., Gould-Saltman, D. J., & Stahl, P. M. (2003). Is the child's therapist part of the problem? *Family Law Quarterly, 37*(2), 39–67.

Greenberg, L. R., Gould-Saltman, D. J., & Gottlieb, M. C. (2008). Playing in their sandbox: Professional obligations of mental health professionals in child custody cases. *Journal of Child Custody, 5*(3/4), 192–216.

Grych, J. H., & Fincham, F. D. (1999). The adjustment of children from divorced families: Implications of empirical research for clinical intervention. In R. M. Galatzer-Levy & L. Kraus (Eds.), *The scientific basis of child custody decisions* (pp. 96–119). New York, NY: Wiley.

Gunderson, J. G. (2001). *Borderline personality disorder: A clinical guide.* Washington, DC: American Psychiatric Association.

Hughes, A. E., Crowell, S. E., Uyeji, L., & Coan, J. A. (2012). A developmental neuroscience of borderline pathology: Emotion dysregulation and social baseline theory. *Journal of Abnormal Child Psychology, 40*, 21–33.

Johansen, K. H. (1983). The impact of patients with chronic character pathology on a hospital inpatient unit. *Hospital Community Psychiatry, 34*, 842–846.

Johnston, J. R., & Campbell, L. E. G. (1988). *Impasses of divorce: The dynamics and resolution of family conflict.* New York, NY: Free Press.

Johnston, J.R. (1994). High-conflict divorce. *Children and Divorce, 4*(1), 165–182.

Johnston, J., Girdner, L. K., & Sagatun-Edwards, I. (1999). Developing profiles of risk for parental abduction of children from a comparison of families victimized by abduction with families litigating custody. *Behavioral Sciences and the Law, 17*, 305–322.

Johnston, J.R., Walters, M.G. & Olesen, N.W. (2005). Is it alienating parenting, role reversal, or child abuse? A study of children's rejection of a parent in child custody disputes. *Journal of Emotional Abuse, 4*(4), 191–218.

Johnston, J. R., Roseby, V., & Kuehnle, K. (2009). *In the name of the child: A developmental approach to understanding and helping children of conflicted and violent divorce* (2nd ed.). New York, NY: Springer Press.

Kernberg, O. (1965). Notes on countertransference. *Journal of the American Psychoanalytic Association, 13*, 38–56.

Lampel, A.K. (1996). Children's alignment with parents in highly conflicted custody cases. *Family and Conciliation Courts Review, 34*(2), 229–239.

Lebow, J. (2003). Integrative family therapy for disputes involving child custody and visitation. *Journal of Family Psychology, 17*(2), 181–192.

Lebow, J. (2005). Integrative family therapy for families experiencing high-conflict divorce. In J. L. Lebow (Ed.), *Handbook of clinical family therapy* (pp. 516–542). Hoboken, NJ: John Wiley & Sons.

Lebow, J., & Black, D. A. (2012). Considerations in court-involved therapy with parents. *Journal of Child Custody, 9*(1–2), 11–38.

Lebow, J. L., & Gurman, A. S. (1995). Research assessing couple and family therapy. *Annual Review of Psychology, 46*, 27–57.

Lenzenweger, M. F., Lane, M. C., Loranger, A. W., & Kessler, R. C. (2007). DSM-IV personality disorders in the National Comorbidity Survey Replication. *Biological Psychiatry, 62*(6), 553–564.

Liebman, R. E., & Burnette, M. (2013). It's not you, it's me: An examination of clinician- and client-level influences on countertransference toward borderline personality disorder. *American Journal of Orthopsychiatry, 83*(1), 115–125.

Linehan, M.M., Comtois, K.A., Murray, A.M., Brown, M.Z., Gallop, RJ., Heard, H.L., Korslund, K.E., Tutek, D.A., Reynolds, S.K. & Lindenboim, N. (2006). Two-year randomized controlled trial and follow-up of dialectical behavior therapy vs therapy by experts for suicidal behaviors and borderline personality disorder. *Archives of General Psychiatry, 63*(7), 757–766.

Maccoby, E. E., Depner, C. E., & Mnookin, R. H. (1990). Coparenting in the second year after divorce. *Journal of Marriage and the Family, 52*, 256–272.

Martindale, D.A. & Gould, J.W. (2008). Countertransference and zebras: Forensic obfuscation. *Journal of Child Custody, 4*(3–4), 69–75.

McCready, K. (1987). Milieu countertransference in treatment of borderline patients. *Psychotherapy, 24*, 720–728.

McIntyre, S.M. & Schwartz, R.C. (1998). Therapists' differential countertransference reactions toward clients with major depression or borderline personality disorder. *Journal of Clinical Psychology, 54* (7), 923–931.

McWilliams, N. (1994). *Psychoanalytic diagnosis*. New York: Guilford Press.

Najavits, L. M. (2000). Research therapist emotions and countertransference. *Cognitive and Behavioral Practice, 7*, 322–328.

Norcross, J. C. (Ed.). (2011). *Psychotherapy relationships that work* (2nd ed.). New York, NY: Oxford University Press.

Olesen, N. W., & Drozd, L. (2012). Prudent therapy in high conflict cases: With and without allegations of intimate partner violence or child abuse. *Journal of Child Custody, 9*, 69–84.

Perlman, G. L. (2012). A judicial perspective on psychotherapist–client privilege: Ten practical tips for clinicians. *Journal of Child Custody, 9*, 126–152.

Pickar, D. B. (2007). Countertransference bias in the child custody evaluator. *Journal of Child Custody, 4*(3/4), 45–67.

Pope, K. S., Butcher, J. N., & Seelen, J. (2006). *The MMPI, MMPI-2, & MMPI-A in court: A practical guide for expert witnesses and attorneys (3rd ed.).* Washington, DC: American Psychological Association.

Quinnell, F. A., & Bow, J. N. (2001). Psychological tests used in child custody evaluations. *Behavioral Science and the Law, 19*, 491–501.

Roseby, V. R., & Johnston, J. (1997). *High conflict, violent and separating families.* New York, NY: Free Press.

Rossberg, J. I., Karterud, D., Pedersen, G., & Friis, S. (2007). An empirical study of countertransference reactions toward patients with personality disorders. *Comprehensive Psychiatry, 48*, 225–230.

Schwartz, R. C. (2000). Psychotherapeutic assessment and treatment of antisocial personality disorder. *Annals of the American Psychotherapy Association, 4*, 6.

Schwartz, R. C., Smith, S. D., & Chopko, B. (2007). Psychotherapists' countertransference reactions toward clients with antisocial personality disorder and schizophrenia: An empirical test of theory. *American Journal of Psychotherapy, 61*(4), 375–393.

Siegel, J. C., & Langford, J. S. (1998). MMPI-2 validity scales and suspected parental alienation syndrome. *American Journal of Forensic Psychology, 16*(4), 5–14.

Strong, D.R., Greene, R.L., Hoppe, C., Johnston, T. Olesen, N. (1999). Taxometric analysis of impression management and self-deception on the MMPI-2 in child custody litigants. *Journal of Personality Assessment, 73*, 1–18.

Sullivan, M .J., & Kelly, J. B. (2001). Legal and psychological management of cases with an alienated child. *Family Court Review, 39*(3), 299–315.

Thylstrup, B. & Hesse, M. (2008). Substance abusers' personality disorders and staff members' emotional reactions. *BMC Psychiatry, 8*(21), 1–6.

Warshak, R. A. (2000). *Obstacles and controversies in the pursuit of children's best interests.* Keynote address to Arizona chapter of Association of Family and Conciliation Courts. Sedona, Arizona. Available through www.warshak.com

PART II

The *Overcoming Barriers* Approach

6

Overview of the *Overcoming Barriers* Approach

PEGGIE WARD, ROBIN M. DEUTSCH, AND
MATTHEW J. SULLIVAN ■

1. INTRODUCTION

After separation and divorce, children may resist contact with a parent for many reasons (Fidler, Bala, & Saini, 2013; Gardner, 1998; Johnston, Roseby, & Kuehnle, 2009; Kelly & Johnston, 2001; Wallerstein & Kelly, 1980; Ward, Deutsch, & Sullivan, 2010; Warshak, 2010). The prevalence of this phenomenon is not known, but the effect on at least two generations of children is becoming better understood (Fidler, Bala, & Saini, 2013). The topic has generated significant public and academic interest as well as controversy. Concerns about interpersonal violence, child abuse, impaired and compromised parenting, and overt or covert attempts by one parent to exclude the other from the children's lives have created debate about distinguishing what might be considered protective gatekeeping from restrictive gatekeeping (Austin, Pruett, Kirkpatrick, Flens, & Gould, 2013; Ganong, Coleman, & McCaulley, 2012).

The research is fairly unequivocal in indicating that children suffer and are harmed when they are in the middle of extremely high-conflict cases where there is no resolution to ongoing exposure to the conflict and where parent access arrangements are uncertain and are being litigated (Amato, 2000, 2001; Cummings & Davies, 2002; Cummings, Schermerhorn, Davies, Goeke-Morey, & Cummings, 2006; Davies, Sturge-Apple, Winter, Cummings, & Farrell, 2006; Deutsch & Kline-Pruett, 2009). High-conflict custody cases often present to professionals involved as situations where one parent is identified as toxic, dangerous, and neglectful and the other parent as alienating. This highly polarized perspective is played out in adversarial court processes while the children endure uncertainty and suffer from impaired cognitive and emotional functioning (Johnston, Walters, & Olesen, 2005; Kelly & Johnston, 2001). Clinicians across the United

States and Canada have worked on models of intervention to help reduce the parental conflict, improve coparenting and interparental communication, and offer tools for families to move from polarized thinking to honest, systemic analysis and working through the specific problem (Judge, Bailey, Behrman-Lippert, Psaila, & Dickel, 2016; Eddy, 2009; Fidler, 2009; Polak, Fidler, & Popielarczyk, 2013; Freeman, 2008; Friedlander, & Walters, 2010; Garber, 2013; Ward, Deutsch, & Sullivan, 2010). However, no one approach has to date demonstrated longitudinal effectiveness. In this chapter we will describe one such program, Overcoming Barriers, including the families it has served, core elements of the approach, and the impact it has had on families who present with these chronic and intractable family systems dynamics.

2. ORIGINS OF OVERCOMING BARRIERS CAMP

Overcoming Barriers (OCB) was first conceptualized as a program in 2007 after a unique attempt at reunification resulted in a failed therapeutic intervention due to parental alienation (This was due to **active parental interference** by the mother specifically and not the more global parental alienation.) This chapter's first author, with the cooperation of attorneys for each parent and with an order from the court, met with the entire family to explain the newly developed plan and a structure for safe involvement of the children with the father during time at a family camp. Both parents agreed that the father would go to Common Ground Center Family Camp in Starksboro, Vermont, where, in the company of other families and with significant staff support, he would meet and spend the week with his two boys, whom he had not seen in many months. The intervention was sabotaged when the mother who was not included in the family intervention at the camp, convinced the children not to participate in this carefully created program.

Despite the lack of success with this family, camp personnel expressed a desire to help develop a program in 2008 along with a group of court personnel, judges, family law attorneys, and mental health professionals. This working group met for several months to develop an intensive program, based on family systems and social science, that would include **all** family members. The program was designed for families for whom the court has determined, despite various allegations against one or both parents, that continued attempts to support shared parenting time are in the best interest of the children. The first OCB camp was held in 2008, and up to 2015 the program has been repeated in six different years at locations in Vermont, California, and Arizona. It has evolved after each camp experience and now includes a significant research element (see Chapter 13) and a training component.

Key elements that define the OCB approach include the following:

1. Inclusion of the entire family system involved in maintaining the status quo of a child's rejecting a parent when the rejection has been

determined to be unjustified by or disproportionate to the child's experience of that parent

2. Intensive single- or multifamily intervention for three to five days in a neutral setting, within a supportive yet challenging clinical and recreational environment where parents and children are in the care of clinical professionals or paraprofessionals 24 hours a day

3. Creation of a safe environment for all program participants where all family members can share their particular concerns without fear of negative consequences

4. The expectation that each family member will participate fully in each aspect of the program, including challenges to strongly held but potentially misconceived beliefs about the rejected parent

5. Specialized clinicians with significant experience in family systems, child dynamics, dynamics of divorce and separation, child abuse and neglect, intimate-partner violence, mental health issues (including personality issues), and parenting and coparenting after separation and divorce, working as a coordinated team with families

6. A careful, thoughtful balance of structure and experiential work in all interventions within a family as well as within and across groups

7. Development of unique, in-the-moment interventions with parents, coparents, children, and families that challenge their strongly held yet polarized beliefs that one parent is all bad and the other all good

8. A strong recreational component to help model and create positive connections between children and the rejected parent

9. Emphasis on whole-family interactions, including eating together and recreational activities with all family members present

10. Psychoeducation relevant to the family issues, using didactic presentation, media, and other materials

11. An aftercare program connecting the family to specific treatment professionals in their local area, who ideally are in place before the family leaves the intervention.

The OCB approach draws from various types of therapeutic approaches. The founders possess a foundation of knowledge and skills that informed development of this innovative program. Theoretical influences include family systems therapy (Ackerman, 1958; Bowen, 1978; Minuchin, 1974; Satir, 1964; Whitaker & Bumberry, 1988) and aspects of cognitive–behavioral therapy (e.g., systematic desensitization and exposure therapy) (Garber, 2015). Group work uses concepts from the scientific literature on learning and memory (e.g., suggestibility, misperception and fallibility) (Goodman, Rudy, Bottoms, & Aman, 1989; Goodman & Schaaf, 1997; Loftus, 1979) and cognitive science (e.g., cognitive distortion and perspective taking) (Burns, 1980; Grohol, 2014). The founders of OCB had many years of experience working with high-conflict populations involved in the family courts and had all previously worked in inpatient and residential settings.

3. CHARACTERISTICS OF FAMILIES AT OVERCOMING BARRIERS CAMP

The families ordered by the court to attend OCB camps, despite clear individual differences, have strikingly similar characteristics. Parent dyads are polarized, with common themes in their impasses. The favored parent's perspective is most commonly organized by what she or he considers a "protective stance" (Ward, Deutsch, and Sullivan, 2010) as it relates to the rejected parent. The favored parent alleges child abuse or neglect (including sexual abuse), parenting compromised by drug or alcohol use or abuse, intimate-partner violence, lack of interest or availability, or inept parenting as the primary reason the child rejects contact with the other parent. From the perspective of the favored parent, almost all negative aspects of parenting reside with the rejected parent and are the only significant reasons for the child's rejection.

Rejected parents assert they are victims of alienation by the favored parent (Fidler, Bala, & Saini, 2013; Kelly & Johnston, 2001). They view themselves as good parents who have historically been positively involved in their children's lives. Rejected parents maintain that the favored parent has directly tried to remove them from their children's lives by portraying them in word and deed as inadequate parents who have abandoned the family. The rejected parent asserts that the favored parent has involved the children in the interparental conflict and untenable loyalty pressures, bad-mouths the rejected parent, has created the impression that the rejected parent is dangerous or sick, and engages in gatekeeping and role reversal with the children (Austin, Fieldstone, & Pruett, 2013; Baker & Sauber, 2013; Garber, 2011; Johnston et al., 2009; Warshak, 2010). Rejected parents allege that the favored parent's agenda is malicious and either impaired by mental illness or driven by retaliatory motives aimed at gaining advantage in divorce issues other than those directly involving the children (e.g., property, support, or relocation). Like favored parents, rejected parents attribute their children's negativity and rejection as emanating exclusively from their coparent.

Children present with varying degrees of expressed hatred, fears, anxieties, and other symptoms of distress. They show extreme resistance to having or total refusal to have any contact with the rejected parent (Ward, Deutsch & Sullivan, 2010). While expressing idealized affection (including boundary diffusion, role reversal, and separation issues) toward the favored parent, many children are overtly hostile and at times aggressive toward the rejected parent. The children accept the polarized stance of the favored parent, seeing that parent as all good and the rejected parent as all bad.[1]

Consistent with other high-conflict families where alienation has been found to be a part of the family dynamic (Kelly & Johnston, 2001), particularly challenging aspects of families who have attended OCB Camp include the following:

1. The child's reaction to the rejected parent seems exaggerated and out of proportion to many of the allegations of misconduct by the rejected parent.

2. There is often some credible evidence, albeit also exaggerated, supporting the favored parent's concerns about the child's experience of the rejected parent.

3. The presenting allegations of each dyad of parents (and of stepparents when they are involved) are rigid, polarized, and so fully incorporated into each parent's beliefs that they are difficult to change.

4. There has been a series of ineffective, failed, or even counterproductive traditional mental health interventions. Families thus come to OCB with at least one parent (usually both) and the children having no belief that another mental health intervention will be helpful. Many are angry at being forced to participate.

5. Many families come to OCB as a "last resort" prior to a potential change in custody to the rejected parent as long as that parent is deemed "good enough" by the Court or to a placement outside either parent's care and control). These families have had one or more neutral court evaluations finding that the child's rejection of one parent was due to a persistent pattern of alienation by the other parent.

While many families come to OCB with court findings or evaluations that define the case as one where alienation is present, a large proportion of the cases sent to OCB come after court-ordered neutral evaluations have found many factors at work in the parent–child contact problem, including poor or inconsistent parenting by one parent and concerns about fear or safety resulting in isolation, overprotection, or role reversal by the other parent. These "hybrid" cases include elements of alienation, estrangement,[2] and often enmeshment (Friedlander & Walters, 2010; Johnston & Goldman, 2010).

4. GOALS OF THE OVERCOMING BARRIERS PROGRAM

The central goal of the OCB approach is to provide a family systems intervention to high-conflict families who are mandated by the court to work to implement a shared parenting plan. The whole-family approach, which may include all family members who know the children and are part of the family system, allows for the greatest impact on the entrenched family dynamic as well as the greatest long-term support of change that occurs in the OCB intervention (Fidler & Bala, 2010; Friedlander & Walters, 2010; Johnston & Campbell, 1988; Johnston et al., 2009; Kelly & Johnston, 2001; Sullivan & Kelly, 2001). Participation of all family members is essential to achieving reconnection between a child and rejected parent.

The OCB approach was formalized through meetings in 2014 with Dr. Michael Saini (Factor-Inwentash Faculty of Social Work, University of Toronto) in consultation with the OCB research group, after an initial pilot evaluation project found that most parents and children expressed having positive experiences with attending camp. Fidelity guidelines and a checklist were developed to ensure that clinicians working in the program followed the OCB approach. Eight key dimensions essential to replicating the model were identified. These are

- facilitator training and experience;
- facilitator adherence to the model;
- target population that fits screening criteria;
- setting with sufficient space to accommodate all clinical and programmatic activities, including whole-family, recreational, and common-area space;
- materials including administrative forms and orientation materials, audio and video access, games and sports equipment, and art supplies;
- delivery of OCB specific components: psychoeducational programs, intensive clinical interventions, and a rich, positive, and structured experience;
- specific number, length, and frequency of programs; and
- aftercare pathways and interventions with identified roles and personnel for follow up care.

The OCB approach evolved directly from the OCB camp model after the critical factors necessary for inclusion were identified. This model includes having whole families come to a neutral setting removed from their usual living context. The program involves a combination of psychoeducation, intensive clinical interventions, and recreational components. Information about families is drawn from each of the above referenced aspects of the program and incorporated into all interventions in real time. Clinical staff meetings take place several times a day to review the family's engagement in the program from the multiple perspectives of clinicians and support staff. These meetings form the basis for the next set of interventions.

As a multiple-family group intervention, the OCB camp can exploit the dynamics that develop across the various relationships between families. Strong relationships develop among the fathers, mothers, stepparents, and children in different families during camp. These systems of identification provide additional therapeutic opportunities for intervening with the intractable relationship dynamics that exist within individual family systems. For example, a boy who vehemently rejects his mother may develop an open and positive relationship with another mother in the camp who has a positive relationship with his mother. Camp staff may use the other mother's relationship with the boy in this case to create a bridge connecting him with his rejected parent, in this case the mother. Similarly, a rejected father may develop a friendship with a favored mother at camp who has developed a trusting relationship with that father's coparent. This triadic relationship system may be useful to the camp staff both in addressing the coparenting relationship and in efforts to reconnect the child in that family with the rejected parent.

Intake screening is a crucial element to ensure that each family has goals consistent both with its specific court order and with the OCB program. Each family member is expected to accept the overall goal of helping to support the shared parenting plan by working on overcoming obstacles to reconnecting children with the rejected parent. The program involves intensive group psychoeducation for all family members; coparenting work with parent dyads (at least daily if possible); family meetings consisting of dyads, triads, and the whole family as appropriate; and carefully crafted "safe connections" between the rejected parent and child within the camp milieu.

5. STRUCTURE OF THE OVERCOMING BARRIERS APPROACH

The camp program is divided into three segments daily. Morning groups, which begin after breakfast in the common area, work separately with favored parents, rejected parents, and children. The ages of the children at camp have ranged between 9 and 18 years, and the children either meet together as a whole or split into age ranges to address more developmentally appropriate issues. We do not allow children younger than 9 years of age to attend camp. Based on our experience, young children lack the cognitive maturity to participate in therapeutic programming. The young child's age-appropriate needs can become a distraction for his or her family members and undermine therapeutic efficacy.

Initially the OCB approach was modeled strictly on an "in" group (the group of favored parents) named East Group and an "out" group (the group of rejected parents) named West Group. Our rationale for this approach was to create a shared experience where these parents could, through shared family experiences and dynamics, develop a sense of intimacy, trust, and commonality within members of the same group. We anticipated that this group cohesion would help members support each other in the process of change and in confronting irrational, ineffective, and distorted beliefs and behaviors. However, these parents developed a sense of cohesion within their own group and a sense of distrust toward the other parent group. This dynamic seemed to mirror the black-and-white, good-or-bad, us-versus-them rigid thinking that had persisted within their families and led them to need an intensive intervention. As a result, in more recent years we have created additional groups that combine both sets of parents for educational components. We continue to consider other methods, such as combining unrelated members of both groups, that encourage healthy identifications and alliances while discouraging splits.

Parent group time provides substantive information about the dynamics of high-conflict divorce, including the deleterious impact of litigation on coparenting and children; current systemic conceptualizations of the alienated child (Kelly & Johnston, 2001); and effective interventions with high-conflict coparents (e.g., parallel parenting models supported by parenting coordination) (Coates, Deutsch, Starnes, Sullivan, & Sydlik, 2004; Sullivan, 2008). We offer parents practical strategies for managing and responding to their alienated child and coparent (Baker & Fine, 2008; Moran, Sullivan, & Sullivan, 2015; Warshak, 2003) and recommend legal and psychological interventions relevant to aftercare support. Group themes focus on goals and motivations; appropriate expectations and possibilities of change; identifying and correcting cognitive distortions; issues of fear, safety, overprotection, and underprotection; strategies for coping with intense affect; and effective tools for direct communication. Didactic presentations, audiovisual media, discussion of shared experiences, role playing, and using the camp experience itself as a "learning laboratory" for developing new behaviors are all part of the psychoeducational component. The power of the group process becomes clear as group members challenge each other (with careful supervision and coaching) on rigidly held beliefs and behavior as well as provide each other with support for change.

The children's group, called Common Ground (after both the name of the camp itself and the aspirational goal of creating a tenable space for the children within their families), combines psychoeducation through group exercises with projects providing a venue for inner reflection as well as group connection. The goals of the group are to shift the child's polarized and rigidly held view of each parent to a more realistic and nuanced view based on actual experience as well as to change behavior such that rejected relationships could be restored. Themes include building group cohesion and trust; understanding different points of view; understanding how thoughts, feelings, and behaviors are related; identifying cognitive distortions; and changing behavior in small (or larger) increments as children's newly learned skills can be demonstrated in either behavior orchestrated by clinicians or spontaneous behavior. In the groups, the children find a sense of belonging and normalcy in sharing their stories and noting common experiences with other group members; this sense is reinforced in their other camp experiences.

Efforts are made to match the themes in the children's group with themes in the rejected parents' group and to begin connections between the children and their respective rejected parents. One exercise aimed at this goal involves the child's writing anonymous notes to the rejected parent. Group leaders read these anonymous notes to the rejected parents who struggle with understanding whether the note is directed to them and if so, how they might respond. Similarity of themes of anger, blame and distortion are discussed. In a separate exercise the rejected parent's write to their child an anonymous statement of understanding and an apology. The group leaders in the children's group read these apologies aloud; the children struggle to believe whether any could be true. This connection, though anonymous and displaced, creates a template for children to speak with their rejected parents and to struggle to tolerate a response that they want to dismiss as "fake" or disingenuous. Dismissing the response is more difficult when the children have observed the other parents and seen no evidence that the other children have toxic, dangerous, or insincere parents. Cognitive dissonance about another child's rejecting stance may help children reflect on their own situations differently.

We observed over time that the children did not see much reason for them to be at camp and that they believed the majority of the issues to solve belonged to their parents. While this placing of external blame had some parallel in the parent dyad, each member of which adamantly held the other responsible for the current difficulties, in many cases it appeared that the child's rationale had merit. If the parents were not locked in rigid and polarized conflict, it is unlikely the child would have become polarized on his or her own. In more recent years of camp, OCB clinicians have discussed ways to better integrate the three groups so as not to mirror the polarized, "I'm in, you're out" dynamic of the family.

In the afternoons, clinicians work with coparents, stepparents, significant others, other family dyads or triads, or the whole family. This work is a fluid process from the time the family enters the program to the minute they leave. The essence of this work is to capture the rapidly changing dynamic within each family, to intervene at the precise time that a goal-related theme has emerged, and to use the limited time available to interrupt and modify rigid, entrenched patterns enough that some change may be possible. These interventions with coparents and other family members (usually one a day for each family) are initially difficult. Most parents have not had any direct engagement outside a courtroom for months or years. Children and parents have not had targeted interventions with therapeutic support from child clinicians and parent clinicians. While initially anxiety provoking for the family members, the family meetings, which may include any members of the family along with their corresponding therapist from the morning group, proved to be sought after by almost all families across all camps. Over the short time at camp, parents and children developed trust in the therapeutic team approach, and many expressed fear of leaving such a supportive environment to try to accomplish the work to be done in "the real world."

Aftercare is a key focus of the clinical team prior to the arrival of each family and throughout the entire camp. Some families have presented to camp with an aftercare team (i.e., parenting coordinators, therapists, family therapists, or a combination thereof) already in place. Other families have arrived at camp with little in the way of a support network in place for the return home, and still others have come with a divided support network. In the latter cases there was typically at least one therapist who was aligned with the favored parent and supported the child's rejection and another therapist who believed the child was alienated. For example, one therapist might have been treating the favored parent for post-traumatic stress disorder, ostensibly the result of an abusive marital relationship, while another involved therapist believed that the favored parent was maliciously preventing the children from seeing the other parent.

It became clear over time that some teams were split and mirroring what each parent or child believed. A common denominator among these fractured teams was a failure to maintain a systems perspective about the entire family, as opposed to multiple, simultaneous therapists operating in silos or with limited or incomplete information. Either these teams had not communicated about the family, or their conversations had not led to a shared understanding of the family system or treatment approach (Greenberg, Gould, Gould-Saltman, & Stahl, 2003; Greenberg & Sullivan, 2012). Aftercare referrals were most difficult in these situations, since the OCB approach is not an evaluation per se and thus clinicians are not in a position to recommend changes to a therapeutic team. However, whenever the OCB team identified problematic dynamics in an aftercare team, OCB clinicians addressed these concerns thoroughly with the coparents, letting them know that without a unified team working together toward their stated common goals, the family was unlikely to succeed.

The OCB approach in the camp setting requires the direction and presence of a highly skilled camp director and camp counselors who take every opportunity to interrupt destructive interactions, reinforce positive messages and behavior, calm anxious or angry family members, and create a safety net for all families. This use of the recreational milieu has roots in the therapeutic milieu common to inpatient hospital programs (see Chapter 7). The OCB milieu also takes advantage of outdoor and indoor space to implement carefully structured recreation, crafts, games, and dining. The clinical team uses camp activities to promote the goal of reconnecting rejected parents and children in parallel activities or larger, more integrated whole-camp activities. Favored parents are encouraged to support these reconnecting experiences, from a rejected parent simply watching a child play with a sibling from 20 feet away to engaging in a whole-family craft-making exercise. Favored parents also participate in recreational time planned exclusively for them (e.g., cooking, crafts, and hikes).

A coordinated team approach is one of the fundamentals of OCB. Clinicians, counselors, and recreational staff members work in almost seamless concert. The families observe, perhaps for the first time, people who support one another, work together toward the same goals, and are able to address any differences they may have. At times, particularly in coparenting and family meetings, the clinicians are able to model successful resolution of disagreements for family members who have been unable to accomplish this in their own relationship. Coordination between the milieu sphere and clinical team occurs through clinical meetings at the beginning, middle, and end of each day that invite input from counselors and recreational staff. These meetings also provide an opportunity to address differences in clinical assessment and ideas for intervention.

Families live in this cohesive, synchronized supportive system for three to five days. This clinically cohesive environment, which supports the whole family, is one they have not experienced as a separated family. Families often express the concern that they will leave this environment only to return to their own dysfunctional systems, where they will not feel safe. Creating follow-up teams that can work well and in a coordinated fashion with the families when they return home is essential to the OCB approach.

The OCB approach involves a variety of daily rituals or routines that we use to provide continuity and community. For example, at the end of each day there is a "closing circle" where the entire staff and families sit together, outdoors if possible, and learn the events planned for the next day as well as hear any important announcements. Family members sit wherever they would like, providing children and coparents with an opportunity to use newly gained skills to view each family member with a new perspective. Often family members wonder or marvel at how well the rejected parent from their family seems to do with other families.

Another important ritual is planning the Big Show, a talent show held on the last night in which staff and family members participate. Teams of people work together to produce their acts in the show, providing an opportunity for children to see a different, more playful side of their parents. Rejected parents get to see talent in their children that they may have missed out on for months or years. Favored parents get to see the ability of the coparent they perceive as "bad" to work with other parents to produce entertaining performances. Children can experience their parents watching the same program in the same room together without overt conflict. Hence the Big Show reinforces a core OCB goal—for family members to experience one another in a different way.

An ending ritual, the "final circle," is held on the last day with all family members, clinicians, and staff present. Throughout the duration of camp, everyone is encouraged to put "affirmations" (positive statements about any person at camp) into a sealed box. These affirmations are read at the final circle. Each family member receives a carefully planned and signed affirmation from a staff person in addition to any other affirmations written (and screened) by recreational or camp staff.

The OCB camp involves intense and emotional work by all. A staff debriefing is the final experience for the clinicians after the families have left. In this group process all staff (clinicians, recreational staff, and counselors) share their high and low moments as well as any other thoughts about family members, the process, and their hopes and disappointments that they choose to bring up with the entire staff. This discussion is confidential and provides a space in which to name and process the strong emotional reactions generated by exposure to serious individual psychopathology in some family members, by the high level of conflict, and by the difficulty of maintaining a neutral stance in the face of pulls for polarization.

6. EVOLUTION OF OVERCOMING BARRIERS CAMP

The OCB approach has evolved since its inception in 2008. Initially our process screening occurred by telephone only; screening now includes a questionnaire that all parents fill out and send in prior to the intake call (see Chapter 2). This allows for a more tailored and specific follow-up call to parents and helps identify important collateral sources and aftercare team members who can provide continuity for the family after they leave camp. The intake questionnaire includes specific questions about intimate-partner violence, drug and alcohol abuse, mental health issues and concerns, parental conflict, and the ability of parents to work together as coparents. Parents with current problems with substance abuse, intimate-partner violence, or severe untreated mental illness, including thought disorders, are screened out. During intake, we explain the expectations of the OCB program and clarify that OCB is not an evaluation per se and that no custody recommendations will be made as a result of the family's participation. Intake interviews broadly address issues of confidentiality, mandatory reporting, and specific fees. If the family is accepted, parents sign a formal agreement about their roles and responsibilities.

By the time a family arrives at camp, they will have received a camper information packet, signed all appropriate releases of information, and spoken with camp staff about the children's needs (medical, psychological, and social). Over the seven years that the OCB camp has operated, clinicians and camp staff have formalized elements of supporting families once they arrive at camp. These include

- providing more structure when families arrive, including assignment of a "buddy" for each parent;
- group educational meeting for all family members on the first day, focusing on expectations and camp structure and requiring all parents to sit in the same room, thereby providing a first step in reducing anxiety through exposure;
- daily coparenting or family (dyad, triad, or whole family) meetings to address specific issues identified by clinicians in group, staff in the milieu, or family members;
- specific attention to clinicians and staff members modeling appropriate interactions for parents and children;
- use of videos and other multimedia during group and in parent meetings to address crucial themes such as perceptions, distortions, and effects of interparental conflict on children;
- evening camp activities such as games, stories, and the closing talent show to build on any cohesiveness achieved during the day;
- structured, often assigned seating at dinner, including camp staff at each table, based on events that transpired within a family during the day;
- closing circle each day with announcements and the agenda of the following day;
- use of the affirmation box, where anyone is encouraged to put specific positive statements about another camper or staff member, to help focus all camp attendees on positive aspects of interpersonal interaction
- morning group meetings including didactic, experiential, and behavioral processing using the "camp as learning laboratory" model;
- identification of broader-context factors (significant others, extended family, and mental health and legal systems) to help the coparents strengthen their relationship while keeping various forms of polarized units ("tribal warfare"; Johnston & Campbell, 1988) in appropriate perspective;
- significant group focus on negative effects of litigation for most families, including the effect of heightened family conflict and decreased parental cooperation;
- planning and recording of aftercare plans and dissemination and discussion of these plans with each family, including an accounting of all interventions provided and agreements made at camp as well as specific

suggestions for professionals or structures necessary for the family when
back in their community;

- agreement to follow up with each family to assist in finding appropriate
professionals for aftercare; and

- consultation by a designated camp clinician with the aftercare
professionals to provide continuity in the transition from the work at
camp to aftercare.

While the general concepts and structure were in place from the start, postcamp evaluations have yielded important information that has provided a basis
for refining the OCB approach. We have found over time that the use of multiple modes of intervention (audio, visual, experiential, didactic, recreational, and
modeling) has increased the richness of the camp experience.

6.1. Didactic and Immersion Training

As demand for OCB programs increased, the need to train more clinicians in
the OCB approach became clear. In addition to the goal of increasing the general
pool of clinicians trained to do this highly specialized work, it was also essential to
ensure the availability of competent clinicians who can provide aftercare services
to build on and reinforce the positive changes that occur for families during the
camp. Overcoming Barriers therefore began offering didactic training as well as
an immersion training on site at camp. Didactic trainings, often offered at the
Association of Family and Conciliation Courts conferences, were made available
to clinicians, attorneys, and judges to increase awareness about the OCB approach
and the crucial need for early intervention for the families it seeks to help.

Immersion training was more labor-intensive. Prospective clinicians applied to
participate in the training, and OCB staff interviewed potential participants, all
of whom had experience working with families in high conflict. Ideally, pairs or
teams of clinicians from the same geographic area participated, so that on returning to their communities they could provide the team care that families from
OCB require. The ten clinicians invited to participate took part in 10 hours of
online seminars offered by the OCB camp founders and then attended camp as
trainees or observers. Trainees observed all aspects of the camp process but had
no direct involvement with families. In our second year of immersion training, six
of the previous trainees were invited to return to the camp as "fellows." In this role,
they facilitated the morning groups in collaboration with the founding clinicians.
Similarly, a fellow and an original clinician did afternoon interventions as a team.
A second group of experienced clinicians, who attended camp as trainees that
year, observed the fellows conducting groups as well as afternoon interventions.

Ensuring ongoing availability of new generations of clinicians is essential,
both to infuse the OCB approach with new ideas as well as to ensure that there
are enough experienced clinicians trained to work with the types of families the
approach is meant for.

6.2. Application of the OCB Approach to Intensive Interventions

Overcoming Barriers began as an intensive residential family model, with all families residing for five days with all clinicians and staff in a family camp setting in rural Vermont. The OCB approach is applicable, however, to other forms of treatment of high-conflict families where a child is resisting contact with a parent. As OCB clinicians and staff recognized that families wanted more rapidly available programs as well as programs tailored specifically to their individual family needs, the concept of *intensive* programs arose (Deutsch, Fidler, & Sullivan, 2014; Deutsch, Sullivan, & Bailey, 2014; Deutsch, Sullivan, & Moran, 2015; Ward, Deutsch, & Sullivan, 2010).

One such model is a two-and-a-half- to five-day "intensive immersion" program with a single family, conducted by two or three clinicians and a staff person with training in recreational work with children and families. There is no one intensive program to fit all family needs. Programs vary from those for families at the more severe end of the alienation continuum (Warshak, 2010, 2015), which require a temporary or permanent reversal of custody and work with the rejected parent and children, to programs that incorporate whole families along many segments of the continuum (Polak, Fidler, & Popielarczyk, 2013; Friedlander & Walters, 2010).

Despite differences in the severity of the family dynamic, the goals for each of the intensive immersion programs that work with whole families are remarkably similar. Each program hopes to (a) repair and strengthen the children's healthy relationships with both parents, (b) keep children out of the middle of their parents' conflicts, (c) address distorted perspectives and memories regarding rejected parents, (d) help children develop critical-thinking skills and apply them to the current situation, (e) develop more effective coparent and parent–child communication, (f) confront and correct black-and-white, polarized thinking that leads to rigid and inaccurate judgments, (g) develop empathy for all family members, and (h) maintain the gains made through the program with an active follow-up component.

The OCB approach to intensive immersion evolved directly from the OCB camp model. Clinicians and staff work with all family members in a setting convenient to the family (e.g., a hotel, conference center, or the family home). A clinical team works with children, coparents, dyads, triads, and the whole family using educational and experiential interventions. A recreational component is carefully integrated with psychoeducational and clinical components. Regular team miniconferences lead to rapidly evolving, targeted interventions that address immediate family needs and goals. When a difference of opinion emerges in the team that would be useful for the family to witness, the clinicians model cohesive teamwork by addressing and resolving their differences in the family's presence. Although intervention themes and structures are well defined and determined prior to each meeting, should a specific unanticipated need arise, the OCB team attempts to incorporate the new information into the intervention.

Key components of intensive immersion programs for an individual family use many concepts of the OCB approach. For programs where the goal is reuniting family members to implement the court-ordered parenting plan, the structure is similar:

- structured intake and follow-up to determine the appropriateness of the particular family to this type of intervention (including availability of all key members of the family);
- didactic and experiential sessions, separated into coparent work and child work to clarify goals of the parent and child sub-groups (with intervention by clinicians as necessary) to reach a mutual goal of the child's having contact with each parent as ordered by the court;
- parent training in active listening and appropriate responses in coparent communication; cocreating a new narrative for the children; resolution or letting go of "past issues"; goals and pathways to forward progress, including managing emotions and behavior; understanding how the family has reached their current impasse; and creation of new ways to work together toward future cooperation and civility;
- child work focused on shifting polarized thinking to allow for willingness to work on reconnecting with the rejected parent, as well as on learning to identify and solve problems and apply that method to difficulties in the child's relationship with one or both parents;
- days and evenings focused on specifically tailored coparent, parent, parent–child, and whole-family work addressing in real time issues that emerge in the clinical work and milieu;
- mealtimes together in shared space; and
- recreation component in which children actively participate with both parents in a positive, enjoyable manner.

Applications to outpatient approaches include the use of a family systems model (i.e., meeting with different individuals, dyads, triads, and the whole family at different times), incorporation of longer meeting times, inclusion of a pleasurable recreational component for the rejected parent and child, work with the favored parent on demonstrated acceptance of the goal of reuniting the child with the rejected parent, and work both within and outside the therapist's office on parenting skills and relationship building. (See Chapter 12 for more detailed discussion of the application of the OCB approach to outpatient treatment.)

Working with the whole family allows the clinician to understand the multiple perspectives and pulls at work in the family system. A collaborative team approach is essential in most cases. Team members can help manage the polarized perspective that may develop in individual work, particularly with a single family member. Meeting times tailored to the family's needs may be longer than traditional outpatient sessions. Many families require two-hour, half-day, or even longer meetings to break through the initial anxieties and defense mechanisms of family members and for meaningful progress to occur. Longer meeting times also allow for out-of-office recreation to occur. Pleasurable experiences involving both the resisting child and rejected parent often evolve from the recreational aspects of this work.

7. CONCLUSION

The essence of the OCB approach remains the same whether in a camp model, in an intensive immersion program, or applied to an outpatient intervention. The approach

- brings a holistic, family systems approach to bear on high-conflict, fragmented families;
- includes a residential component where the family is in neutral territory away from their "home field";
- includes extensive work over multiple days;
- uses a collaborative team of clinicians to ensure effectiveness of the work as well as to model how people can work together and resolve conflict;
- includes extensive training of clinicians, both didactic and experiential, for their work with the highest-conflict families;
- involves a structured approach with elements individually tailored to each family member that targets the family's impasse and works on multiple fronts toward re-establishing connections among family members;
- works extensively and in multiple modes with all members of the family, bringing to bear the way of learning best suited to each member;
- attracts clinicians who work "where others fear to tread" with realistic hopes for positive effects on families, who in turn incorporate this hopeful stance as part of their belief that change can occur;
- focuses on aftercare from the initial intake through the camp or intensive experience, so that families leave the program with a plan as well as specific suggestions for follow-up treatment in place;
- creates an alternative to costly litigation if the family can make use of what they have learned, come to agreements with the help of clinicians and staff, and follow through with those agreements as specified in their aftercare plan;
- endeavors, as part of its commitment to strong aftercare, to find clinicians willing to work in a cohesive team model to avoid polarization and splitting reflective of the family dynamic; and
- has a strong commitment to research and a dedicated research team.

Despite the carefully constructed elements of the OCB approach, it has clear limitations:

- The program is very costly, and it has proven difficult to bring down the cost of the camp and intensives because of the almost 1:1 ratio of clinical and other staff to family members.

- Programs are short: Camp is four to five days long, and intensive immersion programs are two and a half to three days. We don't yet know to what extent these short but intense programs will have long-term on these families.
- The OCB approach is labor-intensive; clinicians and staff work 12- to 14-hour days with the family or families.
- Despite clear goals, it is difficult to measure and determine the success of OCB interventions. Is success evidenced by a decrease in litigation? Increased contact between the rejected parent and resistant child contact? Better coparent communication? Children no longer being caught in the middle? All of the above? And can such changes be successfully measured over time?
- We do not yet know which families benefit most from the OCB approach and whether success is different for different families.
- Though aftercare is critical to the approach, aftercare options range from highly effective to nonexistent. More effective aftercare involves better training in the key elements of the model for clinicians who are local to the family.
- The OCB approach must be adapted to a smaller scale. Camp is not viable in most communities. Intensive immersion is a promising adaptation that could operate in a variety of areas, but it is currently expensive and out of reach for most families. Adapting the OCB approach to outpatient interventions can increase its reach.
- Fundraising, an absolute necessity to bring down costs, is difficult, as families in high conflict who create a dynamic harmful to their children tend not to generate much appeal among philanthropists.

The OCB approach is a promising, innovative addition to the very limited legal and mental health interventions that exist for high-conflict shared-custody situations. The availability of OCB intensive programs among the range of interventions available to the courts has had a benefit for many families who have not even attended an OCB program. Not infrequently, for example, cases referred to OCB notify our administrative staff as intake is underway that there is no need to proceed because the child has started to connect with the rejected parent. In many of these situations, it is clear that the often dramatic change resulted from the favored parent's change in motivation to support the child's connection with a rejected parent when facing the financially and logistically undesirable mandatory involvement in an OCB program.

New approaches can build on the years of work on the OCB approach completed to date. One possibility is to teach family and individual therapists to use the key elements of the OCB approach in intensive immersion weekends as a "jump-start", either prior to therapy or during times when there is no forward movement in ongoing therapy. The "jump-start" may shift the entrenched family dynamics enough to allow the newly evolving connections and communication within the family to take hold thus helping the family make better use of out patient work. Training clinicians throughout the country in the approach could allow for more rapid access to effective treatment closer to each family's home base. With more rapid access to effective treatment and aftercare, it is likely that negative family dynamics will become less entrenched and that children will be able to have a relationship with both parents.

Another possibility is to train court personnel and attorneys to identify families who have many elements of alienation already beginning in their family systems and refer them earlier to family-based treatment, whether intensive or office based. Overcoming Barriers is training attorneys and judges in early identification and has begun to work with clinicians on how to best set up intensive and outpatient interventions to meet the needs of particular families. While some individual or parent–child work may be necessary in some cases, the whole-family concept of treatment is crucial to achieving the stated goals of the OCB approach, which, as agreed to by both parents, are that the child have a positive and ongoing relationship with both parents.

Well-established therapy practices might consider consultation with personnel trained in the OCB approach to establish a team within or across their practices to work in a unified manner with the high-conflict families targeted by OCB. Though working with these very high-conflict, polarized families is difficult, a positive outcome allows the children, caught in situations not of their making, the freedom to have contact and connection with both parents.

NOTES

1. Overcoming Barriers screening rules out families with active intimate-partner violence, active untreated mental illness, and active untreated substance abuse. Families with "justified rejection" of a parent are not candidates for the OCB program. Justified rejection refers to situations where a child's resistance to or rejection of contact is justified by abuse, neglect, or significantly compromised parenting (Fidler, Bala, & Saini, 2013).
2. Fidler, Bala, and Saini (2013) describe confusion between the terms *alienation* and *estrangement* arising from their different meanings among the professional, academic, and lay audiences. They and others have proposed that an alienated child may show contempt toward or withdraw affection from a parent but still be in contact with that parent, whereas an estranged child is physically apart from a parent in addition to being emotionally separated.

REFERENCES

Ackerman, N. W. (1958). *The psychodynamics of family life*. New York, NY: Basic Books.
Amato, P. R. (2000). The consequences of divorce for adults and children. *Journal of Marriage and the Family, 62*, 1269–1287.
Amato, P. R. (2001). Children of divorce in the 1990's: An update from Amato and Keith (1991) meta-analysis. *Journal of Family Psychology, 15*, 355–370.
Austin, W. G., Fieldstone, L. M., & Pruett, M. K. (2013). Bench book for assessing gatekeeping in parenting disputes: Understanding the dynamics of gate-closing and

opening for the best interests of children. *Journal of Child Custody: Research, Issues, and Practice, 10*(1), 1–16.

Austin, W. G., Pruett, M. K., Kirkpatrick, H. D., Flens, J. R., & Gould, J. W. (2013). Parental gatekeeping and child custody/child access evaluation. Part I: Conceptual framework, research, & application. *Family Court Review, 51*(3), 485–501.

Baker, A. J. L, & Fine, P. (2008). *Beyond the highroad: Responding to 17 parental alienation strategies without compromising your morals or harming your child.* Retrieved October 27, 2010, from htpp://www.amyjlbaker.com/index.php

Baker, A. J. L., & Sauber, S. R. (Eds.). (2013). *Working with alienated children and families: A clinical guidebook.* New York, NY: Routledge.

Bowen, M. (1978). *Family therapy and clinical practice.* Northvale, NJ: Jason Aronson.

Burns, D. (1980). *Feeling good: The new mood therapy.* New York, NY: Morrow.

Coates, C., Deutsch, R., Starnes, H., Sullivan, M. J., & Sydlik, B. (2004). Parenting coordination for high conflict families. *Family Court Review, 42,* 246–262.

Cummings, E. M., & Davies, P. (2002). Effects of marital conflict on children: Recent advances and emerging themes in process-oriented research. *Journal of Child Psychology and Psychiatry, 43,* 31–63.

Cummings E. M., Schermerhorn, A. C., Davies, P. T., Goeke-Morey, M. C., & Cummings, J. S. (2006). Interparental discord and child adjustment: Prospective investigations of emotional security as an explanatory mechanism. *Child Development, 77,* 132–152.

Davies, P. T., Sturge-Apple, M. L., Winter, M. A., Cummings, E. M., & Farrell, D. (2006). Child adaptational development in contexts of interparental conflict over time. *Child Development, 77,* 218–233.

Deutsch, R. M., Fidler, B., & Sullivan, M. T. (2014, June). *Interventions when children resist contact with a parent.* Paper presented at Association of Family and Conciliation Courts 51st Annual Conference, Toronto, ON

Deutsch, R. M., and Kline Pruett, M. (2009). Child adjustment and high-conflict divorce. In R. M. Galatzer-Levy, L. Kraus, & J. Galatzer-Levy (Eds.). *The scientific basis of child custody decisions* (pp.353–375), New York: John Wiley & Sons.

Deutsch, R. M., Sullivan, M. J., & Bailey, R. (2014, November,). *Children resisting contact with a parent: Application of intensive interventions.* Paper presented at Association of Family and Conciliation Courts Symposium on Custody Evaluations, San Antonio, TX.

Deutsch, R. M., Sullivan, M. J., & Moran, J. (2015, February). *Practical applications of intensive interventions for children who resist/refuse contact with a parent.* Paper presented at Association of Family and Conciliation Courts California Chapter Annual Conference, Costa Mesa, CA.

Eddy, B. (2009). *Handling alienation in new ways.* San Diego, CA: High Conflict Institute.

Fidler, B. J. (2009, May). *Responding to alienation: Practical solutions in the family justice system.* Invited presentation at the Supreme Court of British Columbia Education Seminar, National Judicial Institute, Kelowna, BC.

Fidler, B. J., & Bala, N. (2010). Children resisting post-separation contact with a parent: Concepts, controversies and conundrums. *Family Court Review, 48,* 10–47.

Fidler, B. J., Bala, N., & Saini, M. S. (2013). *Children who resist postseparation parental contact: A differential approach for legal and mental health professionals.* American Psychology–Law Society Series. New York: Oxford University Press.

Freeman, R. (2008). Children with absent parents: A model for reconnection. In J. B. Fieldstone & C.A. Coates (Eds.). *Innovations in interventions with high conflict families* (pp. 41–81). Madison, WI: Association of Family and Conciliation Courts.

Friedlander, S., & Walters, M. (2010). When a child rejects a parent: Tailoring the intervention to fit the problem. *Family Court Review, 48*(1), 98–111.

Ganong, L., Coleman, M., & McCaulley, G. (2012). Gatekeeping after separation and divorce. In K. Kuehnle & L. Drozd (Eds.), *Parenting plan evaluations: Applied research for the family court* (pp. 369–399). New York, NY: Oxford University Press.

Garber, B. D. (2011). Parental alienation and the dynamics of the enmeshed dyad: Adultification, parentification and infantilization. *Family Court Review, 49*(2), 322–335.

Garber, B. D. (2013). Providing effective, systematically informed, child-centered psychotherapists for children of divorce: Walking on thin ice. In A. J. Baker & S. R. Sauber (Eds.), *Working with alienated children and families: A clinical guidebook* (pp.168–188). New York, NY: Routledge.

Garber, B. D. (2015). Cognitive–behavioral methods in high conflict divorce: Systematic desensitization adapted to parent–child reunification interventions. *Family Court Review, 53*(1), 96–112.

Gardner, R. A. (1998). *The parental alienation syndrome* (2nd ed.). Cresskill, NJ: Creative Therapeutics.

Goodman, G. S., Rudy, L., Bottoms, B. L., & Aman, C. (1989). Ecological issues in the study of children's eyewitness testimony. In R. Fivush & J. Hudson (Eds.), *What young children remember and why* (pp.189 – 206). New York, NY: Cambridge University Press.

Goodman, G. S., & Schaaf, J. M. (1997). Over a decade of research on children's eyewitness testimony: What have we learned? Where do we go from here? *Applied Cognitive Psychology, 11*, S6–S20.

Greenberg, L. R., Gould, J. W., Gould-Saltman, D. J., & Stahl, P. (2003). Is the child's therapist part of the problem? What judges, attorneys and mental health professionals need to know about court-related treatment for children. *Family Law Quarterly, 37*, 241–271.

Greenberg, L., & Sullivan, M. (2012). Parenting coordinator and therapist collaboration in high conflict shared custody cases. *Journal of Child Custody, 9*(1–2), 85–107.

Grohol, J. M. (2014). 15 common cognitive distortions. *Psych Central.* Retrieved September 3, 2015, from http://psychcentral.com/lib/15-common-cognitive-distortions/

Johnston, J. R., & Campbell, L. E. (1988). *Impasses of divorce: The dynamics and resolution of family conflict.* New York, NY: Free Press.

Johnson, J. R., & Goldman, J. R., (2010), Outcomes of family counseling interventions with children who resist visitation: Qn addendum to Friedlander and Walters. *Family Court Review, 48*, 112–115.

Johnston, J., Roseby, V., & Kuehnle, K. (2009). *In the name of the child: A developmental approach to understanding and helping children of conflicted and violent divorce.* New York, NY: Springer.

Johnston, J. R., Walters, M. G., & Olesen, N. W. (2005). The psychological functioning of alienated children in custody disputing families: An exploratory study. *American Journal of Forensic Psychology, 23*(3), 39–64.

Judge, A. M., Bailey, R., Behrman-Lippert, J, Bailey, E, Psaila, C & Dickel, J. (2016, April). The Transitioning Families therapeutic reunification model in non-familial abductions. *Family Court Review, 54*, 232–249.

Kelly, J. (2012). Risk and protective factors associated with child and adolescent adjustment following separation and divorce: Social Science Applications. In K. Kuehnle & L. Drozd (Eds.). *Parenting plan evaluations: Applied research for the family court* (Chapter 3, pp. 49–84). New York, NY: Oxford University Press.

Kelly, J., & Johnston, J. (2001). The alienated child: A reformulation of parental alienation syndrome. *Family Court Review, 39*, 249–266.

Loftus, E. F. (1979). *Eyewitness testimony*. Cambridge, MA: Harvard University Press.

Minuchin, S. (1974). *Families and family therapy*. Cambridge, MA: Harvard University Press.

Moran, J., Sullivan, T., & Sullivan, M. (2015). *Overcoming the co-parenting trap: Essential parenting skills when a child resists a parent*. Palo Alto, CA: Overcoming Barriers.

Satir, V. (1964). *Conjoint family therapy*. Palo Alto, CA: Science and Behavior Books.

Polak, S., Fidler, B. J., & Popielarczyk, L. (2013, May). *Children resisting contact with a parent post separation*. Paper presented at Association of Family and Conciliation Courts 50th Anniversary Conference, Los Angeles, CA.

Sullivan, M.J., & Kelly, J.B. (2001). Legal and psychological management of cases with an alienated child. *Family Court Review, 39*, 299–315.

Sullivan, M. (2008). Coparenting and the parenting coordination process. *Journal of Child Custody, 5*, 4–24.

Wallerstein, J., & Kelly, J. (1980). *Surviving the breakup: How children and parents cope with divorce*. New York, NY: Basic Books.

Ward, P., Deutsch, R., & Sullivan, M. (2010). *Group weekend retreat for alienated and estranged families: An intensive model*. Paper presented at Association of Family and Conciliation Courts 47th Annual Conference, Denver, CO.

Warshak, R. A. (2003). *Divorce poison: How to protect your family from badmouthing and brainwashing*. New York, NY: Harper Paperbacks.

Warshak, R. A. (2010). Family Bridges: Using insights from social science to reconnect parents and alienated children. *Family Court Review, 48*(1), 48–80.

Warshak, R. A. (2015). Ten parental alienation fallacies that compromise decisions in court and therapy. *Professional Psychology: Research and Practice, 46*(4), 235–249.

Whitaker, C. A., & Bumberry, W. A. (1988). *Dancing with the family: A symbolic-experiential approach*. New York, NY: Brunner/Mazel.

Management of the Camp Experience

Tho Integration of the Milieu and the Clinical Team

CAROLE BLANE, M. TYLER SULLIVAN, DANIEL M. WOLFSON,
AND ABIGAIL M. JUDGE ■

1. INTRODUCTION

For many generations, children's summer camp programs have provided a space for children to develop independence, leadership, enhanced self-esteem, and an improved ability to form and maintain peer relationships. Overnight camp programs provide a unique setting in which campers and staff may coexist in a self-contained, natural environment. The Overcoming Barriers Family Camp (OBFC) is one such program with a unique mission and target population: to help families in high conflict and where a child is resisting contact with one parent following separation or divorce.

This chapter focuses on the milieu at OBFC and its integration with the camp's traditional mental health interventions, described elsewhere in this volume (see in particular Chapters 8–11). At OBFC, the *therapeutic milieu* refers to nonclinical staff, recreational activities (e.g., art, music, and games), and the camp physical environment itself. The physical surroundings of OBFC typically encompass a 20-acre family retreat site surrounded by wilderness and including amenities such as a pond, creek, playground, and a basketball court. The therapeutic milieu at OBFC serves a range of programmatic goals: fostering safe connections among estranged family members, generalization of gains made in family and coparenting interventions to real-time settings (e.g., meals, games, and cabins), and fostering systematic desensitization between children and the resisted parent (Garber, 2015).

We start this chapter with a brief history of milieu therapy and a review of the research literature on therapeutic camp programs to provide a theoretical and empirical rationale for the therapeutic milieu at OBFC. Next, we describe the main elements of OBFC's milieu, including roles of key personnel and program components. Although the milieu operates with some independence from the clinical team, the OBFC approach requires a delicate process of communication and integration between the two spheres. We highlight challenges of this process and conclude with suggestions for implementing principles of the therapeutic milieu in traditional outpatient interventions.

2. HISTORY OF THE MILIEU CONCEPT AND ITS RELEVANCE TO THE OBFC APPROACH

The *Oxford English Dictionary* defines *milieu* as an environment or surroundings, especially one's social environment ("Milieu," n.d.). The concept of milieu therapy originated in Germany in the early 20th century as a new hospital therapy for psychiatric inpatients in which nursing staff actively worked with patients (Hoffman, 1982). Originally called *activere behandlugen*, or "more active therapy," milieu therapy emerged from changing notions about psychiatric treatment during the 18th and 19th centuries (Hoffman, 1982). These include the tradition of *moral treatment*, which asserted the then radical notion that psychiatric treatment should involve compassion, minimal physical restraint, and incentives to self-control. Therapeutic benefits were therefore believed to emanate from a carefully maintained milieu (Hoffman, 1982; Showalter, 1985; Tomes, 1994).

Contemporary milieu therapy encompasses many of these early notions: that the entire treatment team, including milieu staff, is critical to treatment; that the therapeutic community is a powerful intervention to shape behavioral change; and that the physical environment of treatment affects therapeutic outcomes. *Milieu therapy* today can refer to treatment in a range of settings, including inpatient psychiatric units, residential programs, token economies, or other common spaces in which the environment is created and leveraged to support clinical change.

In the OBFC model, we use the term *milieu* to describe the recreational activities of camp; the milieu staff who implement these activities, which parallel and deepen the clinical team's interventions; and the physical environment of camp. Our use of the term differs from its traditional meaning in that we are not describing a psychiatric facility per se but rather a carefully orchestrated social environment designed to reinforce clinical interventions, build community, and benefit from the healing properties of nature. We next review research on the psychological benefits of overnight camps for both clinical and nonclinical populations, since this work provides the basis for the OBFC approach.

3. PSYCHOLOGICAL BENEFITS OF THE CAMP EXPERIENCE: CLINICAL AND NONCLINICAL POPULATIONS

Regardless of population, camps are frequently designed to foster participants' self-esteem, social engagement, and positive self-identity and self-confidence. In the professional literature, the term *camp* refers to a wide range of programs, including day camps, overnight camps, programs as short as one weekend or as long as two months, and programs at any time of year. The majority of studies we review describe overnight summer camp programs, since this is the OBFC's model.

Research by the American Camp Association (2005) found positive outcomes following camp for a range of nonclinical populations in a sample of 5,000 children representing over 80 summer camps accredited by the association. Outcomes included improved confidence, self-esteem, and social skills. In one of the largest studies of the developmental outcomes of children's camp experiences, over 3,300 families whose child or children had attended one of 80 summer camp programs completed questionnaires measuring precamp to postcamp growth on a number of measures (Thurber, Scanlin, Scheuler, & Henderson, 2007). Domains included positive identity, social skills, physical and thinking skills, positive values, and spirituality. While many of the effect sizes were small, statistically significant improvements were reported in each of these domains. Results based on this sizable population suggest that summer camp programs may provide a structure for positive youth development for a range of children. Other research describes the positive impacts of summer camp on participants' confidence (Crombie, Walsh, & Trinneer, 2003), self-esteem (Rubenstein, 1977), and peer relationships (Hanna & Berndt, 1995).

Given the positive outcomes associated with camp for nonclinical groups, recent research has investigated the psychological benefits of overnight summer camps for various clinical populations. Improved self-esteem and reduced isolation were found among children and adolescents attending a therapeutic camp for youth with learning disabilities (Michalski, Mishna, Worthington, & Cummings, 2003). A program evaluation of a therapeutic summer camp for youth with attention deficit hyperactivity disorder described campers' improved social skills following camp as compared with a matched control group; participants also reported improvements in peer relationships and measures of self-esteem (Hantson et al., 2012). Other research groups have reported similar findings, including improved social skills and peer interactions among a small sample of youth diagnosed with autism spectrum disorders (Walker, Barry, & Bader, 2010).

As these studies suggest, a recurrent outcome of overnight summer camp for clinically referred youth is improvements in social development (e.g., social skills and peer relationships). Research suggests the unique value of a peer-based environment for youth with social difficulties, isolation, or poor social skills. This is not surprising, given that social difficulties, isolation, or both characterize many disorders or medical illnesses of childhood and that camp provides a unique opportunity to be among other children facing similar challenges.

Convergent results are observed from research on overnight camps designed for children affected by medical illness. These include a study of a summer camp for siblings of children with cancer that used a pre–post design and found statistically significant improvements in campers' emotional functioning, peer interactions, validation of peers' experience, and self-esteem at three-month follow-up (Packman et al., 2004). Similarly, improvements in hope, as measured by the

Children's Hope Scale, were reported following a camp designed for children with chronic illnesses, primarily cancer and kidney disease (Woods, Mayes, Bartley, Fedele, & Ryan, 2013). Both research groups highlighted the normalizing experience of camp for youth who may otherwise feel marginalized from their peers. This may be an important nonspecific factor among all therapeutic camps.

While the majority of available research focuses on therapeutic camps for children and adolescents, benefits have also been reported for certain groups of adults, such as individuals with cerebral palsy (Dawson & Liddicoat, 2009).

A more limited literature exists on programs that use a family camp model. Experiential therapist Virginia Satir pioneered the family camp model in 1976 when she designed the Satir Family Camp for therapists and their families (Haber, 2011). Over time, the camp evolved into a forum focusing on relationships with the self, family, friends, and the camp community. The Satir Family Camp is based on the notion that relationships will deepen in an environment that is free from distractions such as modern technology. Satir's work thus provided an early model for family participation in a camp community where personal and family work may also be facilitated by clinical staff.

Family camp programming that has followed the work of Satir and colleagues emphasizes strengthening family relationships and communication. A mixed-methods study of 60 families who participated in 18 family camp programs reported positive parenting outcomes and the reinforcement of family bonds among participants (Garst, Baughman, Franz, & Seidel, 2013). Participating families identified camp staff as contributing positively to the camp experience by helping family members connect with one another, providing a safe environment, and creating a camp culture of positivity, enthusiasm, and friendliness.

Examined together, the available literature highlights the positive outcomes of overnight summer camps for nonclinical and clinical populations of youth and adults, although the literature on adults is sparse. Program evaluation for family camps is limited but promising and highlights the importance of camp staff in facilitating a supportive milieu.

Several aspects of this literature are particularly relevant to the camp milieu at OBFC. First, the potential for overnight therapeutic camps to promote shared experience and reduce isolation is highly applicable to families in high conflict. Children of high-conflict divorce frequently report difficulty speaking about their experiences with peers of other divorced families because of the unique features that set high-conflict divorce apart (e.g., protracted litigation, extensive interparental conflict, and triangulation of children) (Grych & Fincham, 1999; Maccoby, Depner, & Mnookin, 1990). Parents in high conflict may also feel isolated, particularly the nonfavored or resisted parents. Second, the ability of camp staff to foster a therapeutic milieu in which families may safely experiment with new patterns of interaction is another key finding from this literature that bears directly on the development of the OBFC milieu. As we will highlight later in this chapter, the milieu staff plays a critical role in this process. Finally, a beautiful surrounding that is neutral and distinct from the environments that families associate with distress and the dissolution of marriage and family may afford a needed change of context in which to forge new patterns of interaction. In light of these findings, we now describe OBFC's application of the family camp model to families experiencing high-conflict divorce and where children are resisting contact with a parent.

4. DEVELOPMENT OF THE OBFC MILIEU: STRUCTURE, KEY PRINCIPLES, AND GOALS

In 2007, Overcoming Barriers partnered with Common Ground Center to pilot a family camp for families in high conflict and where children were at risk of losing a relationship with a parent. Common Ground Center is a nonprofit organization that offers family-based camp experiences for a range of family presentations (e.g., autism, homeschooling, and adoption). For the next three years, Overcoming Barriers and Common Ground Center implemented OBFC together and refined the integration of the clinical and milieu spheres of OBFC. Since that time, Overcoming Barriers has operated camps at Common Ground Center as well as at sites in California and Arizona in furtherance of its nonprofit mission.

The OBFC milieu provides a rich environment that is designed both to motivate individual family members to engage in activities and to challenge entrenched behavior patterns. The milieu functions as a space in which families can generalize the clinical coparenting work and clinical family interventions to real-time interactions, with the facilitation and support of milieu staff. For example, a topic identified during morning group or family meeting may inform an afternoon activity in the milieu or a planned seating arrangement during a meal. The greater opportunity for practicing new skills and behaviors in real life and in the moment sets OBFC apart from traditional and office-based outpatient interventions. Clinical intervention in turn is informed by what happens in the milieu, which then offers safe and specifically designed opportunities to integrate that clinical work immediately. And then this milieu work can be processed with clinical staff as needed, and so on.

This feedback loop from clinical work to therapeutic milieu and vice versa is a powerful component of the OBFC model. It requires a high degree of communication between the two spheres of camp and also adaptability in the milieu space and among staff. Indeed, the art of orchestrating the OBFC environment lies in fostering effective integration and feedback between the milieu and clinical teams while simultaneously maintaining boundaries and a practical distinction between the two. This is a key tension and dialectic in how OBFC operates, and we discuss lessons learned from this process throughout this chapter.

Creating clear boundaries between clinical and nonclinical work is important for both campers and staff because milieu staff are not licensed and because campers, children in particular, would be stressed by the pressure of constant clinical supervision. Clinical work is differentiated from nonclinical work within the milieu by space, time, and personnel job descriptions.

Many goals of the OBFC milieu are similar to the goals of any camp experience: for children and families to learn from and about one another, to build social skills, to have fun, and to allow the environment's natural beauty to relieve stress and promote healing. In addition to these general factors, the milieu is designed to consider the unique needs of families where children are resisting contact with a parent. This means providing healthy and safe opportunities to reconnect and enabling every individual in the family to be heard and valued. Other goals specific to the OBFC milieu include

- providing an emotionally and physically safe space;
- creating a space for the clinical work of camp;
- removing families from their normal surroundings, distractions, memories, habits, and social groups that may support the entrenched dynamics, thereby helping family members examine their situation from different perspectives;
- focusing participants intensely on the task of moving the family forward;
- engaging participants in positive and cooperative activities that provide enough motivation or distraction to overcome negative thoughts related to the presence of resisted family members;
- providing specifically designed and varied opportunities for parents and children to practice connecting positively and safely, integrating information they have learned in their psychoeducational groups and agreements they have created in family meetings;
- providing structured and unstructured opportunities for campers to connect with other campers and staff, give them feedback, and get feedback from them, and particularly for children to discover that other kids face similar challenges; and
- sending families home with positive memories that will help them sustain any positive agreements they have made toward overcoming entrenched conflict.

5. ROLES AT OBFC

5.1. Camp Director

The camp director is the program administrator and is usually a family's initial contact with OBFC. The first two authors of this chapter have served as OBFC's camp directors since its initial year of operation. The director fields administrative inquiries about camp and may be the first voice prospective families will hear; as such, the director is a critical liaison to the program. The director has the most interaction with campers before camp, because she or he makes sure all administrative paperwork is completed, questions are answered, and so on. The director also oversees the recruitment and hiring of milieu staff.

During camp, the director maintains responsibility for overseeing effective communication and coordination of goals between the clinical team and milieu staff. Often during camp, campers rely on the camp director as a familiar face and someone who knows their story. This can place the director in a difficult position, since the director must enforce rules as well as tolerate family members' distress, disappointment, and resistance at times. It is therefore important to clarify to campers from the outset, both in initial contact by phone and once families arrive at camp, that the director plays a nonclinical role at camp.

Qualifications for the director position include experience with program administration and the ability to anticipate problems and to make quick and possibly unpopular decisions. Communication skills are of the utmost importance, including facility with public speaking and equanimity in the face of family conflict and polarized perspectives.

5.2. Milieu Staff: "Green Shirts"

Milieu staff are referred to as *Green Shirts* because of the color of the OBFC shirts they wear when working. This title is also used to differentiate their role from that of a clinician,. Families can easily confuse the role of camp counselor with that of clinician, and maintaining this distinction is critical to the work at OBFC. Most Green Shirts have worked in the past with high-risk populations (e.g., emotionally disturbed youth, developmentally disabled populations, or populations with addiction problems), often in camp settings, although past work with such populations is not required. Green Shirts with prior camp experience are likely to find OBFC to be unlike other camp work. As one Green Shirt noted about her experience at OBFC, "This is the first time I've been at camp where people are not happy to be here." Although experience with court-referred populations is not required, willingness to learn about the unique characteristics of these families is essential.

Key qualities for the Green Shirt position include maturity, flexibility, and the ability to follow directions meticulously and work well with a team. Other critical qualities are the ability to maintain composure and protect confidentiality in highly intense and emotional situations.

One of the greatest challenges in selecting Green Shirts is ensuring each milieu staff member's ability to maintain a nonclinical role at camp. This is especially important if the staff person has a clinical background. Role definition, including not overstepping the limits of one's professional competence, is a key aspect of treatment with families in high conflict who are court involved (Association of Family and Conciliation Courts, 2010; Greenberg, Gould, Schnider, Gould-Saltman, & Martindale, 2003). Green Shirts are not qualified, licensed, or insured to work in a clinical role while at camp and must be comfortable with and committed to this expectation. However, role definition does not diminish the critical part that Green Shirts play at camp. Rather, this distinction allows the milieu to function independently from but also informed by the clinical team. Role definition also upholds professional standards of legal and ethical mental health practice.

The camp director selects individual Green Shirts to complement one another and to make sure certain critical skill sets are represented on the team. For example,

Green Shirts with loud and authoritative voices and a charismatic presence are needed to facilitate large group activities. An arts and crafts expert is needed, as are a few Green Shirts who can play guitar to facilitate the iconic musical activities of camp (e.g., informal playing of music, accompaniment for campfires, talent show participation, and helping awaken campers in the morning). Indeed, there is often a Green Shirt who acts as a minstrel, whose job is to provide a calming background soundscape in the milieu. The shared experience of music helps reduce anxiety and foster community (Hughes & Cormac, 2013; Juslin, 2010).

The camp director and clinical team limit the amount of clinical information they share with Green Shirts about each family prior to the start of camp. This practice helps Green Shirts form impressions on their own and interact with families in as authentic and unbiased a manner as possible. Green Shirts can do their jobs most effectively when they support all campers as equitably as possible, providing them with a neutral and supportive "safety net." They are paired as "buddies" with the adult campers: a welcoming presence for a camper to seek out in times of stress or when feeling rejected. Given this role, Green Shirts walk a very fine line. Adults at OBFC are struggling to learn more skillful ways of interacting with coparents and children. Green Shirts model acceptance even in the face of unskilled behavior. When missteps occur, Green Shirts may role-model problem-solving and convey relevant observations to the clinical team.

5.3. Nurse

The camp nurse, who resides on site in case of medical emergency, plays a critical supportive role at OBFC. Very often, the health needs of children in high-conflict families (e.g., allergies, chronic illness, or dietary restrictions) are a source of interparental conflict. When such conflict occurs, the nurse must maintain a calm, nonreactive, and neutral manner while serving as a source of objective medical decision-making. The nurse holds children's medications and over-the-counter products in a secure office and dispenses medications to the children according to the plan agreed upon by their parents.

Children at OBFC often express psychological distress through somatic symptoms. sometimes because physical problems are a fulcrum of interparental conflict. Thus the nurse is in frequent consultation with the director and clinical team to share information and plan interventions. For example, a resisted parent may have been excluded from coparenting around a child's medical issue, and the child may report exaggerated or unfounded beliefs that the resisted parent is not capable of helping with this issue or is indifferent to the child's needs. Accordingly, one intervention at camp may involve the resisted parent's dispensing medication or other treatment to the child with the nurse there to facilitate. Whether at the nurse's office or elsewhere, camp provides a unique opportunity for children to engage in such activities of daily living with the resisted parent. These experiences can help correct the cognitive distortions characteristic of children triangulated in conflict (see, for example, Chapter 10).

5.4. Photographer

A photographer is a welcome addition to the staff and plays a large role in providing memories for the family. The photographer particularly tries to capture shots where a resisted parent and child may be near one another smiling. All pictures taken at camp are used for the therapeutic purpose of providing reminders of the connections that took place at camp. For example, at the end of each OBFC there is a slide show featuring participating families. Pictures are sent home only at the request of families and with the signed release of every family member. Sending photos home is not usually possible, however, since one or more favored parents refuse to give permission to have images of the family shared.

6. KEY COMPONENTS OF THE OBFC MILIEU

6.1. Physical Space

The space at OBFC was originally defined by what Common Ground Center had developed for the broad range of family programs at its facility. Various indoor and outdoor spaces provide for hundreds of activities. Spaces are characterized by their rustic aesthetic and communal utility. Considerations relating to physical space include the following:

- lines of sight that allow staff to keep track of campers and other staff at all times, facilitating communication and chaperoning, and that meets family members' need to see and keep track of one another to feel safe and allow them to take emotional risks;
- sleeping cabins and other accommodations that are not too far or isolated from the rest of the milieu to prevent easy trips back and forth when needed, while not being so close as to provide a distraction or easy "escape";
- an open playing area for active games and gatherings;
- the ability to set up simultaneous activities either indoors or outdoors with privacy or within view of one another to allow for parallel activities;
- diverse indoor and outdoor activity spaces such as a tennis court, climbing structure, archery range, painting studio, community kitchen, or campfire;
- multipurpose spaces such as a stage, amphitheater, barn, dance floor, open field, or forest;
- as many as 10 private meeting spaces for families and small groups to use for psychoeducational groups, staff meetings, and family meetings;
- family-style seating options for meals and activities that require assigned seating;
- beautiful, natural environment with vistas that provide stress relief, opportunities for education and exploration, and hiking trails for vigorous exercise; and

- water-play options supervised by milieu staff, a certified lifeguard, or both, which are particularly important in warm climates (Common Ground Center has both a creek and a pond).

6.2. Safety

Safety, including physical and emotional safety, is a key component of any family camp environment and particularly for OBFC. To prevent distractions or avoidance of participation, it is essential to eliminate any reasonable safety concern that might come up. Providing for safety includes having adequate medical resources on site, emergency medical facilities in close proximity to the site, and well-maintained grounds. Emotional safety is fostered by Green Shirts' respect for and adherence to the daily schedule and camp expectations and also by their supporting families with their genuinely friendly and upbeat morale.

6.3. Balancing Engaging Activities and Human Connection

Engaging activities and a positive, stimulating environment are the cornerstones of OBFC. However, these elements are useful only to the extent that they facilitate connections within and between families. Parents and children may need relief and downtime from the intense family work, but time at OBFC is limited. The camp is designed to help families find solutions and to not collude with their avoidance of challenging therapeutic work. While hosting a program at a site with a network of water slides would provide a lot of fun and excitement, especially for kids, the quality and depth of connection with family members might suffer from such an intense distraction. Thus the novelty of the environment must be balanced alongside the clinical work that families attend camp to accomplish.

6.4. Removal From the Family's Typical Environment

Overcoming Barriers Family Camp seeks to help families change the entrenched patterns of thinking that maintain their family conflict. Clinical staff invite participants to consider new ideas and new perspectives, and the physical milieu and milieu staff serve a similar function, albeit with different tools. Removal from the physical reminders of damaged family relationships may give campers more freedom to relinquish past hurts and focus on present and future functioning.

The camp was also designed for families that have had little success with outpatient therapy, treatment that is usually conducted in offices. It takes advantage of the natural surroundings as much as possible. Whenever possible, clinical intervention happens outdoors, under trees, as long as privacy can be assured. Initially the clinical team had concerns about the camp's lacking privacy, but it turned out that the proximity of nature provided a calming, soothing environment in which to address difficult topics (Hill, 2007).

6.5. Nourishment

It is essential to provide lots of food options and seek camper input on food that will provide nourishment and comfort. Prior to camp, each adult provides information about his or her children's favorite foods, preferences, and dietary restrictions. Camp is physically and emotionally demanding, and campers and staff both require the nourishment that will allow them to perform optimally. Healthy snacks are always available, because individuals may miss meals when meetings run over or because of other unplanned situations. Coffee and tea are available at all hours, since some campers need it to function and staff work long hours.

6.6. Rules and Expectations

Every member of the camp community—staff and camper alike—is entitled to respect at a minimum, and disrespectful behavior is met with a simple reminder like "Remember, we are at camp and we don't treat people that way here." This expectation creates a higher default standard of behavior than generally exists within many families who attend OBFC.

Other than a few child-specific rules, everyone at camp is expected to follow the same rules, and community members are expected to hold each other equally accountable. Staff lead by example and model behavior at all times. Two particularly resonant ways that staff frame the importance of following the rules are reminding parents how critical it is that they model rule following for their children or coparent and reminding both parents and children that the rules exist to keep everyone safe.

One example of how the principle of respect is reinforced at camp began during an activity at the pond. An adolescent camper kicked sand at her mother, the parent she was rejecting. Staff observed the incident and immediately clarified with the child the expectation that everyone at camp must be respectful to others. The mother felt particularly violated and unprotected, perhaps embarrassed as well. Although the adolescent's father, the favored parent, also observed the incident, he did not intervene. The milieu staff shared this observation with the clinical team, who communicated with the father about the effects of his behavior and encouraged him to convey the importance and value of the camp rules to his daughter.

Beyond respect, the following are basic rules that OBFC uses to create a milieu that facilitates the clinical work:

- No cell phones or personal computers are allowed for the duration of camp, except for adults during scheduled times (children and adolescents have no cell phone access).

- All communication between children and parents is monitored by staff.
- Campers are chaperoned by staff at all times.
- Everyone is expected to participate in activities.

Milieu staff anticipate that family members will struggle with these rules. Individual campers often have needs that challenge the camp structure, and staff have to problem-solve to accommodate those needs within the rules. To the extent possible, the intake process identifies special needs so they can be accommodated proactively. Certain circumstances may necessitate that rules be modified at the discretion of the clinical team. For example, one parent who was unable to sleep was given permission to stay up past "lights out" within a lit area in eyesight of the night watch, avoiding the need for any extra staff to stay up all night and preventing other campers from being disturbed. By problem-solving and giving individual needs serious consideration, camp staff offer good role modeling to parents on ways to work together.

The expectation for all campers to remain near a Green Shirt at all times requires some elaboration. Understandably, this rule can cause discomfort for many campers, adults in particular. Even though families are screened for physical safety concerns, adult and child campers often express concerns about their physical well-being to staff. A high number of families present to OBFC following multiple abuse allegations and investigations by child protective services. Given this history, unless campers are assured that OBFC is providing consistent supervision, they will not feel safe and therefore will not be able to take the emotional risks that treatment requires.

To facilitate safety, OBFC provides a high ratio of staff to campers, and staff are easily identifiable by the color of their shirts. Camp rules are clearly explained in intake paperwork, are verbally restated at the outset of camp, and are taken very seriously throughout camp. Staff address any rule violation immediately and directly, and ongoing violations can lead to dismissal from camp. Maintaining a sense of support and safety without making campers feel they are scrutinized is a delicate balance.

Staff safety is equally attended to, and staff are reminded to have a witness to every interaction. Staff do not spend time alone with any camper under the age of 18, and they always let someone know where they will be with any camper. This practice prevents misunderstandings or allegations of improper behavior.

6.7. Accommodations and Cabin Assignments

Before camp begins, cabin assignments are determined by consultation between the clinicians responsible for intake and the camp director. The director balances family clinical needs with camp's limitations.

Child and adult campers sleep in age- and gender-segregated cabins. Adult cabins have approximately one staff person for every three campers, while children's cabins have at least two staff regardless of the number of children, to allow for flexibility in care. Cabin assignments are approved by clinical staff and take into account the potential for any unhelpful situations. For example, a stepmother would not be in the same cabin as her stepchildren's mother unless both agreed this would be acceptable. Sometimes sleeping arrangements are shifted during camp because of loud snoring.

Favored and resisted parents are deliberately mixed in cabins to help prevent excessively polarized late-night conversation, which can spill over into the daytime milieu. Cabin assignments are planned to foster empathy in both directions and challenge assumptions in profound ways. Cabin time allows for unstructured debriefing and connection among adults outside more structured camp activities and clinical time.

No adults except the Green Shirts are allowed in the children's cabin area. Maintaining this boundary is intended to create a space for children to be children. Establishing a protected area for children also provides respite from any real or perceived parental conflict. A night watchperson is stationed outside the children's cabin area.

The children, with the support of their Green Shirts, are responsible for organizing the space, keeping track of their belonging, getting dressed, taking care of hygiene, going to sleep, and waking up. For some children, especially those from families with high levels of enmeshment or other forms of role corruption (Garber, 2010), this is a unique opportunity to engage in those activities without their parents. Families are asked to pack children's clothes and belongings separately from the parents' to prevent lengthy unpacking and ongoing interactions with aligned parents that re-create the dynamics of home and maintain an imbalance between parents. Children often build strong connections with other children at camp. At one camp the children named their area "The Groove" and were always excited to return there for downtime and fun.

Green Shirts who stay in the cabins maintain a healthy level of respect and supervision in the cabins and have time to build relationships with campers. Staff and campers will often share their experiences and perspectives with their cabin mates. One fathers' cabin decided that each night a different person would share his story. Besides the powerful effect the interactions among cabin mates can have by themselves, the deeper and more organic relationships campers form with staff who share their cabins can provide staff with insight that can be useful in the larger effort to help a family move forward.

6.8. A Typical Day

Prior to camp, a template schedule is set up. However, each camp cohort will have different clinical needs, which will inform the schedule. Thus to some extent the schedule must remain fluid and flexible. Notwithstanding the need for flexibility, the following is a fair representation of a typical day at OBFC.

Camp starts early. Instead of the day's starting with a bell or bugle, the OBFC minstrel wanders from cabin to cabin to sing a morning wake-up song or strumming guitar, often accompanied by a group of children. Optional yoga, taught by a certified yoga teacher from off site, or a morning walk is offered to all campers.

Green Shirts monitor campers as they complete morning routines. At Common Ground Center, the bathhouse provides an ideal set of circumstances for families to practice sharing space and for desensitizing the child and resisted parent. While toilets are private and gender specific, the rest of the bathhouse is shared. Male and female campers alternate each day between using indoor and outdoor showers, sharing the sink area. This setup requires family members to negotiate with staff and other campers to achieve their desired level of contact with other campers. For example, a child who does not want to share the sink space with a parent will have to communicate that wish and find a solution. This could be waiting until the parent leaves, asking the parent to leave, or sharing the space with the expectation that they won't talk to each other. Even such seemingly minor interactions help children shift from avoidant strategies to problem-solving, a skill they will need in their relationships with both parents, peers, and others. Similar dynamics appear at the meal buffet and recreational spaces. It is usually the case that children's comfort levels in these settings increase over the course of camp.

The clinical team meets during breakfast and lunch to plan interventions, debrief one another about recent events in the milieu, and share other information. After breakfast, campers attend their respective psychoeducational groups (see Chapters 8–10). This time is crucial for Green Shirts. It is their only time without campers to chaperone and includes planning for the day's activities with the camp director. When available, a clinician attends this staff meeting to allow for real-time feedback between clinical and milieu work (see section 4 above).

Green Shirts plan the afternoon activities with clinical input. The clinical team may tell the Green Shirts, "Campers are not yet ready for an all-camp game" or "Be sure Suze and her dad sit together for dinner," or may determine that a particular family is ready to participate in an activity all together, with a Green Shirt present. Activity planning is aided by children's interest questionnaires, which both parents complete independently before attending OBFC. The degree to which parents provide conflicting or consistent information about their children and family dynamics can be useful for both the clinical and milieu staff, another link between those two spheres.

After morning groups, the Green Shirts always have an active game available for the children to provide a transition back to the milieu and prevent unstructured time, which we have found fosters children's anxiety and makes them more likely to seek out the favored parent. At lunch there is a children's table; all others, including Green Shirts, sit in assigned seats.

Clinical team meetings occur during most meals. These meeting times provide a crucial intersection between therapy and the milieu. During these meetings, an assigned milieu staff person—generally the camp director—will relay information from the milieu that seems relevant for clinical decisions. A significant benefit of the milieu is the opportunity it gives for observations of families interacting in real time, which milieu staff can share with the clinical team to help each family work on its goals. Unlike the once weekly sessions of outpatient therapy, at OBFC the teams—clinical and milieu—are living 24/7 with families and have the chance to observe them in a range of mundane as well as challenging situations. The clinical team may also ask an individual Green Shirt to orchestrate or be present for a family activity. For example, a Green Shirt may be asked to escort a resisted parent and child on a short walk or do a shared craft activity with them. This planning may occur during the morning or lunch team meeting or spontaneous consultation anytime in between between the milieu staff and clinical team.

For the first activity block after lunch, the campers are usually divided into their respective groups (children, preferred parents, and resisted parents), with children and resisted parents being within sight and proximity of one another to allow for connections. At the same time, clinical interventions are ongoing. Thus the milieu provides backdrop activities for all campers not involved in an intervention with clinical staff. The second afternoon block is usually an all-camp activity. It may be a clay craft activity with assigned seating early in the week and may evolve to a game of kickball or time at the pond later on.

After this second activity period, the camp gathers in an all-camp circle for approximately 20 minutes before dinner. A Green Shirt or the camp director typically leads "Circle," which is an important touchstone during the day and serves multiple functions. Circle is perhaps the only time when the entire camp is all together: campers, milieu staff, and clinical staff. As a daily ritual, Circle conveys norms and expectations for the camp community through fun activities and planned expressions of gratitude. Recall that one function of the therapeutic milieu is to create a community in which the work of therapy can be extended, challenged, and internalized. The daily ritual of coming together as an entire camp fosters such community. The Green Shirt who leads Circle will read aloud "appreciations," which campers and staff can submit anonymously. This practice allows staff members and campers alike to acknowledge and express appreciation for something during the day. Resisted parents often take this opportunity to acknowledge their children's accomplishments. The writing of appreciations and sharing them during Circle models respectful communication, the importance of expressing gratitude, and also humor, as submissions are frequently lighthearted. Other traditions of Circle include sharing announcements, meditation, or playing a game all together.

Dinner happens immediately after Circle. Dinner has assigned seating, and sometimes the clinical staff joins as well if they are not meeting as a team. Evenings offer a good chance for casual interactions between the clinical team and campers, as well as giving the clinical staff the opportunity to observe behaviors firsthand.

Dinner is followed by an evening activity, which could be a campfire with singing, game night, the "Big Show" (the OBFC talent show), or a table tennis tournament. Green Shirts work together to showcase the strengths of all campers during evening activities.

Bedtime can be challenging. Children resist separation from the aligned parent. Over time the milieu staff has learned not to formalize the saying of "good nights" between parents and children, since that practice may foster children's seeking out the favored parent in dramatic ways that may be hurtful to the resisted parent. Once in the cabins, however, the children generally relax and share in fun and games.

7. FOSTERING HEALTHY CONNECTIONS IN THE MILIEU

In addition to the extensive clinical work families experience throughout the day, the OBFC milieu provides a safe, structured, and supportive environment in which families can practice interacting in more adaptive ways. The Green Shirts are tasked with planning and engaging campers in cooperative activities and maintaining a positive, upbeat energy in the milieu. This can be challenging, given the court-ordered nature of OBFC and high levels of resistance among children and adults alike. By definition, OBFC families have struggled with engaging positively with one another for an extended period. To overcome the rigid thinking patterns and conflicted emotions of campers, Green Shirts must work collaboratively with one another, leveraging their individual skill sets within the confines of the camp environment and camp structure.

The clinical team oversees and collaborates with the milieu staff to accomplish OBFC's goals. The clinical team works with each family to understand the sources of the clinical impasse that led families to camp and to reach agreements about expected treatment goals for camp and aftercare. The team communicates relevant information about these goals to Green Shirts so that they can provide activities tailored to each family's needs that will help each family member participate and engage positively. Clinicians also communicate expectations and objectives for particular activities to milieu staff, who then work with parents and children to make activities successful. Importantly, milieu staff engage campers in the activity-planning process at every opportunity; whenever possible, activities are camper rather than staff driven. This provides families with the critical practice they need to develop the capacity to plan activities together once camp is over. Communication between the clinical team and Green Shirts facilitates teamwork between these levels of the camp experience.

Clinicians may also be integrated into the milieu for specific activities. This is useful for activities that will be more challenging for a particular group of campers. If an individual needs support for or a reminder of an intervention from an earlier clinical meeting, that support can be integrated in real time. Seating charts and other groupings of campers for activities and meals provide opportunities for structured connection among campers. Fostering interactions between resisted parents and children is prioritized. The milieu presents many opportunities to challenge children to increase contact with a resisted parent, either with other families present or one to one in the presence of a Green Shirt. The clinical team uses principles of systematic desensitization to plan groupings (Garber, 2015), and it often has specific requests for which campers should or shouldn't be assigned to the same group.

Behavior among milieu staff is monitored by the camp director in consultation with the clinical team. As discussed in Chapter 5, families in high conflict can cause strong and often divisive reactions among clinical teams. Great care is therefore taken at OBFC to make sure that milieu staff feel supported and understand that clinical decision-making is done carefully, even if an individual Green Shirt may not be privy to certain clinical details. Transparency and trust between the clinical and milieu teams is essential for the teams to remain intact, nonpolarized, and effective.

8. CONCLUSIONS

The therapeutic milieu at OBFC functions as an independent and complementary sphere to the program's clinical team. Role definition, safety, and the upholding of rules and expectations are critical aspects of milieu management.

The OBFC milieu is rooted in the theoretical foundation of milieu therapy and empirical research on the psychological benefits of overnight camps. The OBFC approach adheres to principles of a therapeutic milieu in a picturesque surrounding to create an environment that removes families from everyday reminders of family trauma and helps them safely experiment with different modes of interaction in real time. Management challenges include maintaining a distinction between the milieu and clinical teams while ensuring the flow of information between these spheres to provide effective and responsive treatment.

The challenges of applying principles of intensive intervention to outpatient practice are described in Chapter 12. Here, we would just like to suggest that certain elements of a therapeutic milieu may inform traditional interventions with the same population of families. For example, therapists might keep an abiding focus on activities of daily living and ways to foster interactions between the resisted parent and child in real-time contexts. Recreational or experiential techniques might also be integrated into traditional outpatient practice (see Chapter 4). Even if clinicians do not have the luxury of a therapeutic milieu, principles of "active therapy" and growth through recreational activity have the potential to create new experiences for families and may help them disengage from long-standing conflict.

REFERENCES

American Camp Association. (2005). *Directions: Youth developmental outcomes of the camp experience.* Retrieved from http://www.acacamps.org/sites/default/files/resource_library/report-directions-youth-development-outcomes.pdf

Association of Family and Conciliation Courts. (2010). *AFCC guidelines for court-involved therapy.* Retrieved from http://www.afccnet.org/Portals/0/PublicDocuments/CEFCP/Guidelines%20for%20Court%20Involved%20Therapy%20AFCC.pdf

Crombie, G., Walsh, J. P., & Trinneer, A. (2003). Positive effects of science and technology summer camps on confidence, values and future intentions. *Canadian Journal of Counseling, 37*(4), 256–269.

Dawson, S., & Liddicoat, K. (2009). "Camp gives me hope": Exploring the therapeutic use of community for adults with cerebral palsy. *Therapeutic Recreation Journal, 43*(4), 9–24.

Garber, B. D. (2010). Parental alienation and the dynamics of the enmeshed dyad: Adultification, parentification and infantilization. *Family Court Review, 49*(2), 322–335.

Garber, B. D. (2015). Cognitive–behavioral methods in high-conflict divorce: Systematic desensitization adapted to parent–child reunification interventions. *Family Court Review, 53*(1), 96–112.

Garst, B. A., Baughman, S., Franz, N. K., & Seidel, R. W. (2013). Strengthening families: Exploring the impacts of family camp experiences on family functioning and parenting. *Journal of Experiential Education, 36*(1), 65–77.

Greenberg, L.R., Gould, J.W., Schnider, R., Gould-Saltman, D.J., & Martindale, D. (2003, December). *Effective intervention with high conflict families: How judges can promote and recognize competent treatment.* San Francisco, CA: Journal of the Center for Families, Children and the Courts.

Grych, J. H., & Fincham, F. D. (1999). The adjustment of children from divorced families: Implications of empirical research for clinical intervention. In R. M. Galatzer-Levy & L. Kraus (Eds.), *The scientific basis of child custody decisions* (pp. 96–119). New York, NY: Wiley.

Haber, R. (2011). Virginia Satir's family camp experiment: An intentional growth community still in process. *Contemporary Family Therapy: An International Journal, 33*(1), 71–84.

Hanna, N. A., & Berndt, T. J. (1995). Relations between friendship, group acceptance and evaluation of summer camp. *Journal of Early Adolescence, 15*(4), 456–475.

Hantson, J., Wang, P., Grizenko-Vida, M., Ter-Stepanian, M., Harvey, W., Joober, R., & Grizenko, N. (2012). Effectiveness of a therapeutic summer camp for children with ADHD: Phase I clinical intervention trial. *Journal of Attention Disorders, 16*(7), 610–617.

Hill, N. R. (2007). Wilderness therapy as a treatment modality for at-risk youth: A primer for mental health counselors. *Journal of Mental Health Counseling, 29*(4), 338–349.

Hoffman, L. (1982). A historical overview of milieu therapy. In L. Hoffman (Ed.), *The evaluation and care of severely disturbed children and their families,* (pp. 1–8). New York: Spectrum Publications.

Hughes, P., & Cormac, I. (2013). Music therapy with long-stay in-patients: Communication issues and collaboration with the clinical team. In S. Compton Dickinson, H. Odell-Miller, & J. Adlam (Eds.), *Forensic music therapy* (pp. 58–72). London, UK: Jessica Kingsley.

Juslin, P. N. (2010). *Handbook of music and emotion: Theory, research, applications.* New York, NY: Oxford University Press.

Maccoby, E. E., Depner, C. E., & Mnookin, R. H. (1990). Coparenting in the second year after divorce. *Journal of Marriage and the Family, 52,* 256–272.

Michalski, J. H., Mishna, F., Worthington, C., & Cummings, R. (2003). A multi-method impact evaluation of a therapeutic summer camp program. *Child & Adolescent Social Work Journal, 20*(1), 53–76.

Milieu (n.d.). In *Oxford English dictionary.* Retrieved from http://www.oed.com/view/Entry/118407?redirectedFrom=milieu#eid

Packman, W., Fine, J., Chesterman, B., vanZutphen, K., Golan, R., & Amylon, M. D. (2004). Camp Okizu: Preliminary investigation of a psychological intervention for siblings of pediatric cancer patients. *Children's Health Care, 33*(3), 201–215.

Rubenstein, R. P. (1977). Changes in self-esteem and anxiety in competitive and non-competitive camps. *Journal of Social Psychology, 102*(1), 55–57.

Showalter, E. (1985). *The female malady: Women, madness and English culture, 1830–1980.* New York, NY: Pantheon Books.

Thurber, C. A. Scanlin, M. M, Scheuler, L., & Henderson, K. A. (2007). Youth development outcomes of the camp experience: Evidence for multidimensional growth. *Journal of Youth and Adolescence, 36*(3), 241–254.

Tomes, N. (1994). *The art of asylum keeping: Thomas Story Kirkbride and the origins of American psychiatry.* Philadelphia, PA: University of Pennsylvania Press.

Walker, A., Barry, T. D., & Bader, S. H. (2010). Therapist and parent ratings of changes in adaptive social skills following a summer treatment camp for children with autism spectrum disorders: A preliminary study. *Child & Youth Care Forum, 39*(5), 305–322.

Woods, K., Mayes, S., Bartley, E., Fedele, D., & Ryan, J. (2013). An evaluation of psychosocial outcomes for children and adolescents attending a summer camp for youth with chronic illness. *Children's Health Care, 42*(1), 85–98.

8

"East Group"

Group Work With Favored Parents

PEGGIE WARD ■

1. INTRODUCTION

The "East Group" at Overcoming Barriers (OCB) camp is made up of parents who are favored[1] by at least one and possibly all of their children. These parents have been required (usually by court order) to attend the OCB camp. To reach the point where the court is involved and orders a family to come to the camp, the child or children usually have to be resisting or refusing contact with their other parent. Thus the relationship between favored parents and their children ranges from enmeshed to highly aligned. In many situations, the favored parents ascribe little to no value to their children's other parent. In the situations where these parents feel the other parent does have some value, it is minimal at best and limited by a rigidly defined set of beliefs and fears centered around protection and safety of their children. Though the OCB staff and clinicians consistently label favored and rejected parents as "coparents," this terminology does not match the experience of the parents in the East Group, who have very little desire to work with their children's other parent.

The parents in the East Group do not participate in the OCB program by choice. Their feelings about participating range from frustration to anger to powerlessness at being ordered into a program they believe that their children do not need and may find harmful. They have unsuccessfully argued (with or without attorneys) in court that their children should have input as to whether they will have a relationship with the other parent. While some favored parents, once at the program, try to make the best of the experience and show real effort, others are more passive in their interactions. Still other favored parents, despite court orders for full cooperation with the program, have an extremely difficult time engaging with any aspect of the program that focuses on their own role in the family dynamic.

The favored parents see little to no reason for changing the family system. They believe their children are doing well and often cite their children's school records and accomplishments in sports or other extracurricular activities to "prove" how well they are doing. On several occasions prior to the OCB camp, the court will have admonished some of these parents that if change does not occur at the OCB program, custody may be switched to the children's other parent. In addition to feeling frustration, anger, and powerlessness, parents facing potential custody reversal have reactions including fear, outrage, and confusion. As a group they tend to believe, based on their extremely negative view of the other parent, that a judge would not possibly order a custody change. Their belief can be expressed as follows: "Why would the court order a change of custody when the children are happy and doing well and the other parent is not competent to take over parenting?"

The favored parents typically present to OCB programs with extremely low expectations that positive interactions will be possible during the program. Many express the belief that any intervention that "forces" contact between a rejected parent and a child is, by definition, harmful. Despite being told in all conversations prior to and at the OCB program that contact between a child and rejected parent is not forced but encouraged, these parents appear unable to let go of the negative and fearful belief that their children will be forced to have such contact. The combination of being forced to attend and their stated fears about potential harm to their children foster primarily negative expectations about the program. Their anger at the other parent for "dragging" them through court and to the OCB program is intense. This anger is initially pervasive and leaves no intellectual or emotional room for alternative views or feelings. Moreover, the favored parents' general negative beliefs about the OCB program extend to anyone connected with the program. For the first day or two, these parents have a hard time trusting any effort by staff or therapists to reach out to them.

This chapter will first identify the characteristics of the parents in the East Group. These include specific personality traits as well as the beliefs, feelings, and attitudes that have coalesced to form their current stance toward their children and the children's other parent. These characteristics present challenges to treatment that the East Group must address. The chapter then examines thoughts, behaviors, and actions that have led to the favored parent's actions, conscious or unconscious, that pull their children closer to them and away from the other parent. In particular, the chapter examines the work done in the group that challenges distorted thoughts and memories and opens up the possibility for alternative points of view and change. This examination includes the specific structured psychoeducational tools used, including metaphorical stories, challenges to cognitive distortions, exercises to enhance parents' ability to cope with triggering thoughts, lessons in managing strong feelings and shielding children from them, active listening and communication, and strategies to increase openness to change. Also examined is the use of role play to create an alternative view of another person and a map for changing behavior, as well as the use of parent coaching for interventions with children and the coparent.

2. DESCRIPTION OF FAVORED PARENTS

While parental alienation can occur with either parent, favored parents are typically mothers[2]. There are many explanations for this disparity. One pertains to social and legal history in the United States. The "tender years doctrine" emerged in late 19th-century family law with the presumption that children under the age of 5 should be in their mother's primary custody. Unless a child would be placed in serious jeopardy through awarding custody to the legally favored parent, the "paradigmatic custody rules at play until the late 20th century allowed the courts to determine the result [of placement of children after divorce] by reference to broad legal norms which favored the mother for custody of young children" (Pruett & DiFonzo, 2014, p.156). Gardner (1998) hypothesized that as time came to be more equally shared between parents, the alienating parent would become more likely to be either parent, and the gender difference would abate. Other authors have posited additional reasons why mothers are more likely to become the favored parent (e.g., Cannon, Schooppe-Sullivan, Mangelsdorf, Brown, & Sokolowski, 2008; Ganoung, Coleman & McCaulley, 2012). These include the importance to mothers of maternal role identity, maternal self-esteem's being more directly connected to maternal role, and fathers' ceding child management to mothers. , studies have shown that spending less time with the father, combined with a mother's view of the father as not competent and interparental conflict, results in more restrictive gatekeeping (Austin, Fieldstone, & Pruett, 2013). Thus historically different parent–child attachments based on gender, high-conflict coparenting with resultant pressure on the child to align with one parent, and the differential in parenting time all currently favor the child's having a closer, although not necessarily healthier, relationship with the mother.

Warshak (2015) notes that the father is the alienating parent in about a third of alienation cases. He states that it is a fallacy in the current perception of alienation cases that children never unreasonably reject mothers and presents data demonstrating that they do. Overcoming Barriers programs have certainly seen cases of rejection of the mother where the father has played a major role in the alienation. However, in our OCB camp samples these are only approximately a fifth of the cases (Overcoming Barriers, 2012).

With respect to personality characteristics, favored parents range from those whose emotional health is compromised by factors occurring during the marriage and breakup (e.g., humiliating separation, intense marital conflict, ineffective coparenting, or a high level of divorce-related litigation) (Kelly & Johnston, 2001) to those with treated but pervasive mental health issues (e.g., bipolar disorder, anxiety, or depression) to those with severe personality disorders. The extensive OCB intake process attempts to screen out families where parents have active and untreated mental health issues. However, many parents in the East Group present with significant personality-based characterological issues that interfere with their perceptions of and actions toward their children and coparent. A study by Gordon, Stoffey, and Bottinelli (2010) showed that alienating parents tend to use more narcissistic and primitive defenses and have poor reality testing compared with rejected parents and other high-conflict parents. Chapter 5 reviews in greater detail the literature on personality traits of parents in high-conflict divorces or separations with parent–child contact problems.

A large number of the favored parents in the OCB sample fit the above description.[3] Their patterns of behavior have generally included a history of long-standing external blame of the coparent; denial of the role of their own actions, thoughts, or beliefs in the family conflict; rigid black-and-white thinking; and other cognitive biases, including memory distortions. For these parents, the structured presentation of material at camp (in verbal, role play, exercise, or media form) provided a container that allowed them to absorb information they had previously not considered or had never heard. Some parents were grateful for new ways to look at their complex family dynamics and were able to accept recommendations and group support to change or at least slightly alter otherwise rigidly held beliefs. Over the years of camp, at least one parent in the East Group had a diagnosis of paranoid or delusional disorder (reportedly resolved before intake), and one exhibited psychotic thinking not previously diagnosed; other favored parents presented with histrionic or borderline personality traits that did not meet diagnostic criteria for the full disorders. This smaller subset of parents in the East Group was more resistant to structured intervention and tended to show little change.

Many types of parents engage in parental alienating behaviors (for a review of these behaviors and their correlates, see Chapter 2). Most believe they are protecting their children from an unfit or frankly dangerous parent. Favored parents self identify as the more capable and responsive of the two parents and as the parent who provides for most of the children's needs and is exquisitely attuned to the children's feelings. It is essential in the OCB screening process to distinguish between justified concerns about the rejected parent and the favored parent's conscious or unconscious desires to rid the child of the rejected parent. Causes of justified rejection include severe negative or abusive parenting, significant intimate-partner violence, and impaired parenting (Fidler, Bala, & Saini, 2013). In these cases the child's rejection is reasonable by definition, given the circumstances. Cases of severe justified rejection are not accepted into the OCB programs.

Common features shown by alienating parents in our sample include self-preoccupation, emotional dysregulation, a high level of mistrust, manipulation, parentification of the child, enmeshment with the child, lack of stable relationships generally, and a highly conflictual relationship with the coparent. They show a lack of understanding of their actions and a lack of empathy for their children's place in the family dynamic. Denial of any involvement in the children's rejection of the other parent is pervasive. Most alienating parents are conflict-engaging and are not able to let go of the other parent completely, or they have a new partner with whom they have created a new family where the rejected parent is seen as an intrusion that has no place.

These characteristics are similar to those found in the literature on alienation. For example, Garber (2011) discusses parentification, which he describes as a "pathological parent–child role change" in which "the parentifying adult enlists the child to fulfill his or her need to be cared for" (p. 324). These parents do not want to be alone. They need their children to stay with them, ignoring the children's needs or desires for growth and independence. Some parents enlist the child in a peer- or partner-like role in the process Garber describes as "adultification." These parents turn to their children much as they would an adult friend. They search for validation, make their children into allies in a war against the other parent, engage their children in dialogue about the other parent, and have the children carry messages to the other parent. Garber (2011) notes that parentification and adultification can "compromise the child's health and development" (p. 324), and research shows the negative effects of role reversal on children's long-term development (Johnston, 1990; Manzi, Vignoles, Regalia & Scabini, 2006; Mayseless & Scharf, 2009). Thus these processes are critical targets of treatment.

Other favored parents present as unable or unwilling to tolerate their perceived abandonment in the marriage (Sauber & Worenklein, 2013). These parents communicate the resultant feelings of depression, anger, or anxiety to the child, who may then identify with some of the favored parent's feelings. These parents are unable or unwilling to shield their children from their feelings and incorporate the child into their dependent stance. Many of these hyperprotective parents feel fearful and anxious. They believe they have experienced severe intimate-partner violence and do not want to be in the same vicinity as their respective coparents. Since severe intimate-partner violence has been ruled out in the screening process, these parents experience disabling and excessive worry in the absence of real threat. Their anxiety involves dysregulation in the physiological, affective, behavioral, and cognitive arenas. This group of parents is easily triggered by the anticipated presence of their children's other parent, whether in coparenting sessions or in meetings with that parent and the children. Their difficulty in regulating their anxious affect and their lack of self-soothing skills are apparent to their children and OCB staff.

Other favored parents show behavior that is motivated by revenge and fury. They are rageful, see only their point of view, and express frankly paranoid ideation about the alienated parent. These intensely hostile favored parents view the other parent as harmful. They are the favored parents who are most likely to engage in repeated allegations of abuse against the other parent despite through investigations finding no abuse (Stahl, 1999).

Almost all parents in the favored parents' group have little or no relationship with their coparents. Many report they last saw the coparent in the courtroom or during a transition of caretaking that resulted in a domestic disturbance. These parents do not value working together with their coparent. Their feelings toward their coparents range from disdain and pity to anger, distrust, and fear. They see no useful purpose that OCB camp can achieve and many reject the work there, at least initially. On initial screening, most of these favored parents have difficulty identifying even one strength of their coparents; some say they cannot identify any strengths. They fail to recognize that a hostile and conflicted coparenting relationship is obvious to their children and puts the children in the position of having to choose between two warring parents. Although some favored parents come to the OCB program with a parallel parenting relationship (Stahl, 2000), communicating in writing by themselves or through a parenting coordinator, they do not appreciate the ways in which this absence of any positive contact and outward hostility toward the other parent has a potential negative effect on their children.

The favored parents in the OCB program have engaged in a variety of thoughts, behaviors, and actions that may be considered parental alienating behaviors. Baker (2005) identifies five general strategies used by alienating parents, and Fidler, Bala, & Saini (2013) combine these strategies, as well as actions identified by Baker and Darnall (2006), into eight groups:

- bad-mouthing the other parent (e.g., portraying the other parent as dangerous, mean, or abandoning);
- limiting or interfering with the other parent's parenting time (e.g., moving away, arranging activities during a scheduled time with the rejected parent, or giving the children a "choice" as to whether or not to have contact);
- limiting or interfering with mail or phone contact with the other parent (e.g., blocking, intercepting, or monitoring calls, texts, or email);
- limiting or interfering with symbolic contact with the other parent (e.g., never mentioning the other parent, removing or not allowing photographs of the other parent, or changing the child's name);
- interfering with information (e.g., refusing to communicate with the other parent, using the child as a messenger, or not giving the other parent important school or medical information);
- emotional manipulation of the child (e.g., withdrawing love, inducing guilt, interrogating the child, or rewarding the child for rejecting the other parent);
- unhealthy alliance with the child (e.g., fostering dependence or having the child spy or keep secrets); and
- miscellaneous behavior (e.g., bad-mouthing to friends, teachers, or doctors; creating conflict between the child and rejected parent; or interfering with child's counseling).

Almost every favored parent in the East Group has engaged in most if not all of these strategies. Moreover, at the beginning of OCB programs, every favored parent in the East group either does not view any of these behaviors and actions as harmful to the child,or denies they are occurring. The parents in the East Group can be defined as "restrictive gatekeepers" (Austin, Fieldstone, & Pruett, 2013) who marginalize, denigrate, and refuse to communicate with the other parent; adhere to a rigid parenting-time schedule (if there is any contact at all); and limit the child's opportunity to develop a relationship with the other parent.

The primary motivation to change among favored parents at OCB programs is external, whether through a court order, an unfavorable custody evaluation, or the recommendation of a parenting coordinator. They feel powerless and trapped in a system that they believe cannot understand their view of their children's needs. They enter the OCB program with very little if any ambivalence and often will do what they can to, in the words of many favored parents, "get through" the program with as little disruption as possible. A subset of these parents may violate OCB rules, which all family members are expected to follow (see Chapter 7). For example, they may make excuses to see their children after bedtime, or they give their children cell phones to contact them when no cell phones are allowed. It is difficult for most of these favored parents to tolerate the separation from their children, and many find ways to let their children (and the staff) know this. Many regularly express concern about the children's experience in sleeping away from them, with other children and a counselor in a cabin, despite hearing from the counselors that the children had engaged with their bunkmates, played cards or games, and gone to sleep. Others express concern at being kept away from their children for too long (while engaged in East Group activities) and that their children will be worried about them.

The East Group parents are therefore caught in a bind, having the "loyalty" and closeness of their children but facing consequences meted out by the court. When they successfully engage with members of the team at camp, they initially try to convince therapists and staff that they are at the program in error and it is the child's other parent who needs all the work. They view the other parent as creating multiple problems, both by past behavior and by current actions within the legal system, and thus pushing their children away. Placing external blame is the predominant presentation of these parents. Moving beyond external blame to accepting some level of responsibility for the current family situation is essential but extremely difficult for members of this group. At least initially, members of the East Group believe that their children favor them because of their exquisite attunement to their children and their ability to listen to and react to their children's needs. The children reject the other parent, in contrast, because of that parent's inability to understand their needs as well as other actions toward the children. (Sometimes these concerns are partially valid.) Transforming blame to acceptance of some personal responsibility, understanding the harm being done to their children, working on emotional regulation, and identifying many cognitive and memory distortions are all essential work for these parents.

3. GROUP INTERVENTIONS WITH FAVORED PARENTS

East Group interventions and afternoon coparent and parent–child interventions focus on getting the favored parents to view their family situation through a child-focused lens. While all East Group parents assert in a myriad of ways that their focus *is* on the children, the reality is that all of them, at some period of time, are self-focused, frightened, and anxious; insistent that their children (sometimes as young as 9 or 10 years old) know what is best for themselves; and convinced that the other parent is at best incompetent and at worst a danger to the children's health and safety. Interventions in group are geared toward refocusing these parents on their children's needs through education (through oral, written, and visual information), role play (putting themselves into their children's or the rejected parent's place), reworking what their children do and do not need (e.g. rewriting the narrative script for their children in conjunction with the work of their coparents), taking responsibility for their part in the current dynamic, understanding the effect of litigation and hostility on their children, and learning a variety of modes of self-regulation.

3.1. Structure and Format

The East Group is initially very structured. Group leaders listen to and try to understand the family story of each member, identifying common themes and common challenges. Structure established by group leaders, such as setting a specific time for each member to speak and intervention to bring past material into the present, helps members stay on task as well as containing group members' affect, which is often dysregulated and could overwhelm either an individual group member or the entire group. Any challenges by the group leaders to a participant's thoughts and perceptions are gentle but direct. Too strong a challenge may lead to a defensive reaction, shame and embarrassment, and withdrawal from participation. Too indirect a challenge will simply be not understood and therefore ignored. Transparency in group leaders' challenges to favored parents is therefore essential. East Group members have little trust in the legal system and by extension the camp. Group leaders must be clear, honest, and direct in any challenges to group members' distorted cognitions or dysregulated affect to keep an alliance with each group member. It is also essential that the leader convey a sense of empathy and understanding.

Ideally, a co-therapist team facilitates the East Group. Co-therapy serves several functions. First, the therapists are able to model collaboration and problem-solving in the way they interact with each other. Second, one therapist can provide a valuable reality check when the other is facing strong internal reactions or bias that may interfere with an objective assessment. Third, the co-therapy model allows group members to react to the two therapists without any possibility of splitting between the therapists, who consult each other before and after each group. Members of the East Group are exquisitely attuned to any form of rejection. The group leaders must constantly observe their own feelings toward group members, address any negative feelings first with colleagues, and be certain their interventions are based on an empathic connection and attempt to help rather than to engage in counterrejecting behavior. Lapses early on in the group can easily result in empathic failure such that the individual group member affected often quickly rejects the group leader. It is essential that the group leaders not be susceptible to a split in which a group member sees one leader as good and the other as bad. The group situation has a great potential for splitting, which would likely mirror the polarized split in the family system. Structure, gentle challenges, empathic connection, and transparency form the initial first steps in group meetings.

Like the children's group and the group for rejected parents, the group for favored parents consists of a three-hour meeting each morning. The clinical team meets before each group meeting to allow for incorporation of information about any events or critical incidents that occurred the previous afternoon and evening. As noted above, groups function best with two leaders. This arrangement is essential for management of group process in a highly charged environment where more than one member may have needs that cannot be contained within the group setting. (For example, if a member becomes distressed and leaves the group, one leader can go with that member in an attempt to calm her or him and help bring the member's issues back to the group.) The clinical team meets after each group to plan the afternoon interventions as well as at dinner to discuss what transpired during each intervention and plan the evening's activities around further interventions that may be necessary.

3.2. Goals

The initial tasks of the East Group are to help group members understand the purpose of and rules for the group and to discuss confidentiality as it pertains to the group. This discussion is aimed at getting all members to feel that group can be a protected space where they need not worry that their thoughts will be shared outside the group setting. While there is no guarantee that members will abide by their commitments to group confidentiality, there has never been a violation of this agreement in the OCB programs. Group members often find commonalities and validation in one another's stories, and this experience facilitates group cohesion—an identified form of therapeutic action in group psychotherapy (Yalom & Leszcz, 2005).

Group rules include maintaining civility within and outside group. Civility with the coparent is stressed as a model for children to observe as well as an important working model for behavior beyond the OCB program. Group members are told that they must act in ways they may not believe in and that in early behavior change it is expected that actions may not feel completely comfortable but are nonetheless necessary to facilitate the next stages of learning. Members are told that if individuals are able to act consistently in a certain manner, they are more likely to incorporate these actions into their belief systems. After discussion of group rules and confidentiality, a short video is shown and discussed to emphasize the nuances and potency of words, setting the stage for the next steps in the group work.

The essential components of the East Group interventions include the following objectives, which we will describe in greater detail in the following sections:

- defining and reframing parents' goals;
- eliciting the family narrative, with a focus on family dynamics, to help parents identify problem areas and move forward;
- addressing cognitive distortions;

- providing psychoeducation about memory and suggestibility;
- enhancing parents' skills for coping with triggering thoughts and strong feeling;
- identifying how thoughts and feelings can lead to inaccurate and entrenched beliefs;
- learning and practicing active listening and positive communication;
- understanding appropriate adult–child boundaries and how to shield children from parental feelings;
- improving parents' understanding of the harm children suffer when triangulated in parental conflict and the importance for children of a nonhostile, civil coparenting relationship;
- identifying alternatives to litigation and building "buy-in" for use of these alternatives; and
- emphasizing the importance of a cohesive and coordinated aftercare team.

3.3. Defining and Reframing Goals and Objectives

Each East Group member states his or her individual goals and goals for his or her children, which are written on flip charts. Over time and with exposure to the OCB program, members add to and refine their goals. The objective of this exercise is to help members cognitively reframe objectives that keep parents locked in litigation of interparental conflict and shift parents to more solution-focused goals (Lebow, 2003). Goals that have been added by some group members include "a better working relationship with my coparent," "having the children get back to being children," "getting out of the court system," and "looking at some of my contribution."

3.4. Eliciting the Family Narrative

The family narrative is elicited in the East Group through family drawings. The purpose of this exercise is to understand each parent's conception of the current issues while allowing the group therapist to comment on family structure and needs for change moving forward. Parents are instructed to draw a picture of everyone she or he considers to be in the family. Group leaders add that this is not an exercise in artistic ability but do not offer further explanation. Each parent explains through the drawing the history of her or his family relationships and how she or he has come to be at the OCB program. Eliminating the verbal explanation of family dynamics often allows a different and less constrained view to be shown: Drawings are thought to be generated from specific areas of the right brain and to access a more emotional perspective than left-brained statements using words do (Edwards, 1999). Moreover, since East Group members have not thought about the purpose of the drawing before putting marker to paper, the results tend to be the favored parent's unfiltered view of the family.

Who parents include and omit from the drawings is discussed in detail in the group. Some parents have put grandparents in the picture in place of the children's other parent; others have drawn a blissful family scene from early days that does not reflect the current reality. A significant number of members of the group leave out their children's other parent. The parent's perspective of closeness to or distance from different family members is discussed. East Group parents usually draw themselves and their children as a unit, with other adults and children (nieces, nephews, close friends) at varying distances away from this unit of favored parent-children... Explanation of the drawing and family history provides a description of boundaries within the family, identifies other family members who have been cut off, and gives an emotionally based overview of the family dynamic. The favored parents' views of their coparents are also discussed in group (whether or not the rejected parent is included in the drawing).

This exercise offers group leaders a concrete opportunity to challenge aspects of a parent's perspective that conflict with stated goals, to bring up issues such as protection and overprotection, and to discuss how one might think about each of these. This process is also useful for beginning to separate out the favored parent's views from the child's views, which are usually merged before the family comes to camp.

3.5. Addressing Cognitive Distortions

Work with inaccuracies in thinking, or cognitive distortions, in the East Group borrows from cognitive–behavioral theory about the relationships between cognitions, emotions, and behavior (Beck, 2011) and from more recent writing that applies this model to parent–child contact problems (Garber, 2015). There are always significant levels of cognitive distortion in group members' perceptions of family history as well as the current situation. These distortions are due to a variety of factors, including personality difficulties and mental health issues, reinforcement of the distortions by others who hear only the favored parent's perspective, and misperception of children's statements when filtered through the favored parent's negative perceptions of the other parent.

Cognitive distortions are addressed in the East Group with the intent of changing the distorted perceptions. Common distortions among East Group members include the following:

- *All-or-nothing or black-and-white thinking.* In this form of distortion, thoughts, feelings, events, and actions are seen as falling into only two categories. There is no nuanced thinking. Group work is designed to help people catch this type of thinking (in any arena) and apply this skill to the realm of coparenting and parent–child dynamics. Parents are asked to think of examples of their use of all-or-nothing thinking. Typical examples among the favored parents include "The other parent is *all bad*," "The children *never* have a good time with the other parent," and "The other parent was *always* at work." When parents in the East Group maintain that their thoughts or feelings are accurate, the group leaders, and often other group members, challenge them as to how they, as "good" parents, were able to manage in these types of situations. Often group members are able to acknowledge that their thinking may not be accurate. However, unless continually challenged, these same members continue to deny that this thinking creates any problems. Most members learn not to use all-or-nothing terms in the group; however, they continue to express themselves this way in the camp milieu, where they may be gently queried about these distortions by staff or at times by other parents.

- *Overgeneralizing.* In this distortion, a negative event is seen as exemplifying a pattern that is always true. Role-playing exercises to deal with overgeneralization include taking on the role of the rejected parent when others make only negative attributions. The member who is labeled this way is often able to share how overwhelming negativity distorts who they really are. (This exercise also deals with the cognitive distortion of *labeling*.)
- *Emotional reasoning.* In this distortion people assume that how they feel accurately reflects how things really are. A pervasive example of this distortion in the East Group can be expressed as "I feel anxious about my child's being with the other parent; because my anxiety is real, something bad must be happening." East Group members affected by this distortion interrogate their children to find times when the children may have felt nervous, call their children at the other parent's home to make certain they are OK, or talk to their children directly about how they must have felt frightened when a particular event occurred. Emotional reasoning is a particularly destructive distortion in these group members who view the other parent as toxic, view their feelings as accurate, and communicate their negative and fearful feelings to their children.
- *Blaming.* In this distortion parents focus all negative feelings and thoughts on the other parent. Common statements are "The other parent never loved the child; it is his [or her] fault that the child is not seeing him [or her]" and "The other parent never understood the child; she [or he] must accept responsibility for never being connected and must understand why the child doesn't want anything to do with her [or him]."

Other examples of cognitive distortions common in East Group members include discounting any positive qualities in the other parent, focusing on "what ifs" (e.g., "What if the other parent is driving recklessly?" or "What if the other parent is ignoring the child's needs?"), and inability to disconfirm (rejecting any evidence that might contradict their negative thoughts).

Cognitive distortions that interfere with the favored parents' ability to view their situation more accurately are addressed in group, subject to challenge by the group leaders, and role-played to get the parents to understand how these thinking errors lead them to be stuck in one position, including continued litigation or the possible loss of their children.

3.6. Psychoeducation About Memory and Suggestibility

Favored parents believe their memory is like a video recorder and is 100% accurate. This position is inconsistent with scientific understanding of how memory functions (Schacter, 1997). Leaders in the East Group explain how memory is fallible and subject to reconstruction, how perceptual errors occur, the power of expectation, and how memories can be tainted. Because group members are extremely defensive, multimedia presentations are often more persuasive about the malleability of human memory than words are. For example, group leaders may discuss the example "Lost in a Shopping Mall," which presents research demonstrating that anyone can be influenced to believe that something that did occur did not (Loftus & Pickrell, 1995). Significant discussion focuses on the possibility that their own and their children's "memories" are not 100% accurate and the implications of this possibility. Many favored parents are persuaded of (if shocked by) the unreliability of eyewitness testimony, yet have a difficult time applying this to their own situations.

3.7. Improving Coping with Triggering Thoughts and Strong Feelings

East Group members are often internally fragile despite how they present to the outside world. In the group, they are asked to identify the strong feelings (e.g., anger, fear, or sadness) they experienced in a specific situation related to their current family context. They are then asked to identify the thought that triggered the feeling. One group member stated that prior to the divorce, whenever she returned home after leaving the children with their father, the homework was never done, the house was a mess, and the children were "bouncing off the walls". She would become angry and tell her husband how many times she had reminded him to make sure the children did their homework, to clean up, and not to give the kids sugar. This memory triggered her anger, and she recognized that she thought of her then husband as lazy, thoughtless, and deliberately setting her up for failure. She also recognized that the connection between her intense anger and her thoughts that her then husband did all this on purpose was unwarranted and that he was not out to harm her. The group was able to role-play the situation with different endings, each resulting in more emotional control by the mother and a different outcome of the situation.

3.8. Approaching Change by Dealing with Thoughts, Feelings and Beliefs

Favored parents start the East Group believing that the children's other parent must change but seeing no reason why they should change anything about themselves. Their almost universal mantra is: "Everything is fine with my child. Everything is fine at home. The only problem is that my ex wants the child to do something the child doesn't want to do. It is all my ex's fault." Consistent with the group's cognitive–behavioral framework, leaders teach that a person's interpretation of an event determines how that person thinks and feels about it. Thoughts and feelings are described as reciprocal, with thoughts creating feelings (internal experiences of emotions), and feelings creating thoughts ("I am anxious; therefore my coparent must be dangerous"). Thoughts and feelings lead to beliefs, which can become stuck and rigid, producing certain behaviors. The group goes through exercises of identifying thoughts, feelings, and behaviors in particular child-related scenarios. Group members are then asked to identify events that support or do not support the conclusions they have come to about the scenarios and whether they might need further information to validate those conclusions. Imaging techniques are used in the group to help members contemplate change.

3.9. Learning Active Listening and Positive Communication

Most favored parents have not been successful coparents. They enter the group asserting they are excellent at communicating with their children. They believe they are able to understand their children's needs and anticipate their children's desires, particularly with regard to the other parent. However, many members see no value in communication with the other parent. They say that the coparent was never around, never cared about the child, was self-absorbed, was angry all the time, could not be trusted, was frightening to them, or was frightening to the child. Rarely does an East Group member believe there is a need for positive communication with the other parent. When challenged, most members report that communication through email or text is tolerable but that nothing more direct would be acceptable.

To address these issues, the group practices active listening, including such skills as restating, summarizing, reflecting, "I" messages, redirecting, and silence. The group also practices recognizing and stopping the use of communication blockers (National Aging Information & Referral Support Center, 2005) such as why questions, advising, digging for information, [and] interrupting (Scheingold, 2003). Group members break into dyads and role-play active, attentive listening to their partners. When the whole group reconvenes, leaders give members a scenario in which the rejected parent tries to talk with them about the child's refusal to visit. Willing group members try to use the tools they have learned to listen to the "rejected parent" rather than shut down communication. They are encouraged to practice the active listening tips with their children when they next see them at a camp event and to imagine what it might be like to actively listen to the other parent. They also are encouraged to try these skills with the other parent at camp if the opportunity arises. Later they report back to the group any successes or difficulties with the task.

3.10. Understanding Adult–Child Boundaries and How to Shield Children From Parental Feelings

Favored parents often believe they have adequately shielded their children from their own feelings. They believe they hide their anxiety, hostility, or frustration well. They tend to think that the other parent has overshared information with the children or said negative things about them to their children. They readily agree that sharing too much with a child is a problem but do not see this as a problem they contribute to. They believe the information they share is for the children's benefit. Favored parents are surprised to learn, often from the camp milieu staff, that some of their children feel burdened by being asked to be messengers or to read court documents. Many are surprised to hear that their children worry about their favored parent's intense feelings. One of the ways these problems are addressed in East Group is through role plays of parent–child dyads. Discussing the children's feelings about exposure to legal documents or negative or anxious feelings about the other parent, often incorporated by the child's exposure to the favored parents words or actions, can help parents understand the burden their children may carry.

Another component of the work in the East Group is setting boundaries around the favored parents' interactions with their children. Each day, parents are given an outline of the day's schedule, noting the specific times when they will be able to spend time with their children. Many favored parents feel they do not have enough time with their children and would prefer to do every activity with them. Leaders tell the group when the children will be in proximity to or engaged in a group activity with the rejected parent (e.g., parallel group activities for children and rejected parents occurring near each other such as cooking, in spaces separated only by a door between rooms, or group hikes for children and rejected parents together). Favored parents often voice anxiety about being kept from their children or about the fear (projected from their own psyche) that their children may feel in the presence of the other parent. Leaders reassure members about the careful planning of each activity, the number of clinical staff involved, and the attention paid to the safety of all participants at camp. Any issues about the safety, protection, and emotional comfort of the children are discussed with a view to helping each member understand the opportunity for a shift in their children's relationship with the other parent inherent in the camp environment. The favored parents are encouraged to support the activities in the camp milieu that are designed to promote the children's gradual desensitization to the parent they have rejected. The favored parents also are challenged to allow the rejected parent to have whatever degree of closeness the child permits. The camp rules and structure become part of a systemic intervention that shifts the favored parents' views so that most see camp as a safe and protected environment for their children, one that interrupts the isolation and restrictions that have surrounded the favored parent–child system.

Afternoon work with the favored parents may include having them use scripted interventions either to encourage contact with the children's other parent in the safe and therapeutically supported environment of camp or to participate in creating a shared narrative that both parents share with the children. Some favored parents are able to accept and work with this challenge, while others, unable to support the work, prefer to withdraw from such activities. At times, a favored parent has been unable to allow contact between the child and rejected parent to occur and either has informed staff of the harm the favored parent believes the

proposed interaction will do to the child or, on a few occasions, has directly sabotaged the designed activity.

Over the course of the OCB program, most favored parents come to appreciate
both the careful planning and execution of the interventions aimed at reconnecting the child with the rejected parent and the importance of those interventions
for achieving that end. Some favored parents are able to support, directly and in
a planned manner, the steps in this reconnection. Other parents remain neutral
but acknowledge the safety of the environment provided by the OCB program.
By the end of camp, almost all favored parents express gratitude for this safe and
supportive environment. They also express fear at having to leave the OCB program and venture into the "outside world," where such total support is not available. Transitioning the families to appropriate aftercare is a challenge and requires
group as well as individualized family discussion.

3.11. Understanding Effects of Conflict on Children and the Importance of a Nonhostile Coparenting Relationship

Most favored parents do not think they are harming their children. They believe
it is the child's other parent who is putting the child in the middle by "dragging
us to court." East Group parents express their wish to avoid the court process as
well as to allow the child to have a say about contact with the other parent. If these
two goals could be accomplished, most favored parents state, the children would
no longer be in the middle of any conflict. Favored parents are very sensitive to
any intimation that they are causing their children harm. Most have been exposed
to these allegations from the other parent and have felt the need to defend themselves with stated and written counterarguments. Once someone has taken a position in court and in writing, it is very difficult to disengage from that position.
Although group leaders show powerful video clips of adolescents who have been
caught in the middle of their parents' battles, most favored parents have difficulty
believing their own children feel the same way as the ones in the clips. In the view
of most East Group parents, the fault for conflict rests solely with the other parent; most group members are unwilling to examine the possibility of accepting
any responsibility for harming their children. Most often, they will realize their
responsibility in aftercare, if at all.

As previously noted, most East Group parents say that the other parent has little
value to the child as well as to themselves. This other parent is viewed globally as
negative in all parts of life. The favored parent has bad-mouthed, denigrated, and
vilified the other parent. They have rarely seen this parent outside a courtroom
since the separation or divorce, and their interactions have been almost all negative. However, when forced to spend time with their respective coparents, which
happens at every afternoon intervention at camp, many favored parents begin to
realize that they have engaged in black-and-white thinking. With careful instruction and guidance by their morning-group therapists, many come to view their
coparents through a slightly different lens. Favored parents who stated during

intake that they would not be able to sit in a room with their coparents not only appreciate the coparent work they do at OBC camp but also ask for more coparent meetings. Many come to see the other parent as having some value in the child's life and as someone with whom they may need to work long term. This shift in thinking comes about through the psychoeducational groups, the hard work of the coparenting interventions, and the support and praise parents receive when any therapist or staff member observes them being civil to their coparents. Further, children often let counselors or parents know of the tremendous relief they experience when they shift from hostility to civility toward the rejected parent.

Thus a shift in the coparenting relationship has inherent extrinsic rewards. It is unfortunate that prior to camp most of the coparents did not have the experience of trying to work together in any format, because therapists and attorneys often support their clients' stated view that one of the parents is afraid of being in the room with the other. Camp staff stress the importance of the emerging coparenting skills for aftercare, whether with a parenting coordinator or with a family therapist.

3.12. Identifying Alternatives to Litigation

Favored parents, having been ordered to camp, are generally displeased with their judge, their attorney, or the legal system. Many have been labeled as alienating parents, some with judicial findings to this effect—a label that East Group parents vehemently deny. These parents thus have tremendous motivation to find an alternative to the legal system, which they now experience as punitive. At the beginning of the first group meeting, it is not uncommon for someone to raise a concern about confidentiality. Group leaders use this concern as an opportunity to discuss alternatives to litigation as well as note their coparents are hearing the same information. Members of the both parent groups learn, there are many downsides to court involvement (Sullivan, 2008). These include the legal system's adversarial stance and accompanying polarization, the win–lose mentality, and the depletion of family resources.

There is often enthusiastic discussion in the group about taking control of the children's parenting back from the court. However, reframing this concern to include both parents is difficult. Identifying the pros and cons of litigation is very informative. Most favored parents agree that litigation reflects the most negative aspects of the separation or divorce. These same parents may have made allegations in court that the child's other parent was neglectful or abusive. Within the group it is not uncommon to hear cons of litigation such as that it is unpredictable and fosters parents' sabotaging and blaming each other Discussion of alternatives to the legal system, by contrast, elicits positive feelings expressed as hopes of "being a real parent again," "having more control," "being able to plan," "working together as coparents if possible," and "focusing on the child." While finding the possibilities generated by alternatives to litigation to be more positive, group members are able to see the court's value in ensuring accountability and in monitoring. They discuss the use of coparenting strategies to help themselves and their children restore some normalcy after the chaos of the months prior to camp.

3.13. Emphasizing the Importance of a Cohesive and Coordinated Aftercare Team

One function of the OCB program is to provide consultation about how best to assemble an effective team for aftercare and, in the case of East Group parents, to motivate them to agree to a trial period for aftercare following camp. Favored parents vary in their beliefs about aftercare. Most do not come to OCB camp with the conception of an aftercare team. Many East Group members have an individual therapist who has supported them in their beliefs about the other parent and may have written to the court on their behalf. Some members have a second therapist who may be a domestic violence advocate or someone they see with their children. Parents who have a therapist or advocate who supports their belief system want this person to remain involved in their care. If the child's therapist is supportive of the child's having no or minimal contact with the other parent, favored parents want that person to remain in place as well. Occasionally, favored parents come to camp with a family therapist or parenting coordinator in place. Often this person has encouraged them to attend camp and is therefore seen in a negative light.

Most favored parents, however, do not understand how a treatment team would benefit them or their children. While some group members recognize that the camp team (a group therapist for each parent and the children's therapists) has been very helpful to the family, these parents are concerned that they will lose the neutrality and child-focused approach they have experienced at camp after they leave the program. When the pros and cons of having a parenting coordinator are discussed, they often become more receptive to this idea, since they want to take control of parenting back from the court and they now recognize (to varying degrees) their old approach has not worked. Many favored parents are also receptive to family therapy when they understand that the therapist will work with dyads, triads, or the whole family as needed. Many leave camp with an agreement with their coparents to try working with an aftercare team., OCB tries to carefully select an aftercare team skilled in working within the family systems model. At time OCB is not able to specify the specific team members but will specify the types of skills necessary for each team member. Most favored parents do not want to relinquish their supportive therapists, a challenge for aftercare providers.

The biggest challenge to writing and getting support for aftercare agreements is overcoming parents' disbelief that an aftercare team could be supportive, neutral, and child focused. Favored parents often express skepticism about the value of aftercare or the possibility of a cohesive treatment team because of past experiences with therapists' becoming polarized in the family dispute—one of many challenges inherent to treatment with court-involved families (Greenberg & Sullivan (2012), Greenberg, L.R, Doi Fick, L. & Schnider, R. (2012), see also Chapter 5 of this volume). Although favored parents may acknowledge that clinicians at camp supported them without taking sides, they do not believe this will be true of therapists they see after camp. It is difficult to reassure this population, who have been through many failed attempts at some form of therapy, that a team approach with open releases for team members to speak with one another could be an answer to their family's difficulties.

Though many parents leave camp with an agreement for a systemic team approach to aftercare, this agreement can fall apart during postcamp litigation. The most successful cases are those where the parents accept the OCB approach as beneficial to each of them and enter the realm of therapeutic work with court involvement only for oversight and accountability.

3.14. Group Closure

Rituals and closure are an extremely important part of the last group meeting. Usually most East Group members have established close relationships with one another, although at times psychopathology in individual group members can interfere with group cohesion. In this final meeting the leaders and the group members offer one another feedback about their experience at camp, give one another advice, and discuss their struggles about leaving. Group members' advice to other members can be surprisingly sage, given that some of those offering advice cannot recognize that they would be well advised to take it themselves. Whether because of the group structure or some shift that has occurred within group members over the course of camp, the blame, externalization of the problem, and refusal to accept any responsibility that were initially present are notably absent from this final meeting. Group members look at their initial goals and often recognize that these were self-focused and did not incorporate the entire family. For some members, however, there is no change. Group members are able to celebrate the successes some parents and families have had at camp and respond with appropriate sadness and frustration to those group members who have not made progress. Group leaders stress to members the importance of engaging with the aftercare team as soon as possible, using the OCB clinician assigned to their family as a bridge, and, perhaps most importantly, that they must expect some regression from the progress made at camp before full commitment to an aftercare team is established.

4. LIMITATIONS AND FUTURE DIRECTIONS

While a systemic treatment model is essential for families where children are rejecting a parent after separation or divorce, some aspects of the OCB camp structure are not ideal. For example, there are both benefits and limitations to separating favored and rejected parents into distinct groups. On the one hand, this separation leads to rapid connection among group members and fosters group cohesion, which then leads to more productive group work. On the other hand, this separation can lead to polarization between the two groups, mirroring the adversarial system that has been detrimental to forward progress so far. Overcoming Barriers has therefore begun integrating the groups more at the beginning of camp and in educational meetings. This change appears to have some positive effect on the past polarization. Though the camp milieu provides opportunities for parents in each group to view those in the other group as less toxic than they have been represented by their respective coparents, additional opportunities to mix the groups may encourage more accurate assessments.

Another limitation of the OCB camp is that involvement with the families, although intensive, is relatively brief; camp typically lasts five days and has been shorter. While learning and shifts in behavior are evident both within people and between parents during camp, it is difficult to know if these changes will persist when the families move into the outpatient arena. Although initial feedback from family members is usually very positive (Sullivan, Ward, & Deutsch, 2010), understanding the program's longer-term impact is an abiding goal. Program evaluation (see Chapter 13) has been in place for three years but does not yet offer a large enough sample to permit assessment of long-term effectiveness.

The cost of the OCB camp is an obstacle for many families. The one-to-one ratio of clinicians and staff to parents and children makes the operation of intensive programs very expensive. However, without 24-hour, day-and-night support it is unlikely that families would feel that OCB camp is a safe and secure environment in which to do the necessary work. Overcoming Barriers is working on getting grants and raising funds to bring down the cost per family.

The dynamics of the interactions between particular families and the group have also been problematic. If one family member, whether a child or a parent, often expresses very negative thoughts in group, these thoughts can result in contagion to the whole group. Although lead clinicians process the contagion as it occurs, and some contagion is inevitable, better screening may rule out families who are too rigidly wedded to their negative belief systems. Similarly, if a family member has severe pathology, other group members may be pulled in the direction of the pathology. For example, when at least two members of East Group are certain their children have been physically or sexually abused (despite these "certainties'" having been investigated and determined to be legally unfounded), other group members may begin to question whether they have missed something similar with their own children.

The more OCB is able to learn from the families in the program and from ongoing research, the more changes we can make to create stronger and longer-lasting outcomes for families in need.

NOTE

1. There is no consensus in the professional literature as to what language most accurately describes each of the parents involved in a situation where there is a parent–child contact problem and parental alienation. Terms such as *favored*, *aligned*, and *alienating*

parent are often used interchangeably, even though doing so may conflate different case dynamics. Despite the inadequacy of any single term, in the interest of clarity this chapter uses the adjective *favored* to describe the parents at OCB with whom children have regular contact and do not resist visitation or have contact problems.

REFERENCES

Austin, W. G., Fieldstone, L., & Pruett, M. K. (2013). Bench book for assessing gatekeeping in parenting disputes: Understanding the dynamics of gate closing and opening for the best interests of children. *Journal of Child Custody, 10*(1), 1–16.

Baker, A. J. L. (2005). A qualitative study of adults who experienced parental alienation as a child. *American Journal of Forensic Psychology, 23*(4), 41–63.

Baker, A. J. L., & Darnall, D. (2006). Behaviors and strategies of parental alienation: A survey of parental experiences. *Journal of Divorce and Remarriage, 45*(1/2), 97–124.

Beck, J. (2011). *Cognitive behavior therapy: Basics and beyond* (2nd ed.). New York, NY: Guilford Press.

Cannon, E. A., Schooppe-Sullivan, S. J., Mangelsdorf, S. C., Brown, G. L., & Sokolowski, M. S. (2008). Parent characteristics as antecedents of maternal gatekeeping and fathering behavior. *Family Process, 47*(4), 501–519.

Edwards, B. (1999). *The new drawing on the right side of the brain.* New York, NY: Putnam Books.

Fidler, B. J., Bala, N., & Saini, M. (2013). *Children resisting contact post-separation: A differential approach.* New York, NY: Oxford University Press.

Ganoung, L. Coleman, M. & McCaulley, G., (2012). Gatekeeping after separation and divorce. In L. Drozd & K. Kuehnle (Eds.), *Parenting plan evaluations: Applied research for the family court* (369–398). New York, NY: Oxford University Press.

Garber, B. D. (2011). Parental alienation and the dynamics of the enmeshed parent–child dyad: Adultification, parentification, and infantilization. *Family Court Review, 49*(2), 322–335.

Garber, B. D. (2015). Cognitive-behavioral methods in high-conflict divorce: systematic desensitization adapted to parent-child reunification interventions. *Family Court Review* 53 (1) 96 – 112.

Gardner, R. A. (1998). *The parental alienation syndrome* (2nd ed.). Cresskill, NJ: Creative Therapeutics.

Greenberg, L.R., Doi Fick, L & Schnider, R (Hon. Ret.) (2012). Keeping the Developmental Frame: Child-Centered Conjoint Therapy, *Journal of Child Custody,* 9, 39 – 68.

Greenberg. L.R. and Sullivan M. J.(2012). Parenting Coordinator and Therapist Collaboraton in High Conflict Shard Custody Cases, *Journal of Child Custody,* 9 82–107

Gordon, R. M., Stoffey, R., & Bottinelli, J. (2010). Findings of primitive defenses in alienating parents. *American Journal of Family Therapy, 36*(3), 211–228.

Johnston, J. R. (1990). Role diffusion and role reversal: Structural variations in divorced families and children's functioning. *Family Relations, 39*, 405–413.

Kelly, J. B., & Johnston, J. R. (2001). The alienated child: A reformulation of parental alienation syndrome. *Family Court Review, 39*(3), 249–266.

Lebow, J. L. (2003). Integrative approaches to couple and family therapy. In T. L. Sexton, G.R. Weeks, & M. S. Robbins (Eds.), *Handbook of family therapy.* New York: Brunner Routledge.

Loftus, E. F., & Pickrell, J. E. (1995). The formation of false memories. *Psychiatric Annals*, *25*, 720–725.

Manzi, C., Vignoles, V. L., Regalia, C., & Scabini, E. (2006). Cohesion and enmeshment revisited: Differentiation, identity and well-being in two European cultures. *Journal of Marriage and Family*, *68*, 673–689.

Mayseless, O., & Scharf, M. (2009). Too close for comfort: Inadequate boundaries with parents and individuation in late adolescent girls. *American Journal of Orthopsychiatry*, *79*, 191–202.

National Aging Information & Referral Support Center. (2005). *Aging I & R/A tips. Tip sheet 1: The art of active listening* [Pamphlet].Washington, DC: National Association of State Units on Aging.

Pruett, M. K., & DiFonzo, H. J. (2014). Closing the gap: Research, policy, practice and shared parenting, *Family Court Review*, *52*(2), 152–174.

Schacter, D. L. (1997). *Searching for memory: The brain, the mind and the past*. New York, NY: Basic Books.

Stahl, P. M. (1999). *Complex issues in child custody evaluations*. Thousand Oaks, CA: Sage.

Stahl, P. M. (2000). *Parenting after divorce*. San Luis Obispo, CA: Impact.

Sauber, S. R., & Worenklein, A. (2013). Custody evaluation in alienation cases. In Amy J. L. Baker & S. R. Sauber (Eds.), *Working with alienated children and families: A clinical guidebook* (pp. 47–70). New York: Routledge.

Sullivan, M.. (2008).Co-Parenting and the parenting coordination process. *Journal of Child Custody*, *5*.(1/2) 4–24.

Sullivan, M., Ward, P., & Deutsch, R. (2010). Overcoming Barriers Family Camp: A program for high conflict divorced families where a child is resisting contact with a parent. *Family Court Review*, *48*(1), 116–135.

Warshak, R. A. (2015. June). Ten parental alienation fallacies that compromise decisions in court and in therapy. *Professional Psychology: Research and Practice*, *46*(4), Aug 2015, 235–249.

Yalom, I., & Leszcz, M. (2005). *Theory and practice of group psychotherapy* (5th ed.). New York, NY: Basic Books.

9

"West Group"

Group Interventions for Rejected Parents

MATTHEW J. SULLIVAN ■

1. INTRODUCTION

The "West Group" at the Overcoming Barriers (OCB) camp is made up of the parents with whom the children are resisting contact. In the most favorable circumstance found among these parents and children, they have some regular parenting time and the parents are implementing the court-ordered sharing of custody, but the child is expressing negative attitudes, beliefs, and emotions (e.g., fear, anxiety, or anger) and demonstrating increasing patterns of resistive conduct toward the parent. Resistance may be active or passive and may include having constant contact with the favored parent when with the rejected parent, not transitioning from the favored parent, or transitioning back early from the resisted parent, among other variants. In more challenging cases, the parent has had no contact with the child for a long period, sometimes years, and the resistance has been unchanged by mental health and legal interventions. For these cases, the referral to camp is a "last chance" intervention to determine the viability of a shared custody arrangement,[1] to determine whether an intensive intervention can facilitate contact with the child, and to address the multiple factors that have contributed to this entrenched situation.

Rejected parents approach their experience at camp with a range of expectations. Some hope that camp will be a "miracle" that will reunite their children with them and result in a healthy shared-custody situation. Other parents expect that someone will finally do something to successfully intervene in the alienating conduct of their coparents, who they believe are the sole cause of their children's rejection of them. Finally, some rejected parents, feeling hopeless after years of unsuccessful struggle in the courts to reconnect with their children, are simply grateful for the opportunity to have a shared experience with the children.

This chapter will describe the characteristics of West Group members that frame the daily group interventions with them at OCB camp. First, the chapter will describe the common beliefs, feelings, and attitudes that organize the rejected parents' responses to their situation. Next, it will explore how the group process challenges these limited narratives to foster opportunities for progress and change. This includes establishing the group as a safe laboratory for rejected parents to explore and practice different approaches to engaging with their children and coparents. Finally, the chapter will describe techniques used in group, including psychoeducational components and in-the-moment coaching of parenting and coparenting skills that the rejected parent will practice throughout the camp experience. This work prepares group members for a series of structured and supported experiences with family members both in the camp milieu and in clinical interventions

2. CHARACTERISTICS OF WEST GROUP MEMBERS

Our experience with the 30 or more families we have worked with in OCB camp over the last several years is that roughly 80–90% of the rejected parents are fathers. Rejected mothers have tended to (a) have older teenage children; (b) have left the spousal relationship, after which the remaining parent felt betrayed, rageful, or desperate but helpless to change the situation and engaged the children in their outrage; (c) have had some type of serious mental health or substance abuse issue or have allegedly abused their children (with or without clear substantiation), after which the children resisted or cut off contact and that dynamic became entrenched; or (d) be in some combination of these circumstances. The gender difference in parent–child alignments is likely due to many factors, including historically differential attachments in the parent–child dyads, with stronger (though not necessarily healthier or more secure) mother–child bonds than father–child bonds; differential percentages of parenting time, with mothers playing greater roles in primary caretaking and residential situations; and high-conflict coparenting that creates pressure to align with a more primary parent. Moreover, by the time families are referred to intensive interventions, this high-conflict coparenting has usually been exacerbated by significant adversarial court involvement and ineffective or even harmful mental health interventions.

The gender homogeneity in the West Group has both negative and positive implications for group process and camp interventions. On the minus side, shared elements of the members' narratives tend to reinforce a sense of victimization by the legal and mental health system (i.e., feeling that mothers receive preferential treatment in the courts). Left unchecked, this tendency could unwittingly maintain rejected fathers' preoccupation with blaming their coparents. The solidarity that derives from shared narratives also can lead to polarization and an adversarial relationship between the West Group and the East Group (for favored parents)—an "us versus them" mentality. This situation is counterproductive in that it mirrors and can reinforce the intrafamilial dynamics that have entrenched the child's resistance to contact with the West Group parents.

We find that this dynamic has been softened when we have had at least one mother among the rejected parents in the camp. Stepparents, who are often included in the camp experience, can have a similar mitigating effect on these gendered obstacles to progress.[2] Regardless of group constitution, steps need to be taken to coach and direct rejected parents to connect positively with favored parents in the camp milieu and to build relationships across the potential "divide" in the coparenting relationship to bridge and humanize the experience of aligned and rejected parents.

On the plus side of the West Group's gender homogeneity, their shared experiences increase the potential for fathers to identify with other fathers. Fathers develop strong supportive relationships with one another during camp. The commonalities in their experiences with their children, their coparents, and the courts act as an antidote to the isolation of what they often have felt to be unique and horrific personal experiences. West Group fathers often become "foxhole buddies" whose compassion and empathy for one another's painful situations support their individual work at camp. West Group members tend to build deep bonds with one another that often endure beyond camp.[3] They routinely exchange email addresses before leaving camp and continue to correspond with and provide support to one another as they move into their more hopeful but still uncertain futures with their children and coparents.

Despite the fact that almost every West Group parent comes to camp with the perspective that he (or occasionally she) was a good parent whose malicious coparent turned his children against him, we have found that West Group members *always* have contributed to their children's rejection and have a responsibility to do individual work if the family situation is to change. Because rejected parents function on a continuum of parental competence, from highly attuned and skillful to neglectful and abusive (with most parents falling somewhere in the middle), it is critical to have some accurate information about their psychological functioning prior to their arrival at camp. The staff responsible for the OCB intake process work hard to obtain as much information about family members as possible, reviewing legal documents and custody assessments and interviewing mental health service providers and family members themselves. One function of obtaining this comprehensive intake information is to rule out rejected parents with serious, unmanaged mental health issues or active substance abuse or addictions. If the rejected parent has perpetrated domestic violence, child abuse, or both, that can be a reason to exclude the family from involvement in the camp.

A common problem in this intake process is that information about the rejected parent from custody evaluations (if they have been conducted) and the courts may not be accurate. For example, an evaluation may focus, legitimately and validly, on the restrictive gatekeeping and alienating behaviors of the favored parent and determine (with the court concurring) that the child's rejection of the other parent is due solely to the favored parent's alienating conduct. Sometimes the parenting behavior of the rejected parent is not even assessed. During the many days and hours of camp, where campers are observed in varied settings, the clinical and milieu staff get a fairly informed sense of the parenting strengths and weaknesses of both East and West Group members, often more accurate than what was derived from a custody evaluation protocol or previous outpatient treatment.

Rejected parents typically arrive at camp after enduring an arduous and costly legal struggle to compel their coparents and children to attend. The stakes are therefore high for rejected parents, who often consider camp their last chance to save their relationships with their children; it is not uncommon for them to cover all of the costs of camp to remove that obstacle to family attendance. Rejected parents often arrive at camp with both high hopes and skepticism that any change can occur. The court may have told them that if the camp intervention is unsuccessful, the court may or will change custody, possibly awarding it to the rejected parent. This message from the court can lead to motivations and conduct in the rejected parent that are contrary to the goals of the camp, which are to explore the viability of shared parenting moving forward and to work to reconnect the rejected parent and child. The rejected parent may "play both sides of the fence" because of crosscurrents of motivation ("If the camp fails, I can go back to court to request a change in custody; if the camp succeeds, there is a hope of normalizing a shared-custody arrangement"), affecting their involvement throughout the intervention.

Managing rejected parents' unrealistic expectations is a constant issue in the clinical work at OCB camp. They come into the program hoping for a miracle and have a variety of problematic reactions to the inevitable disappointments in their moment-to-moment camp experience: frustration, anger, blame, despair, and desires for staff to call out and punish the favored parent. Ironically, this dynamic tends to become more problematic as progress is made, because having a taste of the desired connection with the child after so much disappointment and failure can create more hope and build unreasonable expectations for progress during camp. These feelings can lead the rejected parent to push the staff or the child too hard and too fast to connect with eachother, with the result that the child's resistance to connection increases.

The rejected parents' perspective about their children's rejection tends to be narrowly and externally focused. Their blame of the coparent for the problem is the most significant obstacle to change. The rejected parent puts considerable energy into convincing everyone in the camp (staff and other parents) that the favored parent is the problem—is malicious, manipulative, playing a game, and so on—and that the child 's response is just an extension of the favored parent's attitudes and behaviors toward the rejected parent. Since there is usually evidence that the rejected parent's claims about the favored parent's contributions to the child's rejection are at least partially valid, either from past verification (e.g., custody evaluations, feedback from mental health professionals, or patterns of alienating behavior) or from the parent's own behavior at camp, it is crucial to help rejected parents move beyond assignment of blame and its derivatives (e.g., not taking responsibility for personal change, working to align OCB staff with their perspectives, or acting in hostile manner toward their coparents). West Group work emphasizes challenging rejected parents' overreliance on blame and shifting them to other approaches for dealing with the favored parents' contributions to the parent–child contact problem.

Accordingly, West Group interventions refocus the rejected parents on what *their* work is and what *they* can do to improve the situation moving forward (while reinforcing that work is being done with the other parents on what their contributions are and what work they need to do). The critical work with the rejected parents lies in challenging them with evidence, both historical and in the ongoing camp experience, of their parenting, coparenting, and interpersonal strengths and deficits and in helping them shift from victimization—helplessness and projection of responsibility for change on others—to more active and adaptive coping with their difficult family situations.

3. DESCRIPTION OF THE WEST GROUP INTERVENTION

The West Group meets daily after breakfast for three hours, with a midmorning break. This group meets at the same time as the group for favored parents (East Group) and the children's group (Common Ground). The West Group has two group leaders, which is essential for adequate management of the group process (e.g., managing a group member who becomes upset and abruptly leaves the group). We have used both a co-therapist model with two experienced clinicians and a model where one clinician is an "understudy" involved in more practical support during the group.

The first task of the group leader[4] is to orient the group members to the group experience and to set the parameters for effective group work. Confidentiality is discussed as it pertains to the group. The leader explains the importance of having a safe context to share personal information in and how maintaining the confidentiality of the other group members is essential to that safety and protection. In our experiences at OCB camp, when asked to abide by a commitment not to share personal information outside the group, all members have made that commitment.

In addition to this parameter, a number of rules about camp involvement are presented and discussed with the group. Rules are framed in terms of how to get the most out of the camp experience to minimize resistance and foster investment in the therapeutic process. The rejected parents' ability to follow these behavioral directives is a significant prognostic indicator for a positive outcome. If a parent cannot learn to follow these rules (even with the intensive support of camp staff), the likelihood of reconnection with the child is low. There are two main categories of directives:

1. *Conduct vis-à-vis the coparent.* The West Group parents are directed to call the other parent their "coparent" from now on (not "my wife," "my ex," "him," "her," and so on). This terminology is consistent with building a more businesslike and respectful coparenting relationship during camp. The rejected parents must respect the personal boundaries of their coparents at camp, even if they do not agree with the rationale for those boundaries, and must not initiate direct interaction with their coparents

without guidance from the clinical staff. This directive is particularly important when the coparent has made allegations of domestic violence, whether substantiated or not, in the past. West Group parents are directed to be impeccable in their respectful conduct toward their coparents in all camp interactions. We ask that they refrain from bad-mouthing the coparent to anyone at camp, and we impress upon them that any attempts to share negativity about the coparent with the staff, other parents (favored or rejected), and children in the camp to enlist and align them in vilifying the other parent will be counterproductive to their goals.

2. *Engagement with their children.* The West Group members are told to follow the directions of clinical and milieu staff with respect to their proximity and approach to their children. Engagement with the children at camp is a delicate, well planned, and supported process unique to each family situation. Rejected parents are instructed from the moment they arrive at camp that they must be aware of and respectful of their children's personal space (which is different for each parent–child dyad) and must engage with the child only with the direction and coaching of staff. An important psychoeducational message involves understanding parent–child connections in a broader context than just direct interaction. There are a range of connections that have an impact on the goal of reconnection, from the least engaged (being at camp together and having an enjoyable family experience) to having varying degrees of proximity in the same "field" (in the dining hall, at "Circle"— the daily all-camp gathering before dinner—and at all other camp activities) to having parallel involvement (competing on opposing teams, doing a craft activity, watching children play, or going on a hike with a group) to having increasing degrees of direct involvement in the milieu (instantaneous interaction in a fast-paced game or sustained interaction while playing table tennis or a card game) to the intense engagement of parent–child interaction in a clinical session.

The West Group parents are educated about how the clinical interventions and milieu experience work together at camp and form a template for continued progress in reconnection in aftercare. West Group members are directed to participate in the camp milieu fully and passionately. Though the rejected parents' understandable focus is on reconnecting with their own children, engaging enthusiastically in the milieu by making connections with staff, other parents, and other children (who have more positive connections with their children) and by participating in camp activities creates indirect "bridges" of connection to their children. Put simply, by making positive connections with everyone in camp, they increase the possibilities for connection with their children.

The West Group parents are instructed to follow the lead of camp staff, who will create and provide supported experiences in the basic structures of camp intervention, implementing the powerful combination of a positive family experience in the milieu and focused clinical interventions. The group leader introduces this intervention strategy at the outset of the group, explains why we construct the camp experience around these two basic components, and then works with the rejected parents for the rest of camp to exploit the benefits of this experiential–clinical intervention model. Since parents typically do not appreciate the power of the experiential component of the intervention at first, efforts to increase their appreciation (and conscious exploitation of the connections with their family members that occur in the camp milieu) are a primary, ongoing focus of group work. Even if these parents have reasonably good parenting skills, significant coaching (described in section 4 below) is necessary for them to be effective in rebuilding a connection with their children and coparents.

The importance of parents' "compartmentalizing" their engagement in the milieu and in the clinical interventions is a critical lesson at camp and for after-care. The basic formula is to maximize enjoyment and manage and minimize neg-ativity (avoidance, conflict, opposition, etc.) during parenting time and to avoid any engagement during parent–child contact that involves processing or dis-cussing the difficulties in the relationship unless it concerns management of the immediate situation. That aspect of relationship building is reserved for clinically supported forums (parent–child dyadic therapy and family therapy) and includes addressing past issues and ongoing debriefing from and preparing for scheduled parent–child contact at camp. If we can educate West Group members in this model and give them some successful experiences implementing it while at camp, this increases the likelihood that they can continue to make progress in aftercare.

4. ESSENTIAL COMPONENTS OF THE WEST GROUP INTERVENTION

The objectives of the West Group intervention are

- to elicit each group member's narrative and then use that narrative to build group cohesion;
- to build confidence in the group leader so that group members believe that the therapeutic team has knowledge and experience that they will bring to bear on supporting the best interests and goals of each member;
- to build working alliances between each member and the leader and between group members; and
- to provide psychoeducation about the common components of the members' problems.

These objectives support the following clinical goals for the West Group members:

- having reasonable expectations for progress and change,
- broadening their perspectives on how change will occur by working on change in the coparenting relationship,

- reconnecting with their children,
- having alternatives to court involvement, and
- assessing existing mental health interventions and designing an effective aftercare plan.

Psychoeducation relevant to these goals and objectives is presented in group and then applied during camp, with intensive, coordinated support. The West Group becomes a safe, supportive context in which to prepare for and debrief from the intensive experiences group members are having in the other components of camp.

4.1. Eliciting the Narrative

Each West Group member takes some time (20–30 minutes) to share his (or her) personal history, how the relationship with his child and coparent has deteriorated, the family's history of legal and psychological interventions, what the current situation is, and what his goals are for the camp. This structured sharing of common experiences builds trust and intimacy among group members. It allows the group leader to establish the role of manager of the group process by keeping each member's narrative on track, limiting some members' desire to push beyond the time parameters, and to use the narratives to challenge aspects of members' perspectives that are obstacles to achieving their goals. The systemic diagram (see Figure 2.1 [this volume]) kept on the wall of the meeting room is a useful psychoeducational tool for working with common themes and broadening group members' understanding of their situations to create more opportunity for change.

Parents come into West Group with a range of perspectives on the history of their relationship with their children. Some state that the relationship was close and positive and that they were shocked when it deteriorated, gradually or abruptly. These parents say they are unaware of any precipitant of that change other than that they came to believe subsequently that the coparent caused the shift in the child's attitudes. Other parents report having had a close and positive parent–child relationship until some dramatic and negative incident caused a breach in the relationship. This event could have been a harsh, perhaps verbally or physically abusive, response to the child's oppositional or defiant behavior. These parents can acknowledge some contribution to the child's negativity but feel that the rejection is significantly disproportionate to that contribution and are at a loss for how to repair their breach with the child. Still other West Group parents acknowledge serious past problems in the parent–child relationship as a result of the child's past (sometimes years ago) exposure to domestic violence, their substance use, their mental health issues, or their poor parenting practices. The perspective of these parents is that they have addressed these concerns personally but the child will not forgive them for their past transgressions.

There is always some degree of distortion in group members' narratives, either because they represent only a partial perspective or because of the parent's personality pathology and the reinforcement of the parent's distortions by significant

others, children, attorneys, evaluators, consultants, treating mental health professionals, or other individuals. The more distortion in a West Group member's narrative, the more challenging the work with that parent will be.

The West Group leader challenges parents to be honest about their historic
contributions to the child's rejection (regardless of other contributors), stresses
that the initial step in connecting with the child is to acknowledge their responsibility for the child's response, and prepares the parents to address this obstacle.
Regardless of the history of the parent–child relationship, the rejected parent now
has to deal with the reality of trying to reconnect with a child who opposes that
reconnection. That current reality, regardless of the causes of the child's rejection, puts the parent in a very difficult parenting situation. Parents require help to
acquire the skills needed to manage the reconnection, even when the history of
the parent–child relationship was objectively positive until the rejection (Moran,
Sullivan, & Sullivan, 2015). The leader educates West Group parents about these
formidable challenges and coaches them in implementing those essential parenting skills during camp. Group support of the work between the child and rejected
parent at the camp is described in sections 4.5 and 4.6 below.

Another universal theme among the West Group parents is that the favored parent has undermined, damaged, or even destroyed the relationship between the child
and the rejected parent. Statements such as "My attorney has told me that this is the
worst case of parental alienation he has ever seen" are common. Often the court, in
ordering the family to attempt OCB camp, has made a finding that the favored parent has engaged in alienation and has sometimes weighed a custody change. The
West Group parent typically vilifies the favored parent as "the" problem and does
not trust that the favored parent's participation in the camp intervention will have
any positive impact on the child's rejection. If the favored parent has stated that he
or she is supportive of the camp's goals, the West Group parent has no faith that this
pledge is anything other than further manipulation and deceit. When describing
their coparenting relationships, West Group parents share stories of campaigns of
denigration and malice against them, often including false allegations of physical
or sexual abuse or domestic violence that have been found to be unsubstantiated
after being investigated by the authorities and evaluators and addressed in court
hearings. Rejected parents state that the coparent, who has substantial or sometimes all of f the parenting time, does not share any information with them about
the child and makes unilateral decisions about the child's health, education, and
other matters, eliminating them from any meaningful parental involvement. This
marginalization of their parental role happens despite court papers that more often
than not provide for shared legal custody. Rejected parents have in common extensive histories of court involvement encompassing the most adversarial processes in
family court, often including custody evaluations, custody hearings, trial, criminal
contempt proceedings, and more. The court involvement with the coparent has
reinforced their view that the favored parent is an enemy and adversary. Finally,
West Group parents describe histories of failed coparenting interventions, from
counseling to parenting coordination, and place responsibility for these failures
exclusively on the coparent's conduct.

A central focus of West Group work creating a less adversarial and more functional coparenting relationship. Group members are challenged to engage their coparents in a respectful, businesslike relationship moving forward. The concept of "parallel parenting" (Fidler, 2012; Ricci, 2013; Sullivan, 2008) is introduced and discussed in group, including the principles that stress shared involvement in decision-making, information exchange, and communication guidelines and protocols appropriate for high-conflict coparents (Arizona Chapter of the Association of Family and Conciliation Courts [Arizona AFCC], 2011; Eddy, 2014; Sullivan, 2014). Parallel parenting is an attractive idea for rejected parents who have felt very disenfranchised in their coparenting experience, and buy-in to adopt this model and practice it in camp is easily obtained. The notion that building a more functional bridge in the coparenting relationship is an essential component of reconnecting with their children tends to increase rejected parents' motivation to undertake this difficult task, despite their distrust of and anger at their coparents.

The West Group members are only at the OCB camp because of successful court involvement. Since nearly all families who attend camp have been ordered by the court to do so, these parents come to camp with a view that court involvement has been the only effective process in addressing their problem. Many are pleased that their coparents have finally been identified as engaging in alienation; it validates their perspective on who is to blame and satisfies their desire for retribution for the coparent's perceived malicious conduct. They express satisfaction that the court has finally given them an experience of empowerment in the midst of an otherwise pervasive experience of victimization. Because this is a common attitude among West Group members, they fail to appreciate the downsides of court involvement and the appropriate role for the court moving forward.

The group members' narratives about court involvement validate the court's determination (usually only after considerable investigations from child protective services, family court evaluations, multiple court hearings, and review of interventions) that a shared custody arrangement is in the child's best interest as a critical starting point for moving forward. With this determination clearly articulated by the court, the mandate that the OCB camp program will work to reconnect the rejected parent and child is essential to the family member's expectations about goals for the camp program and for aftercare. The West Group leader validates this mandate as a positive result of court involvement from an accountability standpoint but also challenges group members to shift their energy and resources into therapeutic interventions with an accountability component even as the court continues to monitor and oversee compliance and progress.

The leader explains the rationale for shifting away from court involvement in the future by stressing that court involvement has many downsides. Table 9.1 lists opposing characteristics of litigants and coparents that explain why continued court involvement is antithetical to building functional coparenting and so works against the goal of shared parenting time (Sullivan, 2008). Put simply, litigants don't make good coparents, and staying involved in the legal-adversarial context for any purpose other than oversight and accountability will likely continue the pressures on the child to align with the favored parent.

Table 9-1. CONTRASTING CHARACTERISTICS OF LITIGANTS AND COPARENTS

Litigants	Coparents
Representation by attorney–advocacy	Self-representation–parenting
Distrust	Trust
Sabotage of coparent	Support of coparent
Win or lose	Give and take
Chaos	Structured flexibility
Avoidant and crisis oriented	Proactive and plan oriented
Unilateral action	Collaborative action
"In the name of the child"	Child focused
Blame	Problem-solving
Depleted resources	Conservation of resources

4.2. The Essential Role of Parenting Coordination in Aftercare

The presentation of the downsides of continued involvement in adversarial court processes flows logically into a description of the role of parenting coordination in high-conflict cases and how engaging with a parenting coordinator is an essential component of aftercare. The linkage to the court's authority, with the expectation of the court's receiving ongoing feedback about compliance with mental health interventions and progress on mandated goals, provides more accountability than do mental health services without parenting coordination. Having an alternative dispute resolution process for predictable problems in implementing the parents' custody plan, having a specialist to design and implement a parallel-parenting model (with adequate sharing of child-related information through email, coordination of scheduling of parenting time and children's activities, etc.), and having a professional who can coordinate mental health interventions are critical to the effectiveness of these aspects of aftercare (Friedlander & Walters, 2010; Greenberg, Gould, Gould-Saltman, & Stahl, 2003; Greenberg & Sullivan, 2012).

Parenting coordination as an essential role in aftercare is also introduced to the West Group as a resource to continue to support the positive changes in the coparenting relationship that usually occur at camp. Again, very few cases, despite the chronicity and severity of the high-conflict coparenting dynamics, have had effective parenting coordination prior to camp. The group leader explains the role and functions that help the parenting coordinator to structure, support, and provide accountability in implementing a parallel-parenting plan. The role is particularly well received by the rejected parents because they understand that past therapeutic interventions in their situation have failed as a result of a lack of coordination, therapists' becoming aligned, and favored parents' withdrawing their support of therapy (often precisely because progress is being made).

West Group members come to camp with a legacy of failed mental health treatment interventions. The sharing of their experiences with these interventions gives the group leader the opportunity to assess campers' past and current treatment, educate group members about what likely contributed to treatment failures, work with the clinical team on providing a potent experience of effective therapeutic intervention at camp, and contribute to the design of aftercare based on the camp experience. This last role may include developing strategies for addressing current problematic mental health treatment—working to get it back on track, add components, change the providers, or terminate the treatment (Greenberg & Sullivan, 2012). The group leader, who is an experienced forensic mental health professional, gives the rejected parents advice about and assistance in addressing problematic treatment (whether child therapy, reunification therapy, family therapy, or a parent's individual therapy), which might include providing consultation to current therapists if they are involved in aftercare or even encouraging the parent to terminate treatment by a mental health professional involved with the family.

West Group members' stories have several themes in common about the shortcomings of previous and current mental health interventions. One such theme is the provision by inexperienced and poorly trained therapists of ineffective treatment that sometimes does not meet professional standards (Association of Family and Conciliation Courts, 2011; Greenberg & Sullivan, 2012). In child therapy, for example, the therapist may do intake and then treat a child in a high-conflict shared-custody situation without the knowledge, consent, and balanced involvement of both parents; may provide opinions about psycho-legal issues beyond their scope; or may fail to recognize that in times of court involvement, parents can arrange therapy for their children not for child-focused reasons but because of their personal, court-based agendas (e.g., obtaining full custody, relocating, or using the child as a pawn in disputes with the coparent).

In other cases, mental health treatment has been insufficient. Given the complexity and severity of the issues in the families who come to OCB camp, mental health interventions are often inadequate to address the problems in the family system. Problems with having multiple providers without any expectation of or structure for coordinating interventions are not uncommon (Greenberg et al., 2003; Greenberg & Sullivan, 2012). Unfortunately, poorly coordinated treatment by multiple providers can cause multiple problems, including mirroring and thereby reinforcing the high-conflict dynamics of the family that result in the child's rejection of the West Group parent (see Chapter 5). The OCB camp program is an exceptional and unique context for the optimization of effective treatment, in that it provides adequate mental health support, coordination of treatment goals and objectives for each component, careful implementation, review of progress, and reformulation of goals and objectives as needed.

Finally, problems have arisen in many cases when there has been no accountability or support of treatment by the court. Family members are often in treatment involuntarily, so a linkage to court authority to have sufficient accountability for compliance is an essential component of effective treatment (Arizona AFCC, 2013; Sullivan & Kelly, 2001). A common pitfall in the history of these cases is not having treatment court ordered with service agreements that structure the work effectively and have expectations of compliance, as is having effective treatment terminated when it is brought back into the court for review (Greenberg et al., 2003).

4.3. Using the Group to Support Members' Goals During Camp

The focus of the daily morning group can be broken down into work on the relationship with the favored parent (coparenting) and work on the relationship with the child (parenting). The group provides a safe and supportive context for developing new coparenting and parenting skills that are essential to the rejected parents' goal of reconnecting with their children. The beauty of the total camp program is that parents have immediate and repeated opportunities to implement the skills they learn in group in "real life" as they engage in the other components of the program. The working alliances that develop between the group leader and group members and between group members create significant therapeutic leverage to support risk taking by members and change in their perceptions and behaviors as they work in the rest of the program on the challenges of their difficult relationships with their coparents and children. More specific descriptions of West Group work in these two areas follow.

4.3.1. Coparenting Focus
Significant group time is spent supporting the rejected parent's involvement in coparenting sessions, family sessions, and interactions with coparents that occur during the camp experience. Group members use group time to prepare for and debrief from these experiences. The processing of the members' engagement with their coparents brings up intense emotional issues that, when addressed in the group, contribute to their understanding of how they can become triggered by their coparents. The group leader focuses each group member on what is coming up that day in camp with regard to engagement with the coparent and prepares the member to interact more functionally with the favored parent by identifying goals for that engagement. The engagement in question may involve a milieu-based experience or a clinical session later that day.

Milieu-based experiences might include working with the coparent to collaboratively plan a birthday celebration for their child (if the child happens to have a birthday during camp) or working in a session with the coparent to prepare for a joint connection with the child in the milieu, such as sharing a meal together or playing a game in the evening as a family. Coparent clinical work might include a rejected parent's being coached to apologize to the coparent for past violent or emotionally abusive behavior or to acknowledge the impact of continued litigation on the coparent.

The West Group helps rejected parents prepare for all of their coparenting sessions. In every case, the group prepares the parent to work with the coparent on developing a shared narrative to deliver to the child and, if possible, negotiating parenting time after the camp. Preparation might include helping the rejected parent understand the emotional triggers that create reactivity and using role play or peer feedback to practice more functional responses with the coparent. For example, another group member might share how they managed a situation like one the member in question is facing or might play the role of the coparent in a difficult interaction while others observe and critique the other member's responses. The leader may coach members in communication skills that are deficient in the coparenting relationship, such as making proposals or active listening. In debriefing coparenting interactions that have occurred in the camp program, the group has the benefit that the group leader (or staff who provide feedback about milieu experiences between coparents) knows exactly what happened. Thus the debriefing, which might include corrective or critical feedback as well as positive reinforcement for a job well done, is based on accurate information about the rejected parent's behavior in those experiences outside the group.

As a follow-up to education about the principles and implementation of parallel-parenting and parenting coordination work, the leader coaches West Group parents in applying that model in coparenting sessions while at camp. In the group sessions, the rejected parents prepare issues and agendas for coparenting meetings, rehearse how to present those matters in a constructive (nonblaming, present-focused, and child-focused) manner, and practice how to respond to behavior by their coparent that may be emotionally triggering. The subsequent coparenting sessions are processed in the next group meeting, with the group leader and group members offering the rejected parent feedback to help him or her prepare for the next coparenting session. This intensive training in more functional engagement with the coparent at OCB camp creates a foundation that a competent parenting coordinator can build upon in aftercare.

4.3.2. PARENT–CHILD RELATIONSHIP FOCUS
The daily morning group for rejected parents supports their work on building more direct, positive connections with their children. These connections occur in the milieu, where proximity to and engagement with the child is carefully planned based on the unique situation between that parent and child. Some parents are reconnecting after periods of complete disconnection from their children, while others are dealing with increasing negativity and resistance in children who have some connection with them. The parent–child work in the clinical sessions has the goals of addressing the obstacles that drive the child's resistance and creating a plan for connection after camp.

A common initial camp intervention between the rejected parent and child that is supported in the West Group process is an exchange of letters. In their morning group, the children write letters to the rejected parent listing all of the reasons they do not want to have contact with that parent and what that parent would need to do to address these issues. Framing this exercise in terms of communicating the objections they have to reconnecting with the parent already shifts expectations significantly, since the child is now considering opening the door to connection. The children's letters are typically filled with negativity, blame, and distortion. However, the letters usually communicate the children's feelings and thoughts in a reasonably respectful manner, as the children's group leaders have worked hard to set an expectation for the tone. The letters often contain a litany of complaints from the past, which may include allegations of violence, abuse (physical, sexual, emotional, or a combination), or neglect (including not paying enough support to the favored parent) and references to court involvement for which they blame the rejected parent. Some letters address a specific incident that caused the rejection, sometimes acknowledging that the relationship was more positive prior to that incident.

The children's letters are delivered to the West Group, where each parent reads the letter from her or his child and then writes a response, with input from the group. This exchange is often the first contact the parent has had with the child for quite some time and is highly emotional. Group members are supported in reframing what is often devastating and hurtful to receive to something positive (e.g., that in responding to these letters they are getting what they want, which is a connection with their children, and that the intensity of the childrens' negativity suggests a strong emotional connection). As group members work together on their written responses, they are coached to acknowledge the child's feelings, take responsibility for any of the issues that are valid, provide a heartfelt apology for those transgressions, and commit to working on a healthier relationship in the future. With regard to issues they do not think are valid (i.e., significant exaggerations or complete fabrications), rejected parents are coached to state that though they don't agree about what occurred in the past, they understand the child's beliefs and concerns, that it's not likely to be helpful at this point to debate their differing perspectives, but that the parent is committed to not having those issues arise in their relationship moving forward.

The exchange of letters lays the groundwork for the next, more intense connection, which is a meeting between the West Group parent and child to have the child directly express her or his issues and concerns about reconnection to the parent. Again, the group work helps prepare the parent to respond sensitively. This session often requires the rejected parent to apologize for his or her contribution to the child's rejection and make a sincere commitment to move forward in a sensitive and child-focused manner. The emotional intensity of these parent–child meetings can be extreme, and the West Group leader, who is at all the clinical sessions and in the debrief with the group, provides essential support for the parent, who may feel battered and bruised by this experience with their child.

The final way in which the West Group supports the parent–child work is helping parents focus on their connection with their children after camp. Though the camp experience is almost always successful in creating some connection between the rejected parent and the child, we try to have the final clinical connection between the rejected parent and child address the postcamp connection. West Group members use the group to develop proposals for postcamp connections (both in therapy and out) and to prepare for a meeting with their child to explore the possibilities and, ideally, come to some agreement. Like the other clinical connections with their children, these meetings require West Group parents to exercise parenting skill within a very precarious parent–child relationship. The group, including the leader and fellow members, helps parents to come up with reasonable proposals; present them in a sensitive manner; and respond to the child's reactions, engage in negotiation, and manage their expectations (and often their disappointments) without getting emotionally triggered. By this time in the group process, most group members find this support invaluable.

After having a positive set of connections at camp, a father and his 17-year-old daughter, with whom he had previously had no contact for several months, put a plan in place, with the support of camp clinicians, for the two of them to visit several college campuses on their way back home. The coparenting work had progressed to the point where the mother was able to be supportive of this plan, which would give the father and daughter a two-week period of positive connection, centered around an activity that the daughter had a high investment in occurring that summer, prior to their returning to the home situation.

4.3.3. Reconnection Work With the Rejected Parent and Child in the Milieu

In parallel and integrated with the group's focus on the clinical connections between the parent and child, there is a focus on planning positive contact in the camp milieu. This planning involves a progression from indirect to more direct and sustained contact in the camp activities and in arranged parent–child activities (taking a hike, shooting baskets, preparing food, eating a meal together, etc.). When the clinical staff set a goal for a connection between a particular parent and child, the West Group leader announces the plan during that member's group time, and work is done to prepare the parent for that connection. For example, the parent may be coached on skills like working with a resistant child on selecting an activity (a very difficult but essential parenting skill for rejected parents) and on skills needed for successful engagement in the activity. The latter skills may include being mindful of physical contact and proximity, physical approach (greeting and ending the connection), optimal verbal interaction (perhaps none at all), letting the child take the lead, dealing with the competitive element of the activity (if there is one), and handling negativity (Moran et al., 2015).

The group time with the rejected parent after a connection in the camp milieu is used to give the parent feedback to increase her or his understanding of and skill with connections. The group leader receives a full report on the connection, so the debrief can address any distortions the parent may reveal in their retelling and assessment of how things went. An added benefit of the group work is that in processing each group member's experiences in the milieu and in clinical interventions, all group members learn essential knowledge about their common situation and skills for dealing with it.

4.4. Group Closure

When possible, the West Group meets for a short period the last morning of camp. Typically, group members have built considerable camaraderie over the course of camp and are also quite anxious about what the future holds for their relationships with their children. The final group meeting provides a structure for each member and the leader to give final feedback to every member of the group. This group sharing is usually poignant, with members giving one another as much support as they can muster to help with the difficulties they anticipate when they go back home. The group celebrates the triumphs of the more successful reconnections some parents have had and shares the sadness of the reality that other parents have made little progress and are unlikely to have connections with their children in the foreseeable future. Every member gives specific feedback about the progress each other member has made in addressing his (or her) contribution to the rejection by his child and to the conflicted relationship with his coparent.

The feedback session is testament to the significant shifts in perspective, from blame and victimization to personal responsibility and empowerment, that have occurred over the course of camp. This final sharing provides the group leader with an opportunity to reinforce critical messages as members prepare to leave the group, including (a) the importance of keeping the court involved or introducing a parenting coordinator to provide more accountability in both parents' adherence to agreements and court orders, (b) the need to engage the recommended aftercare team as soon as possible (c) the need to connect with the designated member of the Overcoming Barriers clinical team to assure continuity of care, and (d) expecting some regression in the relationship with the child and coparent as part of the transition back home.

For several years of camp, West Group members have exchanged emails to maintain connections beyond the camp experience. Overcoming Barriers staff encourage these ongoing connections, and anecdotal reports by parents indicate that such connections have provided important support to West Group members. One year, the West Group planned a reunion several months after camp to continue to support each member's journey.

NOTES

1. *Shared custody* refers to any arrangement where the child has access to both parents.
2. Stepparents and significant others who live with parents may be invited to camp based on information derived from intake. Their attendance cannot be court ordered, but they often come. They can be very helpful to achieving the family's goals, or they can be a major obstacle to those goals that require significant intervention to overcome.
3. A poignant example of this strong positive group bond is the fathers' performance of the following song to the full camp at the "Big Show" (the talent show on the final evening of camp):

> DAD'S SONG (sung to the tune of the Beatles' "Hey Jude")
> Hey campers, we love you all
> Here at camp we came to have a good time
> Remember, we hold you in our hearts
> Because you are all so beautiful
> Hey campers, let's build a plan

Like the boats we launched into the river
Even if it's hard we must give love a chance
For it is love that makes it better
And anytime you feel the strain
We'll be there with this refrain
We want you to know we're here forever
So let it out and let it in
We should begin
The memories you made will stay forever
Nah, nah nah, nah nah nah nah . . .
Copyright 2010 Overcoming Barriers, Inc. Reprinted with permission.

4. Throughout this chapter, *leader* refers to the co-therapist team.

REFERENCES

Arizona Chapter of the Association of Family and Conciliation Courts. (2013). *Co-parenting communication guide*. Retrieved from AZafcc.org/wp-content/uploads/2013/09/AzAFCC-Coparenting-Communication-guide.pdf

Association of Family and Conciliation Courts. (2011). Guidelines for court-involved therapy. *Family Court Review, 49*(3), 564–581.

Eddy, W. (2104). *BIFF: Quick responses to high-conflict people*. Scottsdale, AZ: High Conflict Press.

Fidler, B. J. (2012). Parenting coordination: Lessons learned and key practice issues. *Canadian Family Law Quarterly, 31*(2), 237–273.

Friedlander, S., & Walters, M. (2010). When a child rejects a parent: Tailoring the intervention to fit the problem. *Family Court Review, 48*(1), 98–111.

Greenberg, L. R., Gould, J. W., Gould-Saltman, D. J., & Stahl, P. (2003). Is the child's therapist part of the problem? What judges, attorneys and mental health professionals need to know about court-related treatment for children. *Family Law Quarterly, 37*, 241–271.

Greenberg, L., and Sullivan, M. (2012). Parenting coordinator and therapist collaboration in high conflict shared custody cases. *Journal of Child Custody, 9*(1–2): 85–107.

Kelly, J. B., & Johnston, J. R. (2001). The alienated child: A reformulation of parental alienation syndrome. Family Court Review, 39, 249–266.

Moran, J., Sullivan, T., & Sullivan, M. (2015). *Overcoming the co-parenting trap: Essential parenting skills when a child resists a parent*. Natick, MA: Overcoming Barriers. Available from www.overcomingbarriers

Ricci, I. (2013). *The coparenting toolkit*. San Ramon, CA: Custody and CoParenting Solutions. Available from www.thecoparentingtoolkit.com

Sullivan, M. J. (2008). Coparenting and the parenting coordination process. *Journal of Child Custody, 5*(1–2), 4–24.

Sullivan, M. J. (2014.) Strategies for working with difficult clients. In S. A. Higuchi & S. J. Lally (Eds.), *Parenting coordination handbook* (pp. 77–92), Washington, DC: Publisher.

Sullivan, M. J., & Kelly, J. B. (2001). Legal and psychological management of cases with an alienated child. *Family Court Review, 39*, 299–315.

10

"Common Ground"

The Children's Group

ROBIN M. DEUTSCH, ABIGAIL M. JUDGE,
AND BARBARA J. FIDLER ■

1. INTRODUCTION

The children who come to Overcoming Barriers (OCB) camp, like those who attend outpatient reunification therapy, do so with great resistance, little hope, and a sense of loss of control. The control they previously felt originated from maintaining their resistant or rejecting stance. Their parents have generally been ordered by the court to attend OCB programs, and the favored parent, with whom they primarily live, has almost always actively fought or strongly resisted the court order. The children are then told they must attend OCB camp. Parents may explain participation at camp to children in different ways. For example, sometimes parents tell children if they do not attend, the favored parent will go to jail; sometimes they are told that they will just have to go through the motions; and sometimes they are told this is a chance to make things better in their family. The explanation they get can inform how children present when they arrive to camp.

This chapter will describe common characteristics of the children in the family system that help frame the work done in the children's group at OCB camp. We focus on the model of using the power of the group to shift perceptions and reframe experiences to create new possibilities. We describe the goals of the psychoeducational groups and the processes and activities that form the morning group work. This work provides a foundation for any parent–child and family interventions that occur throughout the duration of camp and may inform coparenting interventions as well.

The children's group at camp is referred to as "Common Ground," not only because that is the name of the campground where OCB camp originally took place but also because the children are quite literally the primary, and perhaps the sole, source of common ground between their parents (Sullivan, Ward & Deutsch,

2010). This name for the group captures the camp's abiding focus on coparenting, even in the context of high conflict and where dynamics of resistance, refusal, alignment, and alienation exist. We explain the group's name to children to highlight that despite the many areas in which their parents disagree, the entire family is attending camp to address this common ground.

2. THE CHILDREN'S DILEMMAS

Children's refusal to have or resistance to having contact with a parent after a separation or divorce can have complex and multiple origins linked to developmental, psychological, and family influences. These include parenting style, attachment, systemic processes of communication, and the child's and parent's role in the family system. The children in the families we work with at OCB camp are shaped by multiple experiences throughout their life; we must remember and consider that the point in time when we see a child is just that moment in the child's developmental trajectory of adaptation. When litigation has been intense and focused on the child's refusal or resistance to have contact with a parent, the history of parenting and coparenting, the child's role in the family, and their exposure to the details of the litigation shape where the child is, emotionally and psychologically, when he or she arrives at camp.

There is a significant research suggesting that high conflict between parents results in a higher incidence of maladjustment or psychopathology in children (Cummings & Davies, 1994; Deutsch & Kline Pruett, 2009; Grych, 2005; Harold, Shelton, Goeke-Morey, & Cummings, 2004; Johnston, Roseby, & Kuehnle, 2009; Kelly, 2012). Children who are alienated from a parent tend to have more behavioral problems and show poor reality testing, inaccurate perceptions, illogical reasoning, simplistic and rigid information processing, inaccurate or distorted interpersonal perceptions, difficulty modulating intense emotions, and coping deficits (Johnston, Walters, & Olesen, 2005). In addition, children exposed to conflict between their parents, whether it occurs when the parents' relationship is intact or when they are separated, often have more difficult and negative relationships with their parents than do children in low-conflict situations (Buehler & Gerard, 2002; Grych, 2005). When parents are in high conflict, their communication with each other about their children is ineffective, limit setting is often compromised, and they are unable to expose their children to a supportive coparent relationship. Witnessing these confusing processes and the negative expression of emotions often leads children to have poor, ineffective, and inappropriate ways of processing information and regulating their own emotions. Accordingly, our child group interventions focus on two important components: modulation of emotion and accurate processing of information.

Often the children are part of an enmeshed family system where the child receives a great deal of support and responsiveness but must give up some autonomy and ally herself or himself with one parent (or system) hostile to the other to receive the responsiveness the child needs and desires (Minuchin, 1974). In these families it is not uncommon to see one parent who is disengaged, with traits of low demandingness and low responsiveness (Maccoby & Martin, 1983), or authoritarian, with high demandingness and low responsiveness, and one enmeshed parent with high demandingness and high and inconsistent responsiveness. The child is attracted to or coerced by the parent who provides high responsiveness, sometimes inconsistently, no matter what else. Children from disengaged or enmeshed families have higher rates of maladjustment (Jacobvitz, Hazen, Curran, & Hitchens, 2004; Johnson, 2003), which increase over time, than do children from cohesive families (Sturge-Apple, Davies, & Cummings, 2010). The maladjustment we typically observe includes oppositionality—often only in the family context—and anxiety.

As a group, the children who are aligned with one parent and resisting or rejecting the other parent present with many of the same characteristics. They often give trivial or unelaborated reasons for their rejection of a parent. They adhere rigidly to their view of the rejected parent and refuse to openly consider alternative explanations for the rejected parent's behavior or their relationship with that parent even when the claims they make are unconvincing. They repeat their extreme rationales in a way that sounds rehearsed. Often, they extend their rejection to the rejected parent's extended family. These children show little or no ambivalence or guilt when expressing their exaggerated views (Kelly & Johnston, 2001; see also Appendix 2.A in Chapter 2 of this volume).

Often, the children who come to camp have been involved in failed family therapy interventions or have had their own therapists or series of therapists. Sometimes the child's therapist has been part of the family polarization and has supported the child's rationales even when what the child reports runs counter to the therapist's own perceptions and experiences. Often, the individual therapy has not focused on the development of healthy coping skills but has endorsed and supported adaptive but growth-inhibiting and developmentally inappropriate coping skills. As a result, many children reach Common Ground highly skeptical of therapy or even hostile to it. We deal with this fact by validating their past experiences and then expressing our hope to accomplish something different during camp.

Developing skills needed to be a functioning adult is the core concept in therapeutic intervention for children involved in a high-conflict parenting situations (Greenberg, Doi Fick, & Schnider, 2012). In their child-centered conjoint therapy model, Greenberg, Doi Fick, and Schnider (2012) endorse a structure that focuses on

> validating the child's independent feelings, promoting feelings of safety and security, establishing boundaries, identifying and making distinctions among family members' perceptions and emotions, encouraging discussion about specific behaviors and problems, and altering both parents' and children's behavior to promote healthy adjustment in the child. (p. 40)

This perspective informs the key interventions of Common Ground, detailed later in this chapter.

Coping with anger and anxiety through avoidance is one of the major dynamics in the high-conflict families who come to us when a child is resisting contact with a parent. The favored parent, and sometimes extended family, therapists, and others, reinforce the child's avoidance, interfering with the development of competence and confidence. Often there is a family history of anxiety. Because anxiety is often a central issue for the child, in whom it may be covered up by anger, and often an issue for the favored parent as well, it can create a pathway for intervention. We find that the child's anxiety is maintained and intensified by five factors (Vasey & Dadds, 2001):

1. Avoidance, which reduces anxiety but prevents mastery and ensures perpetuation of the anxiety
2. A failure to master and develop competencies in multiple domains, including the emotion regulation skills that would allow the child to tolerate and conquer fears
3. Cognitive biases or distortions that serve to maintain anxiety by focusing attention on anxiety-arousing cues, interpreting ambiguous information as threatening, and leading the child to avoid corrective experiences
4. Actual negative experiences and criticism or rejection from others that arise from the child's lack of competence
5. Overprotectiveness on the part of parents, teachers, extended family, or a therapist that prevents exposure to the anxiety-provoking situation and mastery of fear.

The parent–child dynamic perpetuating this process is that the anxious child pulls for one parent (and possibly extended family and therapists) to protect him or her from the other parent, in response to an incident or pattern of behavior and the favored parent's anxiety and/or substantiation of the child's anxiety, avoids or rejects the second parent, and trains the first and favored parent to accommodate his or her fear, which amplifies the child's tendency toward and reliance on avoidance (Deutsch, 2014; Fidler & Bala, 2010; Garber, 2015). Alternatively, the parent may avoid or express fear or concern about the other parent and lack good affect regulation skills the child imitates the parent with heightened emotion and a disproportionate response. Finding the child's anxiety stressful, the anxious parent may have difficulty calming himself or herself in response to the child's distress and may become irritable, further exacerbating the child's anxiety.

Anxiety in these cases needs to be treated systemically. At camp, everyone in the family is exposed to each other in safe, titrated ways, ranging from minimal exposure while sharing the same space to face-to-face structured interventions. For the children, the goal is to replace avoidance as a functional coping skill with mastery and competence. This requires emotional regulation and accurate cognitive processing. The child must be able to accurately distinguish what is safe from what is unsafe to avoid the unsafe while being able to master what may be uncomfortable but safe.

By the end of our group work, children are facing dilemmas and asking questions like *How do we know what is true? When is it all right to not tell the truth? How do we trust that we can be safe again? How will the legal system intervene and change our lives? How do we integrate new information or changes? Is my parent's behavior fake or a lie?* These questions suggest to us that the children are making distinctions among the perceptions and feelings of different family members, are engaging in autonomous thinking, and are attempting to have more control over their lives.

3. GOALS OF THE CHILDREN'S GROUP

At OCB camp, we focus on children 9–18 years old, broken into two groups when we have a broad age range. The division is based on gender, sibling groups, and developmental status. Typically, we have one group for children from 9 to 13 or 14 years old and one group for children 14 years and older. Like the favored parents (East Group) and rejected parents (West Group), the children meet in group for three hours each morning, with a break in the middle for snack and movement to provide an outlet for and regulation of emotions (Perry & Hambrick, 2008).

One of the goals of Common Ground is to relax, shift, or change an inappropriate or destructive coalition in the child's family. This process begins with experiences that create a path for desensitization to the rejected parent. The path is created by giving the child exposure to the rejected parent in the milieu in nonthreatening ways (e.g., in the same dining space or while playing fast-moving games buffered by the presence of other children and parents). As the camp and interventions progress, the child sees both parents working together in a safe way. In group, we reinforce the camp rules of participation in all activities and cordial and respectful communication. We also help the children manage their anxiety through group processes including identifying thoughts, feelings, and behaviors; learning about cognitive distortions; and participating in problem-solving exercises. Changing one element of a process will not only change other elements but also will promote understanding. As Bronfenbrenner (1979) noted, "if you want to understand something, try to change it." (p. 37).

Boxes 10.1 and 10.2 summarize the goals and objectives of the work done with children at OCB camp. Over the course of camp we seek to decrease the child's fear, anxiety, and anger toward the rejected parent and to improve the parent–child relationship. The latter aim can be satisfied in many ways, from the child's becoming comfortable spending time with the rejected parent to producing an agreement of no contact. In addition, we give the child opportunities to have less polarized, more nuanced views of the favored parent. The ultimate goal is better well-being of the children in the long term.

Box 10.1

GOALS OF COMMON GROUND

- Alter child's polarized, rigidly held view of each parent as all bad or all good into a more realistic, nuanced view based on child's actual experience
- Improve child's well-being

---

4. STAGES OF THE GROUP PROCESS

The first stage of the group work is dedicated to establishing rapport and creating common ground among the children, who enter the group mistrustful and angry at being there. We are attempting to establish a trusting, caring relationship between them and the group leader(s) and among the group members. The leader sets the stage, letting the children know we care about them and want this group to provide a space for them to share thoughts and feelings. Through "icebreaker" activities, the children begin to get to know each other. We establish ground rules, providing the first few and asking the children to contribute more. We describe the ground rules as the basics of respect and cordial communication and explain that they parallel the rules in the whole camp.

In this first meeting, children also describe their families and situations, and we accept their descriptions as we attempt to understand what they mean to the children, who shares their views, and the bases of their views. They each have a story and generally they want to tell it. We ask each child to share what makes his or her family unique and how his or her family is like other families. We may ask who knows the most in their family and how decisions get made. We have the children create lifelines using a piece of wire to depict ups and downs from the beginning

---

Box 10.2

OBJECTIVES FOR CHILDREN IN COMMON GROUND

- Understand child's family, e.g., who is favored and who is rejected and how that came to be
- Understand roles family members play through role play and role switching
- Identify cognitive distortions
- Learn to modulate emotions
- Learn problem-solving
- Become less reactive to rejected parent
- See both parents working together in a safe way

---

to the present. They share their lifelines with the group, often revealing information about the levels of stability and conflict at different points in their lives. This
is an important initial exercise for the children, who become energized by reciting
the negative behaviors and characteristics of the rejected parent. For the remain-
der of the group time, it is a challenge to honor the children's need to tell their
stories and the entirety of the group process without getting stuck in this dynamic.

We also introduce an ongoing project in the first meeting. Each child receives a
cigar box and has access to many art and collage materials. The task, during time
allotted each day, is to create a box that reflects the inside and the outside of the
individual. This project has a few objectives, including making the differences
between the seen and the unseen conscious, using activity to regulate emotion
and make connections, and providing an opportunity for nonverbal exploration
of feelings. One very quiet boy demonstrated his rage with sharp nails sticking out
of the inside of a fully painted black box. Another child pasted words cut out of
magazines inside her box, referring to them as her secrets.

Day 2, and the second stage of the group work, focuses on introducing the children to the relationships among thoughts, feelings, and behaviors; helping them
understand different points of view; and introducing the concepts of cognitive
distortion and selective attention. Using pre-made situations on notecards, we ask
teams of four children each to participate in a role-playing exercise. One child is
the director, two are parents, and one is the child. The children then switch roles to
experience another perspective. In each role the actors are asked what they were
thinking and feeling, including what they were thinking and feeling about each
of the other two actors. They are asked how their thoughts and feelings affected
how they behaved and how their behavior affected their thoughts and feelings.
The role plays lead to discussion about viewing situations from multiple points
of view and how thoughts, feelings, and behaviors influence one another. Often,
this discussion leads to a discussion of "mirror neurons" (how emotions are con-
tagious). Children are asked to recall times with peers when one child was angry
or frightened and how that influenced their feelings. Often a child comes up with
a scenario where there was a potential danger in the child's community, and we
process how they heard about it and how the frightened person's rate of speech,
body posture, and tone of voice changed. We ask how the child felt when that
person looked frightened, and how it affected the child's thoughts, feelings. and
behaviors. After the role plays, it is often a good idea to bring in some short videos illustrating compassion or empathy to generate a discussion about how they
might relate to any of the role play scenarios or the feelings the actors portrayed.
These videos may portray different species of animals or human interactions.

In this second day we also ask the children to write notes to their respective
rejected parents. The note should identify what the child feels the parent must do
for reconnection to occur or what the child wishes would change. The only rule
is that the notes must be written respectfully, though they can certainly include
complaints. By writing about the barriers to connection, the children are considering connection as a possibility. These notes are brought to the West Group (the
rejected parents) for discussion, and the children are told their parents will write

back. The child's note is often the first direct communication a child has had with her or his rejected parent in some time, and it often sends a negative message. However, the next day we return to concepts of empathy and compassion, discussing what it was like for the children to receive the messages from their parents and what it might be like for the parents to receive their messages. This exercise is the first step toward a parent–child meeting where the child is coached and supported to directly share his or her concerns and issues with the rejected parent. The notes also provide a link to discussion of cognitive distortions, memory fallibility, and selective attention using short videos and optical illusions. This psychoeducational approach, moving from experiential and more emotionally laden material to a more intellectual level, allows the children to maintain some distance from their own situations.

On Day 3 we shift the role plays to scenarios scripted by the "director" (one of the children), who directs each of the "actors" what to say and how to behave. We ask each actor what she or he thought and felt and how those thoughts or feelings influenced her or his behavior. Again, asking the actors to shift their roles give them insight into other perspectives and may lead to discussion of selective attention and perceptual errors We continue the practice of switching roles so that each child has the opportunity to be the director.

We then move into the next stage with problem-solving practice. The steps of problem-solving are posted and explained. A volunteer poses a problem, which could relate to something in the volunteer's family or could arise from a current camp experience. The first task the group is given is to shape the problem into something that can be solved. The group then brainstorms solutions; discusses the efficacy of each one; begins the process of eliminating those that are impractical, illegal, or not useful; and finishes by choosing the best solution. During the brainstorming it is not unusual for the suggestions to be strong, exaggerated, and negative at first, followed by more moderate and attainable proposals.

Sometimes the problem-solving exercise leads to an intervention at camp for a specific family or for the camp as a whole. For example, we once had a situation at camp where one child set up a "tattoo" booth where anyone at the camp could get a tattoo except for her rejected parent. The camp director closed the tattoo booth, as the camp rule is that everyone must be included in all camp activities. The child wanted to reopen the booth, so we used the problem-solving model to come up with a proposal and invited the camp director to hear it. The camp director approved the new structure, and the booth was reopened. (This exercise in fact required side conversations between the group leaders and the camp director so that by the time the children came up with a viable solution we knew the child would find success.)

The process of breaking problems down and solving them is tied to the ability to modulate negative emotions, which requires shifting from feeling overwhelmed with emotion to identifying a problem and taking specific steps to solve it. We describe how this process can be a helpful tool for the children to use on their own when they are feeling stuck. We also use this process to prepare children for family or parent–child meetings, so that they can go into the meetings with an idea of how to respectfully propose solutions to their particular parent–child problems.

Day 4, or the fourth phase, is about moving forward as the children leave camp. Sometimes a child has come up with a real problem that he or she would like to solve with the problem-solving steps learned the day before. We may discuss the group experience in general. The children are invited to share their observations of the group and about how each group member may have changed. They are asked what messages they have for the next group of children coming to camp. Every child expresses her or his hopes for each other member of the group. The group leaders participate in this ending ritual in parallel by providing an affirmation to each child, either written on a card or verbally, while giving the child a special stone. A common theme of these hopes and affirmations is confirming the bravery the children demonstrated by opening up their hearts and minds, taking appropriate risks, trying to understand other perspectives, and giving up their well-worn defenses of avoidance and withdrawal. The children note that the group provided support from other kids going through similar situations, that they liked feeling "normal" with "normal kids," that it was reassuring to confirm that everyone has his or her own problems; and sometimes that they felt supported in sorting out what is true and what may be false or exaggerated.

5. CONCLUSION

At the time children enter Common Ground, they are strongly aligned with their East Group parents and strongly resisting or even rejecting their West Group parents. Clinical staff observe and assess the parenting dynamic throughout the camp and ultimately bring it to light with the children and the parents. Specifically, we consider the parenting dimensions of demandingness and responsiveness (Maccoby & Martin, 1983) to understand how parents can assert power. More specifically, we evaluate the extent to which the child is exposed to high demandingness and low responsiveness in an authoritarian parent, low demandingness and high responsiveness in a permissive parent, or high demandingness and high or inconsistent responsiveness in an enmeshed parent. Further, we look into whether inconsistently highly demanding and highly responsive parenting has created a coercively controlling dynamic. (In one enmeshed parent–child relationship, the child was so fearful of violating the favored parent's demands and expectations that she refused to participate in any group relaxation exercise that might reduce her vigilance.) To the extent that the children can see each of their parents more realistically and can claim their own thoughts and feelings, they have a better prognosis for continued growth than do children who maintain a dependent and enmeshed view of their family.

Understanding the parent–child dynamic is useful in determining how to intervene with the parent–child dyad, with each parent individually, and with the coparenting dyad where possible. Yet unless children learn new information about family relationships, the interaction among thoughts, feelings, and behaviors, cognitive distortions, and problem-solving, they will not be exposed to the alternative perspectives or have the opportunity to experience the novel feelings, thoughts, or behaviors needed to interrupt their status quo. The psychoeducational group is designed to improve the children's skills for coping with the interparental conflict, help them develop independent thoughts and feelings, and empower them to identify and solve problems. These new skills ideally lead to improved emotion regulation and cognitive processing.

REFERENCES

Bronfenbrenner, U. (1979). *The ecology of human development: Experiments by nature and design.* Cambridge, MA: Harvard University Press.

Buehler, C., & Gerard, J. M. (2002). Marital conflict, ineffective parenting, and children's and adolescents' maladjustment. *Journal of Marriage and the Family, 64*, 78–96.

Cummings, E., & Davies, P. T. (1994). *Children and marital conflict: The impact of family dispute and resolution.* New York, NY: Guilford Press.

Deutsch, R. M. (2014, November). *Children resisting contact with a parent: Application of intensive interventions.* Invited presentation at Association of Family and Conciliation Courts Symposium on Custody Evaluations, San Antonio, TX.

Deutsch, R. M., & Kline Pruett, M. (2009). Child adjustment and high-conflict divorce. In R. M. Galatzer-Levy, L. Kraus, & J. Galatzer-Levy (Eds.), *The scientific basis of child custody decisions* (2nd ed., pp. 353–373), Hoboken, NJ: John Wiley & Sons.

Fidler, B. J., & Bala, N. (2010). Children resisting post-separation contact with a parent: Concepts, controversies and conundrums. *Family Court Review, 48*, 10–47.

Garber, B. D. (2015). Cognitive–behavioral methods in high conflict divorce: Systematic desensitization adapted to parent–child reunification interventions. *Family Court Review, 53*(1), 96–112.

Greenberg. L. R., Doi Fick, L., & Schnider, R. (2012). Keeping the developmental frame: Child-centered conjoint therapy, *Journal of Child Custody, 9*(1–2), 39–68. doi:10.1080/15379418.2012.652568

Grych, J. H. (2005). Interparental conflict as a risk factor for child maladjustment: Implications for the development of intervention programs. *Family Court Review, 43*, 97–108. doi:10.1111/j.1744-1617.2005.00010.x

Harold, G., Shelton, K., Goeke-Morey, M., & Cummings, E. (2004). Marital conflict, child emotional security about family relationships, and child adjustment. *Social Development, 13*, 350–376.

Jacobvitz, D., Hazen, N., Curran, M., & Hitchens, K. (2004). Observations of early triadic family interactions: Boundary disturbances in the family predict symptoms of depression, anxiety, and attention-deficit/hyperactivity disorder in middle childhood. *Development and Psychopathology, 16*, 577–592.

Johnson, V. K. (2003). Linking changes in whole family functioning and children's externalizing behavior across the elementary school years. *Journal of Family Psychology, 17*, 499–509.

Johnston, J. R., Roseby, V., & Kuehnle, K. (2009). *In the name of the child: A developmental approach to understanding and helping children of conflicted and violent divorce* (2nd ed.). New York, NY: Springer Press.

Johnston, J. R., Walters, M. G., & Olesen, N. (2005). The psychological functioning of alienated children in custody disputes: An exploratory study. *American Journal of Forensic Psychology, 39*(3), 39–64.

Kelly, J. (2012). Risk and protective factors associated with child and adolescent adjustment following separation and divorce: Social science applications. In K. Kuehnle & L. Drozd (Eds.), *Parenting plan evaluations: Applied research for the family court* (pp. 49–84). New York, NY: Oxford University Press.

Kelly, J. R., & Johnston, J. R. (2001). The alienated child: A reformulation of parental alienation syndrome. *Family Court Review, 39*(3), 249–266.

Maccoby, E. D., & Martin, J. A. (1983). Socialization in the context of the family: Parent–child interaction. In P. H. Mussen (Series Ed.) & E. M. Hetherington (Ed.), *Handbook of child psychology: Vol. IV. Socialization, personality, and social development* (4th ed., pp. 1–101). New York, NY: Wiley.

Minuchin, S. (1974). *Families and family therapy.* Cambridge, MA: Harvard University Press.

Perry, B. D., & Hambrick, E. (2008). The neurosequential model of therapeutics. *Reclaiming Children and Youth, 17*(3), 38–43.

Sturge-Apple, M. L., Davies, P. T., & Cummings, E. M. (2010). Typologies of family functioning and children's adjustment during the early school years. *Child Development, 81*, 1320–1335.

Sullivan, M. J., Ward, P. A., & Deutsch, R. M. (2010). Overcoming Barriers Family Camp: A program for high-conflict divorced families where a child is resisting contact with a parent. *Family Court Review, 48*, 116–135.

Vasey, M. W., & Dadds, M. R. (2001). An introduction to the developmental psychopathology of anxiety. In M. W. Vasey, & M. R. Dadds (Eds.), *The developmental psychopathology of anxiety* (pp. 3–26). New York: Oxford University Press.

11

Coparenting, Parenting, and Child-Focused Family Interventions

MATTHEW J. SULLIVAN, ROBIN M. DEUTSCH, AND PEGGIE WARD ■

1. INTRODUCTION

The Overcoming Barriers (OCB) intensive camp program uses a combination of interventions (likened to inpatient treatment) to address the entrenched dynamics of the family system that contribute to a child's resisting contact with a parent. The focus of this chapter is on those interventions. In scheduled daily sessions with individual families and spontaneous responses to incidents that occur in the camp milieu, multiple combinations of clinicians design and deliver intensive interventions to each parent, to the coparent dyad, to the parent–child dyads, and to the child, both separately and jointly with the parents. The potency of these interventions is significantly augmented by the therapeutic camp context in which they are delivered. As described in Chapter 7, this highly structured milieu is customized to work with the unique issues each family presents.

In the parenting, coparenting, and child-focused work at OCB camp, the clinicians provide substantial practical and emotional support (through psychoeducation and coaching), encourage healthy risk-taking and problem-solving, and provide corrective feedback to family members. One key element to effective clinical intervention is the rapid development of a strong and positive therapeutic alliance with staff and other campers resulting from each family member's immersion in the groups and milieu. This intense working alliance can make the OCB approach a powerful and effective intervention for families in which prior legal and psychological interventions have failed to address the intractable dynamics that have led to a child's rejecting a parent.

While the intake process provides the information that leads to a family's being accepted for OCB camp, it is limited to information from third parties and self-report. It lacks direct observation of the family process. Working with accurate information about individual functioning and relationship dynamics within each family is critical for appropriate intervention. At camp, essential information comes from the family's participation in the milieu and feedback derived from family members' participation in group and individual-family work. The clinical team process, described later in the chapter, ensures that accurate, comprehensive information about the functioning of the family system is available throughout the camp program to guide interventions.

In later sections of this chapter we address the specific steps each family must go through in the camp environment. However, there are two critical components in the referral process that determine family motivation and thus success or failure in the camp program. The first is the court order (or other stipulation) stating that the goal of the program is to reconnect the rejected parent with the child. The second is the order for full and complete participation in the program. Parents must know coming into the program that they are mandated by the court (or agreement) to affirmatively assist the children in every way they are directed by camp staff to enable the child to re-establish a relationship with the rejected parent.

The clinical intake is a thorough process that derives information about each family prior to their arrival. Assuming that the family is determined to be an appropriate referral (see Chapter 2), the intake professional distills information from interviewing each parent, reviewing court documents (particularly any neutral, child-focused reports from a guardian ad litem or child custody evaluator), and interviews with past and current mental health providers and presents it to all clinicians prior to the families' arrival at camp. The clinical team gathers essential information about the historical aspects of the family system and any external factors (involvement in family court, child protection processes, and past and current mental health interventions) that are relevant to the child's rejection of a parent. The team then generates hypotheses that guide the initial interventions with the family. These hypotheses focus on the following questions:

1. What are the individual psychological strengths and vulnerabilities in the parents and children and in the parent–child relationship dynamics?
2. Do the coparents have any functional engagement?
3. When was the last time the child had contact with the parent, and was there a specific incident that caused the breach between parent and child?
4. What has caused the failure of mental health interventions? Are particular therapists more of an obstacle to reconnection than a support?
5. How has the court addressed the custody issues historically? Is the court considering a change in custody if the OCB program is not successful?

Are the parents returning to court for a review after their work at
OCB camp?

6. What is each parent's narrative about the reason for the child's current
resistance to having a relationship with the rejected parent? Are issues of
child abuse, domestic violence, or alienation central to those narratives?

7. What are the expressed attitudes and goals of each family member as he
or she anticipates involvement at the OCB camp?

As soon as the family arrives at camp, hypotheses about the family dynamics
generated by the intake process are tested. Since families arrive in the afternoon,
considerable information can be gathered about each family's process by the time
the first family interventions are developed and implemented the next afternoon.
The initial clinical interventions are guided by systematic and observable information about family members' individual functioning (e.g., what they say, how
they are interacting with others at camp, and their engagement in milieu activities like sports, music, and crafts); affiliations with campers, milieu staff ("Green
Shirts"), and clinicians, both problematic and positive; and manifest behaviors
(e.g., avoidance, panic, oppositional behavior, or somatic symptoms). Camp clinicians gather this information by direct observation and from verbal reports by
Green Shirts working in the cabins, meals, and milieu and by other staff, such as
the nurse or night watchperson.

For example, a Green Shirt might report that one of the teenagers cried all
night, saying she could not sleep without her mother; that a teenager was texting
his aligned father on a prohibited cell phone; or that two coparents were talking
intensely alongside the barn. The nurse might report observing a parent giving a
child food not permitted by the child's reported dietary restrictions or giving a
child medication that only the nurse can administer at camp. The camp director
might note that a rejected father approached a child and the child listened to the
father with head down and a sullen facial expression. The camp director typically
is charged with pulling together this type of information and reporting it to the
clinicians in the "situation room" the private space at the camp where the clinicians meet at regular intervals during the day so that they can integrate it into
their intervention plans.

2. PLANNING, COORDINATION, AND SUPPORT OF INTERVENTIONS

In every OCB camp, the entire clinical staff meets as a group several times a day—
in the morning, at lunch, and throughout the evening during camp activities—to
formulate and implement family interventions. During the intake process, a team
of clinicians is assigned to work with each family (one clinician for each parent
and often one clinician for each child, unless the children are in the same morning
group). This team of clinicians then participates in all of the interventions involving that family that occur during camp, though there are often some shifts in

clinical assignments to particular members of a family based on the working alliances that are built in the morning groups and engagement between clinicians and individual family members in the milieu. The entire clinical staff works together in the regular situation room meetings to formulate initial and subsequent goals and objectives. With each family intervention, new information about the family dynamics emerges to inform the next intervention. Flexibility in the focus of these interventions is critical to the process, as is exploiting the opportunities for change in the family system that present themselves as the family engages in the camp program.

For example, the initial family interventions typically focus on the favored parent's work with the child to engage with the rejected parent. These interventions may involve group and individual work with the favored parent (including specific coaching when the parent is working with the child) to overcome resistance to supporting engagement. If this focus of intervention does not succeed (as determined by the favored parent's taking more authentic actions to support some form of engagement with the rejected parent), a central goal of the camp and expectation of the court will not be realized.

Assuming this initial objective is met and the child is freed from a bind between the parents, the focus of the next set of clinical interventions is the relationship between the rejected parent and the child. This set of interventions typically centers on the child's sharing the reasons for not having contact with the rejected parent and on what the rejected parent needs to do for the child to be open to reconnection. The initial connections between the child and rejected parent are carefully choreographed and intensively supported by clinicians (before, during, and after meetings) to maximize the likelihood that a progression of positive and healing experiences of engagement occurs during the camp program.

Because particular clinicians work with the West Group (rejected parents), East Group (favored parents), and Common Ground (children), tensions and conflict typically emerge between clinicians as the work progresses. These tensions are generated by the clinicians' identification with individual family members and with the culture that develops in each group. For example, the rejected parents' group narrative almost always coalesces around their victimization by their respective alienating coparents in the East Group. This focus, though often having some validity, can mobilize considerable negative feelings in both the West Group clinicians and the Common Ground clinicians. East Group parents who continue to disparage and denigrate their respective West Group coparents when the basis of those perspectives has been determined (by prior evaluation or court findings, as well as from the West Group parent's behavior at camp) to be distorted and to stem from serious psychological issues, such as delusions, borderline personality disorder, or malice, can mobilize considerable anger in Common Ground and West Group clinicians.

The East Group clinicians, whose intense involvement with the favored parents engenders more empathy and compassion for them, can become defensive about and resistant to critical feedback of the rest of the clinical team. Similarly, the strong identification and of the clinicians working with the West Group, which tends to be incited by the group members' sense of victimization, can mobilize them to take an advocacy stance in relationship to these parents. This can diminish their objectivity when assessing and working with the vulnerabilities and problem behaviors these parents contribute to their families' problems. The children's clinicians often experience more negative feelings (anger, fear, disappointment, etc.) that the children themselves are not expressing or even aware of, leading these clinicians to feel anger toward the East Group parents for the ways they undermine the goals of reunification, toward both parents for the children's chronic exposure to interparental conflict, and, less often, toward the West Group parents for the disappointing ineptitude they display when given the opportunity to connect with their children.

The clinical team must identify and manage these polarizing forces in order not to replicate the polarized dynamics of the family system. In addition, the camp staff can have very intense reactions to family members based on their own histories. It is therefore essential to effective staff functioning to discuss those reactions with the staff and to assist them with managing those reactions in their work with the individuals in question.

3. PARENT PREPARATION FOR PARENT–CHILD INTERVENTIONS

Each day after the morning group meetings, the clinical team plans the family interventions that will occur at camp that day, based on observations and information from the groups and reports from the milieu. The discussion among the clinicians identifies which family member(s) and which clinician(s) will be part of each intervention and when it will take place. Interventions may include any combination of parents, stepparents, and children. Parents and children are always supported by their group clinicians in family meetings. Sometimes a parent and clinician meet separately to prepare for the meeting, but often this preparation has been a part of the morning-group intervention.

For example, the favored parent may need to give permission and support to the child prior to the meeting between the child and the rejected parent, and the East Group clinician and the child's clinician may be present to provide additional support at the meeting. The favored parent must shift from an initial stance of protecting the child from emotional or physical harm to actively encouraging contact between the children and the rejected parent. Often the motivation to make this change must come from the court's mandating that the favored parent may lose custody if she or he does not help the child recognize that the rejected parent has much to offer and that the favored parent has made some mistakes. With the mandate for reconnection issued prior to camp, the clinician working with the favored parent can expect that parent's compliance in work to encourage contact between the child and the rejected parent. If the favored parent is not willing to support contact, she or he is engaging in alienation, which the court has already identified as problematic. If the parent does attempt to support reunification but is unsuccessful, this is a parenting issue (a problem with exerting effective authority or behaving appropriately when in charge) that the clinicians at camp can work with.

To prepare the favored parent to deliver a message encouraging reconnection to the child, individual work (coaching) may be necessary to help that parent develop a rationale for the about-face. The child may experience this new stance, which is in stark contrast to the alienating messages the favored parent has historically given the child, as a betrayal of the alliance with the favored parent to reject the other parent. Favored parents must be able to tell their children convincingly that they now realize the importance of the child's reconnecting with the other parent and that because the staff has reassured them that any connections during camp will be safe and supported, the child should follow the staff's direction in reconnection efforts.

The above example is typical of initial family work at OCB camp. In this example, the favored parent's clinician may coach that parent to respond to intense challenges by the child to the parent's change in attitudes about the other parent and the child's need to reconnect with them. Often what emerges from this work is that in colluding with the child to reject the other parent, the favored parent has lost the parental authority needed to require the child to engage with the other parent. The inappropriate empowerment of the child, which is a common problem for favored parents, then becomes the focus of the parent–child work.

If these interventions with the favored parent and child are successful, the rejected parent will have the opportunity to connect with the child. The focus of clinical work then shifts to the rejected parent–child dyad. What is usually evident as this work commences is that the rejected parent may have limited parenting skill in general and often is a stranger to the child if they have had little to no involvement for some time. In addition to these issues, the skills the rejected parent needs to reconnect and build a sustainable relationship with the child are quite specialized relative to "normal" parenting.[1] The initial connections in the family meetings require the rejected parent and child to receive considerable preparation to address the obstacles to reconnection in their particular family dynamic.

Preparation of the rejected parent, both in morning group meetings and in individual meetings, may include getting the parent ready to respond to the litany of complaints that the child may advance as why he or she does not want a relationship with that parent. These complaints typically fall into three categories: (a) issues or events that have substantial validity; (b) issues or events that have kernels of truth but have been exaggerated into more serious reasons to reject the parent, often with the assistance of the favored parent, whose poor boundaries around adult issues have poisoned the child's relationship with the rejected parent (Warshak, 2015); and (c) issues or events that that never occurred but which the child either believes because they have been incorporated into his or her memory or is lying about to justify the rejection. Each type of complaint requires an effective response from the rejected parent if the corresponding barriers to reconnection are to be overcome. The following paragraphs describe the work done to address each kind of issue.

Issues or events that have substantial validity or create understandable negative feelings in the child toward the rejected parent include situations where the parent has been violent or abusive (sexually, emotionally, or physically) toward the child, the child's siblings, or the favored parent; has been harsh, insensitive, or punitive in parenting the child or the siblings; has had extramarital affairs; has not seen the child or children by his or her own decision (abandonment); or has had problems with drug or alcohol abuse. For the court to mandate reconnection between the parent and child, and for OCB to determine the family to be appropriate for our intervention, the court and professionals obviously must no longer consider these issues to preclude efforts to work on reconnection. Moreover, there must have been a determination that despite any past issues, it is in the child's best interests to have a relationship with the rejected parent. Predictably, issues that have been assessed as substantially valid create major obstacles to the clinical work at camp. In these situations, rejected parents must take responsibility for their past behavior (expressing their understanding of its negative impact), provide a sincere apology, and make a commitment not to engage in that behavior in the future. They must respond to the child's skeptical and often derisive response to their apology in a manner that recognizes that the child's rejecting responses are understandable and acceptable.

Issues or events that children cite to justify their rejection of a parent that have kernels of truth but have been exaggerated over time include (a) the degree of blame the rejected parent deserves for the separation and divorce, (b) incidents of poor parenting (losing one's temper and yelling, using corporal punishment, etc.,), (c) the parent's engaging in mutually escalating verbal and physical interparental conflict that the child now characterizes as true domestic violence (Drozd & Olesen, 2004; Hardesty & Chung, 2006; Johnston & Campbell, 1993), (d) alcohol use that is not objectively problematic, (e) financial issues (child support and standard-of-living discrepancies that the child now resents), (f) court involvement initiated to address the violation of court orders by the favored parent but that the child blames exclusively on the rejected parent, and (g) alienation and loss of contact with the child. Some examples of complaints that children express to justify rejection but that have no substantiation or validity are (a) allegations of abuse, domestic violence, or substance abuse that have been comprehensively investigated and determined to be unfounded[2] and (b) events in the child's life that the favored parent has twisted to represent irresponsible, neglectful, or even dangerous parenting by the rejected parent. When the child raises these types of issues with the rejected parent, they often have a rehearsed quality that suggests they are more strategic than heartfelt reasons for the rejection.

In situations where the child's complaints center on fabricated, exaggerated, or recharacterized issues or events, clinical work coaches the rejected parent not to debate the "facts" or attempt to convince the child of the fabrications and distortions in their perceptions. The rejected parent is also strongly directed not to implicate the favored parent in fostering these distortions, even if that has been found to be the case. Saying to the child, "You sound just like your mother" in these situations is a nonstarter for reconnection. It will evoke in the child a militantly protective response of the favored parent and intensify the rejection of the other parent. A productive response to these types of barriers to connection is to listen to and acknowledge the child's reasons for resisting connection so that the child feels "heard" and understands what affect her or his perceptions have on engaging with the rejected parent. Based on that understanding, the parent must reassure the child that in moving forward in the relationship, she or he doesn't have to worry about the issue in question occurring. Work during camp and afterward between parent and child on building such reassurance follows from the work on identifying barriers to connection. Shifting from a past to a future orientation in addressing these relationship issues is a critical step in the parent–child work.

4. CLINICAL WORK WITH CHILDREN

Preparing children for parent–child sessions and debriefing them afterward is critical work both in group and individually. Sessions for which this work is necessary include ones where (a) the favored parent is encouraging the child to connect with the rejected parent, (b) the child is meeting with the rejected parent to share the child's complaints and conditions for working on the relationship, (c) the child is listening and responding to the parents' new narrative about the past and moving forward, and (d) the child is hearing about and perhaps having input into an aftercare plan (e.g., a contract between a rejected father and his daughter to have six months of conjoint therapy after camp as a condition for her then being permitted to change her last name).

For some of these parent–child or family sessions, preparation occurs within the group and involves problem-solving (e.g., how can the child best say what he or she wants to say and have the parent or parents listen, and how can they together ultimately come to a resolution that the child can accept). Preparation may involve further rehearsal for the upcoming session outside the group as well. Some preparation may involve discussion between just the children's group therapist and the child of the format, process, and intention of the parent–child or family session and of ways to manage anger and anxiety for the most effective session. In each case the clinician helps the child prepare to interact respectfully rather than avoid the problem, in the interest of reaching a more effective resolution. In addition, group work focuses regularly on bringing an open heart and open mind to a relationship while maintaining boundaries and moving at a gradual pace. For some children the first step of reconnection is contact and sharing grievances and feelings, while for others it is just having an initial contact in which the child feels some control. During the family session, the child clinician sits next to and serves as a touchstone for the child, representing a known and safe adult who can provide direct support if the child feels anxious or overwhelmed or loses track of her or his plan of interaction. The therapist may ask the child a question to elicit a planned narrative, may ask for a break so the child can compose herself or himself, and may facilitate the interaction with general questions or thoughts.

As an example of this work, a 14-year-old girl prepared for a session with her mother in the group by brainstorming all the possible interactions she could have with her mother, given that she had made an agreement with her father that she would have some contact. The options ranged from sending an impostor to bringing her older sister or her father. The group identified two options that met the criteria of feeling safe and contained and not feeling trapped,(i.e., being able to leave if she felt her mother was too intrusive and having a time limit). This girl became very anxious whenever she saw her mother, whom she described as "always judgmental," harsh, and selfish. Before the mother–daughter session, the girl and a trusted recreation counselor went for a long walk. Using activity, particularly rhythmic activity such as walking, bouncing, or swinging, to regulate the arousal system and reduce anxiety can be extremely helpful for children and adults before engaging in an emotionally difficult task or experience. The child and clinician met 10 minutes before the family session to review the plan and then together met with the mother and her clinician. The mother had been coached to respond in a welcoming way, to accept the child's small step, and to negotiate with the child a frequency and duration of mother–child contacts, as opposed to making demands or referencing the court order.

In another example, an 11-year-old boy yelled at his father in the dining room to stay away from him and his friends. A staff counselor intervened and took the boy outside. The boy began to cry, saying that seeing his father was very painful. The father came out to apologize, expressed his understanding to the boy, and said the boy had control over what interactions the father had with him. The boy then agreed to play tennis with his father the next day in the company of a recreation counselor. The clinician met with the child to prepare him for the activity, anticipating any difficulties, supporting his willingness to take a step, reminding him that it would take place in a safe public space, and discussing the short- and long-term benefits of taking part in the activity (e.g., it was fun activity the boy and father used to do, was something they could do going forward, and made use of his father as the good teacher he once was). The next day the children's group was debriefed on the activity. Other group participants praised the boy for taking a "risk," and one boy said he wished his father played tennis.

These examples have common themes of helping children to regulate their emotions, including managing anxiety by moving from avoidance to approach as a step in desensitization, and to appropriately express anger so it can be heard without evoking a purely reactive response. By enabling the children to be heard and understood accurately, these skills help open the door to a new connection.

Another aim of the family sessions which requires preparation prior is for the parents to gain or regain age-appropriate control and influence in the parent–child dynamic. Both parents must be willing to listen to their child and to help the child understand that some things must be negotiated. The parents' job is to help their child grow up to be a healthy adult. Sometimes that job requires setting expectations and limits that the child does not like, does not want to follow, and may not find easy or comfortable. The parents can support the child in taking these steps and risks in the reconnection process with the rejected parent, always with a focus on achieving safe, healthy adjustment. The parents are essentially taking charge of the child, who has been inappropriately empowered by the "skew" in the coparenting relationship (in which the favored parent–child coalition undermined the executive element of coparenting).

5. COPARENTING INTERVENTIONS

The coparenting relationship is the bridge that the child needs to traverse to reconnect with the rejected parent in order to healthily rebalance their involvement with both parents. That bridge does not exist for the child as these families enter camp, and the coparents in each family are a major focus of the clinical interventions. Without both some detente between the parents and the favored parent's support of the reconnection work between the child and the rejected parent, there is little chance that work will succeed. Most coparents when they arrive at camp are in entrenched high conflict. Many are not in contact with each other (except in court or through their attorneys), or whatever engagement they do have is hostile, strategic, and completely dysfunctional. In many cases, there has been a history of alleged emotional abuse or physical violence (sometimes substantiated, sometimes not) by one or both of the parents toward the other parent, the children, or both. Significant disputes over financial issues may be unresolved. There is usually a legacy of litigation, and court involvement may be pending to consider changing custody to the rejected parent if progress is not made in the OCB camp program. The stakes are high, and the polarities in the relationship are fertile ground for loyalty pressures for the child to align with the favored parent.

5.1. Work on Enabling the Coparents to Re-engage With Each Other

If either or both of the coparents have engaged in behavior in the past that is antithetical to functional coparenting in shared custody, work is done in coparenting sessions to enable the parent or parents to acknowledge this behavior, take responsibility for its impact, and make a commitment to moving forward in a more functional way. This apology may apply to incidents or patterns of domestic violence; harsh, insensitive, or neglectful parenting; alienating behaviors (which both the rejected and favored parent may engage in); or other issues that either parent identifies as barriers to functional engagement.

Often the parents' perspectives about their separation are discrepant and form a major obstacle to establishing a functional coparenting structure. This is particularly true when the separation was particularly traumatic for one or both parents. Separations involving affairs, financial impropriety, or allegations of separation-induced violence often lead to an entrenched conflict in which these issues have been the source of repeated court involvement. Most importantly, they can be significant contributors to a child's rejection of a parent, if the child's beliefs, feelings, and attitudes about these controversial past issues in their parents' lives align with those of the preferred parent.

There is a daily conjoint session with each coparent dyad along with ad hoc interventions that may occur as a result of issues that arise as the family moves through the program. These family sessions are conducted by one clinician each from the West and East groups, and a child clinician may be involved if the child is part of the session (or to bring the child's perspective into a coparent session). One or both parents often resist meeting together, and considerable preparation may be required to have such meetings occur.

For example, in a more extreme case where the rejected parent had perpetrated domestic violence several years before and restraining orders had precluded direct engagement between the coparents for a period of time, the coparents, who shared legal custody, had continued to have no contact after the restraining orders expired. As a result, the rejected parent had no knowledge of any aspect of their children's lives (education, health, social involvements, and even residential location). The coparenting intervention involved stepwise progressive engagement between the parents, beginning with separate and parallel meetings with clinicians, who moved back and forth between the parents as proxies while they discussed child-related issues. With considerable work with each coparent between sessions, this format evolved into the parents' being in the same room with no direct interaction but with clinicians acting as intermediaries in their exchanges. (Each parent talked to his or her clinician, who would then address the other parent, who would then talk to her or his clinician while the other parent listened.) This progressed by the end of the camp program to the parents' being able to speak directly to each other with considerable support from the two clinicians in the room. Throughout this desensitization procedure, the favored parent's anxiety and fear were worked with to make sure they were manageable. As in most cases, the goal for this coparenting relationship in aftercare was to establish a supported parallel-parenting model that would be emotionally safe for both parents by having their engagement highly structured and supported by a competent parenting coordinator (Deutsch, 2014; Deutsch, Coates, & Fieldstone, 2008; Sullivan, 2008, 2014).

An essential part of the coparenting work at OCB camp is successfully managing the expression of the strong emotions that are nearly always triggered when direct engagement between coparents occurs in the coparenting sessions. The coparents must have an experience at camp that these intense emotions can be managed and to some extent resolved. If the coparents repeat the same conflicted experience of engagement, there can be no progress. The two experienced clinicians working in these meetings therefore must be well versed in being active and directive in addressing strong emotions. When these emotions are triggered, they need the skill to intervene quickly to calm the affected parent, enhance his or her self-regulation, and coach responses that are more functional than simply reacting (slowing the process down, breathing, taking a break, etc.) (Fonagy, Gergely, Jurist, & Target, 2002; Siegel & Bryson, 2011). The clinicians also intervene to prevent interruptions, accusations, and blame; to refocus interactions on the present and future rather than the past; and to keep the content of sessions centered on coparenting (the business of raising a child).

We use the frame of "opening a new chapter" to help bound interaction that will likely trigger and escalate conflicted engagement. The goal is to make the coparenting interaction more manageable (safer and more functional). The teaming of East and West group leaders in coparenting sessions has proven successful in giving parents at camp a more effective experience of engaging with their coparents, giving many hope that a new chapter in their relationship is possible.

5.2. Work Toward Parallel Coparenting After Camp

For most coparents, the interventions during the camp program provide both psychoeducation about and an experience of a parallel model of coparenting (Ricci, 2013; Sullivan, 2008, 2014). Though their coparenting after camp will be highly structured and disengaged, there is an expectation that they will share involvement in raising their child (through child-focused information sharing and joint decision-making). Exclusion and marginalization of the rejected parent is not permissible, and the favored parent's reluctance to engage with the rejected parent is addressed by creating structures of engagement based on a businesslike, respectful, and child-focused relationship. The parents are given the support to manage intensely emotional interactions by having their respective clinicians sitting next to them in the coparenting sessions to manage their emotional triggers (as discussed above) and keep them in a rational, child-focused place.

Several common areas of work with coparents are focused on moving them from high-conflict to parallel engagement. Coparents are given a didactic explanation of parallel parenting, with the clinicians covering the essentials of the model:

1. Disengaged communication about child-focused issues is necessary to support shared custody. Communication is exclusively through email, and the parents follow rules about what content is acceptable in communicating with the coparent (Arizona Chapter of the Association of Family and Conciliation Courts, 2011; Eddy, 2014).
2. A highly structured parenting plan (custody order), often several pages in length, must be developed to clearly define all of the structures needed for shared custody and to reduce the amount of engagement between coparents.
3. A neutral professional is needed to support coparenting, ideally with some delegation of court authority, by assisting the parents with implementation of the parenting plan, monitoring coparenting communication, and providing an alternative dispute resolution process.

When the parents are unable to make decisions about their child(ren),
they first go to the coparent counselor or parenting coordinator to
attempt resolution, reducing the need for attorneys or the court.

In addition to this psychoeducation about parallel parenting and the coparenting work that supports this model, the coparenting sessions provide an
experience of working within this model. The clinicians are both experienced
parenting coordinators, and the coparenting work at camp seeks to provide parents with a potent and positive experience of engaging with their coparents.
Highly structured sessions begin with addressing camp-based issues such as
developing a shared strategy to have the child connect with the rejected parent and progress to build on that connection. Increasing the parents' capacity
to communicate, problem-solve, come to agreements, and implement them is
the goal of these sessions, which culminate in some cases in agreements about
a custody schedule and mental health interventions that will continue to support the meaningful involvement of both parents with their child after the camp
intervention.

5.3. Work to Support Reconnecting the Rejected Parent With the Child

For every family, a critical focus of the coparenting work is to assist the parents
in creating a shared narrative about the separation and the issues that created the
favored parent–child alignment (e.g., the involvement of a new intimate partner;
the favored parent's intent, shared with the child, to relocate or have more parenting time; or the favored parent's message to the child that he or she has discretion
to spend time with the rejected parent or not). It is the job of the clinicians and
parents alike to agree that the parents are responsible for reconciling their conflict over these issues. After agreeing that such a unified narrative is necessary,
the parents work, with the support of the clinicians, to develop a narrative that
communicates their shared responsibility for the child's rejection of one parent
and the expectation that the family will work toward re-establishing meaningful
parenting time with both parents. This coparenting work creates a foundation for
the child's reunification with the rejected parent. The parents deliver the narrative
to the child in a family session that is carefully choreographed to have each parent
present particular parts, taking responsibility for his or her own contributions to
getting the family to this point and making a commitment to move the family in
a better direction.

The following is an example of such a narrative:

FATHER: Your mother and I have been doing a lot of work at camp with Drs. X
and Y. We wanted to have a meeting with you because we understand the stress
and hardship that our conflict has caused you over the years and to tell you that
we are committed to moving the family to a better place.

MOTHER: I realize how important it is for you to have a relationship with your father and regret that our conflict and involvement in the court system has created a situation where you are not spending time with him in a meaningful way.

FATHER: I know that I've done some things when we were living together as a family before your mom and I separated, like losing my temper and not spending much time at home with you guys, that made you question whether I was committed to you as a father and whether it was safe to spend time with me. I want to tell you I regret behaving in that way. I've done a lot of work in therapy to handle my anger, and I'm totally committed to building back trust with you guys, even if it takes a while to do so.

MOTHER: I want to tell you guys that I regret many things I said to you that made you feel bad about your father. I now realize that it was unfair and hurt your relationship with your father to share court papers with you and to show you emails that were part of our communication as parents. You kids should not have been shown those things, and I'm sorry I did that.

FATHER (WITH MOTHER REINFORCING THIS MESSAGE): Your mom and I are very sorry for what we've put you through and would like to use the experience at camp to work on making your experience with both of us happier for you.

The child typically has some "pushback" against the favored parent, since the alignment they have had based on the rejection of the other parent is now called into question. Feeling that the shift to supporting the rejected parent is a betrayal of that alignment, the child may become quite angry toward the favored parent. The clinician's work when this occurs is to assist the favored parent in remaining steadfast in sharing her or his realization that continued rejection of the other parent is not in the child's best interest, along with the rationale behind that realization.

This coparents and child also work in this session to develop a plan for implementation of contact between the rejected parent and the child, which will begin immediately afterward. The parents' clinicians offer considerable support to keep the parents unified and functional in generating proposals for possible connections and problem-solving. Similarly, the child's clinician is present to support the child if the child expresses opposition due to anxiety or anger about the mandate for contact.

The camp milieu offers a rich environment for various manageable and pleasurable joint activities that the recreation counselors (Green Shirts) can support to optimize a good experience for both the child and the rejected parent (and to ensure accurate feedback to the clinical team about what occurred in an activity). The interplay between the family sessions (sometimes dyadic between the rejected parent and the child, but usually triadic, involving both parents and the child) and the sequential building of reconnection with the rejected parent and child is a cornerstone of the reunification work at camp.

Work in the coparent sessions results in experiences for the child in the camp milieu of the parents' working together on the child's behalf. For example, a pair of parents might work in a session on a birthday celebration for their daughter, whose birthday falls during camp. In this case, the work with the parents will focus on planning each one's involvement with the child and with each other at the presentation of a birthday cake at an all-camp meal. Issues like who will present the cake, where the parents will stand in relationship to each other, what they will say, whether one or both will have physical contact with the child are all addressed and sometimes negotiated in this joint exercise. This kind of work provides parents with the skills for engagement that are the building blocks of functional coparenting around other issues, and they provide children with new and healthier experiences of their parents. These experiences are also witnessed and supported by the camp community.

One example that raised several challenges and opportunities for shifts in the coparenting dynamics had to do with the parental management of a girl who had serious juvenile diabetes and was resisting one parent's efforts to manage her care. This resistance had led to a cutoff of contact, because the child had repeatedly require emergency care at the hospital when in that parent's care. The child's opposition was not due to that parent's lacking skill or competence in managing her diabetes but rather was a manipulation of the situation to prevent spending time with that parent. Clinicians worked with the coparents to have them work together during camp on various aspects of their daughter's diabetes management. At first they were jointly in charge of her care, and then they negotiated with the child shared responsibility for blood monitoring, going to the store to get supplies, administering insulin, and working with the on-site nurse. This process challenged the parents to work together functionally and gave the child a strong message that her parents were both committed to involvement in managing her health.

Based on the stated mandate for the coparents to build a connection between the child and the rejected parent, we work with the coparents to create a series of increasingly direct and engaged connections that the favored parent supports, either directly or indirectly. Sometimes we use opportunities that arise at camp, like having the child and rejected parent engage first in parallel play (e.g., the rejected parent, in a group of parents, watches the child play volleyball) or indirect engagement in play (e.g., the parent and child play on different teams in an all-camp evening game). Their proximity is carefully gauged based on the child's resistance to connection, but it is progressively increased to more direct involvement (e.g., taking a walk in the woods, playing basketball or tennis, or doing a crafts project together). These experiences are designed to be pleasurable and to give the rejected parent and child practice interacting in a safe and supervised way as they take their first, tentative steps toward reconnection. The connections between the rejected parent and child involve considerable preparation (both in groups and individually), are supported by staff while they are occurring, and are then debriefed by clinicians and family members in preparation for the next connection at camp.

The camp program has recently added a segment during each day when the entire camp—clinicians, Green Shirts, and all family members—meets for a media-based intervention. Clinician pairs are responsible for developing and presenting to the campers psychoeducational content on general conceptual material like perspective taking and empathy (through video clips); more practical skills like nonblaming communication, apologies, and listening; and more specific topics like alienation and estrangement. The presentations are sequenced to progress from more general and less directly confrontational content to more provocative material that is more challenging for family members to take in and whose relevance to their situation is more difficult for them to consider.

For example, a media presentation to the entire camp focused on alienation dynamics might start with two roughly five-minute video segments. Clinicians might follow this with some explanation of alienation dynamics and then show a film clip in which a mother undermines a daughter's affection for her father, leading to the daughter's refusing to visit him the next weekend; the clip ends with the father sitting alone in a neighborhood park with his head in his hands, crying.

The goal of such media presentations is to help family members access previously disavowed affects and cognitions related to the parent–child contact problem, which clinicians can then address in group sessions or coparenting or child-focused interventions. We have observed that this use of media to illustrate such themes and dynamics can help "unstick" entrenched and unaddressed factors that are maintaining a child's unwarranted rejection.

6. CLOSING THE CLINICAL WORK WITH THE FAMILY

Typically, positive momentum builds in the various aspects of the family work at OCB camp: the coparenting work, the parent–child work with the favored and the rejected parent, and the whole-family work. This progress needs to be channeled into closure of the camp's clinical work and transitioned into aftercare for the family. It is not uncommon for family members to regress in anticipation of camp's ending (and of returning home), and staff frequently observe signs that children's rejection of a parent is increasing and coparenting conflict is escalating. It is important to recognize this regression as something expected and not indicative of a lack of progress in the family process during camp. Knowing that regression is "normal" can help assuage the mounting anxiety that family members understandably feel as they face the uncertainty of their postcamp future.

Though a successful camp experience can catalyze significant changes in the factors that led a child to reject a parent, those changes can be quickly undone. Sustaining and building on those changes is the difficult work of aftercare. Therefore, at the end of camp the focus of the family interventions shifts to issues relevant to leaving camp. These include managing all family members' expectations about the future, dealing with disappointments in the camp experience (e.g., a rejected parent's not having as much contact with the child as the parent would have liked), and doing as much planning for the family's actual departure as possible. How will the child say goodbye to the rejected parent? If the child is leaving with the favored parent or the family is on the same flight, what are transportation arrangements home? When will the next contact between the rejected parent and child be?

Clinicians also focus on components of an aftercare plan that are essential to supporting changes catalyzed by the camp experience. Specific and documented suggestions are made to coparents in an aftercare meeting on the last day of camp that closes the coparenting work. For almost every family involved in camp, a recommendation for a parenting coordinator is made to the parents. As discussed above, the parents have already received psychoeducation about the role a parenting coordinator plays in assisting with ongoing coparenting work (e.g., functional child-focused communication and decision-making) and the coordination of mental health interventions (e.g., reunification work and child and parent psychotherapy). In addition, coparents have had multiple coparenting sessions in which they have hopefully experienced more functional engagement around their children, making them more optimistic that they can work together in a new way and reduce or eliminate their dependency on court processes.

Another focus of the family's work as the camp experience is drawing to a close is how to transition the intensive and comprehensive clinical work of the camp to the aftercare team. The aftercare meeting with the parents addresses and provides suggestions about two aspects of this transition. First, aftercare may include components essential to continued progress that were not part of the interventions the family had previous to camp. Parenting coordination is one such intervention. Other types of interventions may focus directly on supporting reunification, such as seeing a family therapist to continue the reconnection process begun at camp or individual therapy (or parent coaching) to address essential parenting skills for parents in these high-conflict situations. Some suggested interventions have less direct relevance to reconnection and come instead from concerns about the child that we think should be followed up on. An example of this type of suggestion might be obtaining a neurological or psychoeducational assessment of the child if the child's involvement at camp was suggestive of learning or processing issues. Another example might be suggesting that a parent have a psychopharmacological consult if she or he has manifested behavior that raises concern about untreated mental health issues (e.g., anxiety, depression, bipolar illness, attention-deficit). Second, the aftercare plan provides the parents with a suggested structure for the aftercare team, discussing the rationale for each intervention, explaining the type of professional role needed, and exploring whether and how the parents can implement this aftercare plan immediately, so as not to lose the momentum of any progress that has occurred at camp.

The parents are assured in their aftercare meeting that a representative of the camp's clinical team will connect with the professionals providing aftercare to brief them on the family's experience at camp, the status of reunification, and the immediate goals and objectives for continued family work. This consultation to the aftercare team is included in the camp cost and is critical to improving the effectiveness of future interventions. The knowledge that this consultation will take place is particularly reassuring to the rejected parent, who tends to be fearful that any progress during camp will be quickly undone when the family returns home. When possible, our clinicians may be able to make referrals to specific specialized professionals local to the family in the written aftercare plan (see example in Appendix 11.A). Another helpful safeguard to prevent a relapse to the precamp status quo is for the court to have a status conference or hearing scheduled immediately after camp. This court oversight helps with the good-faith follow-through on the verbal agreements for aftercare that parents typically make as they complete the camp program.

NOTES

1. Chapter 5 of Moran et al. (2015) provides additional description of the clinical work with the favored parent.
2. Unfounded allegations of sexual abuse, physical abuse, or domestic violence are particularly difficult to address, because the child and favored parent may continue to assert that the events in question occurred and that the child protection and family court systems have just failed to substantiate the truth.

REFERENCES

Arizona Chapter of the Association of Family and Conciliation Courts. (2011). *Coparenting communication guide*. Retrieved from http://azafcc.org/wp-content/uploads/2015/12/AzAFCC-Coparenting-Communication-Guide.pdf

Deutsch, R. (2014). The process of parenting coordination. In S. A. Higuchi & S. J. Lally (Eds.), *Parenting coordination handbook* (pp. 63–75). Washington, DC: American Psychological Association.

Deutsch, R., Coates, C., & Fieldstone, L. (2008). Parenting coordination: An emerging role. In C. Coates & L. Fieldstone (Eds.), *Innovations in interventions with high conflict parents: Clinical practice* (pp. 187–223). Madison, WI: Association of Family and Conciliation Courts.

Drozd, L., & Olesen, N. (2004). Is it abuse, alienation and/or estrangement? A decision tree. *Journal of Child Custody, 65*, 65–106.

Eddy, W. (2104). *BIFF: Quick responses to high-conflict people*. San Diego, CA: High Conflict Institute Press.

Fonagy, P., Gergely, G., Jurist, E. L., & Target, M. (2002). *Affect regulation, mentalization, and the development of the self*. New York, NY: Other Press.

Hardesty, J., & Chung, G. (2006). Intimate partner violence, parental divorce and child custody: Directions for intervention and future research. *Family Relations, 55*, 200–210.

Johnston, J., & Campbell, L. (1993). A clinical typology of interparental violence in disputed custody divorces. *American Journal of Orthopsychiatry, 63*(2), 190–199.

Ricci, I. (2013). *The coparenting toolkit*. San Ramon, CA: Custody and CoParenting Solutions. Available from www.thecoparentingtoolkit.com

Siegel, D. L., & Bryson, T. P. (2011). *The whole-brain child*. New York, NY: Bantam.

Sullivan, M. J. (2008). Coparenting and the parenting coordination process. *Journal of Child Custody, 5*(1–2), 4–24.

Sullivan, M. J. (2014). Strategies for working with difficult clients. In S. A. Higuchi & S. J. Lally (Eds.), *Parenting coordination handbook* (pp. 107–123). Washington, DC: American Psychological Association.

Warshak, R. (2015). Ten parental alienation fallacies that compromise decisions in court and in therapy. *Professional Psychology: Research and Practice, 46*, 235–249. http://dx.doi.org/10.1037/pro0000031

OVERCOMING BARRIERS FAMILY CAMP

Summary of Interventions and Agreements
XXX family

Father
Mother
Child 1
Child 2

The components of the following recommended aftercare plan were
presented and discussed with the parents as part of the Overcoming
Barriers psycho-educational program on July 17, 2016. They are based on
the clinical staff's work with the family in the program and designed to
provide professional support for the family's parenting plan.

It is essential that all of the professionals selected to provide the following
services discuss the family's experience at the Overcoming Barriers
program with a representative from our clinical staff to assist them with
the onset of their work with this family.

CLINICAL INTERVENTIONS

7/17/16: Parents orientation group 30 min. Group led by Drs. X, Y, and Z.

7/17/16: Group intervention for each parent. 90 min. Drs. X, Y and Z.
Introductions, general expectations and anxieties about coming to camp;
answered any questions remaining from orientation.

7/17/14: Children's groups; 90 min.; Drs. A, B, and C 7/14/14: Supportive
intervention following interactions in the milieu regarding cabin
assignments; 30 min. Dr. X.

7/18/16: Group intervention for each parent; 3 hrs. Drs. X, Y and Z. Parents
told their story in group.

7/18/16: Group therapy for each child; 3 hrs. Drs. A and B

7/18/16: Co-parent intervention; 50 min; Drs. X and Y; The issues of
lack of trust between the parents, not adhering to agreements made,
parentification of the children when they are unable to agree and be
unified were addressed. Both parents expressed the fear that they could
lose custody or parenting time with the children. Mom feels that she is
under the extreme scrutiny and Dad feels that child's anxiety symptoms
are being used as a way to reduce his parenting time.

7/18/16: Family intervention: 30 min. Drs. X, Y & child counselor. Talked about
the parentification of the two older children regarding younger child's anxiety.
Parents agreed about the sleeping arrangements for child at camp due to her
distress. Parents also agreed upon father having contact with child.

7/18/16: Preparation for older child for family meeting; 15 min.; Dr. B.

7/18/16: Group intervention; 3 hrs. Drs. Y and Z. Discussed how the coparenting & family interventions were going. There was also a discussion about goals for the family that could be worked on in camp as well as an understanding of the goals we have at OB.

7/18/16: Group therapy for each child; 3 hrs. Drs. A, B, and C

7/18/16: Family intervention; 50 min.; with Drs X, Y and A and B. The impact on the children (parentification) regarding the parents' inability to manage parenting time problems was discussed.

7/18/16: Co-parenting intervention; 50 min.; with Drs. A and Y. Discussed the need for parents to manage the children's problems with their father so that the children did not have to take responsibility for managing younger child's anxiety& other issues. Parents were encouraged to think about what would be best for the children regarding a parenting plan.

7/18/16: Dr. A had an intervention with older daughter; 30 min.

7/19/16: Group intervention for each parent with Drs. X, Y and Z; 3 hrs.

7/19/16: Co-parenting intervention with Drs. X and Y. 50 min. Discussed plans for after camp with primary focus upon the trip home as a model for coparenting.

7/19/16: Family intervention with Drs. X, Y and A; 50 min. Discussed the trip home and which children would go home with which parent.

7/19/16: After-care planning meeting; 75 min. Drs. X and Y; Discussed after-care plan for the family.

7/19/16: Children's wrap-up group 1.25 hours. Drs. X, Y, A and B.

AGREEMENTS

1. Both parents agree to share information with each other about child-related issues in a timely fashion and prior to making any commitments to the children about those issues if they involve the other parent in any way.

2. Younger child will fly home with Mother after camp and Older child will drive home and go on the car trip with Dad.

3. Dad will return home from car trip on July 30, 2016, unless he determines that older daughter needs to return sooner.

4. During the time period when each parent will have an 11-day absence with a child/children, the children will be able to call either parent when they want to. Both parents will be respectful of the other's parenting time when it comes to the amount of calls/texts between the children and the other parent. This agreement will supersede the prior recommendations by the Parenting Coordinator.

OVERCOMING BARRIERS ADVISES THE PARENTS
TO CONSIDER THE FOLLOWING

Continued work be done to develop a parenting plan, including timeshare schedules for each child once school starts, and other components of a parenting plan to support a parallel parenting model.

Intensive therapy for mother with a focus on her personal adjustment to the family's transition and the normalization of her relationships with the children and father.

Continued individual therapy for father to support his personal adjustment to the families transition and the normalization of his relationships with the children and mother.

A behavioral medicine professional (therapist) with expertise in anxiety disorders be engaged to help younger child become independent in managing her anxiety.

It is critically important for all professionals who will undertake the suggested work to consult as soon as possible (or as part of their intake process) with a representative of the OB clinical team.

Sincerely,

Drs. X, Y and A

12

Translating the *Overcoming Barriers* Approach to Outpatient Settings

BARBARA J. FIDLER, PEGGIE WARD, AND ROBIN M. DEUTSCH ∎

1. INTRODUCTION

Clinical interventions for separating and divorcing families have tended to be eclectic, drawing on different treatment modalities (e.g., psychodynamic, psychoanalytic, cognitive–behavioral, psychoeducational, and family systems based) used with individuals, couples, families, and groups. Recognizing gaps in existing effective treatment for parent–child contact problems, Dr. Peggie Ward initially conceptualized the Overcoming Barriers Family Camp (OBFC) for high-conflict separated and divorced families in 2008, and Drs. Robin Deutsch and Matt Sullivan subsequently developed it (Sullivan, Ward, & Deutsch, 2010).

From its inception, the Overcoming Barriers (OCB) approach drew from existing treatment modalities used with separating and divorcing families. These antecedent modalities informed and provided impetus for the development of an innovative, immersion-type whole-family intervention. They included group therapy (Yalom & Leszcz, 2005), psychoeducational groups for parents (Goodman, Bonds, Sandler, & Braver, 2004) and children (Deutsch & Roseby, 1986; Johnston & Roseby, 1997; Pedro-Carroll, 1997; Pedro-Carroll & Cowen, 1985; Roseby & Deutsch, 1985), and various iterations of family therapy (Darnall, 2010; Freeman, Abel, Cowper-Smith, & Stein, 2004; Gardner, 1998, 1999, 2001; Johnston, Walters, & Friedlander, 2001; Lebow & Rekart, 2007; Sullivan & Kelly, 2001).

Having their own precursors, these various therapies and the OCB approach have integrated elements of behavior therapy and cognitive–behavioral therapy for anxiety and phobias (Francis & Beidel, 1995; Silverman, Pina, & Viswesvaran,

2008; Wolpe, 1958; Wolpe, Brady, Serber, Agras, & Liberman, 1973). In addition, experiential, structural, and strategic systemically based therapies dating back to the first generation of family therapy (e.g., Bowen, 1978; Haley, 1973; Haley & Hoffman, 1968; Minuchin, 1974; Satir, 1964; Whitaker, 1958; Whitaker & Bumberry, 1988) have been extremely instrumental in our work with high-conflict families. The OCB has incorporated more recent interventions with separating and divorcing children and parents, which have been influenced by second-generation systemically based interventions such as solution-focused, integrated problem-focused, and narrative therapies (Berg, 1994; de Shazer, 1988; Pinsof, Breunlin, Russell, & Lebow, 2011), relaxation techniques (Benson & Klipper, 2000), mindfulness and meditation training (Kabat-Zinn, 2005), and motivational interviewing (Brodsky, 2011; Miller & Rollnick, 2012), which may be helpful for more resistant clients.

Family interventions[1] for parent–child contact problems used in outpatient settings have been elaborated in Canada and the United States (Albertson-Kelly & Burkhard, 2013; Baker & Sauber, 2013; Carter, 2011; Fidler, 2009, 2011; Friedlander & Walters, 2010, 2014; Garber, 2015; Gottlieb, 2012, 2013; Greenberg, Doi Fick, & Schnider, 2012; Walters & Friedlander, 2012; Warshak, 2010a; Warshak & Otis, 2010). In addition, several primarily psychoeducational approaches and programs have emerged for rejected parents (Baker & Fine, 2008, 2013; Goldberg & Goldberg, 2013), for children in the school setting (Andre & Baker, 2009; Baker & Andre, 2013), and for families (Eddy, 2009, 2010, 2011, 2014; Warshak & Otis, 2010). Overcoming Barriers has published an instructive guide on essential parenting skills for preferred and rejected parents (Moran, Sullivan, & Sullivan, 2015).

Both the OCB approach and outpatient-setting interventions are evolving, each building on the other reciprocally. We learn and grow not only from our successes but even more so from our failures and challenges.

While clinical interventions are likely to be less expensive than litigation, many families, for reasons such as logistics, insufficient funds, or lack of court support, will not have the opportunity to attend an OBFC or an intensive, multiday single-family intervention (often referred to as an *intensive*[2]), both of which are brief interventions that in most cases require aftercare treatment. In this chapter, we identify the essential and unique features of the OCB approach, discuss how these can be applied to whole-family interventions in the outpatient setting, and illustrate these applications with case examples.

2. SCREENING, INTAKE, CONTRACTING, AND TREATMENT PLANNING

2.1. Preliminary Screening and Clinical Intake

As elaborated in Chapter 2, cases referred for clinical intervention to remedy parent–child contact problems require legal structural components and informed systematic clinical protocols for managing referrals, beginning with a preliminary screening and followed by a more thorough clinical intake. Thoughtfully developed protocols will assist in screening out cases likely to be inappropriate for an outpatient-setting family intervention. These protocols will vary depending on the referral source and on whether a child custody evaluation has been conducted. When there has been no custody evaluation, a more through clinical assessment by the therapist for the purpose of treatment planning is needed.

With cases that appear to be more severe, at least during the preliminary screening, the clinician may choose to conduct a more thorough clinical consultation before accepting the case for outpatient therapy. This consultation will involve meeting with the child and parents individually (and sometimes together), reviewing relevant documentation and reports, and contacting key collateral sources (a previous custody evaluator, previous or current therapist(s), etc.) The therapist then provides feedback to the lawyers and parents about *possible* options for intervention (e.g., outpatient multi-faceted family therapy, multiday whole-family intensives, whole-family sequential intervention, no family therapy, individual therapy or addiction counseling for one or more of the family members, or legal remedies), including the risks and benefits of each. See Chapter 2 for further elaboration on these options.

The nature and severity of the parent–child contact problem will point to the differentiated intervention response. Generally, irrespective of the nature of the contact problem (affinity, alignment, alienation, realistic estrangement, or a hybrid), mild and moderate cases are likely to be appropriate for a family intervention, such as an OBFC, intensive single-family intervention, or multifaceted family therapy in an outpatient setting.

In some more severe cases, while some progress may be observed in the office or community, often any positive changes are short-lived once the child returns to the orbit of the favored parent, who is usually the custodial parent. Consequently, as discussed in Chapter 2, when the rejected parent is a good or "good enough" parent, the severest cases are likely to require a change in custody to the rejected parent combined with a temporary interruption in contact with the alienating parent, often using a sequential intervention model such as Family Bridges (Rand & Warshak, 2008; Warshak, 2010b), Transitioning Families (Judge et al., 2016) or Stable Paths (Judge & Bailey, 2015) to assist with the transition of care. In some of these cases, the child may be placed in a neutral setting before being transitioned to the rejected parent's care. These brief but intensive approaches begin with an intervention (clinical, educational, or both) with the rejected parent and child, followed by reintegration of the child with the previously favored parent if and when that parent has demonstrated the willingness and ability to discontinue her or his parental alienating behavior and to facilitate the child's relationship with the other parent. When integration of the child back with this parent is possible, the alienating parent may have participated in individual therapy and education to learn what alienation is, what its negative impact on children and adolescents is, and how to modify her or his own behavior. Coaching is used to help the parent apply newly taught verbal and behavioral tools.

Box 12.1

PRELIMINARY SCREENING RULE-OUT CRITERIA FOR OUTPATIENT
FAMILY INTERVENTION

- Restraining order without exception for contact noted
- Clear presence of threats of abduction, violence, or both
- Clear history of power and control dynamics
- Clear untreated major mental illness; may include
    - fixed belief or repeated unsubstantiated allegations of sexual abuse
    - ongoing alcohol or substance abuse
- Refusal of some members of families to participate or sign consent agreement for services, including stipulation it is in the child's best interests to have a good relationship with both parents[a]
- Failed previous outpatient treatment efforts; may be due to fixed and unyielding beliefs re abuse or repeated allegations of abuse, including sexual, that, after investigation, have proven unsubstantiated
- nability to pay for services

[a]If one or both parents cannot provide this stipulation, then the therapy cannot proceed, because there is a dispute about what is in the child's best interests. There may need to be a finding from the court or recommendations from a custody evaluator as to what is in the child's best interests before the therapy can begin.

Chapter 2 provides checklists for preliminary screening and clinical intake protocols. Factors or areas of inquiry indicating that an outpatient family intervention is likely to be inappropriate are shown in Box 12.1. While there is no bright line, the longer the duration of no contact or of significant disruptions in contact has been, the more severe the case will be, and the greater the likelihood is that family therapy will be ineffective. Related factors to consider include the child's age, communication abilities, and any special needs or vulnerabilities.

Exploring the previous legal, educational, or clinical efforts to remedy the problem is essential to the preliminary screening and clinical intake. Common sense tells us it is counterproductive to repeat similar efforts that have been unsuccessful; often our attempted solutions then become the problem (Waltzlawick, 1974). Moreover, repeated unsuccessful interventions are likely to exacerbate the parent–child contact problem: The longer the problem persists, the more entrenched and resistant to change it becomes (Fidler & Bala, 2010).

2.2. Contracting: Legal Structural Components

In parent–child contact problem cases, clinical intervention must be accompanied by a detailed service agreement, which is part of the required informed-consent process. Some cases will have the added benefit of a court order for the treatment, though typically these orders have insufficient detail—hence the need for the detailed service agreement if it is not possible to incorporate the necessary clauses into an order. In cases with active court involvement, signaling at least moderate severity, it is prudent for the parents' consent agreement to be made into a stipulation or on-consent court order. For cases where court involvement has yet to occur, and it is reasonably clear the contact problem is of milder nature, commencing a court application may be ill-advised, as doing so may exacerbate the conflict. Still, best practice requires a detailed and unambiguous consent service agreement (AFCC Task Force on Court-Involved Therapy, 2011).

Providing a sample treatment agreement to the referring source in response to the initial query for a clinical intervention will be instructive and practical in terms of time taken during the early stages of a referral. The agreement can be relied on for the parent consent agreement or as a template for a court order for treatment if the case is already in court or there are plans to take it to court (Greenberg, Deutsch, Gould-Saltman, & Cunningham, 2013). Some jurisdictions have therapy court order forms. (See Appendix 12.A for an example of treatment agreement and order.) The checklist in Box 12.2 may assist parents, lawyers, or the court during the referral, preliminary screening, and clinical intake phase.

The presence or absence of a detailed and unambiguous parenting plan or court order for parenting time will significantly affect any therapeutic intervention. A court order or consent agreement for therapy requires a stipulation that it is in the child's best interests to have a good relationship with both parents and further, that each parent agrees to participate fully towards that mutual goal. If there is any question as to what is in the child's best interests in this regard, a custody evaluation may be necessary prior to commencing an intervention or further direction from the court.

A court order or consent treatment agreement authorizing the reintegration or family therapist to determine (or even make recommendations for) the parenting time schedule, though not uncommon, is ill-advised; doing so places the therapist in an unethical dual role (Greenberg, Gould, Schnider, Gould-Saltman, & Martindale, 2003). Arbitrating or determining parenting time is an evaluative or forensic role, while the therapeutic role includes, among other things, attempting to implement the previously ordered or agreed to parenting time. If there is no order or agreement for parenting time and there is an expectation that the therapist will determine or make recommendations for parenting time, it is likely the therapy will be obstructed, because the favored parent, child, or both are likely to continually lobby the therapist to make a recommendation or determination for no or highly restricted contact with the other parent. Further, making recommendations about legal custody or parenting time is contrary to best practice (AFCC Task Force on Court-Involved Therapy, 2011), because the therapist would not have completed a comprehensive child custody evaluation and consequently does not have a sufficient basis on which to make recommendations. We caution mental health professionals in this regard: A therapist's making recommendations for custody or access is one of the most frequent complaints about professionals by disgruntled litigants.

Box 12.2

CHECKLIST FOR COURT ORDER FOR FAMILY INTERVENTION IN
PARENT–CHILD CONTACT PROBLEM CASES

1. Provide structured and specified parenting plan, or pathway to return to court for determination after specified duration of therapy.
2. Identify objectives of therapy or intervention.
3. Identify minimum duration for therapy or intervention, or clarify terms for parents' withdrawal from services and procedures for selecting new therapist.
4. Identify the names of professionals who will provide therapy or intervention; failing that, specify a process for selecting professionals in the event parents cannot agree. Process may include provision for no unauthorized introduction of new therapists.
5. Identify specific role of each professional, including scope of decision-making powers, if any.
6. Name any specific seminars or educational programs parents are to attend.
7. Name each family member who is to participate in therapy or intervention.
8. State that professionals are entitled to communicate with one another as deemed necessary by therapists and that parents will execute any necessary authorizations to allow exchange of information.
9. State that parents will cooperate with therapist.
10. Clarify limits of confidentiality, if any, including reporting requirements to court.
11. Identify enforcement clauses (e.g., sanctions, consequences for noncompliance, and options to prevent change of custody).
12. Specify any grievance procedures.
13. Clarify details of payment for services.

NOTE. Adapted from Fidler, Bala, Birnbaum, and Kavassalis (2008).

In some cases, there will be a detailed court order or consent agreement for parenting time, but the specified time is not or is only partially occurring. In other cases, there will be no order, and the child's contact will be limited to seeing the disfavored parent during the therapy as determined by the therapist. Once the family intervention has occurred, the case would return to court or the previously retained parenting coordinator or arbitrator for determination of the parenting time going forward.

Unlike with traditional therapies, best practice dictates that with clinical interventions in parent–child contact problem cases, treatment agreements or orders will include terms permitting the court to monitor progress and permitting the therapist to provide reports to the court when necessary. It bears reiterating that repeated unsuccessful intervention is likely to exacerbate the problem: The longer alienation lasts, the worse it becomes. If therapy does not begin in a timely manner (as stipulated in the order or consent agreement) or if some progress does not occur after about two or three months, consideration should be given to a return to court and alternative remedies. For cases that have not yet involved the court, setbacks or a lack of progress will be a red flag pointing to the need to seek the court's assistance before what was thought to be a minor contact problem becomes full-fledged alienation.

The preliminary screening and clinical intake for family reintegration therapy are critical opportunities for the potential therapist to provide information to referring sources about the requirements for accepting referrals for the particular family intervention the therapist provides. The rule-out criteria noted in Box 12.1, indicating that the case is more severe, or the absence of or inability to obtain the necessary and sufficient structural legal components summarized above is a red flag for the therapist. It is prudent for the therapist to exercise caution when accepting referrals. While the therapist wants to be helpful, some referrals are inappropriate for the family reintegration therapy and should not be accepted. These cases may be referred back to the lawyers or court for legal remedies or for other interventions designed for more severe cases, as elaborated in Chapter 2.

2.3. Initial Interviews

Once the referral has been accepted, as elaborated in Chapter 2, the therapist will begin with the informed consent process with each family member (Lebow & Black, 2012) by carefully reviewing the detailed treatment agreement and order, if any, including the specific treatment goals, limits of confidentiality, reporting and payment terms, and other terms (see Appendix 12.A).

While protocols will vary depending on the family circumstances, specific allegations, and the severity of the contact problem, often the therapist will see each parent individually at this stage, beginning with the favored parent, who may be feeling blamed and resistant to therapy. In more mild cases, the therapist may choose to see the parents together at first to review the treatment agreement or order, followed by individual meetings with each parent. The therapist will make efforts to build rapport and develop a working alliance with each parent as that parent discusses her or his own narratives, perceptions, concerns, fears, and anxieties. While it is important for the parent to feel that her or his concerns are heard, well-paced redirection to the future and goals is imperative. The requirements to cooperate with therapy and for parent accountability noted in the consent agreement or order need to be made clear to the parents and children, including any potential consequences for lack of cooperation. These may include a return to court and the possibility of a change of custody, which in itself can be an important and effective incentive for change (Fidler, Bala & Saini, 2013).

While it may be possible to see the child the first time with both parents together, or with the child and the rejected parent, in most cases the child will attend her or his first interview, where confidentiality and goals are explained, with the favored parent; an individual interview with the child may follow the joint introductory meeting or on another day. Before this first interview with the child, it is necessary to explore the extent to which the favored parent will be able or willing to adequately explain the purpose of the family therapy (to repair relationships and reconcile with the rejected parent) to the child during the interview. (If the parent is unable to provide this explanation, the therapist may need to meet with the child alone the first time.) Coaching may be necessary to help the parent develop an age-appropriate script. Once confident the parent can deliver the message correctly, the therapist will ask the parent to explain her or his expectations for the child's cooperation and participation. It is likely the therapist will need to assist the favored parent in imparting these important ground rules to the child. Reminders about what the therapist's role does and does not entail (e.g., not making recommendations about or determine parenting time) are imperative at this stage to address the child's expectations and anticipated empowerment. The therapist can fill in any gaps, clarify any uncertainties, and conduct an age-appropriate informed-consent process explaining the limits of confidentiality, the therapist's role, and the limits of that role.

2.4. Family Intervention Goals, Developing the Treatment Plan, and the Clinician's Tool and Resource Kit

Generally speaking, the goals for therapeutic and psychoeducational interventions when children are resisting or rejecting a parent are consistent across various models (e.g., Albertson-Kelly & Burkhard, 2013; Blow & Daniel, 2002; Carter, 2011; DeJong & Davies, 2012; Everett, 2006; Fidler, 2009, 2011; Friedlander & Walters, 2010; Garber, 2011, 2013; Gottlieb, 2012, 2013; Greenberg et al., 2012; Johnston et al., 2001; Lebow & Rekart, 2007; Sullivan et al., 2010; Walters & Friedlander, 2012). The sample family treatment agreement in Appendix 12.A lists the typical goals, stated generally as

- fostering overall healthy child adjustment;
- restoring or developing adequate parenting (roles and boundaries) and coparenting skills (communication, problem-solving, and conflict resolution); and
- removing the child from parental conflict.

Based on the OCB goals (Sullivan et al., 2010) and the outpatient literature cited above , Chapter 2 includes a chart (Table 2.X) listing the treatment goals for individual or group work as they apply to each parent, the child, coparents, or all family members (dyads or the full family). To accomplish these goals, interventions are designed with the following concrete objectives:

- decrease the child's feelings of fear, anger, discomfort, or anxiety toward the rejected parent;
- expand the child's and parents' perspectives;

- shift the child's perceptions and feelings toward a less polarized view of each parent;
- reduce polarized views of each parent's contribution to the child's resistance;
- decrease parental conflict;
- improve individual parenting skills;
- improve parent alliance, coparenting relationship, and conflict management;
- improve parent–child relationships, develop or repair appropriate parent–child boundaries, and correct alignments;
- decrease parent–child conflict;
- improve communication and problem-solving among all family members; and
- enhance empathy and foster compassionate relationships.

During the clinical intake and contracting, treatment goals may need to be adapted or augmented to meet the family's specific needs and circumstances. The information obtained during the preliminary screening and clinical intake will assist in treatment planning. While designing a treatment plan is essential, the plan should be seen as organic and invariably will be modified throughout the process as new information is obtained, themes emerge and expand, and the intervention pathways uncover what may or may not be working. Careful planning in between sessions will augment the effectiveness of the treatment.

Psychoeducation, support, and coaching of children and parents are essential parts of the therapist's repertoire for any intervention model, whether the group camp, multiday intensives, outpatient settings. The therapist will select specific interventions, educational materials, and other resources from her or his own "clinician's tool and resource kit" to address the identified treatment goals with the family members, whether individually, in dyads (i.e., parent–child or coparents), or as a whole.

The tools and resources used will vary from therapist to therapist and be continuously augmented as the therapist participates in peer consultation (or supervision), attends continuing education, or discovers more material. These psychoeducational materials will include varied content and principles intended to teach the family members about

- affect identification and regulation;
- the impact of separation or divorce and of loyalty bind;
- differentiation of parent–child contact problems and the multiple factors that contribute to these;
- cognitive distortions, perceptual errors, selective attention, and multiple perspective taking;
- critical-thinking skills;
- effective problem solving, communication, and conflict management;
- social conformity and suggestibility;
- memory construction and fallibility;

- adolescent brain development; and
- compassion, empathy, and hope.

The form this content takes will vary and includes written educational handouts and checklists; videos and YouTube clips; bibliographies; books for children and parents; metaphorical stories; exercises; and educational websites (e.g., pertaining to parenting, coparenting communication, conflict resolution, problem-solving, or adolescent brain development). The possibilities for the clinician's tool and resource kit are endless; exploring options can be inspiring, fun, and educational, and a necessary but insufficient part of the therapy development process (e.g., Fidler, 2011; Polak, Fidler, & Popielarczyk, 2013).

3. APPLYING ESSENTIAL COMPONENTS OF THE OCB APPROACH TO OUTPATIENT SETTINGS

In this section, we discuss ways the three essential components of the OCB approach can be translated to whole-family (reintegration) interventions in outpatient settings. These components are

1. An intensive, whole-family approach
2. Experiential and recreational activities
3. A coordinated case management and team approach.

3.1. Intensive, Whole-Family Approach

As discussed more extensively in Chapter 6, OBFC is a group residential program for several families at one time, lasting three to five days (Sullivan et al., 2010; www.overcomingbarriers.org). By contrast, one family at a time participates in outpatient settings, over a duration ranging from 6 to 24 months, sometimes longer. Individual family intensives may be three to five days long. Given that OBFC and intensives are by design brief, developing and coordinating aftercare plans for implementation in the family's home jurisdiction are integral to the intervention goals. Outpatient setting models can provide these aftercare interventions subsequent to OBFC or an intensive, which may have occurred out of the family's state or province.

The OCB approach and outpatient settings involve the whole family, both those living in the same home, and sometimes other family members such as grandparents, new partners, or older siblings, who have been identified during the screening and intake to play a critical part in maintaining the family dysfunction. Since the OCB approach is residential and immersive, it is necessarily intensive. In outpatient settings, the intervention, while not residential, still has an intensive quality: The whole family is involved in various combinations, usually in longer blocks of time than the one hour per week schedule typical of more conventional therapy that may be bound by insurance parameters.[3] Like a juggler, the therapist coordinates, manages, balances, and synchronizes the process, including the sequence of sessions; which family member or combination of members attends and when they attend; and the specific tools, strategies, or resources used at a particular time.

The essential components of each of the OBFC morning psychoeducation groups—East Group for the favored parents, West Group for the rejected parents, and Common Ground for the children—are discussed in Chapters 8, 9, and 10, respectively. After lunch, these three-hour group sessions are followed by recreational activities (led by the milieu staff) and parenting, coparenting, and child-focused clinical interventions designed to build connections and address each family's specific themes and issues. Relying on the building blocks of the morning sessions, these afternoon clinical interventions, elaborated further in Chapter 11, may involve conjoint parent meetings, parent–child dyads, or the whole family. These sessions are led by one or more of the East Group, West Group, or Common Ground therapists. These morning-group therapists help the family members feel supported in their individual work that occurs during the morning group process and then again during the intensive afternoon family work.

In outpatient settings the "team" may comprise one or more therapists; the child and one or both parents may each have an individual therapist. The entire family is involved in office sessions in various combinations as determined by the therapist(s): individual meetings with each parent, conjoint coparenting meetings with the parents, meetings with parent–child dyads, and,whole-family meetings. Meetings or telephone calls with collateral sources may also occur.

Family intervention in cases of parent–child contact problems, particularly in the earlier phases, requires a significant commitment of time, usually several hours each week as the therapist sees the family members in various combinations, reviews court and other documentation, and obtains key information from collateral sources (e.g., a child protection agency, previous or current therapist(s), a guardian ad litem, a custody evaluator, teachers, or a parenting coordinator). This time commitment affects not only the cost of the therapy but also the logistics. Children, favored parents, or both are often resistant, and the need to miss school or for extended time to travel to and from the therapist's office after school adds stress. To avoid the stress related to lengthy travel, particularly during high-traffic times or after school, it is preferable for the family to live reasonably close to the therapist's office (though in some cases no alternatives are available). When therapists do not work evenings or weekends, close proximity may also be helpful for parents who do not have flexible work schedules. Models enabling fewer visits to the office by combining longer (full or half-day) sessions with homework and follow-up sessions several weeks later may be suitable for some families, depending on the nature and intensity of the contact problem.

3.2. Experiential and Recreational Activities

In Chapter 4, Drs. Abigail Judge and Rebecca Bailey elaborate the rationale, benefits and techniques of experientially based therapies for families in conflict. In

Chapter 7, Tyler Sullivan, Carole Blane, Dan Wolfson, and Judge discuss the recreational milieu component of the OCB approach—perhaps its most distinctive element—and how this component is coordinated and integrated with the clinical components of the camp program.

The choices for structured recreational and experiential activities in family interventions, including OBFC, intensives, and outpatient settings, are endless. OBFC provides opportunities for such activities in the afternoons, at meals, and during evening programming. In outpatient settings, recreational activities can easily be incorporated into office sessions and outside the office in the community or other locations. As discussed in previous chapters, movement and nature provide significant opportunities for healing and change (Jordan, 2015). We know from brain research that to regulate emotion, we must start with patterned rhythmic activity. And regulation must be in place if individuals are to reason effectively (Perry, 2001). We intentionally and strategically provide interventions using sensorimotor parent–child interactions, such as walking, running, swinging, and jumping, to regulate the child's arousal. The use of animals (see Chapter 4) for rhythmic petting, walking, or riding, both independently and with a parent or parents, offers children opportunities for regulation and for experiential learning about power, control, letting go, and trust.

Structured and planned recreation is intended to create an opening or "space" where family members can experience opportunities for new or corrective positive experiences and connections. Within this structure, children can be given choices or a range of ways to engage, to foster their willingness to participate and preserve their sense of control. Often, connections can be achieved more easily through doing than through talking. Talking elicits defensive posturing, and repeating old narratives tends to keep rigid beliefs and scripts entrenched (in keeping with the neuroscientific maxim "Neurons that fire together, wire together"). Through doing, new or different experiences redirect family members away from their worries, rigid beliefs, and hurt feelings, paving the way for a positive shared experience.

Recreational experiences also "make points" about important principles related to relationships, boundaries, perspective taking, cognitive distortions, empathy, cooperation, communication, and so on, without the points' actually being stated. Because children and their favored parents are likely to be resistant and defensive, a more indirect and nonjudgmental approach is likely to be more effective than confronting them "head-on," which often activates their defenses of denial and projection. In addition, positive new experiences can trigger memories of previous positive experiences that the child may be denying, not remembering, or negatively reconstructing. With recreation, doing, and movement as foundations creating positive experiences and solidifying them in memory, family members may be more willing to address hurt and angry feelings and to learn better communication and problem-solving skills during subsequent sessions.

Behavioral change often comes from doing, not just thinking. Strong beliefs, especially when publicly stated, are prone to remain unchanged (Warshak, 2010b). Activities allow the child to ease into building connections and having a good time with the rejected parent while being permitted to save face, an essential piece of the work. Where appropriate, family members can be given immediate feedback or corrective information, resulting in their learning better communication and more appropriate ways to interact with others. There may also be opportunities for one or both parents to apologize for experiences that created distress or mistrust.

In many cases, the child may not have seen the rejected parent for some time. In other cases, the contacts that have occurred have been paired with negative feelings, thoughts, and behaviors. Recreational activities provide an opportunity for the child and rejected parent to share a corrective experience. The child can observe firsthand that the resisted parent has some capacity to be loving, warm, understanding, and sensitive to the child's needs and feelings. Direct experience can demonstrate to the child that the rejected parent is not blaming or criticizing the other parent.

Activities need to be carefully planned, structured, and paced, taking into account the child's and the parents' varying degrees of anxiety, fear, and discomfort. Clinical experience and recent research (Wier, 2011) have demonstrated it is not uncommon for there to be a disconnect between what a child states or protests against and how they behave once they are with the resisted parent. While forcing a resistant child to engage with a parent is never permissible, when a child can be cajoled, it is not uncommon to discover he or she is not in fact anxious or fearful: "Jumping in" may work well, and better than expected. In other cases, connections have to be more gradually titrated.

As discussed in Chapter 2, a polarized child resisting contact with a parent often is anxious, fearful, or phobic; these feelings play out in the mutually escalating dynamic with the favored parent. Sometimes, the fears and anxieties have a basis in the child's actual experiences (e.g., in cases of mild or moderate realistic estrangement or hybrid cases). However, at other times, when the aligned parent seizes on past negative episodes with the resisted parent and exaggerates them, the child's reaction is irrational or disproportionate to the actual experience (in alienation cases). Regardless of the cause of their anxieties, children must be reassured safety comes first and they will not be physically forced into face-to-face contact with the resisted parent. However, with the support of the favored parent, the child can be prepared to have face-to-face contact when they can have some control over the setting and plan. The child's phobic symptoms must be addressed and in cases where some abuse or trauma has occurred, children should not be retraumatized by being pushed too vigorously to reunify. In some cases the child is more willing to engage with the parent they are resisting in the favored parent's presence, while in other cases the child can feel free to engage with the resisted parent only once they are apart from the favored parent.

Allegations of past abuse, regardless of the nature or severity, do not mitigate the need to address the favored parent's protective behavior, whether it is justified or needlessly protective. Restrictive gatekeeping, even if the parent truly believes the child is at risk, can be harmful to a child, particularly when it is not warranted. In the subset of more severe alienation cases where the allegations are known to be false, the therapy must also address the alienating parent's underlying motivation to destroy the rejected parent's relationship with the child and/or preserve their own at the exclusion of the other parent.

Systematic desensitization and exposure have proven effective in the treatment of anxiety and phobias (Wolpe, 1958; Wolpe et al., 1973).[4] These therapies can be applied in parent–child contact cases by replacing avoidance with gradual, planned contacts that are consistent with the child's current level of comfort; as a result, the child gains mastery and has positive experiences (Deutsch, 2015; Garber, 2015). Relaxation techniques (Albertson-Kelly & Burkhard, 2013; Garber, 2015) and pairing positive reinforcements, such as snacks or positive activities, with indirect exposure can assist with the systematic desensitization process (Wolpe, 1958). These methods, used with the child individually and with the child–rejected parent dyad, while in some cases effective, must not be used in isolation; they must be combined with essential pieces of reintegration therapy, including the legal structural components and work with the favored parent.

As elaborated in Chapters 6 and 7, there are many ways to orchestrate connection building. In outpatient settings the process can begin with indirect contact with the rejected parent, such as viewing photographs or family videos (DeJong & Davies, 2012; Fidler et al., 2013), and gradually move to telephone or video chat, parallel play, and interactive engagement (Chase, 1983). Activities as simple as a walk in the neighborhood or to a nearby park to see the spring blossoms or get ice cream, for example, can be within a child's comfort zone while permitting connections to be built first through parallel experience. As the child desensitizes, activities involving more engagement, such as throwing a ball or playing a game, can be phased in. Other options include sharing a picnic inside or outside the office, watching movies together, drawing or building, playing board games, preparing a snack, or cooking together. The possibilities are endless; each activity can involve a range of experiences, from parallel to fully interactive.

Weitzman (2004, 2013) describes a nonconfidential outpatient protocol for treatment of anxiety disorders that uses observation through a one-way mirror, allowing the child to initially view an alienated or estranged parent without being seen, as a tool to reintroduce children to the estranged parent. Weitzman (2004) states, "The one-way mirror provides a physical and psychological barrier from direct contact with a parent whom the child fears and allows the clinician to more easily control the pace of the reunification process" (p. 27). Viewing the resisted parent from behind the one-way mirror can reduce the child's anxiety, permitting reunification to proceed gradually. The parent and child can talk to each other through a speaker system. Using the mirror and audio equipment is also fun for many children, assisting with the process of reunification. The child can observe the parent with the therapist, and when ready, the child can ask the parent questions. After informed consent and confidentiality are addressed, the protocol involves the following stages:

1. The therapist meets initially with the parents.
2. The therapist meets with the child.
3. The therapist orients the child to the viewing room.

4. Use of the one-way mirror begins with the child observing the resisted parent.
5. The resisted parent is interviewed in the child's presence.
6. Additional interviews occur with other resisted family members, initially from behind the mirror if necessary.

Once the parent–child relationship is re-established, the child's contact with the previously resisted parent can occur in public places or during family therapy.

In cases of parent–child contact problems, children develop an anticipatory anxiety due to the lapse in contact combined with the phobic memory, whether real or suggested. As Weitzman and others have shown replicated, empirically based evidence indicates we can reasonably expect symptom reduction in children who are genuinely anxious or fearful from behavioral, systematic desensitization, and exposure therapies, even when the symptoms result more from the favored parent's fears, anxieties, or vindictive behavior than from the child's own experiences. When, however, the child's resistance does not abate or even increases, it is likely that the problems are not caused by actual anxiety or fear but result from unrelenting parental alienating behavior continuing between therapy sessions. At that point, it will likely be useful for the therapist to explain to the aligned parent that increases in anxiety symptoms in response to gradual exposure are inconsistent with true anxiety and, further, to remind the parent of the court's expectation that the parent will make her of his best effort at cooperation and of the potential consequences for noncompliance (Weitzman, 2013).

Outpatient family reintegration therapy is not a quick fix; it can take anywhere from six months to two years (Fidler et al., 2013). Sustainable change may require progress combined with minor setbacks, which then become grist for the therapy. Despite preliminary screening and thorough clinical intake, in some cases the inappropriateness of a case for family intervention or the futility of the therapy will become evident only sometime after the treatment has been attempted. Therapy needs to be monitored carefully for indications of the attainment of the treatment objectives, with expectations that some change in the desired direction will occur within the first two months. Belaboring therapy in the absence of reasonable progress is likely to further entrench the alienation. Delays in implementing the more appropriate legal, clinical or psychoedcational remedy will compound the problem, and in such situations a referral back to court for more appropriate legal remedies or other interventions is indicated.

In outpatient settings, just as with the OCB approach, direct debriefings with the favored parent after the child's engagement with the rejected parent are needed to correct unnecessary protective behavior and the mutually escalating dynamic of anxiety and to reinforce the child's mastery. During OBFC or an intensive, the favored parent is easily accessible for any needed debriefing. In outpatient settings, by contrast, it is imperative to plan for sufficient time for debriefing the favored parent after any community or office dyadic work with the child and rejected parent. Debriefing may occur when the favored parent picks up the child after a session, either with the parent alone while the child waits or with the parent and child together; by telephone while the rejected parent is returning the child to the favored parent and well enough before the child arrives; or in a subsequent meeting or call. The therapist will provide education, coaching, and support, sometimes using role plays and carefully crafted scripts, to assist the favored parent with managing and responding to the child's inevitable complaints.

CASE EXAMPLE

Nine-year-old Sarah's parents, Mary and Steven, were divorced when she was 6 years old. An incident involving aggression precipitated the separation. Mary alleged Steven had hit her. He acknowledged there was a nasty argument with both parents exchanging nasty insults, but denied he had hit her and alleged she had used physical aggression with him. The police were not involved.

Before the separation, Mary rarely allowed Sarah to be alone with Steven, fearing he could not adequately care for her asthma. After the parents separated, Mary was protective, and Sarah had contact with her father only for very brief periods, usually in Mary's presence. Often Mary made excuses or scheduled activities that resulted in lengthy interruptions of contact between Sarah and her father. Although prior to the separation Sarah and Steven were developing a secure attachment, afterward, with the limited contact, opportunities to further develop the relationship were lost despite Steven's efforts to make himself available.

After Steven's conciliatory efforts proved unsuccessful, he concluded he had no choice but to resort to litigation. Mary felt threatened and her anxiety increased, resulting in Sarah's own anxiety and fears escalating, much like a snowball picking up more snow. It was not too long before Mary advanced abuse allegations against Steven on the basis of statements Sarah had made to her and a neighbor. The police and the child protection agency became involved. After a thorough investigation, the allegations were not substantiated, and the police did not charge Steven. Mary could not be reassured her daughter was not at risk, and consequently neither could Sarah.

In the meantime, feeling depressed, Steven had moved away and was living on the other side of the country, where he was able to have the support of his parents and siblings. He was not advancing a claim for custody but did want to develop a schedule of gradually increasing time with Sarah, including one weekend a month where Sarah lived and, eventually, half the holidays. The lawyers referred the family for reintegration family counseling.

From the outset, Sarah was extremely anxious and appeared to be afraid of her father. Eventually, after many hours of office work with the family in various combinations, the therapist accompanied Sarah and Steven to the nearby park. In what seemed like a miracle, Sarah engaged her father in kicking a ball and appeared to be gleeful. In retrospect, the therapist questioned if it would have been better to introduce this activity far earlier. At one point Sarah fell down and scraped her knee, which also brought on a coughing episode. She cried briefly until her father ran to her, cared for the injury, and administered her inhaler. She rebounded quickly and resumed laughing and playing soccer.

Sarah complained about having to leave the park and said she wanted to play with her father more. On the way back to the office, Sarah started to become anxious and distant from Steven. When Sarah, Steven, and the therapist arrived back at the office, Steven was asked to wait in one room, as Mary refused to be near him. As Mary entered the office, before she could even sit down, Sarah ran to her and alleged that her father "took hours" to provide her inhaler. The therapist quickly mobilized to convene a session with Sarah and her mother to discuss what had actually happened at the park. Sarah's need to misrepresent what had actually happened was reframed as her need to say what she thought her mother needed to hear. Mary, who was suspicious of the therapist and unable to recognize Sarah's predicament, was encouraged to give Sarah permission to enjoy her time with her father. A follow-up session was booked with Mary to provide further intervention, and conjoint sessions with Sarah and Steven continued.

Just as the child's exposure to the rejected parent can be titrated, so too can the participation of the therapist. At first the therapist may accompany the child alone into the community to participate in planned recreational activities, and later the rejected or favored parent may join them. Then the child and resisted parent can engage on their own in the office or in the community, combined with brief sessions with the therapist before and after the contact. Another variation at this stage is for the parent and child to be left on their own to play a game or do an activity while the therapist in an unplanned manner comes in and out of the room periodically. Brief sessions with the resisted parent and child on the Friday before a weekend contact and then again the Monday after (before the child sees the favored parent) can provide some containment and an opportunity to address any issues or setbacks that may have arisen before they escalate. Subsequently the office can be used as a location for transitions, with the favored parent dropping the child off and leaving the premises and the resisted parent picking the child up from and returning the child to the office.

3.3. Coordinated Case Management and Team Approach

Both historically and currently, many professionals are typically involved in high-conflict and alienation cases. This can be confusing and stressful to the family members. Conflicts and alignments can form among well-intentioned professionals that mirror the family and adversarial system dynamics (Sullivan & Kelly, 2001). Poorly coordinated services can be wasteful, escalate conflict, and be harmful to children (Greenberg et al., 2013).

In the OCB systemic approach, systematic planning, coordination, and organization take place among multiple professionals in four related ways:

1. During the preliminary screening and clinical intake, the clinician communicates and coordinates with relevant collateral sources (e.g., the custody evaluator, guardian ad litem, lawyers, child protection agency, and other therapists).
2. Throughout OBFC, the clinical team (the child and parent group therapists) exchange information and plan interventions several times each day. This process sometimes includes referring back to obtained reports or contacting collateral sources for clarification.
3. Throughout the camp, mutual exchanges of information occur between the clinical team and the recreational director about the family's experiences in the therapeutic and recreational milieu, and these updates are integrated into the subsequent clinical and recreational programming. This mutual feedback and integration between the clinical team and the milieu staff are unique to the OCB approach and key to its process and outcomes.
4. Professional planning, coordination, and communication take place between the OCB clinical team and potential aftercare therapists.

In outpatient settings, protocols for coordinated planning and communication among the professionals are essential and will vary depending on the circumstances of the family. In addition to the family therapist, one or both parents and the child may have individual therapists. Other professionals periodically involved with the family over the course of the therapy may be physicians, teachers, tutors, child protection workers, mediators, supervised access workers, parenting coordinators, and lawyers. Careful planning, coordination, and communication between the family therapist and the other involved professionals are necessary to prevent professional splitting and polarization (Greenberg & Sullivan, 2012).

In some cases, there will be one or more therapists actively involved along with a parenting coordinator (or arbitrator), who has the authority to make child-related decisions within a limited scope as per the parenting coordination agreement or order (Coates, Deutsch, Starnes, Sullivan, & Sydlik, 2004). When a parenting coordinator is assigned to facilitate implementation of the parenting plan, they may function as the leader of the professional team and assist with intervention planning and communication among the actively involved professionals (Greenberg & Sullivan, 2012). When there is no parenting coordinator, the family therapist needs to assume the important function of team leader.

The family therapist needs to exercise caution when becoming involved in ongoing parenting plan conflicts (e.g., over changes in the parenting time schedule, scheduling of holidays, telephone contact, extracurricular activities, travel consent, or transfer of clothing and belongings between the parents' homes). This is sometimes easier said than done. For example, there may be no order or agreement for an imminent Christmas school break, and although some progress was made during therapy, a noticeable setback occurs as the parental conflict over parenting time escalates during the holiday. Naturally, the parents, and sometimes their lawyers or the court, turn for assistance to the therapist, who they believe is in the best position to provide direction. It is essential that the outpatient therapist understands the critical issues involved in playing a dual role and not allow herself or himself to be put in a position to mediate conflicts of this sort or offer definitive recommendations or determinations. Taking on this dual role may compromise the therapist's neutrality and impede therapeutic progress. In cases where parenting plan conflicts are frequent, the therapist may find it appropriate to recommend a mediator or parenting coordinator.

When parenting coordinators are involved, the court order or consent agreement will necessarily permit the therapist to provide progress reports to the parenting coordinator, who may then rely on the information to make decisions or recommendations within the scope of the stipulation. Parenting coordinators can offer additional benefits to families receiving family therapy for parent–child contact problems (Sullivan, 2008):

- The parenting coordinator may have the authority to recommend or determine the treatment team at the outset of the therapy or, once the family therapy has started, to make changes needed to address problems.
- The coordinator can act as a buffer to the child's therapy: The therapist can communicate with the parenting coordinator, who shares information with the parents on a discretionary basis.
- The coordinator can reinforce changes in parent and coparenting behavior addressed during the family therapy.

CASE EXAMPLE

Fifteen-year-old Benjamin refused to see his mother after learning (by viewing text messages on his mother's phone) his mother had been having an affair with the recently divorced mother of one of his friends, with whom Benjamin's mother had been friends for many years. He described his mother's infidelity as "immoral and reprehensible" and began to reject not only his mother but also his mother's Jewish religion, in which he had been raised. His father was devastated by the affair and described how he could not believe his wife would sacrifice her morals for both infidelity and homosexuality. The mother acknowledged that the romantic relationship between her and her now-girlfriend had begun two years earlier and was a cause of the girlfriend's recent divorce and the mother's own wish for the same.

The court ordered a shared parenting plan corresponding to the parents' work schedules. The paternal grandmother moved into the family home to care for Benjamin and quickly joined with the father in his shock and beliefs about the immorality of the mother. Soon after the grandmother moved in, Benjamin refused to follow the parenting plan. His father vocalized emphatically that Benjamin had strong beliefs and should not be forced to do something that violated his morals and belief system. The court ordered reunification therapy and a parenting coordinator.

The reunification therapy began with individual sessions with each parent, including multiple sessions with the father focused on educating him about the long-term effects on Benjamin of not having a relationship with his mother. These sessions were followed by a meeting with both parents to plan the therapist's meeting with Benjamin. Benjamin then had two sessions that focused initially on decision-making and how decisions affect both ourselves and others; on wondering with him how he might express his feelings to his mother; and on having mixed feelings. Benjamin had his own individual therapist, and the parenting coordinator communicated with both the individual and the reunification therapist. The initial meeting between Benjamin and his mother occurred at a coffee shop they used to frequent together. It lasted 10 minutes before Benjamin left. The parenting coordinator then ordered the mother to take Benjamin to school on her two or three parenting days. Initially Benjamin refused, but with the coordinator's directive to each member of the family, he began to go with his mother but did not speak to her. The mother attended his soccer games and on one occasion took him home from soccer.

Meanwhile, conversations continued between the father, the parenting coordinator, and the reunification therapist about the father's view of the mother's immorality and betrayal of the family and the importance of the mother's role in Benjamin's life, and about how the father might be able to imagine a continued relationship between Benjamin and his mother. Work with Benjamin's mother focused on thinking long term, not just short term; continually expressing her love and care for Benjamin in texts; and considering ways she could understand how difficult her decision was for Benjamin and his father. The court order included provisions for the family dog, who would move with Benjamin between his two homes. The father began to allow the mother to pick up the dog on her scheduled parenting days. On one occasion she needed to leave town quickly because of a family emergency, and Benjamin picked up the dog from her apartment (which was within walking distance of his school).

Benjamin's entry into his mother's apartment shifted something in him. With his father's encouragement, he began to meet the mother for reunification therapy in the presence of the family dog. Having the dog with him made things easier for Benjamin. Much of the mother–son treatment was now focused on her decisions that as recited by Benjamin, "destroyed our family." Benjamin and his mother began to walk the dog after the therapy sessions. Although Benjamin was still not complying with the parenting schedule, he was seeing his mother at the therapist's office. The father was referred for parent coaching, while the parenting coordinator managed the treatment team and made recommendations for increased contact between the mother and son.

5. SUMMARY

There is no one-size-fits-all intervention for cases involving strained parent–child relationships in high-conflict separation or divorce. The nature and severity of the contact problem informs the differentiated clinical and legal intervention response. Mild and moderate cases of affinity, alignment, alienation, or realistic estrangement, and mixed or hybrid cases of similar severity, *may* be suitable for whole-family systems-based psychoeducational intervention. These interventions may occur in outpatient settings or may begin with a multiday family intensive intervention, followed by aftercare outpatient multifaceted family therapy. The family systems-based model necessary for contact problem cases draws on and necessarily incorporates elements from various iterations of family therapy (e.g., structural or strategic) combined with other treatment modalities, such as psychodynamic therapy, cognitive–behavioral therapy (e.g., systematic desensitization), psychoeducational child and parent group work, coparenting counseling, solution-based therapy, narrative therapy, and mindfulness and meditation.

In this chapter we have described considerations and protocols for preliminary screening, clinical intake, and contracting (including the legal structural components); identified treatment goals; and provided an overview of various tools and resources that will help the clinician implement a treatment plan customized to the needs of each family. The illustrative case examples show how elements of the OCB approach—specifically the whole-family approach, use of experiential and recreational activities, and coordinated case management—are translated to outpatient settings to promote healthier family functioning, including relationship healing, repair, and reintegration.

NOTES

1. As noted in Chapters 2 and 3, different names have been used to describe these multifaceted family therapy interventions, often referred to generically as *reintegration therapy* or *reunification therapy*. While reintegration of the child with the rejected parent is one important intervention goal, in this chapter we refer to these therapies interchangeably as *family therapy* or *family intervention*, using the terms.
2. See Chapter 6 for further elaboration on intensives.
3. Therapists should advise clients to check with their insurance carriers for any rules or restrictions relating to the duration of each session.
4. See articles by Weitzman (2004, 2013) for discussion of the use of desensitization for several decades in child welfare reunification cases where family preservation is the mandate where possible. Weitzman notes that the same codified reunification interventions have yet to be established in family law domestic cases. See Warshak (2015) for some further cautions and considerations, particularly when the child is not actually fearful or anxious despite his or her claims otherwise.

REFERENCES

AFCC Task Force on Court-Involved Therapy. (2011). Guidelines for court-involved therapists. *Family Court Review, 49,* 564–581. Also available from http://www.afccnet.org/pdfs/Guidelines%20for%20Court%20Involved%20Therapy%20AFCC.pdf

Albertson-Kelly, J., & Burkhard, B. (2013). Family reunification in a forensic setting. In A. J. L. Baker & S. R. Sauber (Eds.), *Working with alienated children and families: A clinical guidebook* (pp. 232–252). New York, NY: Routledge.

Andre, K., & Baker, A. J. L. (2009). *I don't want to choose: How middle school kids can avoid choosing one parent over the other.* New York, NY: Kindred Spirits.

Baker, A. J. L., & Andre, K. (2013). Psycho-educational work with children in loyalty conflict: The "I Don't Want to Choose" program. In A. J. L. Baker & S. R. Sauber (Eds.), *Working with alienated children and families: A clinical guidebook* (pp. 149–165). New York, NY: Routledge.

Baker, A. J. L., & Fine, P. (2008). *Beyond the high road: Responding to 17 parental alienation strategies without compromising your morals or harming your child.* Retrieved from http://www.amyjlbaker.com/index.php

Baker, A. J. L., & Fine, P. (2013). Psychotherapy with targeted parents. In A. J. L. Baker & S. R. Sauber (Eds.), *Working with alienated children and families: A clinical guidebook* (pp. 90–107). New York, NY: Routledge.

Baker, A. J. L., & Sauber, S. R. (Eds.) (2013). *Working with alienated children and families: A clinical guidebook.* New York, NY: Routledge.

Benson, H. & Klipper, M. Z. (2000). *The relaxation response.* New York, NY: Harper Collins.

Berg, I. K. (1994). *Family based services: A solution-focused approach.* New York, NY: W. W. Norton.

Blow, K., & Daniel, G. (2002). Frozen narratives? Post-divorce processes and contact disputes. *Journal of Family Therapy, 24,* 85–103.

Bowen, M. (1978). *Family therapy in clinical practice.* New York, NY: Jason Aronson.

Brodsky, S. L. (2011). *Therapy with coerced and reluctant clients.* Washington, DC: American Psychological Association.

Carter, S. (2011). *Family restructuring therapy: Interventions with high conflict separations and divorces.* Scottsdale, AZ: High Conflict Institute Press.

Chase, G. A. (1983). Previsitation anxiety, postvisitation depression, visitation phobia, visitation conflicts: Preludes to child custody consents. *Conciliation Courts Review, 21*(1), 81–86.

Coates, C., Deutsch, R., Starnes, H., Sullivan, M. J., & Sydlik, B. (2004). Parenting coordination for high conflict families. *Family Court Review, 42*(2), 246–262.

Darnall, D. (2010). *Beyond divorce casualties—reunifying the alienated family.* Lanham, MD: Taylor Trade Publishing.

DeJong, M., & Davies, H. (2012). Contact refusal by children following acrimonious separation: Therapeutic approaches with children and parents. *Clinical Child Psychology & Psychiatry, 18*(2), 185–198.

de Shazer, S. (1988). *Clues: Investigating solutions in brief therapy.* New York, NY: W. W. Norton.

Deutsch, R. M. (with Sullivan, M. & Moran, J.). (2015, February) *Practical applications of intensive interventions for children who resist/refuse contact with a parent.* Invited pre-conference institute presentation at Association of Family and Conciliation Courts California Chapter Annual Conference, Costa Mesa, CA.

Deutsch, R. M., & Roseby, V. (1986). Cognitive skills training for children of divorce. *Manitoba Journal of Counseling, 12*(3), 26–32.

Eddy, B. (2009). *New ways for families in separation and divorce: Professional guidebook for judicial officers, lawyers and therapists.* Scottsdale, AZ: High Conflict Institute Press.

Eddy, B. (2010). *Don't alienate the kids! Raising resilient children while avoiding high conflict divorce.* Scottsdale, AZ: High Conflict Institute Press.

Eddy, B. (2011). *BIFF: Quick responses to high conflict people.* Scottsdale, AZ: High Conflict Institute Press.

Eddy, B. (2014). *So, what's your proposal? Shifting high-conflict people from blaming to problem-solving in 30 seconds!* Scottsdale, AZ: Unhooked Books.

Everett, C. A. (2006). Family therapy for parental alienation syndrome: Understanding the interlocking pathologies. In R. A. Gardner, S. R. Sauber, & D. Lorandos (Eds.), *The international handbook of parental alienation syndrome* (pp. 228–241). Springfield, IL: Charles C Thomas.

Fidler, B. J. (2009, May). *Responding to alienation: Practical solutions in the family justice system.* Invited presentation at the Supreme Court of British Columbia Education Seminar, National Judicial Institute, Kelowna, BC.

Fidler, B. J. (2011, June). *Children and divorce: The voice of the child and interventions when children resist parental contact.* Presentation at Loyola University Chicago School of Law's Civitas Child Law Center and Association of Family and Conciliation Courts (2 days), Chicago, IL.

Fidler, B. J., & Bala, N. (2010). Children resisting post-separation contact with a parent: Concepts, controversies and conundrums. *Family Court Review, 48,* 10–47.

Fidler, B. J., Bala, N., Birnbaum, R., & Kavassalis, K. (2008). *Challenging issues in child custody disputes.* Toronto, ON: Carswell Thomson.

Fidler, B. J., Bala, N., & Saini, M. (2013). *Children resisting contact post-separation and parental alienation: An evidence-based review.* American Psychology–Law Book Series. New York, NY: Oxford University Press.

Francis, G., & Beidel, D. (1995). Cognitive–behavioral psychotherapy. In J. S. March (Ed.), *Anxiety disorders in children and adolescents* (pp. 321–340). New York, NY: Guilford Press.

Freeman, R., Abel, D., Cowper-Smith, M., & Stein, L. (2004). Reconnecting children with absent parents. *Family Court Review, 42*(3), 439–459.

Friedlander, S., & Walters, M. (2010). When a child rejects a parent: Tailoring the intervention to fit the problem. *Family Court Review, 48*(1), 98–111.

Friedlander, S., & Walters, M. (2014, February). *Intervention with children who resist or refuse post-separation contact with a parent: Current status.* Paper presented at the Association of Family and Conciliation Courts–California Chapter Annual Conference, San Francisco, CA.

Garber, B. D. (2011). Parental alienation and the dynamics of the enmeshed dyad: Adultification, parentification and infantilization. *Family Court Review, 49*(2), 322–335.

Garber, B. D. (2013). Providing effective, systemically informed, child-centered psychotherapies for children of divorce: Walking on thin ice. In A. J. L. Baker & S. R. Sauber

(Eds.), *Working with alienated children and families: A clinical guidebook* (pp. 166–187). New York, NY: Routledge.

Garber, B. D. (2015). Cognitive–behavioral methods in high conflict divorce: Systematic desensitization adapted to parent–child reunification interventions. *Family Court Review, 53*(1), 96–112.

Gardner, R. A. (1998). *The parental alienation syndrome* (2nd ed.). Cresskill, NJ: Creative Therapeutics.

Gardner, R. A. (1999). Family therapy of the moderate type of parental alienation syndrome. *American Journal of Family Therapy, 27*, 195–212.

Gardner, R. A. (2001). *Therapeutic interventions for children and parental alienation syndrome.* Cresskill, NJ: Creative Therapeutics.

Gottlieb, L. J. (2012). *The parental alienation syndrome: A family therapy and collaborative systems approach to amelioration.* Springfield, IL: Charles C Thomas.

Gottlieb, L. J. (2013). The application of structural family therapy to the treatment of parental alienation syndrome. In A. J. L. Baker & S. R. Sauber (Eds.), *Working with alienated children and families: A clinical guidebook* (pp. 209–231). New York, NY: Routledge.

Greenberg, L. R., Deutsch, R. M., Gould-Saltman, R., & Cunningham, D. (2013, May 5). Poor planning produces (predictably) poor results: Systematic intervention planning. *Association of Family and Conciliation Courts (AFCC) e-News.*

Greenberg, L. R., Doi Fick, L., & Schnider, R. (2012). Keeping the developmental frame: Child-centered conjoint therapy. *Journal of Child Custody, 9*(1–2), 39–68.

Greenberg, L. R., Gould, J. W., Schnider, R.A., Gould-Saltman, D. J., & Martindale, D. A. (2003). Effective intervention with high-conflict families: How judges can promote and recognize competent treatment in family court. *Journal of the Center for Families, Children and the Courts, 4*, 49–65.

Greenberg, L. R., & Sullivan, M. J. (2012). Parenting coordinator and therapist collaboration in high-conflict shared custody cases. *Journal of Child Custody, 9*(1–2), 85–107.

Goldberg, W., & Goldberg, L. (2013). Psychotherapy with targeted parents. In A. J. L. Baker & S. R. Sauber (Eds.), *Working with alienated children and families: A clinical guidebook* (pp. 108–128). New York, NY: Routledge.

Goodman, M., Bonds, D., Sandler, I., & Braver, S. (2004). Parent psychoeducational programs and reducing the negative effects of interparental conflict following divorce. *Family Court Review, 42*(2), 263–279.

Haley, J. (1973). *Uncommon therapy.* New York, NY: W. W. Norton.

Haley, J., & Hoffman, L. (Eds.). (1968). *Techniques of family therapy.* New York, NY: Basic Books.

Johnston, J., & Roseby, V. (1997). *In the name of the child: A developmental approach to understanding and helping children of conflicted and violent divorce.* New York, NY: Free Press.

Johnston, J. R., Walters, M., & Friedlander, S. (2001). Therapeutic work with alienated children and their families. *Family Court Review, 39*(3), 316–333.

Jordan, M. (2015). *Nature and therapy: Understanding counseling and psychotherapy in outdoor spaces.* New York, NY: Routledge/Taylor & Francis Group.

Judge, A. M. & Bailey, R. (2015) Clinical Protocol for Stable Paths: A *Transitioning Families* Program. Unpublished manuscript.

Judge, A. M., Bailey, R., Behrman-Lippert, J., Bailey, E., Psaila, C., & Dickel, J. (2016). The Transitioning Families therapeutic reunification model in non-familial abductions. *Family Court Review, 54*(2), 232–249.

Kabat-Zin, J. (2005). *Full catastrophe living: Using the wisdom of your body and mind to face stress, pain, and illness.* New York, NY: Random House.

Lebow, J., & Black, D. A. (2012). Considerations in court-involved therapy with parents. *Journal of Child Custody, 9*(1–2), 11–38.

Lebow, J., & Rekart, K. N. (2007). Integrative family therapy for high-conflict divorce with disputes over child custody and visitation. *Family Process, 46,* 79–91.

Miller, W. R., & Rollnick, S. (2012). *Motivational interviewing* (3rd ed.). New York, NY: Guilford Press.

Minuchin, S. (1974). *Families and family therapy.* Cambridge, MA: Harvard University Press.

Moran, J., Sullivan, T., & Sullivan, M. (2015). *Overcoming the co-parenting trap: Essential parenting skills when a child resists a parent.* Available from www.overcomingbarriers.org

Pedro-Carroll, J. (1997). The Children of Divorce intervention program: Fostering resilient outcomes for school-age children. In G. W. Albee & T. P Gullotta (Eds.), *Primary prevention works* (pp. 213–238). Thousand Oaks, CA: Sage.

Pedro-Carroll, J., & Cowen, E. (1985). The Children of Divorce intervention program: An investigation of the efficacy of a school based prevention program. *Journal of Consulting and Clinical Psychology, 53,* 603–611.

Perry, B.D. (2001). The neurodevelopmental impact of violence in childhood. In D. Schetky & E. P. Benedek (Eds.), *Textbook of child and adolescent forensic psychiatry* (pp. 221–238). Washington, DC: American Psychiatric Press.

Pinsof, W., Breunlin, D. C., Russell, W. P., & Lebow, J. (2011). Integrative problem-centered metaframeworks therapy II: Planning, conversing, and reading feedback. *Family Process, 50*(3), 314–336.

Polak, S., Fidler, B. J., & Popielarczyk, L. (2013, May). *Children resisting contact with a parent post separation.* Workshop presented at Association of Family and Conciliation Courts 50th Anniversary Conference, Los Angeles, CA.

Rand, R., & Warshak, R. (2008). *Overview of the family workshop—2.2.* Unpublished manuscript.

Roseby, V., & Deutsch, R. M. (1985). Children of separation and divorce: Effects of a social role-taking group intervention on fourth and fifth graders. *Journal of Clinical Child Psychology, 14*(1), 55–61.

Satir, V. (1964). *Conjoint family therapy.* Palo Alto, CA: Science and Behavior Books.

Silverman, W. K., Pina, A. A., & Viswesvaran, C. (2008). Evidence-based psychosocial treatments for phobic and anxiety disorders in children and adolescents. *Journal of Clinical Child and Adolescent Psychology, 37,* 105–130.

Sullivan, M. J. (2008). Co-parenting and the parenting coordination process. *Journal of Child Custody, 5*(1/2), 4–24.

Sullivan, M. J., & Kelly, J. B. (2001). Legal and psychological management of cases with an alienated child. *Family Court Review, 39*(3), 299–315.

Sullivan, M. J., Ward, P. A., & Deutsch, R. M. (2010). Overcoming Barriers Family Camp: A program for high-conflict divorced families where a child is resisting contact with a parent. *Family Court Review, 48,* 115–134.

Walters, M., & Friedlander, S. (2012). Finding a tenable middle space: Understanding the role of clinical interventions when a child refuses contact with a parent. *Journal of Child Custody, 7*, 287–328.

Waltzlawick, P. (1974). *Changing families*. New York, NY: Basic Books.

Warshak, R. A. (2010a). *Divorce poison: How to protect your family from bad-mouthing and brainwashing*. New York, NY: Harper Collins.

Warshak, R. A. (2010b). Family Bridges: Using insights from social science to reconnect parents and alienated children. *Family Court Review, 48*(1), 48–80.

Warshak, R. A. (2015). Ten parental alienation fallacies that compromise decisions in court and in therapy. *Professional Psychology: Research and Practice, 46*(4), 235–249.

Warshak, R. A., & Otis, M. (2010). *Welcome back, Pluto: Understanding, preventing and overcoming parental alienation* [DVD]. Available from www.warshak.com

Weitzman, J. (2004). Use of the one-way mirror in child custody reunification. *Journal of Child Custody, 1*(4), 27–48.

Weitzman, J. (2013). Reunification and the one-way mirror. In A. J. L. Baker & S. R. Sauber (Eds.), *Working with alienated children and families: A clinical guidebook* (pp. 188–208). New York, NY: Routledge.

Whitaker, C. A. (1958). Psychotherapy with couples. *American Journal of Psychotherapy, 12*(1), 18–23.

Whitaker, C. A., & Bumberry, W. (1988). *Dancing with the family: A symbolic-experiential approach*. New York, NY: Brunner/Mazel.

Wier, K. (2011). High-conflict contact disputes: Evidence of the extreme unreliability of some children's ascertainable wishes and feelings. *Family Court Review, 49*(4), 788–800.

Wolpe, J. (1958). *Psychotherapy by reciprocal inhibition*. Stanford, CA: Stanford University Press.

Wolpe, J., Brady, J. P., Serber, M., Agras, W. S., & Liberman, R. P. (1973). The current status of systematic desensitization. *American Journal of Psychiatry, 130*, 961–965.

Yalom, I., & Leszcz, M. (2005). *The theory and practice of group psychotherapy* (5th ed.). New York: Basic Books.

APPENDIX 12.A

FAMILY THERAPY INTERVENTION AGREEMENT

Between: _____ **and** _____
                    [Mother's Name]   [Father's name]

Court File Number _____

OBJECTIVES

1. The parents agree the objective of the family therapy intervention is not to determine IF it is in the child(ren)'s best interests to have contact with one of the parents. Rather, the parents agree it is in the child(ren)'s best interests to have meaningful relationships with *both* parents. The family therapy intervention is intended to help the child(ren) have healthy and meaningful relationships with both parents.

2. To meet the goals listed below, the parents agree to engage the services of [therapist's name] _____ (also referred to as "the therapist" in this Agreement) and will contact the therapist no later than _____ to provide consent to proceed with the clinical intake and engage in the informed consent process. Once both parents have contacted [therapist's name] _____ office, intake questionnaires will be sent to each parent to complete. The parents agree to complete the intake questionnaires within 7 days of receiving them. Once both sets of completed intake questionnaires and any supporting documentation (e.g., relevant court orders, custody/access or Guardian ad Litem reports, etc.) have been received, appointments will be scheduled.

3. The family therapy intervention provided for in this Agreement has been court ordered, in the [name of court] _____.

4. Any other particulars of this matter can be addressed in the court order, this Retainer Agreement, by way of attachment, or future correspondence.

5. The role of the therapist is to assist with the family intervention therapy and not as a custody assessor, arbitrator, parenting coordinator, or consultant for litigation.

6. The goals of the therapy may include to:
   a. foster overall healthy child adjustment;
   b. facilitate the implementation of the previously agreed-to or court-ordered parenting time schedule, dated _____;
   c. restore, develop, or facilitate adequate parenting and coparenting functioning and skills;
   d. assist the parents to resolve relevant parent–child conflicts;
   e. develop family communication skills and effective approaches to problem-solving;

f. assist the parents to fully understand the child(ren)'s needs
   for healthy relationships with both parents and the negative
   repercussions for the child(ren) of a severed or compromised
   relationship with a parent in their young lives and as adults;
g. restore or facilitate contact between [rejected parent's name]
   _____ and [child(ren)'s name(s), age(s), and date(s)
   of birth] _____,_____,_____.
h. assist the parents and their child(ren) to identify and separate each
   child's needs and views from each parent's needs and views;
i. work with each family member to establish more appropriate
   parent–parent and parent–child roles and boundaries;
j. correct the child(ren)'s distortions and replace these with more
   realistic perceptions reflecting the child's actual experience with
   both parents;
k. assist the child(ren) to differentiate self from others and exercise
   age-appropriate autonomy;
l. assist each parent to distinguish valid concerns from overly negative,
   critical, and generalized views relating to the other parent;
m. other (specify)_____.

7. While the parents may have different views about the causes or reasons
   for their child(ren)'s reluctance or refusal to have contact with [rejected
   parent's name] _____, they agree not only to the
   objectives defined above but also that they each need to be part of the
   solution to meet those objectives.

PROCESS

8. The parents agree to the involvement of the entire family, in various
   combinations, as directed by [therapist's name] _____.
   The process will include meetings with each parent and the child(ren)
   individually and jointly. The process may include meetings with other family
   members as deemed necessary by [therapist's name] _____.
9. [Therapist's name] _____ will *not* be making decisions
   regarding the child(ren)'s parenting time with each parent (access) or
   legal decision-making (custody) as this is outside her role. Rather, as
   therapist she will be assisting to implement the previously agreed-to
   or court-ordered Parenting Plan. Notwithstanding, the parents agree
   [therapist's name] _____ may [here scope of authority,
   if any, e.g., to determine the nature of transitions, rules of parental
   communication or engagement, location and pacing of the
   parent–child contact consistent with the court-ordered Parenting
   Plan, etc.] _____. [Therapist's name] _____
   may make recommendations deemed helpful to the child(ren) in
   implementing the court orders or the current agreed-to Parenting Plan.

10. [Therapist's name] _____ may provide a report to the parents, lawyers, or the court describing the parents' and child(ren)'s progress and cooperation, including any obstacles preventing the therapy from beginning or continuing. This may include specific statements and behaviors which [therapist's name] _____ deems necessary to adequately support other content or statements in her report. Recommendations may be provided regarding additional services or counseling where deemed appropriate. Any opinions or recommendations reported will be limited in scope to matters for which the therapist has obtained sufficient information.

11. The parents will provide all records, documentation, and information requested by the therapist as soon as possible upon request.

12. [Therapist's name] _____ may choose to contact other previous or current professionals involved with the family members to receive and obtain information to better meet the aforementioned treatment goals. Toward this end, the parents will sign all consent forms permitting [therapist's name] _____ to exchange information with the relevant professionals.

13. [Therapist's name] _____ may make recommendations for the involvement of additional professionals (e.g., individual therapist for parent or child, educational specialist, coach for parent education).

14. The therapist may make recommendations for the termination of therapists who may be currently involved.

RESPONSIBILITY OF THE PARENTS

15. The parents agree to fully cooperate, support, and wholeheartedly participate in the family therapy intervention. This includes, but is not limited to: (1) paying for services in a timely manner in accordance with the fee agreement executed by the parents with [therapist's name] _____; (2) ensuring the child(ren) are transported to and from scheduled therapy appointments in a timely manner; and (3) exercising parental authority to require the child(ren) to attend and cooperate with the therapy.

16. The parents are advised the court may consider the good-faith efforts and the parents' demonstrated behavior during the therapy as a factor in determining any decisions about the child(ren)'s best interests, including legal custody (decision-making) or access (parenting time).

17. The parents have been advised the therapy requires each parent to make changes in their own behavior and parenting to support their child(ren)'s needs. [Therapist's name] _____ may request specific changes in such areas as setting appropriate limits for the child(ren), encouraging the child(ren) to express feelings and solve problems appropriately, listening to the child(ren)'s concerns

and actively supporting the child(ren)'s independent relationships, and shielding the child(ren) from parental conflict. The parents agree to make reasonable efforts to cooperate with the therapist's requests in these and any other relevant areas. If either parent disagrees with requests or recommendations made by the therapist, the parent will discuss those concerns privately with the therapist, and will not allow the child(ren) to witness or overhear the concerns.

18. Both parents will overtly support the therapy and [therapist's name] _____ to the child(ren). This includes respecting the child(ren)'s right *not* to discuss the therapy with their parents and not asking the child(ren) for information about their sessions.

19. The parents will refrain from scheduling new after-school activities, lessons, or events during the scheduled therapy appointments. Reasonable efforts will be made to schedule appointments so the child(ren) do not miss school or their currently scheduled extracurricular activities. However, this may not always be possible.

20. Given the risks of information being taken out of context or being incomplete, the parents agree they and their lawyers will *not* restate, summarize, or paraphrase in court documents any feedback or statements provided by [therapist's name] _____ during the therapy. If necessary, a report may be requested, permitting the therapist to communicate about the therapy to the court as per this Agreement and the court order.

21. There shall be no audio or visual recording of the therapy, unless agreed to in writing by the therapist. Unauthorized recording of any kind may be sufficient basis for the therapist to terminate the treatment and provide a report explaining the reasons.

22. Both parents acknowledge they have had an opportunity to review this Agreement and to ask any questions they may have concerning [therapist's name] _____ approach to counseling and other available alternatives.

DURATION OF SERVICES

23. The therapy shall continue for at least ___ months from the commencing of the therapy unless the therapist determines an earlier termination is in the child(ren)'s best interests. Neither parent may unilaterally withdraw from this Agreement prior to the completion of the term identified. However, with their joint consent in writing, both parents may terminate this Agreement.
OR

24. In the event either parent wishes to terminate the therapy, they will provide 15 days' written notice to the therapist and the other parent. The parents will attempt, with the assistance of their lawyers, to agree on an alternate to replace [therapist's name] _____. If the parents

are unable to agree within 30 days, an alternate will be appointed by ["the court" or the specific name of the Arbitrator or Parenting Coordinator for determination in a summary fashion] _____.

25. With four (4) weeks' notice in writing, [therapist's name] _____ may resign if she determines this to be in the best interests of the child(ren), in which case a referral may be made to another therapist if [therapist's name] _____ deems appropriate.

CONFIDENTIALITY

26. While [therapist's name] _____ is bound to maintain confidentiality and not disclose information to anyone who is not involved in the process, the parents understand the process may involve the therapist and the other relevant professionals (previous or current) sharing information (e.g., custody evaluator/assessor, parent's or child's therapist, teacher, parenting coordinator, Guardian ad Litem, etc.).

27. The therapist may use her discretion to disclose information obtained from the participants in the therapy to the other participants in the therapy.

28. [Therapist's name] _____ shall be free to disclose all information, documentation, and correspondence generated by the process with the lawyer for each parent and with the court, and may speak with the lawyers ex parte. This signed Agreement serves as the parents' informed consent for [therapist's name] _____ to obtain information from the court, counsel, and both parents AND for [therapist's name] _____ to provide information received from all sources verbally or in a report to the court, counsel, and the other parent.

29. The parents understand [therapist's name] _____ is required to report to the appropriate child protection service or agency if she has a reasonable suspicion a child is being physically, sexually, or emotionally abused or neglected. In addition, the therapist is obliged to notify the proper authorities if she has a "reasonable suspicion" a client may harm himself or herself, or the other parent.

ELECTRONIC PROVISION OF SERVICES

30. Scheduling may be done by email or telephone. Electronic provision of services includes email and secure video contacts (e.g., VSee) or communications by telephone and may be provided with your informed consent. The risks include insufficiency, misunderstandings due to lack of visual clues, and technology failure. The benefits include appropriateness, avoiding the need to travel, taking less time off work, services continuing while the therapist is away, convenience, and

comfort. Alternatives to the provision of electronic services include in-person services only or local services from an available health service provider of the same or different discipline.

31. While efforts are made to protect privacy during the electronic provision of services, the same degree of confidentiality provided during in-person office sessions is not possible; limitations include the possibility of interceptions of communications.

32. Please keep in mind others may be able to access information, sensitive or otherwise, communicated electronically between you and the therapist in your own home or workplace. By signing this consent Agreement you are confirming to the therapist you have taken reasonable steps to secure your own electronic devices you choose to use to communicate with the therapist (phones, iPads, computers, etc.). This would include having a confidential password and adequate firewalls. Any communications sent by the therapist are intended for you and not for others, unless agreed to otherwise.

FEES

31. Fees shall be charged for all professional services performed pursuant to the terms of this Agreement, including administrative matters (record-keeping, long-distance telephone charges, photocopying, courier charges, postage, and disbursements), document and correspondence review, writing memos to the file, reports, preparation between sessions, voice mail, email correspondence, in-person sessions with family members and collateral sources, and telephone calls. Fees may be charged retroactively for any services rendered prior to the receipt of the initial retainer. Disbursements shall be paid to professionals who require remuneration for their participation, and for any agency/hospital/police reports.

32. The hourly rate for services is $_____.00 per hour. The fees shall be shared equally unless otherwise agreed to by the parents or ordered by the court at the time this Agreement is executed.

33. Each parent will provide an initial retainer of ____hours of services, that is, $____.00, no later than during their first meeting with [therapist's name] _____. At all times each parent shall maintain a retainer of at least $_____.00 (two hours) in the account of [therapist's name] _____, who shall advise in advance when a further retainer is required. A monthly statement of account will be provided to the parents. If the above terms are not satisfied, the therapist may choose to postpone all services until the retainer terms are satisfied. Nonpayment of fees shall be grounds for the resignation of [therapist's name] _____.

34. Appointments canceled without at least 48 (forty-eight) business hours' advance notice may be charged at full fee independent of the reason for the cancellation (i.e., Monday and Tuesday appointments must be canceled by 5:00 p.m. on the previous Friday to avoid the possibility of this charge). The parents will each be responsible for bills arising from their own cancellation with insufficient notice or failure to attend a scheduled appointment.
35. A parent may request a report. The parent who makes this request will be responsible for paying fully for the report in advance by retainer at the hourly rate identified in #32 above, or otherwise as ordered by the court.
36. The parents agree all testimony or appearance at court of any kind provided by [therapist's name] _____ shall be considered expert testimony. Fees related to preparation for or attendance at court (e.g., trial, settlement conference, discoveries) are billed at $_____.00 per hour. Fees for attendance at court, testifying in court, or discoveries are billed by a minimum half-day rate of $_____.00. Any court-related fees (i.e., preparation time, attendance, and travel) shall be provided in advance by retainer by the parent requesting [therapist's name]'s _____ attendance at court. A separate contract for these services (detailing cancellation policy, etc.) may apply and be provided at the time of any request.

INDEPENDENT LEGAL ADVICE

37. Each of the parents confirms they have received independent legal advice prior to executing this Agreement, or is aware they have a right to do so.
38. Both parents:
    a. understand their rights and obligations under this Agreement and the nature and consequences of the Agreement;
    b. acknowledge they are not under any undue influence or duress; and
    c. acknowledge they are signing this Agreement voluntarily.

RISKS & LIMITATIONS

39. Informed consent requires disclosure of potential risks and limitations. By signing the Agreement, the parents acknowledge the therapist cannot guarantee physical safety during the family therapy intervention. The parents further acknowledge the therapist cannot guarantee against bad faith or abuse of process by any participant. The parents understand there is no guarantee the family and coparenting functioning and the

parent–child contact problem will be resolved during family therapy. The parents acknowledge they may not be fully satisfied with the outcome of the services provided.

INFORMED CONSENT

40. Having read the above, I hereby consent to:
    a. willingly continuing with this family therapy intervention process;
    b. informing my legal counsel, or if acting Pro Se, advising the court in writing to let them know I choose to withdraw from the therapy;
    c. advising the therapist in writing if I choose to withdraw consent for this therapy;
    d. all information and communication provided by me being done so on a 'with prejudice' (not confidential) basis and for this information to be used in court if required;
    e. [Therapist's name] _____ seeking full and active participation from me and other family members as she deems necessary.
41. I understand:
    a. what is expected of me and the relative risks of the information being used in court or this legal matter;
    b. the nature of this therapy, fees associated, cancellation policy (48 hours), mutual responsibilities, confidentiality issues and limitations, benefits, and risks, the consequences of non-action, the option to refuse or withdraw, and the elements of the "with prejudice" nature of this therapy;
    c. the signing of this Agreement/Informed Consent by me is further acknowledgment of informed consent as it dictates the professional activities the therapist will be conducting.

TO EVIDENCE THEIR AGREEMENT, THE PARTIES HAVE SIGNED THIS AGREEMENT BEFORE A WITNESS.

DATE: _____

_____   _____
Witness   [Print Name]

DATE: _____

_____   _____
Witness   [Print Name]

13

Program Evaluation, Training, and Dissemination

MICHAEL SAINI AND ROBIN M. DEUTSCH ■

1. INTRODUCTION

Given the well-established associations between strained parent–child relationships and negative child adjustment, there has been an international focus on designing interventions for both parents and children to mitigate the negative impact of conflict and to improve parent–child relationships (Deutsch, 2008). Despite the growing interest in how these interventions may work, few have been rigorously evaluated (Saini, Johnston, Fidler, & Bala, 2016). Interventions claim varying levels of success (Baker, Burkhard & Albertson-Kelly, 2012; Gardner, 2001; Kumar, 2003; Rand, Rand, & Kopetski, 2005; Reay, 2015; Sullivan, Ward, & Deutsch, 2010; Toren et al., 2013; Warshak, 2010), but there remains inconsistent attention and adherence to standard methods for delivering these interventions, a lack of theoretical foundations for the programs, and a lack of clear linkages between targeted risks and protective factors for parents and children with strained relationships.

Strained parent–child relationships are not a homogenous entity. Fidler, Bala, and Saini (2012) described many forms and pathways of strained parent–child relationships, including developmental factors such as separation anxiety for younger children, alignment with a parent, gender preference or affinity for a parent, a child's reacting to parental conflict, and a child's refusing or resisting contact with a parent because of the parent's conduct. As Fidler et al. noted, each of these forms of strained parent–child relationships can result from a complex interaction of many factors, and many of these factors can overlap. As a result, evaluation of interventions to address strained parent–child relationship is complicated and needs to be based on a coherent and comprehensive plan for testing effectiveness.

Using a program evaluation framework, the purpose of this chapter is to highlight key considerations for developing an approach that captures both treatment process and outcomes. We focus on operationalizing key indicators for short- and long-term success, creating a fidelity checklist to measure the process and implementation of an intervention, and the use of evaluation designs to answer specific questions about the intervention. Using the program evaluation of the Overcoming Barriers (OCB) camp as a case illustration, we propose that a transparent and methodologically sound approach is needed to capture program change and to make program adjustments as needed. As part of the case illustration, we present findings from the 2013 and 2014 program evaluation of OCB camp to demonstrate the kinds of results that can be gained from a comprehensive evaluation of a complex intervention for strained parent–child relationships.

2. REVIEW OF EVALUATION STUDIES OF INTERVENTIONS FOR STRAINED PARENT–CHILD RELATIONSHIPS

Several programs have been developed to improve strained parent–child relationships, but few of these have been rigorously evaluated. The evaluation studies of effectiveness that have been completed are both broad and diverse, defining outcomes differently and sometimes from the limited perspective of one family member. Although most published interventions have reported success, outcomes have ranged from complete restoration of the child's relationship with both parents to partial softening of the child's negativity and resistance toward the rejected parent to reversal of parent preference (Saini et al., in press).

2.1. Evaluations of Non-OCB Interventions

To evaluate outcomes of change of custody within the legal system for severe cases of alienation, Gardner (2001) analyzed his own clinical cases. Based on a sample of 99 children from 52 families, Gardner reported that the court chose either to restrict the children's access to the preferred parent or change custody in 22 cases, which led to the reduction or even elimination of alienation in all of these cases. In 77 cases, the court chose not to reduce access to the preferred parent or transfer custody. Gardner noted an increase in alienation in 90.9% of these cases.

Kumar (2003) evaluated Smart Parenting, a therapeutic supervised-visitation program for visitation-resistant children, to examine the factors that seemed to interfere with resolution of visitation refusal. The sample consisted of 105 families attending the Smart Parenting office because of a child's refusal to have contact with a parent. All participants completed the survey and consented to a passive observational design using archival data. Results showed that 60% of the children reconciled with the rejected parent after the program. The results also showed that children older than 13 years old were less likely to reconcile with their parents compared to children under the age of 13 years of age. The length of time since visits and the level of parental conflict had little impact on reconciliation. Kumar found that the more willing parents were to communicate and ameliorate their relationship with the other parent, the more likely the children reconciled with the rejected parents.

To evaluate the efficacy of structural and therapeutic interventions for interrupting parental alienation in more severe cases, Rand et al. (2005) recruited 45 children from 25 families from custody evaluation files of one of the authors. The results suggested that the mothers were considered the alienating parent in 18 cases and the fathers were considered the alienating parent in 7 cases. At follow-up, 20 children, from 12 families, experienced an interruption in the alienation process and 11 children, from 5 families, had "mixed outcomes". The court's decisions with respect to custody and visitation were viewed as essential for interrupting or preventing alienation. Rand et al. found that when therapy was the primary intervention, it was ineffective for interrupting alienation and sometimes made contact problems worse.

Warshak (2010) evaluated Family Bridges, his court-mandated four-day educational program for alienated children and their rejected parents. Family Bridges is a brief, intensive workshop based on social psychological principles (e.g., common errors in perception, suggestibility, response to authority, and negative stereotype formation) that teaches critical thinking, communication, problem-solving, and parenting skills. Cases were selected based on Warshak's involvement with families during the intervention. From 12 families, including 23 children, who were referred by court orders mandating children's participation with the rejected parent, 10 of the 12 rejected parents provided updates and documents such as report cards, award certificates, and photographs in a follow-up period ranging from months to several years. Results showed that by the end of the workshop, 22 of the 23 children had restored a positive relationship with the rejected parent, as evidenced by the children's own statements and by the observations of the rejected parent, workshop leaders, and the aftercare specialist. According to Warshak, 4 of the 22 children regressed after the court renewed their contact with the preferred parent.

In 2015, Warshak reported on an updated and ongoing evaluation of Family Bridges with a larger sample of 57 children. Results of this preliminary evaluation were similar to the previous findings reported above. According to Warshak, 95% of the children recovered a positive relationship with the rejected parent at the end of the intervention, with 82% of the sample continuing to enjoy good relationships with the previously rejected parent at follow-up.

Baker et al. (2012) compared 19 children who were referred for reunification therapy with 21 other children chosen based on their self-reported feelings and beliefs regarding their parents. The latter children were referred for evaluations ($n = 4$), supervised therapeutic visitation ($n = 10$), and individual therapy ($n = 7$). The evaluation focused on the behaviors of the children once they began to receive services. To capture the children's extreme rejection of one parent and extreme idealization of the other, Baker et al. administered the Baker Alienation Questionnaire (BAQ). They found that the reunification therapy group had statistically significantly higher BAQ total scores than the comparison group and that children resistant to treatment had experienced more extreme alienation than those who were not resistant to treatment.

In an evaluation of a four-month, 16-session therapeutic program for alienated children and their parents, Toren et al. (2013) compared 38 parents and 22 children with a group enrolled in a standard community treatment. To be included in the treatment group, children were considered to be alienated if they had refused to visit the rejected parent for a minimum of four months and were referred to the clinic by the court or social welfare authorities. Toren et al. found that anxiety and depression levels of children with parental alienation decreased significantly compared to the comparison group at one-year follow-up and they had increased levels of parental cooperation.

Reay (2015) evaluated the Family Reflections Reunification Program, a four-day intensive treatment program to reconcile children with their rejected parents and to foster a healthy relationship between them. The sample included 6 rejected mothers, 6 rejected fathers, and 22 children (14 boys and 8 girls) from 12 families who participated in a pilot study in 2012. The families were followed up at 3-, 6-, 9-, and 12-month intervals. Based on the 21 children of the 22 who remained in the treatment, the reported results suggest that there was a 100% success rate: All 21 were able to re-establish a relationship with the once rejected parent as evidenced by statements made by the children and the parents as well by observations by the multidisciplinary team at the program.

2.2. Previous Evaluation of OCB Camp

Sullivan et al. (2010) did a previous evaluation of OCB camp, which in that case consisted of a five-day intensive educational and therapeutic group intervention for both parents and their alienated children. Families were recruited for the program by word of mouth through the authors' professional networks and selected for pragmatic reasons (e.g., timing, cost, and availability). All participants were approached to complete a satisfaction survey at the completion of the camp, one month later, and six months later; group leaders also completed rating forms. The sample consisted of 10 families, including 21 parents (5 families per camp offering). The adult ratings of the camp experience in general were positive (all 4–5 on a five-point scale). According to Sullivan et al., preliminary results showed a decrease in parent–child relationship difficulties and an increase in normalizing visiting arrangements.

2.3. Summary of the Current Evidence

Given the variations in approach and selected outcomes, it is difficult to aggregate the overall findings across the intervention studies discussed above. Several outcome variables have been considered, including the satisfaction of the children and parents engaged in the interventions, the rebuilding of strained parent–child relationships and the reduction of alienating behaviors, improved communication between the parents and the parents' level of cooperation, children's overall anxiety and depression levels, and children's overall adjustment after attending the interventions.

Almost all of these studies employed weak research design, including posttest-only treatment evaluations of interventions designed by the researchers, small samples, a lack of clarity about inclusion criteria (especially regarding the method for assessing the presence of strained parent–child relationships). Only two studies used a comparison group (Baker et al., 2012; Toren et al., 2013). Further, there was little systematic control for many other variables that might have affected outcomes.

3. THE NEED FOR A COMMON APPROACH TO EVALUATE INTERVENTIONS

Despite the growing evidence regarding interventions to address strained parent–child relationships, there remains no standard approach to evaluating these interventions. Methodological improvements to the evaluations are needed, and the field would benefit from a common framework for evaluation. Consistency of evaluation designs, methods, measures, and choice of outcomes would allow results to be aggregated and compared across interventions and in different settings. The goal would be to document successes using a consistent approach and to enable intervention programs to learn from other programs by using common definitions and indicators about process and outcome variables to build the knowledge base in this critical area of evaluation.

3.1. DEVELOPING A ROADMAP FOR AN EVALUATION APPROACH TO EVALUATE INTERVENTIONS FOR STRAINED PARENT–CHILD RELATIONSHIPS

The purpose of developing a common evaluation framework is to establish a standard evaluation design that will provide better insight into the experiences and outcomes of children and families who participate in these interventions. To begin the process of establishing a common framework, the OCB evaluation strategy was developed, based on key indicators of effectiveness and efficiency of OCB camp. This strategy aims to evaluate process, implementation, and outcomes of this intervention to assist families where a child is resisting contact with a parent.

For each indicator of success, a set of key questions were identified according to the OCB logic model (see Appendix 13.A). Key evaluation questions included the following:

- *Relevance:* Is OCB camp relevant to the stakeholders involved in family disputes (children, parents, judges, lawyers, mental health professionals, etc.)?

- *Program implementation:* How has OCB camp been implemented with reference to the original objectives?
- *Program administration and operation:* Are the services offered by OCB camp administered and operated satisfactorily from the viewpoint of clients and stakeholders?
- *Impact:* What impact has OCB camp had on the families and stakeholders engaged in family court matters?
- *Sustainability and expansion:* Is OCB camp adequately designed to support the development of new and expanding services as required?
- *Costs and productivity:* What are the costs of delivering the services, and are the services cost-effective for families involved in family courts?

An evaluation can be completed for two primary reasons. The first is to specify, document, and analyze a program's processes. This "process evaluation" focuses on the internal characteristics of the intervention. These characteristics include the structures (e.g., intervention manuals) that guide the operation, the resources that support the intervention, the program's goals and objectives, the target group, and the approaches and strategies that represent the program's core elements. The second reason is to identify the outcomes of the intervention. This "impact evaluation" detects whether the intervention's desired effects are evident in the targeted population.

3.1.1. PROCESS EVALUATION

Process-related evaluation is designed to facilitate the replication of the intervention and to produce recommendations for how best to increase the likelihood of achieving desired outcomes. The *output* performance measures are the goods and services produced by the intervention. They include a description of the characteristics and attributes (e.g., timeliness) established as best practices for achieving effectiveness. The following process questions were proposed for the OCB camp evaluation strategy:

1. *Intended target group:* Was the target group reached? Were there members of the target population who were not reached? Did the project attract the participants it had anticipated?
2. *Staff training:* Did the staff receive adequate training to implement the intervention as planned?
3. *Engagement with participants:* Did the staff engage with families so to enhance continued participation in the services?
4. *Implementation of the intervention:* Were the activities implemented as planned?
5. *Dosage:* Were the intensity and duration of the intervention sufficient for achieving effectiveness?
6. *Fidelity:* Was the intervention delivered consistently?
7. *Participant satisfaction:* Were the participants satisfied with the intervention?
8. *Replicability of the program:* Can the intervention be replicated in other settings?

3.1.2. Outcome Evaluation

Outcomes describe the intended results or consequences of carrying out the intervention or activity. While performance measures should distinguish between outcomes and outputs, there should be a logical connection between them, with outputs supporting outcomes in a logical fashion. Outcomes may relate to the specific beneficiaries of the intervention (i.e., children and parents). Table 13.1 shows the key outcomes measured in the OCB evaluation.

3.2. Developing the Logic Model

To better evaluate and understand the short-, intermediate-, and long-term outcomes of an intervention, the assessment of changes in strained parent–child relationships should be based on a logic model to capture data on the various intervention components. A logic model provides a tool for choosing evaluation methods that best fit the key mechanisms of change according to the vision and approach of the intervention.

In the case of the OCB camp intervention, the OCB logic model (Appendix 13.A) was used to operationalize the goals and objectives of the services and to document the change process. The logic model provides a visual depiction of the activities for the target population. The program evaluation collects and reports on data sources linked to the logic model, namely inputs, activities, outputs, and outcomes (immediate, intermediate term, and long term). For each of those components, the evaluation matrix (see Appendix 13.B) summarizes the logic model in chart format, which includes a description of indicators; data collection sources, methods, and instruments; and timing of data collection. The chart provides the reader with more granular information on the logic model.

Based on the OCB logic model, the OCB research advisory group developed a fidelity guideline and checklist to ensure that key components of the OCB intervention would be implemented consistently over time and in different settings. The consistent delivery of programming helps control for threats to the internal validity of future interventions. Therefore, the logic model and fidelity checklist are critical to the successful expansion of the OCB intervention to other professionals and settings across North America.

3.3. Measuring Strained Parent–Child Relationships

One of the greatest challenges in evaluating interventions for strained parent–child relationships is the lack of consensus regarding how best to measure changes in the relationship. To date, there has been little systematic development of instruments with reports of adequate psychometric properties. The identification of alienation has produced a set of concordant findings from researchers with diverse perspectives (Baker & Ben-Ami, 2011; Baker et al., 2012; Baker & Darnall, 2006; Baker & Verrocchio, 2013; Braver, Coatsworth, & Peralta, n.d.; Hands & Warshak, 2011;

Table 13-1. KEY OUTCOMES FOR EVALUATING INTERVENTIONS FOR STRAINED
PARENT–CHILD RELATIONSHIPS

Parent knowledge and attitudes

1. Being more informed about benefits of protecting children from the conflict.

2. Increased knowledge about tools for affect regulation and self-care.

3. Increased knowledge about specific triggers that set off conflict and how to manage them.

4. Increased knowledge about how to recognize cognitive distortions and see issues from multiple perspectives.

5. Increased knowledge about how reality becomes distorted for a child and what can be done to change these distortions.

6. Increased knowledge about the relationships among feeling, thinking, and acting.

7. Increased knowledge about how courts and the legal system are not usually the answer to a family systems problem.

8. Increased knowledge of communication strategies, problem-solving strategies, and emotional management.

Behavioral and emotional changes

Child related

1. Decrease in child's feelings of fear, anger, discomfort, or anxiety toward rejected parent.

2. Change in child's perception or feelings toward a less polarized view of favored parent.

Parent related

3. Reduction in parents' polarized views of each parent's contribution to parent–child problems.

4. Reduction in parents' polarized views of child's time with the other parent.

5. Decreased parental conflict.

6. Improved parenting skills.

7. Improved coparenting relationship.

Family related

8. Improved parent–child relationships.

9. Decreased parent–child conflict.

10. Improved communication among all family members.

Long-term changes

1. Improved well-being of child.

2. Improved well-being of favored parent and rejected parent.

3. Improved family functioning.

4. Agreement about a parenting plan.

5. Decreased litigation.

6. Compliance with court orders and parenting plans.

Johnston, 2003; Johnston, Walters, & Olesen, 2005a, 2005b; Laughrea, 2002; López, Iglesia, & Garcia, 2014; Moné & Biringen, 2006; Moné, MacPhee, Anderson, & Banning, 2011; Rowen & Emery, 2014; Whitecombe, 2014), but there remains little evidence about whether these measures can reliably assess changes in strained parent–child relationships from before to after an intervention within an evaluation design. To reduce the threat to internal validity of changing instruments, pilot testing should be conducted before establishing baseline data.

Given the lack of standardized tools to capture all OCB program components, the OCB evaluation used an instrument package including a number of both standardized and nonstandardized tests (see Appendix 13.C) to capture the process and outcome variables in accordance to the key outcomes being measured as shown in the logic model (Appendix 13.A).

3.4. Choosing an Evaluation Design

Some evaluation designs provide better evidence than others when seeking answers to specific questions. For example, qualitative methods of interviewing participants about their experiences of attending an intervention are preferred for understanding participants' unique experiences. Given the small samples required to gain a rich description of the experiences, qualitative studies are not well-suited for making inferences to a larger population (Saini & Shlonsky, 2012).

Random sampling to survey participants' responses about their experiences can be a more valid way to make inferences to the larger population about the observation of associational data. The most valid observational studies use both random sampling and randomized control groups to isolate any differences in associational relationships between the target sample and the comparison group. Because of the closed-ended questioning required to manage data collection and analysis of large samples, observational studies, unlike qualitative studies, often do not provide the rich context of these relationships.

Questions about effectiveness, such as the effectiveness of interventions for strained parent–child relationships, are best answered using randomized controlled trials (RCTs) to isolate the salient variables and minimize the risk that confounding factors will influence the results. RCTs are often considered to be the most valid method for finding the true effect of an intervention. These controlled experiments permit an investigation to detect a hypothesized cause-and-effect relationship by determining whether the manipulation of a condition (e.g., providing parents and children with an intervention) causes another variable to change (e.g., improvement in children's relationship with parents).

For evaluating OCB camp, a randomized controlled experimental design was not feasible given that the program was not able to withhold services to children and their parents for evaluation purposes. Instead, the evaluation employed a mixed-methods within-subjects design (no comparison group) that included pre-intervention, postintervention, and follow-up assessments and qualitative interviews with parents and children.

The benefit of the one-group design is that it can provide the time order of the data. This design assesses the dependent variables before and after the stimulus (intervention) is introduced. Although this design assesses correlations among factors and can tentatively establish causal time ordering, it does not account for factors other than the design independent variables that might have caused change between pre- and posttest results—factors usually associated with the following threats to internal validity: history, maturation, and testing effect. This evaluation design best met the needs of the OCB stakeholders because it ensured that all program participants received the intervention.

Although this methodology does not include a comparison group, the use of repeated measures does provide support for determining potential temporal order by considering statistical trends in the results. Strategies have been developed to address threats to internal validity that can occur as a result of the design. These strategies include the use of multiple testing, the use of fidelity checklists to assess whether interventions with higher levels of fidelity make greater changes, and the use of triangulation through the development of additional instruments, use of qualitative methods, and case studies.

3.5. Assessing Program Fidelity

Assessing program fidelity is important in program evaluations because it establishes whether the intervention was conducted as planned and whether there was appropriate adherence to the intervention's goals and purposes (Nigg, Allegrante, & Ory, 2002). For program evaluators to make inferences about the results of their studies, they must first establish whether threats to the internal validity of the evaluation were controlled for so that the study's findings can be attributed to the intervention rather than other factors (Polit & Hungler, 1999; Santacroce, Maccarelli, & Grey, 2004). Evaluators should acknowledge when threats to internal validity might influence study results (Polit & Hungler, 1999).

Interventions designed to ameliorate strained parent–child relationships are complex, as they include a number of sessions across various settings and including multiple contacts with various family members. As intervention designs become more complex, variation in intervention delivery increases, resulting in a heterogeneous approach (Santacroce et al., 2004)

Program fidelity checklists give the evaluator the opportunity to measure whether participants received all essential elements of the intervention and whether the intervention was delivered in a comparable manner to all participants (Kerns & Prinz, 2002). Regular monitoring of the intervention using a program fidelity checklist provides the evaluator with information about variations from the intent of the intervention plan and to suggest corrections (Nigg et al., 2002).

The OCB fidelity checklist, shown in Appendix 13.D, was developed to ensure that the intervention would be implemented consistently with the manner in which it was developed to be effective. The fidelity guidelines specify eight key dimensions of how the program was implemented when it demonstrated evidence of effectiveness: (a) facilitator adherence, (b) facilitator training and experience, (c) target population, (d) location and setting, (e) materials, (f) delivery, (g) dosage, and (h) aftercare.

3.6. Planning for Cost Analysis

Coupling program costs with effectiveness data to calculate savings is increasingly part of the demand for accountability. After a program has demonstrated effectiveness in producing the desired outcomes, cost analyses are done to describe the program costs in relation to benefits.

Cost analysis for interventions within family court–based services has been limited because of the lack of extensive information on the societal costs of prolonged litigation. There is also limited evidence regarding the potential cost–benefit balance of the diverse menu of court-based services to prevent prolonged litigation (e.g., mediation, custody assessments, parenting coordination, and interventions for families). Although estimates of societal costs are underdeveloped, the best available data provide a sense of the extensive individual costs resulting from litigation. For example, Fried (2005) reported in the July 2005 issue of *Money* magazine that the average divorce costs to be $3,000–10,000 for a divorce mediation, $16,000 for collaborative law, $35,000 for traditional attorney-to-attorney negotiation, and a minimum of $20,000–50,000 for a trial.

These estimates do not address the economic burden of litigation over the lifetimes of the children and families involved (e.g., medical costs, productivity losses, mental health costs, special education costs, criminal justice costs, and quality-of-life costs), but they do provide a starting point for assessing the potential cost–benefit balances of interventions for strained parent–child relationships.

The OCB evaluation strategy includes collecting information about the estimated cost of delivering the service (cost per family, staff cost, resource cost, etc.) to enable cost–benefit comparisons with similar interventions and other court-based services (e.g., litigation).

4. RESULTS OF THE OCB PROGRAM EVALUATION

The evaluation of OCB camp was conducted in the summers of 2013 and 2014 in Vermont. A total of 20 parents and 24 children participated in the evaluation. In the 2013 evaluation, 9 of the 10 parents (5 mothers and 4 fathers) participated in the preintervention and postintervention surveys, and all 11 children agreed to be interviewed by a member of the third-party research team on the last day of the camp. In the 2014 evaluation, 11 of the 14 parents (4 mothers and 7 fathers) participated in the evaluation, and all 13 children agreed to complete a post-only online survey on iPads on the last day of the camp.

Most parents and children expressed that attending the camp had been a positive experience. Although the brief time frame of the evaluation and the small sample size were not sufficient to permit observation of behavioral changes on the measures selected for the evaluation, there were non-statistically significant positive changes on all outcomes. Parents specifically seemed to benefit from the opportunities to meet with the clinicians, and children seemed to benefit from the support of peers experiencing similar family dynamics.

4.1. Experiences of Parents

4.1.1. UNDERSTANDING OF THE PURPOSE OF OCB CAMP

The majority of parents reported that the purpose of OCB camp was to improve overall communication and reduce the level of conflict between parties. Several parents believed that finding "common ground" with their coparents would increase their ability to effectively coparent and limit the potential or occurrence of parent alienation. Along with educating parents about the effects of alienation on the parent–child relationship, some parents believed the program would foster improved family unit relationships, repair and facilitate parent–child relationships, and mend previous misunderstandings between family members. One parent reported that the purpose of the program was to remain focused on the children and that the program was dedicated to hearing and supporting the needs of the children. Some parents were not as clear about the purpose of the OCB intervention and wished to find out more information after the program commenced.

4.1.2. GOALS FOR ATTENDING OCB CAMP

Because family members attended the program for different reasons, their goals for completing the program also differed. Many parents felt that their experience in the program allowed them to develop the tools and skills required to meet their initial goals. Those goals included improving communication with the other parent, increasing the ability to effectively coparent, and mending and building the parent–child relationship.

Several parents commended the ability of program staff to teach effective communication tools, reporting that it had helped them be able to effectively coparent after leaving the program. It appeared that many parents felt that sessions with staff were beneficial, provided answers to their questions, and equipped them with the knowledge and information they required to continue making progress in their coparenting efforts. One parent stated, "I believe that things can get better if both myself and my coparent use some of the skills that we have learned and continue to work with professionals in the near future."

While some parents reported accomplishing their goals for participating in the program, others did not. It appeared that at the end of the OCB intervention, parents who still experienced levels of conflict had difficulty maintaining effective communication with each other as well as repairing their relationships with their children. One parent stated that while the other parent had been cooperative throughout the intervention, the parent did not believe that the other parent was committed to their coparenting agreement and felt that this lack of commitment affected both their relationship and their relationship with their children.

Of the parents who reported feeling they had not reached their program goals, the majority stated that the true effects of the program would only become known after they returned home. Since program staff had not provided aftercare plans and recommendations for the future to all of the parents at the time of the survey, many parents felt unsure about the long-term implications of participating in the program. One parent stated:

> My goal was that my kids would gain insight into their situation and that such insight would lead to an improved relationship with me. I can't answer this question without (1) knowing the recommendations that will come from the camp staff and (2) seeing whether there is any improvement in my relationship with my kids once we return home.

One parent reported that because the program was court-ordered, the parent did not have any goals established other than remaining positive and maintaining the belief that the children should have the opportunity to hear and understand the parent's experiences of the divorce process.

4.1.3. Struggles with Attending OCB Camp

The most common concern for parents after the completion of the OCB program appeared to be whether it would be possible to maintain the improvements in family relationships achieved while at the camp and to continue to move forward in a positive direction. It seemed that because several families had entered the program with issues of alienation by one parent toward the other, some rejected parents feared that the alienating behavior would continue despite the family's attendance at the camp. These cases included ones in which parents did not have access to their children after the program and cases in which continued interparental conflict resulted in ongoing undermining of the parent–child relationship and failure to implement the aftercare recommendations. One parent reported that court involvement might be necessary to ensure that such recommendations are enforced, but noted that the court order would be "followed by a deterioration in relations with my daughter as a result of a perceived attack" on the preferred parent.

Parents who felt more collaborative with the other parent and perceived their family circumstances as evolving stated that the work of reintegration of family members would likely present an ongoing challenge. A number of parents saw maintaining the accountability of agreements made with their coparents as an integral part of moving the family dynamic in a positive and healthy direction. While parents agreed that progress made in the program was valuable and hoped it would continue after the camp was over, some noted that not dwelling on past issues would present a challenge. One parent stated that because of the loss of trust and respect for the other parent due to that parent's ongoing demeaning behavior, communication of any kind would be extremely difficult. One parent suggested that the biggest challenge would be to continue making progress and developing skills without the support and program staff available at the camp.

4.1.4. BEST FEATURES OF ATTENDING OCB CAMP

Of all the features of OCB camp, parents repeatedly reported the professionalism, competence, and emotional support of the staff as the most influential. Parents commended the staff on their ability to effectively and efficiently operate the program. One parent stated that there was a "very excellent logistic coordination of activities and people. Running a camp with this many moving parts in the manner in which you did was astounding! Great job!" Parents appeared to feel safe and comfortable in the environment created by the staff and were able to use the camp as an opportunity to bond with both their family and other members of the program. Several parents also appreciated the outdoor aspect of the program.

When asked about their favorite part of the program, parents reported that the clinicians' ability to provide counseling and interventions to family members was helpful in addressing issues surrounding strained parent–child relationships. Parents also appreciated the emotional support that the staff provided to the children. One parent reported: "I felt like, when the kids had a problem, there were competent staff available, that when they came to me, I could hand them off and their voices would be heard. This might be a counselor who would give them emotional support or a therapist." Parents also appeared to value the opportunity to meet other parents in similar situations and stages of divorce. Several parents noted that parents used each other for support, assisting each other in moving forward with their own challenges in their family situations. Highlighting the fact that parents found multiple features of the program beneficial and valuable, one parent reported that the best features of camp included "the food, the yoga, the pond, the children . . . and [parents] support of each other."

4.1.5. CLOSENESS WITH FAMILY MEMBERS AFTER ATTENDING OCB CAMP

When asked if participating in the OCB program created closer bonds between family members, parents responded in a mixed fashion. Several reported that the program provided the opportunity for a "breakthrough" in the parent–child relationship in which the parent felt closer to the child (or children) and hopeful that this closeness would continue after the program. Some parents reported that their family unit as a whole was strengthened as a result of their shared experiences within the program. It appeared that several parents felt they were better able to focus on their children and move forward in a collaborative fashion with the other parent after attending the program.

In other cases, although parents felt a closer connection to their children after participating, several reported feeling more distant from the other parent. Some parents alleged that the other parent's behavior throughout the program was a "performance" and did not reflect that parent's personality and actions outside the program. The resulting sense of distrust made it difficult for these parents to establish meaningful communication or relations with the other parent. One parent stated that the former spouse was unreceptive to the notion of coparenting and thus placed little effort into doing so, which was reflected in the other parent's attitudes during joint interactions and protests against attending the program. This same parent also believed their negative joint interactions affected their ability to bond with their child.

A minority of parents reported feeling more distant from their children after attending the program. This result appeared to be related to the scheduling of activities and group interactions at the camp.

4.2. Experiences of the Children

4.2.1. Hopes for Attending OCB Camp
Many children reported that in attending OCB camp, they had hoped to meet other children in similar situations and for their voices to finally be heard. Some were hoping for less conflict in the family and changes in their parents' behaviors.

4.2.2. Best Features of OCB Camp
The majority of the children reported that having the other children present at the camp was the best feature of their camp experience. The children reported that they connected and bonded with other children through the sharing of similar experiences. Because they understood what each of them was going through, they were mutually supportive, gave one another advice, and acted as one another's confidants. Among their comments were that "I liked best that the kids were very supportive and understood what I was going through"; "It was helpful to have them because one could relate"; and "I also enjoyed bonding with the other kids, helping them with difficult problems, and receiving advice from them as well." Some children also reported appreciating the support they received from counselors and therapists.

4.2.3. Desired Improvements in OCB Camp
Most of the children wished that there had been more downtime or breaks in the cabins each day, especially after family meetings and group therapy, to unwind, rest, and relax; read; write in their journals; listen to music; play games; or just simply talk and share with the other children. They also desired some "alone time" and did not like the camp counselors (Green Shirts) following them everywhere, wanting them to constantly stay active and engaged in activities. They expressed the need to recuperate mentally and physically after difficult events such as therapy sessions and family meetings, and they wanted the program to go more at their own pace. One child said, "I would like to have a rest time in the cabin area after group to unwind and talk to the other kids or sleep," and another complained, "The Green Shirts badger you to always stay active and play activities and sometimes you need a break." A third said: "I would add a rest hour to the days at camp. It would be effective.... Since there is so much going on, a break to relax or rest is helpful."

4.2.4. LESSONS LEARNED FROM ATTENDING OCB CAMP

Most children reported learning that they were not alone in their family circumstances and that there were other children who can understand them and relate to their situations because these children have had similar experiences. One child stated that "support from people that are going through the same problems really helps." Other children took away from the camp that "time plays a huge role," that it's important "to go at your own speed," and that "everything will eventually work out."

4.2.5. NEW INSIGHTS ABOUT THEIR PARENTS AFTER ATTENDING OCB CAMP

While some children said their estranged parents would never change (one said the parent was "still the same asshole"), others felt that their estranged parents felt bad for the pain their estranged parent experienced. Some children also felt that the estranged parent had a serious problem and was finally getting the help the parent needed. Most children had more positive things to say about their preferred parents, stating that the preferred parent was present for them and truly cared about them. The children also reported learning that the preferred parent was strong, loving, and resilient and that it was very important for them to have the preferred parent in their lives.

4.2.6. FAVORITE MEMORIES FROM OCB CAMP

Almost all of the children reported their best memories were of the late-night talks and games they played with each other in the cabins. Among the things children cited were "talking and playing games with all the other kids in the camp" and "being able to hang out in the cabin with all the kids before bed, [from] talking and playing games to just relaxing from the day."

4.2.7. PLANNING TO DO THINGS DIFFERENTLY AFTER LEAVING OCB CAMP

A lot of children mentioned that after camp they intended to focus more on themselves and on what makes them happy—for example, "I plan to concentrate on my life and do things that will benefit my future." Many stressed the importance of communicating better and staying open-minded to all perspectives, mentioning, for example, "explaining my worries more" and "be[ing] sure to take a third look at different perspectives, rather than just two." Some said they would attempt to restore some sort of relationship with the estranged parent, while others said they would not do anything differently and would "still stay away."

4.2.8. ADVICE FOR OTHER CHILDREN ATTENDING OCB CAMP

Most of the children would advise other children attending OCB camp to be active in the process, express themselves, and be open to the other children and the Green Shirts by sharing thoughts and ideas. They also stressed the importance of staying strong and positive and approaching the process with an open mind. One child said: "Be open to the other kids. They are invaluable and a gift. Help each other, love each other, learn together." Another advised, "Come to camp with an open mind and willing to take risks."

4.2.9. How to Get the Most out of OCB Camp

The children said that other children would get the most out of OCB camp by expressing themselves, communicating with the other kids at camp, and keeping a positive, open-minded attitude. "Don't shut yourself off from everyone," said one. "Be open and talk to the other kids. . ... Ask questions and get to know each other."

4.3. Summary of Results

The expectations of parents and children prior to attending OCB camp seem to have a major influence on their subsequent perceptions of their camp experience. Those who thought the OCB staff were going to "fix" preexisting strained parent–child relationships seemed less positive about their experiences of attending the camp. Others, however, appreciated the opportunity to observe their family members in a different context and appreciated the small changes in how they perceived the other members of their families.

The evaluation confirmed that the overall purpose of the OCB intervention is to plant seeds of hope and help families on the road to repairing strained relationships rather than to fix strained relationships within the limited time frame of the camp.

5. CONCLUSIONS

There is insufficient outcome research on interventions for parent–child contact problems, including affinity, alignment, justified rejection, and alienation (Fidler et al., 2012). In addition, small samples and methodological challenges have resulted in varying results across published reports of outcomes related to strained parent–child interventions.

Although the OCB evaluation continues to face similar challenges in determining the program's effectiveness, it incorporated several advances to increase the rigor and credibility of the findings. First, the evaluation was developed and carried out by an independent third-party evaluator that was not part of the delivery of the services. Independent third-party evaluators can provide an "outside view" of a program and can bring credibility because of their independence or expertise. Second, the evaluation was developed based on a transparent and systematic evaluation protocol that outlined the key features of the evaluation design. Given the complexity of strained parent–child relationships, programs for addressing these cases need to be able to demonstrate the key mechanisms of change. Third, the evaluation was guided by a logic model to capture data on the various intervention components so as to better evaluate and understand the short-, intermediate-, and long-term outcomes. Fourth, the evaluation includes a fidelity checklist to enable the evaluator to measure whether participants received all of the essential elements of the intervention and whether the intervention was delivered in a comparable manner to all participants.

Interventions for severe strained parent-child relationships are often more intrusive than other types of interventions and thus ought to be held to a higher research standard than other interventions. The OCB camp intervention is short, and follow-up is critical to maintaining any changes that occurred at camp. To research the longer-term outcomes requires information about the type of and compliance with aftercare. More and better research that identifies and differentiates levels of severity, intervention goals, and short- and long-term outcomes is needed for all interventions.

The OCB evaluation provides a framework for documenting the progress of the program, identifying baseline, midpoint, and posttest results, and for making adjustments to the delivery of the program based on the lessons learned. The evaluation design includes an emphasis on the implementation of triangulation techniques (e.g., combining qualitative and quantitative results) and on the influence of program participation data (e.g., number of sessions and types of services received). There is also emphasis in the analysis on monitoring the minimal dosage and other program-level factors captured in the fidelity checklist for each family to explore how the various components contribute to the key outcomes related to parent–child, coparent, and family change. As well, the inclusion of a fidelity checklist provides better evidence of whether the program is being implemented as planned.

The material discussed in this chapter has important implications for building theory about the conceptualization of interventions for strained parent–child relationships. Only a limited number of such programs are available, and there is no consensus on matching the goals of interventions with the severity of the relationship problem, the components of interventions, the need for targeting content and methods, and the salient features of parenting and coparenting knowledge and attitudes that these programs should address. The results from OCB evaluation provide a solid foundation for identifying the theoretical basis of content, structure, screening, and delivery of programs, which is essential to developing intervention programs tailored specifically to the unique needs of families where a child resists or refuses contact with a parent.

The following are the key lessons to be drawn from this chapter:

- Given the lack of clarity about the context of strained parent–child relationships, it is difficult both to develop comprehensive interventions to address those relationships and to test the effectiveness of those interventions.
- The development and evaluation of interventions (both legal and psychological) are in their formative stages; outcomes are inconclusive or unreliable at this time, mainly because of very weak evaluation methodology.
- Evaluation designs should consider process and implementation variables that may influence the strengths and challenges of interventions for strained parent–child relationships.
- Evaluation designs should include a logic model and fidelity checklist to guide the implementation and evaluation of these interventions.

- Parents should be given a detailed orientation on the expectations of a reintegration intervention so that their own expectations about potential changes to parent–child interactions from the intervention are realistic.
- Children attending interventions should be given opportunities to build social connections with other children experiencing strained parent–child relationships.
- Follow-up surveys with parents and children are important for assessing any long-term gains of participating in interventions for strained parent–child relationships.

REFERENCES

Baker, A. J. L., & Ben-Ami, N. (2011). To turn a child against a parent is to turn a child against himself: The direct and indirect effects of exposure to parental alienation strategies on self-esteem and well-being. *Journal of Divorce and Remarriage, 52*(7), 472–489.

Baker, A., Burkhard, B., & Albertson-Kelly, J. (2012). Differentiating alienated from not alienated children: A pilot study. *Journal of Divorce and Remarriage, 53*(3), 178–193.

Baker, A. J. L., & Darnall, D. (2006). Behaviors and strategies employed in parental alienation: A survey of parental experiences. *Journal of Divorce and Remarriage, 45*(1–2), 97–124.

Baker, A. J. L., & Verrocchio, M. C. (2013). Italian college student–reported childhood exposure to parental alienation: Correlates with well-being. *Journal of Divorce and Remarriage, 54*(8), 609–628.

Braver, S. J., Coatsworth, D., & Peralta, K. (n.d.). *Alienating behavior within divorced and intact families: Matched parents' and now-young adult children's reports.* Retrieved November 2015 from http://www.uea.ac.uk/swp/iccd2006/Presentations/tues_pm/ ps12%20High%20conflict%20&%20Enforcement/Braver%20summary.pdf

Deutsch, R. M. (2008). Divorce in the 21st century: Multidisciplinary family interventions. *Journal of Psychiatry and Law, 36*, 41–66.

Fidler, B. J., Bala, N., & Saini, M. A. (2013). *Children who resist postseparation parental contact: A differential approach for legal and mental health professionals.* New York, NY: Oxford University Press.

Fried, C. (2005). Getting a divorce? Why it pays to place nice. Money Magazine, July, 48–50.

Gardner, R. (2001). Should courts order PAS children to visit/reside with the alienated parent? A follow-up study. *American Journal of Forensic Psychology, 19*(3), 61–106.

Hands, A. J., & Warshak, R. A. (2011). Parental alienation among college students. *American Journal of Family Therapy, 39*(5), 431–443. doi:http://dx.doi.org/10.1080/ 01926187.2011.57533603

Johnston, J. R. (2003). Parental alignments and rejection: An empirical study of alienation in children of divorce. *Journal of the American Academy of Psychiatry and the Law, 31*, 158–170.

Johnston, J. R., Walters, M. G., & Olesen, N. W. (2005a). Is it alienating parenting, role reversal or child abuse? A study of children's rejection of a parent in child custody disputes. *Journal of Emotional Abuse, 5*(4), 191–218. doi:10.1300/J135v05n04_02

Johnston, J. R., Walters, M. G., & Olesen, N. W. (2005b). The psychological functioning of alienated children in custody disputing families: An exploratory study. *American Journal of Forensic Psychology, 23*(3), 39–64.

Kerns, S. E. U., & Prinz, R. J. (2002). Critical issues in the prevention of violence-related behavior in youth. *Clinical Child and Family Psychology Review, 5*, 133–160.

Kumar, S. (2003). *Factors affecting reconciliation in visitation refusal cases* (Doctoral dissertation).Available from Dissertations and Theses: Full Text. (Publication No. AAT 3069406)

Laughrea, K. (2002). Alienated Family Relationship Scale: Validation with young adults. *Journal of College Student Psychotherapy, 17*(1), 37–48. doi:10.1300/J035v17n01_05

López, T. J., Iglesias, V. E. N., & García, P. F. (2014). Parental alienation gradient: Strategies for a syndrome. *American Journal of Family Therapy, 42*(3), 217–231. doi:10.1080/01926187.2013.820116

Moné, J. G., & Biringen, Z. (2006). Perceived parent–child alienation: Empirical assessment of parent–child relationships within divorced and intact families. *Journal of Divorce and Remarriage, 45*(3–4), 131–156.

Moné, J. G., MacPhee, D., Anderson, S. K., & Banning, J. H. (2011). Family members' narratives of divorce and interparental conflict: Implications for parental alienation. *Journal of Divorce and Remarriage, 52*(8), 642–667.

Nigg, C. R., Allegrante, J. P., & Ory, M. (2002). Theory-comparison and multiple-behavior research: Common themes advancing health behavior research. *Health Education & Research, 17*, 670–679.

Polit, D. F., & Hungler, B. P. (1999). *Nursing research: Principles and methods* (6th ed.). Philadelphia, PA: Lippincott.

Rand, D. C., Rand, R., & Kopetski, L. (2005). The spectrum of parental alienation syndrome, Part III: The Kopetski follow-up study. *American Journal of Forensic Psychology, 23*, 15–43.

Reay, K. M. (2015). Family reflections: A promising therapeutic program designed to treat severely alienated children and their family system. *American Journal of Family Therapy, 43*(2), 197–207.

Rowen, J., & Emery, R. (2014). Examining parental denigration behaviors of co-parents as reported by young adults and their association with parent–child closeness. *Couple and Family Psychology: Research and Practice, 3*(3), 165–177.

Saini, M., Johnston, J., Fidler, B., & Bala, N. (2016). Empirical evidence of alienation. In L. Drozd, M. Saini, & N. Olesen (Eds.), *Parenting plan evaluations: Applied research for the family court* (2nd ed.). New York: NY. Oxford University Press.

Saini, M., & Shlonsky, A. (2012). *Systematic synthesis of qualitative research: A pocket guide for social work research methods.* New York: Oxford University Press.

Santacroce, S. J., Maccarelli, L. M., & Grey, M. (2004). Intervention fidelity. *Nursing Research, 53*, 63–66.

Sullivan, M., Ward, P., & Deutsch, R. M. (2010). Overcoming Barriers Family Camp: A program for high-conflict divorced families where a child is resisting contact with a parent. *Family Court Review, 48*(1), 116–135. doi:10.1111/j.1744-1617.2009.01293.x

Toren, P., Bregman, B., Zohar-Reich, E., Ben-Amitay, G., Wolmer, L., & Laor, N. (2013). Sixteen-session group treatment for children and adolescents with parental alienation and their parents. *American Journal of Family Therapy, 41*(3), 187–197.

Warshak, R. A. (2010). Family Bridges: Using insights from social science to reconnect parents and alienated children. *Family Court Review, 48*(1), 48–80. doi:10.1111/j.1744–1617.2009.01288

Warshak, R. A. (2015). Parental alienation: Overview, management, intervention and practice tips. *Journal of the American Academy of Matrimonial Lawyers, 28,* 181.

Whitecombe, S. (2014). *Powerless: The lived experience of alienated parents in the UK* (Unpublished doctoral dissertation). Teesside University, Middlesbrough, UK.

APPENDIX 13.A

LOGIC MODEL FOR OVERCOMING BARRIERS CAMP

	Program plan				Outcome plan			Measurement
Target group	Inputs	Activities	Outputs		Outcome statements			Measurement
	Resources and budget lines	Activities, tasks, and strategies	Deliverables	Short term	Mid-term	Long term		Design
• All members of restructured family system (including parents, spouses, and stepsiblings) • Evidence of strained parent–child relations • Court ordered	**Funding** • Donations • Family tuition **Facilitators** • Seasoned clinical psychologists who provide pro bono or highly-reduced-fee commitment	• Intake process to begin setup work with families • Screening for issues of abuse and safety and initial work with the entire family • Programs • Multinight family camp program • Weekend intensive • One-day follow-up • Psychoeducation • Intensive clinical work • Parallel parent–child work • Strategic use of activities to engage children and parents • Enjoyable camp experience • Role play • Aftercare activities	• Referrals • No. of referrals • No. of participants • No. of family members/ children • Duration/ dosage/ intensity • No. of hours in sessions • No. of follow-ups • Timing of intervention within court process • Full or partial parenting plans, agreement, or both • No. of aftercare referrals • Consultation for aftercare (courts, parenting coordinator, therapist)	• Overall satisfaction with OCB experience • Child has safe interaction with rejected parent • Child sees (or hears about) both parents working together in a safe way • Child becomes desensitized to rejected parent • Increased child and parent knowledge of communication, problem-solving, & emotional strategies • Parents' improved knowledge of impact on conflict on children • Parents' increased knowledge of factors for strained parent–child relationships	• Decrease in child's feelings of fear, anger, & anxiety toward rejected parent • Reduction in polarized views of parenting • More realistic views of parenting plans • Improved parent–child relationships • Decreased parental conflict • Decreased parent–child conflict • Improved parenting skills • Improved coparenting relationship	• Improved well-being of child • Improved well-being of favored parent and rejected parent • Improved family functioning • Decreased litigation	• Mixed-methods design • Pre–post group surveys • Fidelity checklist • Administrative data analysis • Follow-up

APPENDIX 13.B

EVALUATION MATRIX FOR OVERCOMING BARRIERS CAMP

Desired outcome	Key evaluation questions	Indicators	Data sources and collection methods	Timing of data collection
Creating public awareness	• What activities were undertaken to improve public awareness? • What new communication tools, methodologies, or approaches were developed and implemented to improve public awareness?	• Evidence of activities directed at improving public awareness of Overcoming Barriers • Evidence of clients and resource network using new information tools	• Google Analytics	Ongoing
Experiences of parent–child dynamics	• What are the experiences of parent–child dynamics, and how do these experiences shape the participants' experiences of the camp?	• Experiences of children and parents as positive • Evidence of strained relationships at beginning of camp that gradually stabilize	• Interviews with children and parents before and after they have attended camp	Pre–post and follow-up
Parents' knowledge and attitudes about importance of child having a relationship with both parents	• Do parents increase their knowledge of parenting when children are in two homes?	• Increase in parents' knowledge of caregiving skills and needs of children when parents are in conflict	• Survey • Qualitative interviews	Pre–post
Parental conflict	• Has intervention assisted in reducing parental conflict?	• Parents' indication that conflict between parents has decreased after camp	• Survey	Pre–post
Parents' alliance	• Do parents improve their working relationship for children involved in the custody dispute?	• Increased alliance between parents to be more cooperative in meeting needs of the children	• Survey • Qualitative interviews	Pre–post
Parent–child conflict	• Has intervention assisted in decreasing parent–child conflict?	• Decreased parent–child conflict	• Survey Qualitative interviews	Pre–post

Desired outcome	Key evaluation questions	Indicators	Data sources and collection methods	Timing of data collection
Child's resistance to rejected parent	• Does child experience improved relationship with rejected parent?	• Decrease in child's feelings of fear, anger, anxiety toward rejected parent	• Qualitative interviews	Pre–post and follow-up
Child's well-being	• Does intervention assist in increasing overall child well-being? • Does intervention assist in decreasing child's emotional and behavioral problems?	• Decrease in child behavioral and emotional problems	• Qualitative interviews	Pre–post and follow-up
Parents' well-being	• Does intervention assist in increasing overall parent well-being? • Does intervention assist in decreasing parents' emotional and behavioral problems?	• Increase in parents' feelings of self	• Qualitative interviews	Pre–post and follow-up
Family cohesion	• Has camp helped improve family functioning and cohesion?	• All family members indicate better family dynamics after attending camp	• Survey	Pre–post
Alternatives to litigation	• Has family decreased repeated reliance on the courts to solve parenting-plan issues? • Is there a decrease in motions following intervention?	• Frequency of litigation	• Survey	Pre–post
Cost of program	• Is program more or less costly than other types of therapies? • Is program more or less costly than litigation? • Do people use the scholarships? • What is the cost savings for families? • What is overall cost–benefit balance for families?	• Indication of costs and benefits for families involved	• Cost–benefit analysis	Posttreatment

APPENDIX 13.C

OVERCOMING BARRIERS CAMP PARENT SURVEY

A. For the following questions please select (1) vastly better, (2) somewhat better, (3) remain the same, (4) somewhat worse, (5) vastly worse since attending OCB camp

	Vastly better	Somewhat better	Remain the same	Somewhat worse	Vastly worse
Friendliness toward your children's OP (other parent)	O	O	O	O	O
Children's feeling friendly toward the OP	O	O	O	O	O
Disputes with OP about gifts to the children	O	O	O	O	O
Disputes about parenting-time schedule	O	O	O	O	O
Communication with OP	O	O	O	O	O
Feelings about the competency of the OP	O	O	O	O	O
Time with the children and both parents	O	O	O	O	O
Children's satisfaction with the parent–child time	O	O	O	O	O
Disputes about parenting practices	O	O	O	O	O
Relationship with children after spending time with the OP	O	O	O	O	O
Disputes in the presence of the children	O	O	O	O	O
Children taking sides in disagreements between you and the OP	O	O	O	O	O

	Vastly better	Somewhat better	Remain the same	Somewhat worse	Vastly worse
Disputes about child-support payments	○	○	○	○	○
Children's feelings toward the OP	○	○	○	○	○
Children exposed to information about the legal dispute	○	○	○	○	○
Angry disagreements with the OP	○	○	○	○	○
Hostility toward the OP	○	○	○	○	○
OP hostility toward you	○	○	○	○	○
Communication about the children	○	○	○	○	○
An amicable separation/divorce	○	○	○	○	○
Disputes about pickups and drop-offs of the children	○	○	○	○	○
Pressure on children about living arrangements	○	○	○	○	○
Adjustment to the separation/divorce from the OP	○	○	○	○	○
OP's adjustment to the separation/divorce from you	○	○	○	○	○

B. For the following questions please select (1) vastly better, (2) somewhat better, (3) remain the same, (4) somewhat worse, (5) vastly worse since attending OCB camp

	Vastly better	Somewhat better	Remain the same	Somewhat worse	Vastly worse
My understanding of the impact of strained parent–child relationships on my child(ren)	○	○	○	○	○

Statement	○	○	○	○	○
My ability to take responsibility for my own contribution to the strained parent–child relationship problems	○	○	○	○	○
My ability to regulate my emotions	○	○	○	○	○
My ability to communicate with the other parent	○	○	○	○	○
My understanding of effective coping strategies	○	○	○	○	○
My taking responsibility for the rejection of the child(ren) toward a parent	○	○	○	○	○
My ability to deal with the rejection of a child toward the parent in a positive manner	○	○	○	○	○
My ability to build positive, healthy supports for myself	○	○	○	○	○
My ability to work with the other parent outside of court	○	○	○	○	○
My ability to work on a parenting plan that works best for my child	○	○	○	○	○
My ability to be flexible to make sure the parenting plan meets the needs of my child	○	○	○	○	○
My concept of family (who is in and who is out)	○	○	○	○	○
My ability to protect my child from the conflict	○	○	○	○	○
My ability to be empathetic toward the other parent	○	○	○	○	○
My ability to problem-solve with the other parent	○	○	○	○	○

APPENDIX 13.D

OVERCOMING BARRIERS CAMP FIDELITY CHECKLIST

Date	Location	Service provider			Number of parent & child participants

Referral and screening factors	Yes	No	N/A	Additional comments
Did all parents complete a separate intake form?				
Did all court orders stipulate in detail the expectations about the family involvement?				
Did all court orders stipulate in detail the expectations about the follow-up contact with OCB?				
Did each child participant have at least some contact with both parents in the four years prior to attending the program?				
Did the program screen for immediate threat of violence and safety issues?				
Did the program screen for current restraining orders preventing contact between the parents and/or the children?				
Did the program screen for substance abuse?				
Did the program screen for mental health issues and psychotic disorders?				
Other, please specify:				

Fidelity of implementation

Dimension	Implementation consideration	Yes	No	N/A	Additional comments
Facilitator adherence	Did the service provider agree to the requirements to be associated with OCB?				
Facilitator training and experience	Did the service provider have the minimum training and experience to provide OCB services?				
	Has the service provider previously attended an OCB training?				
Target population	Were the inclusion and exclusion criteria applied before providing service to the family to ensure they were eligible for the service?				
	Has there been some contact among all family members in the past four years?				
	Was each family member screened for the presence of risk (e.g. violence, substance use, mental health problems)?				
Location/setting	Was the location/setting consistent with the OCB framework?				
	Did the children sleep in locations separated from the parents?				
	Did the location provide opportunities for extracurricular activities?				

Dimension	Implementation consideration	Yes	No	N/A	Additional comments
Materials	Did the service provider have sufficient materials to deliver the service as per the OCB framework?				
	Were there sufficient materials to support recreational activities?				
Delivery	Did the delivery of service include psychoeducation individually for each family member?				
	Did the delivery of service include a component of family therapy?				
	Did the delivery of service include opportunities for parallel play?				
	Did the delivery of service include common activities (including meals) for all family members?				
	Did the delivery of service provide private space for each family member?				
Dosage	Were at least 3 hours of the service devoted to psychoeducation?				
	Were at least 3 hours of the service devoted to clinical intervention?				
	Were at least 30 minutes devoted to family intervention?				
	Were at least 3 hours devoted to social/ recreational/ group /common group activities?				
Aftercare	Was there an aftercare pathway developed with the family members?				
	Was a plan developed for follow-up?				

14

Conclusion

JANET R. JOHNSTON ∎

1. INTRODUCTION

This book describes a model of clinical intervention for families of separation and divorce where a child strongly and persistently resists or refuses contact with one parent for little or no substantial reason It draws upon the collective experience of well-seasoned clinicians and is informed by a wide range of research evidence that appears to be relevant to understanding and treating these kinds of problems.

Historically this problem has been mired in political controversy, in that powerful organized interest groups for mothers and fathers (and their scholar advocates) have argued along gendered lines as to whether these children—often referred to as *alienated children*—are *realistically estranged* victims of abuse and witness to violence by the rejected parent or whether they are participants in a campaign of malicious indoctrination instigated by an angry ex-partner, the pre-ferred parent (typically referred to as *parental alienation* or *parental alienation syndrome*). In accord with a more nuanced view of these families that has been espoused by clinicians and researchers more recently, this book eschews this sim-ple dichotomy and transcends the highly politicized context in which the problem has typically been conceived: It proposes a conceptual model in which multiple factors are implicated in the etiology, maintenance, and escalation of the child's negative attitudes and behavior (see Chapters 2 and 5). It is also entirely non-partisan when it comes to prescribing treatment, drawing upon the full range of educational methods, therapeutic strategies, and case management options (see Chapter 4). Most important, it begins to ask the question of who needs what kind of intervention and under what circumstances.

This concluding chapter will (a) highlight the conceptual formulation of the problem that underlies the treatment approach, (b) suggest what the important components of the intervention model are, (c) identify conundrums in clinical practice, (d) comment on limitations in available empirical evidence to inform policy and practice and (e) explore how to go about pursuing ethical practices and informed decision-making on these matters while awaiting more definitive direction from accumulated research.

2. CONCEPTUAL FORMULATION OF THE PROBLEM

The parent–child relationship problems in this book are described as analogous to a "perfect storm" of meteorological factors that feed back into a process to magnify its own intensity (see Chapter 5). Here, the perfect storm is a confluence of individual intrapsychic and intrafamily conflicts that tend to expand into social networks beyond the family and escalate to a stalemate after they enter the adversarial legal system. In these cases, attempted solutions can become part of the problem.

Child alienation cases illustrate the quintessential system dynamic of a chronically conflicted postseparation family in which the parents are unable or unwilling to form a parental alliance. Instead, an alliance forms between one parent and the child(ren), and the other parent is excluded. The architect of this edifice can be one or both parents, and the construction materials are the highly negative, polarized views, attitudes, and beliefs about each other that they have fashioned, often with the help of the child and supportive others who hear only one side of the story. The access arrangement provides the opportunity for the alliance to be constructed. The edifice is cemented by the rigid defenses the family members erect as these vulnerable individuals try to cope with feelings of anxiety, fear, shame, helplessness, and loss that are invoked around the time of separation, especially in response to custody litigation. With the passage of time, the cement hardens.

The following case vignette illustrates how the origins of the storm can be recognized in the way parents chronicle the history of their relationship and how individuals with psychological vulnerabilities reframe critical incidents in the family in the aftermath of parental separation. It also shows how parents' extremely negative attitudes, beliefs, and alliances with children form and act as self-fulfilling prophecies, how children's responses increase the parental dysfunction, and how networks of "helpers" can solidify rather than resolve the problem.

CASE ILLUSTRATION: THE B FAMILY

Early origins. The mother in the B family described ongoing parental conflict over childrearing ever since the birth of "her" children, a son now 10 years old and a daughter now 5 years old. She said the father was "inept and unavailable," so she had to "assume the role of homemaker and Super Mom." The father said he was "kicked out of the marital bed and nursery by 'Mother Earth'" and "retreated to his office and worked." He complained that his wife had "mollycoddled" his son, compared to his daughter. Consequently the boy "took his mother's side" in family disputes whereas his daughter had been closer to him.

Personality vulnerabilities. By both accounts, the father was insulted by being marginalized and rendered powerless, and he resorted to several acts of coercive control (pushing and shoving the children) to gain more influence over them. When the father had an affair and filed for divorce, the mother's loss of status and humiliation triggered her anxiety and borderline defenses. Prone to labile emotional states of anger and emptiness, she turned to her eldest child for emotional support.

Negatively reconstructed beliefs and alliance formation. When the father filed for shared custody, the boy influenced his sister to join him in the protective alliance with the mother. The children and mother shared their negative views of the father with one another, supported by family stories about his "abusive" and "manipulative" behavior. They deemed court-ordered time with the father "boring" or "miserable" and often sabotaged visits with him by making alternative plans. The son complained that he "always got sick" when he went to his father's house.

Increased parental dysfunction due to children's symptoms. Although both parents freely disseminated their negative convictions and "bad-mouthed" each other among their separate networks, the children were more exposed to the mother's increasing negativity and her fear that the judge would be duped by the "other side" and change custody. The children became more resistant to and phobic about any contact with the father. Physical struggles between the father and children erupted when he tried to enforce visitation: He slapped the son for swearing at him and dragged the boy bodily to his car. In response to the children's defiant behavior, he locked both of them in his house "to prevent them from running away." The mother became more overprotective and permissive to compensate for what she viewed as the father's "harsh, rigid, and abusive" disciplinary practices. When the father tried to "regain closeness with [his daughter] by insisting on a good-night kiss and body hug," she told the mother that he had climbed into her bed and "touched her privates." Contact was suspended during investigation of these allegations, which were unable to be substantiated.

Spread of Dispute Through Parents' Networks and Stalemate in Court. During the custody litigation that followed, the children refused all contact with the father. The mother's therapist submitted testimony that she was appropriately protecting herself and her children, who were realistically "estranged" from their father. This position was supported by the child therapist who had been treating the children for post-traumatic stress disorder consequent to their father's "abuse." The father's attorney claimed the children were alienated by their mother, citing the custody evaluator's report. The judge concluded that the father's acts of coercive control, although perhaps unwise, did not rise to the level of child abuse and that the children were disproportionately negative toward their father.

Experienced clinicians know there are no simple fixes for long-standing multi-dimensional problems like those in the case illustration. Adversarial litigation reinforces the struggle to vindicate one parent and indict the other. Nonintervention will reinforce the children's phobic avoidance of the rejected parent. Simple court orders for individual counseling, father-child reunification therapy, or change of custody are usually insufficient to dissolve this stalemate, and relieve the children's fears and resistance to contact. Parents' distrust and negative convictions of each other's parenting are reaffirmed by overly permissive mothering and coercively controlling fathering. Court mandates and sanctions for noncompliance *by themselves* will not improve parental capacities to be warmly empathic and appropriately authoritative with their children; nor will these measures restore coparental communication and cooperation. Rather, an entire re-engineering effort is needed to interrupt the vicious cycle and put in place a new parent management structure.

This Herculean task is complex and multifaceted. The authors of this book are fully aware that within each family and across the spectrum of cases, there is considerable variation in the psychological functioning of parents and children and the nature of the forces that contribute to the storm. These variables are delineated to devise focused, strategic interventions for each family (see Chapter 2).

3. FEATURES OF THE CLINICAL FORMULATION

In this concluding chapter, it is important to highlight some of the important features of the clinical formulation of the problem that inform the nuanced intervention model—in particular, the type and range of variation in the factors that are implicated in children's resistance and refusal to have contact with one parent. Some of these features are well-known clinical presumptions and understandings; others are relatively new clinical insights. Together these features help the intervention transcend the simplistic paradigmatic controversy that views parental abuse and parental alienation as binary alternative explanations for children's behavior.

3.1. The Source, Type, and Veracity of Negative Beliefs

It is common for separating individuals to review and revise the failed relationship and reach new "insights" about themselves and their ex-partner. High-conflict individuals rewrite history to derive particularly negative, polarized views of the ex-partner, which are consolidated as narratives when shared with others, including children. This is the stuff of bad-mouthing and the curriculum for a campaign of indoctrination by those parents with an agenda of disrupting or terminating the child's relationship with the other parent. Before assuming this singular motivation, therapists in child alienation cases need to consider the extent to which these negative views and attitudes may be inaccurate and undeserved and for what reason.

Despite attempts to screen out family violence and abuse cases, some slip through the cracks, in which event negative portrayals of the other parent may be more or less accurate and justify a parent's protective stance. Many evaluations for abuse, however, are inconclusive, in that the facts are unclear, clouded in defensive forgetting, and unable to be proven one way or the other and parents' suspicions are not allayed. Moreover, no bright line distinguishes abuse from nonabuse cases. Many behaviors are deemed "bordering on abuse," "inappropriate," indicative of "poor judgment," or even "thoughtless." Critical incidents in the family can be denied, minimized, excused, or justified when they happened but surface later, before or after separation, at which time they are disclosed to significant others, reviewed, and reclassified. These borderline cases can be claimed by advocates for victims of both parental alienation and child abuse syndromes. Emotional abuse in particular is difficult to identify reliably, and alienating parental behavior has only gradually been more widely acknowledged as a form of emotional abuse.

3.2. Motivations for Erroneous and Extreme Attitudes and Beliefs

Some negative beliefs are honest but mistaken assumptions arising from incomplete knowledge of the ex-partner after separation. Other allegations of the rejected parent's misconduct are outright fabrications fueled by malicious anger. Some allegations may be due partly or wholly to defensive processes that, under stress, can evolve to paranoid delusions of psychotic proportions. While some parents' alienating behaviors are conscious and deliberate, other parents seem to be unaware they are transmitting their negative attitudes indirectly by innuendo and body language. While simultaneously voicing the acceptable rhetoric of supporting the child's relationship with the other parent, parents may be conveying a range of confusing and scary messages to the child that the other parent is unimportant, irrelevant, untrustworthy, dangerous, or even toxic.

3.3. The Presence and Level of Personality Disorder

In one or both parents, personality disorders can contribute to the amount of distortion in the reconstructed image of the other parent as well as to parenting problems. This is especially true of narcissistic, sociopathic, and paranoid disorders, all three of which have narcissistic features that are particularly reactive to the humiliation of the rejection inherent in a separation or custody dispute. It is theorized that this experience triggers intense anger, defensive splitting, and projection of all blame onto the "bad" ex-partner in order for the individual to feel "good" and vindicated. Children tend to be seen as either extensions of the "good victim self" or under the total control of the "bad other parent." Also implicated in child alienation are parents with borderline personality traits and disorders who tend to react to separation and threat of loss with intense anxiety emotional deregulation, and instability in interpersonal perceptions and relationships, including those with their children. (see Chapter 5).

3.4. Transmitting Negative Attitudes and Beliefs to Children

Negative attitudes toward and convictions about the other parent are consciously or unconsciously conveyed to children directly or indirectly, by word and deed, in countless ways, along with the aligned parent's acutely heightened anxiety about the threats imposed by impending contact with the other parent. Alternatively, children's behavioral disturbances after visits with the other parent can trigger negative beliefs about the ex-partner's being the cause and invoke corresponding overprotectiveness.

However, there is a wide range in the extent to which children respond to attempts to interfere in and sabotage their relationship with the other parent. In some cases a negative campaign of indoctrination backfires on the parent delivering it, resulting in the child's silently and strategically distancing herself or himself from the alienating parent. Role reversal is more common, with children becoming reciprocal comforters and protectors of the anxious parent, although in this role they do not always lose their emerging capacity to differentiate themselves. Children are also used as buffers and messengers and conditionally rewarded with empathic attunement, permissive parenting, or both to the extent they reflect the aligned parent's views. Close scrutiny may reveal such a child to be in a means-oriented alliance to gain those rewards rather than alienated.

3.5. Parent–Child Enmeshment

Enmeshment occurs when psychological boundaries dissolve and parent and child are codependent and function as one unit. They share identical feelings and views about the rejected parent while taking an "independent thinker" stance. To varying extents depending on temperamental disposition, developmental stage, and attachment history, one or more children in a sibling group can become psychologically enmeshed with the needy parent. More extreme cases may involve a folie à deux wherein a child shares the aligned parent's psychotic delusions about the rejected parent.

All of the above cases clearly need to be distinguished from situations where the child has been traumatized by the aligned parent's abusive behavior. It is not uncommon for children who have been directly abused, emotionally terrorized and/or witness to family violence by a parent to identify with the aggressor. In this case they can assert loyalty to the abusive parent, and vilify an innocent parent who is usually a victim of the same abuser.

3.6. The Influence of Significant Others

Other significant individuals can profoundly influence anxious, vulnerable family members whose world is in flux from the multiple stresses inherent in parental separation that culminates in custody litigation including abuse and alienation allegations. Ideally, counseling by advocates and investigative, evaluation, and litigation processes provide a powerful context for effecting change. However, if the "helpers" involved in these processes lack adequate training in the dynamics of these families and if there is an absence of case coordination and system management, outcomes can range from ineffective to disastrous (see Chapter 11).

3.7. Summary of Variable Features in Child Alienation

In sum, there is a wide range of variability in the factors involved in child alienation cases. These factors include the pernicious intent of the alienating behavior of the aligned parent and the level of distortion in each parent's perceptions of the other. Also varied are the capacities of each parent to be warm and authoritative (rather than authoritarian or permissive) and the extent to which one or both aligned and rejected parents have engaged in critical incidents and patterns of abusive behavior." There is further variability in the extent to which one parent's polarized, negative beliefs and behaviors have undermined the child's relationship with the other parent. Some children are clearly emotionally distressed and behaviorally disordered or at risk for future difficulties. Others seem to be coping reasonably well, but the longer-term risks to their future development are a matter of concerned conjecture. Professional mismanagement and the adversarial legal process itself may be implicated to varying extents in the consolidated stance of the alienated child.

4. IMPORTANT COMPONENTS OF THE INTERVENTION MODEL

The OCB approach was developed specifically for the intractable cases of alienation, often conceived as a last-ditch effort to help in cases where all other efforts have failed to reunify the parent and child, at times under threat of a change of custody to the rejected parent. However, the most severe cases (e.g., where children are in acute risk of danger from a psychotic or sociopathic parent) are excluded. The 3- to 5-day intensive therapeutic experience is provided within a summer camp or residential setting, isolated from children's everyday activities and their home, school, and neighborhood environments (see Chapters 6 and 7.)

The goals of this family treatment model extend beyond reunifying the alienated child with the rejected parent and establishing a mutually beneficial access arrangement. They also include transforming the polarized "good or bad" beliefs and attitudes of family members into more realistic ones and restoring more appropriate parenting and coparenting roles in the family to support the child's development.

Families come to the OCB program with extensive litigation histories, investigations, and custody evaluations, which are previewed by OCB staff. Court orders, with or without parental stipulations, mandate program attendance. One to three family groups participate in the program together, having been screened to exclude inappropriate cases like those with severe intimate-partner violence, child abuse, untreated mental illness, and substance abuse. Interventions are focused on specific goals, fidelity of process is monitored, and relevant outcome data are gathered from different sources (see Chapter 13). The following components of the OCB model, as a group, differ from many other approaches to parent–child contact problems (see Chapter 3):

1. *The intervention is tailored to the individual family* and is based on an individualized assessment of the pattern of elements that are hypothesized to have caused and maintained the particular case of a child's resistance or refusal to have contact with a parent (see Chapter 2). It involves strategically picking apart and dissolving the elements at points of impasse, choosing key elements that are most amenable to change and are likely to have positive ripple effects and circumventing those that are not. For example, personality vulnerabilities like narcissism are least amenable to change, but by taking care not to confront and shame parents with these traits, one can avoid triggering their defensive anger, projection of blame, and paranoia. For another example, conferring with key individuals in the networks of the disputing couple to ensure a unified approach to the family can generate multiple positive ripple effects. Throughout the intervention, there is ongoing review by the OCB team of what is working and what is needed.

2. *Interventions are delivered in a protected, secure setting using the principles of milieu therapy* (see Chapters 4 and 7). This is likely to decrease the excessive vigilance, rigid defensiveness, and anxiety that are the hallmarks of family members at impasse. The goal of milieu therapy is to maximize pleasure and create opportunities for the family to pursue enjoyable, fun activities together. Pleasurable experiences for the family as a group have been long absent, and their re-emergence provides a foundation for hope that change is possible.

3. *All family members are mandated to participate* in the program, including both the rejected and preferred parent and children ages 8 years and older (see Chapters 8–10). Involvement of the preferred parent, who is usually an unwilling attendee, is a departure from many other reunification therapies, which include only the child and rejected parent. From the outset the team's message is, "Whether or not you are part of the problem, you need to be part of the solution," and expectations are conveyed that good parents not only refrain from interference and sabotage but also help repair and promote the child's relationship with the other parent, no matter how difficult this is for them. After being supported in their feelings of loss, frustration, and injustice, rejected

parents are expected to relinquish their victim stance and assume accountability for their own contributions to the problem. They are confronted to answer questions like "What reason might your child have for not wanting to see you?," "What kernel of truth might there be to your child's complaint X?," and "What could you do differently to change that?"

4. *Interventions are delivered within peer groups*, using the powerful group dynamic to provide social support while exerting influence to effect changes in attitudes and beliefs (see Chapter 7). Group members tend to normalize (rather than demonize) one another's feelings and behaviors. They are more likely to acknowledge their own behavior when it is mirrored in others, and they respond to confrontation by peers less defensively than they would to others. Group treatments are also usually more efficient in effecting change and correspondingly less costly.

5. *Intervention is delivered by an empathic, supportive, unified team* (see Chapters 6 and 7). Team members are positive role models in spirit and in deed. Clients are provided with an initial opportunity to tell their stories so that they feel heard. They are treated with respect (not "shamed and blamed"). Based on this experience they are encouraged to let go of their defensive vigilance during the intervention and trust the clinicians to protect their children.

6. *Interaction between family members is highly structured* through living arrangements, prescribed tasks, and orchestrated family activities (see Chapters 8–11). For example, family members reside separately from one another and meet initially with just their peers, only later meeting in selected dyads and triads with other members of their own families. This structured interaction provides a sense of safety and predictability that lowers defensiveness. It also blocks the re-enactment of old pathological patterns of behavior. Carefully designed tasks, scripts, and role plays, drawn from experiential therapies (see Chapter 4), substitute new, more positive behavioral responses for old negative ones. Each component of the family group experience is highly structured in a series of exercises and orchestrated to maximize the likelihood of progress toward the family's goals in a milieu of enjoyment.

7. *Cognitive beliefs that support negative behaviors are gently challenged* with psychoeducation and experiential exercises demonstrating common errors and distortions in perception, attribution, and memory from social psychology (see Chapters 8–11). A wide range of counseling techniques are drawn from cognitive–behavioral therapies (including systematic desensitization of phobic behavior) and employed to deconstruct the negatively biased beliefs and attitudes family members have toward one another that support the child's alliance with one parent and contribute to the exclusion of the other.

8. *New coparenting and parallel-parenting skills are introduced and practiced*
   (see Chapter 11). It is acknowledged that tearing down dysfunctional
   patterns of cognition and behavior is insufficient and that family change,
   if any, will be short-lived unless the scaffolding for a new, more functional
   parenting edifice is erected. Significant attention is therefore given to
   developing after-care for families that may include a comprehensive
   parenting plan and appointment of a parenting coordinator.

4.2.1. Helping with Reality-Testing in Perception and Memory

Overall, the focus of the OCB intervention is creating opportunities for family
members to experience each other in new, more pleasurable ways in the present
and future, not mull over past grievances. However, the extent to which beliefs
about the prior nefarious behavior of the rejected parent are rooted in fact as
opposed to the product of cognitive distortion with malicious intent by the preferred parent remains a disputed issue despite numerous prior investigations. It is
a mistake for clinicians to gloss over, ignore, or deny this issue. Nor should they
be enticed to reinvestigate and render an opinion on it.

Rather than take sides in these disputes, the clinician's role is to help anchor parents' and children's reality testing and resolve profound differences in perception and
memory amongst family members. The child's (and the aligned parent's) crystalli-
zation of intense anger and disappointment toward the other parent into extreme
attributions that vilify, demonize, and in some cases dehumanize that parent need
to be deconstructed. The clinician also challenges family members' proclivity to
manage conflict within their family by cutting off the difficult relationship through
avoidance and exclusion. The tools for this demolition task are carefully chosen
to suit the individuals involved. More effective strategies for dealing with intoler-
able feelings and managing conflict are offered by the OCB program to replace the
old ones. For example, alienated children can be affirmed for their compassionate
caretaking relationship with the aligned parent and at the same time encouraged to
move out of this burdensome role into more gratifying activities with their peers.

To the extent that there is some truth to family members' ongoing complaints,
the intervention involves helping the target parent acknowledge mistakes, issue
apologies, make amends, commit to change, and repair the parent–child relationship. Typically these repair rituals are treated with skepticism, seen as disingenuous and likely to represent short-lived changes by the child and aligned parent.
This is understandable: Trust takes time to rebuild. Meanwhile, aligned parents
are asked not only to refrain from alienating parental behavior (by interfering in
and sabotaging the other parent's relationship with the child) but also to fully support and promote the child's reconnection with the other parent, who may indeed
have residual deficits and eccentricities. The clinician can engage both parents in
a exercise of figuring out how to talk about one other to the child in a charitable
but realistic way and imparting coping strategies that are more effective but also
protective of the child.

4.3.2. Some Conundrums of Clinical Practice

1. *Sustaining Long-Term Change.* The apparent potency of the OCB program is likely due, in part, to the fact that it is a brief, intensive, highly structured, all family member-inclusive intervention by a highly experienced team of clinicians. The initial intensive residential therapeutic experience for a small number of families for a 3- to 5-day period is perceived as crucial to shifting the family impasse and abating the forces driving the "perfect storm". Developing an aftercare model and finding staff to implement it in the geographical locale of each family form a central agenda of the therapeutic team who recognize that many parents will need their executive functioning shored up over the longer term (see Chapter 11). Children may also need direct ongoing support. In fact the availability of appropriate follow-up services has been, at times, a criteria for admitting a family to treatment in the first place.

2. *The Affordability of the Intervention.* The OCB intervention is delivered by a team led by highly experienced clinical psychologists, who work closely with interns, recreational counselors, and other support staff. There is a 1:1 ratio between faculty or staff and family members. Obviously, this is a costly intervention that can be afforded by very few families; often it is paid for by the more motivated (i.e., rejected) parent. Although its cost-effectiveness may compare favorably with the cost of litigation, it is out of reach of the vast majority of clients in family courts with similar problems. Perhaps the program's strongest merit with respect to cost is that it provides excellent opportunities for staff training in work with the most difficult cases of parent–child contact problems. The treatment approach has been adapted to outpatient settings (see Chapter 12) but without the benefit of many of its special features, like the therapeutic milieu and group setting. It might be possible to streamline the intervention by evaluating the contribution of the component parts to outcomes and discarding those that are less effective. This would require an evaluation design where subjects are randomly assigned to different components of the treatment (e.g., individual-family versus multifamily treatment).

3. *Clinical Experience and Training Required.* The OCB model was designed by experienced clinicians who are recognized as national leaders and educators in the family law field. It derives from a composite of what some of the best clinicians and legal professionals know about how to intervene in alienation. This fact raises concerns about what costs might be accrued and what damage might be done by the involvement of less competent, inexperienced clinicians and allied professionals. How can one tell at the outset if a clinician is well qualified and capable of handling the problem? What protections can be afforded to family members who become victims of a process that has derailed or stalemated progress?

As pointed out in Chapter 5 and illustrated in the case example of the B family above, in alienation cases there is some danger that the involvement of helping professionals can be iatrogenic, that is, contribute to the problem. As a result of the intense countertransference reactions typically provoked by intensely polarized, disputing parents, unwary therapists working with different family members can easily be induced to take sides, mirror family splits and alignments, and work at cross purposes to one another. It is the responsibility of clinicians to process their countertransference reactions to their clients rather than act them out and to use the resulting insights wisely in the intervention—for example, to deepen their existential understanding of how children might feel when caught between parents with annihilating anger.

Unless helping professionals work closely together as a unified team, they can multiply in number and stalemate progress, all the while placing exorbitant costs on the family. A good coparenting agreement can forestall this happening. Otherwise, the court may be the only agent with the authority to end the stalemate, hold helping professionals accountable, and reassemble a unified approach to intervention using any and all methods available—court orders, judicial conferencing, and case management.

5. STATE OF THE RESEARCH EVIDENCE

There is a voluminous body of literature about parental alienation (or parental alienation syndrome) and alienated children for both professionals and the wider public that extends across national borders, attesting to the high salience of this matter as a social policy issue. However, closer scrutiny indicates that the bulk of this literature consists of clinical opinion, descriptive and anecdotal accounts, and polemics heavily influenced by advocates. The most comprehensive review of empirical studies on alienation to date (Saini, Johnston, Fidler, & Baler, 2016) shows only 44 studies plus 11 dissertations. Moreover, systematic rating of the quality of these empirical studies indicates that as a group they are methodologically weak, so that there is very limited ability to generalize from the results. Saini et al. (2016) write that the extant studies are "plagued by small non-random samples, data analyzed retrospectively, the use of descriptive statistics, a lack of consensus on the definitions of alienation, and the use of varying, non-standardized measures and procedures" (p. 4). The following statements summarize the state of research on interventions for alienation:

1. In the absence of large, representative samples and randomly drawn comparison or control groups, there are no defensible estimates of the prevalence of alienation, so that all arguments about expected proportions of alienation in different populations are speculative.
2. Although it is commonly agreed that substantiated abuse and intimate-partner violence rule out a diagnosis of child alienation, there is little agreement about whether methods for categorically excluding cases of

family violence or controlling for this variable in the samples studied were valid or reliable.

3. Although there is empirical evidence that the symptoms of alienation cluster together to form a characteristic behavior pattern among some children and that alienating parental behaviors can be reliably measured, the development of standardized measures for these variables is in its infancy.

4. There is insufficient research and consensus on the etiology, progression, prognosis, and treatment of alienation. Although there are emerging findings on the personality profiles of aligned parents, the jury is still out on the extent to which alienated children are more clinically disturbed on standardized measures than nonalienated children within samples of chronically conflicted custody-disputing families. On the other hand, reports by adults who retrospectively identify having been subjected to a parent's alienating behavior as a child are correlated with a number of negative mental health measures.

5. Outcome evaluation of treatments of alienation is also in its infancy (as documented in Chapter 13). To date these studies have employed the weakest possible research design (i.e., a posttreatment evaluation designed by researcher-clinicians who derive small samples from their own caseloads). Few studies have used a comparison or control group or standardized measures of outcome. Further, these studies have included no systematic controls for many other variables that might have affected outcome (Saini et al., in press).

5.1. Implications of Limited Empirical Research for Clinical Practice

It is apparent there is a vast gap between the complex, nuanced clinical insights and conceptual models that inform clinicians' approach to alienation cases and the sparse empirical research directly addressing interventions for this population. To fill this gap, research findings from other behavioral science fields—developmental psychology, social psychology, personality and mental disorders, and theories of attachment and trauma—have been extrapolated and applied to the understanding and treatment of alienation. While this is a scientifically acceptable way of generating hypotheses about the problem, it does not constitute "evidence-based" support of the clinical theories and interventions espoused for alienation, including the ones formulated in this book. One can call interventions "evidence based" only when research questions have been systematically evaluated and replicated by high-quality research methods and the evidence directly supports a given practice or policy. At this time, this intervention can be described at best as "research informed" by related behavioral sciences. (The term "evidence informed" is used when systematic evaluations of the specific research question or treatment are unavailable but where accumulated findings from related bodies of evidence are logically extrapolated to inform decision-making.) Overcoming Barriers compares favorably with other treatment models relying on "speculative" evidence—that which is only weak, hypothetical, or preliminary because it represents relatively new, nonreplicated findings.

5.2. Threat of Scholar-Advocacy Bias

The OCB model is informed by the best and most recent empirical research evidence available, but as explained above, because the research base as a whole is methodologically weak, interpretation of this evidence and its application to individual families can be reframed and heavily biased by the advocacy positions of clinicians. In essence, clinicians decide which factors they want to highlight and which remain silent in the background. Clinical interpretations about an individual family that do not follow standard guidelines for systematic specialized assessments of intimate-partner violence, child abuse, psychological testing, and custody evaluations open the door to advocacy-biased interpretation from all perspectives.

Scholar-advocacy bias occurs when an expert bends (or spins) research evidence to fit an advocacy agenda at the expense of scientific accuracy, espousing speculative evidence as support for "evidence-based" practice. One can recognize such bias when the expert selectively references and overly simplifies research findings, states them as unconditional knowledge claims, does not acknowledge study limitations, and draws conclusions that exceed what the data will support— all in the service of advocacy goals. Bias is also characterized by "absolute" testimony often conveyed as numerous contradictory factoids. These include claims such as that a child is either alienated or abused, that all alienated children are or are not psychologically disturbed and need treatment, that teenagers should or should not be able to decide whether to have contact with a parent, that change of custody should always or never be an option, that rejected parents are or are not architects of their own fates, and that aligned or favored parents are always or never responsible for alienating their children. Scholar-advocacy bias should be suspected when one can guess the conclusions reached in a custody evaluation of a child who refuses to visit a parent simply by knowing who the evaluator is. Unbiased clinicians, on the other hand, are experienced but still prepared to be surprised by the findings.

6. SOME PRINCIPLES FOR ETHICAL INTERVENTIONS INTO ALIENATION CASES

The problem of children's strident rejection of a parent has been widely recognized in democratic societies across the globe, where it invokes ongoing debates about a myriad of human rights and ethical issues. These include whether one or both parents should be held accountable for the problem; parents' rights to contact versus children's rights to contact; whether the child's attorney should represent the child's "voice" or the child's "best interests"; how much authority family courts should have to order parents and children into therapy against their will; what is the appropriate use of contempt proceedings and sanctions for noncompliance with court orders; who should bear the burden of costly litigation and court-ordered interventions; what protection should be given to victims of abuse and violence; questions of violation of civil rights, gender bias, and procedural injustice in family courts; and what criteria to apply for court orders for enforced parent–child contact and change of custody. In sum, these cases pose many legal, ethical, and child welfare dilemmas and are among the most difficult for family courts and helping professionals to resolve to the satisfaction of all parties and for the well-being of children.

In that empirical research studies shed a relatively narrow shaft of light on many of these debates, ethical practice requires that the limits of scientific evidence be acknowledged. It serves neither our family court clients nor scientific progress itself to pretend we know more than we do. Instead of research evidence, decision-makers can bring to bear a number of principles about children's best interests that govern family law policy and authorize practice, including relevant laws, community norms, and family values, together with more mundane criteria about what is expedient, less costly, and feasible. These rationales for everyday family court decisions and clinical practice can and should be articulated and separated from claims of research evidence. For example, rather than stating that "research says that a child needs two parents," the clinician can point out that "without evidence to the contrary the law assumes that frequent and continuing contact with both parents is in children's best interest" and ask "how is that unfair?" Rather than invoking the authority of social science, one can draw upon the family's own values and religious beliefs: "Children should be taught to obey adults and honor their parents"; "Human decency requires every person to be treated with dignity and respect"; "It seems only fair to give him a second chance"; and "There is no harm in trying X."

6.1. Towards a Calculus of Principles for Justifying Treatment Mandates in Parent-Child Contact Disputes

Legal principles and precedents provide the framework for intervention with families, and when those principles and precedents are unclear, family courts increasingly turn to social science for direction in determining what is in "the best interests" of children. When science cannot yet address what is in the child's best interests, the default assumption is a matter of values. With respect to the problem of alienated children, where research evidence is thin, parent–child contact is resisted, and treatments are refused, how can intervention measures be imposed on unwilling individuals on the basis of values? To address this question, it seems reasonable to begin with the basic ethical edict of "*Do no harm*". Beyond that *the least restrictive intervention measure that protects the safety and promotes the well-being of children can clearly be mandated.* Table 14.1 outlines a way of responsibly justifying mandated treatments and more intrusive interventions including court orders for restricted visits, parenting counseling, treatment of any kind, case management, and change of custody.

Table 14-1. Principled Decision-Making: A Framework for Imposing Unwanted Interventions, Custody Change and Mandated Treatment on Families with Parent-Child Contact Problems

Goal Priority	Criteria Justifying Intervention Measures
1. Protect safety and well-being of the child SOME MEASURES TO ACHIEVE GOAL 1. Suspend parental contact or impose high security supervision for the disturbed, abusive parent, Give decision-making authority and child care (custody) to the non-abusive parent. Mandate participation in corrective, rehabilitative treatments as pre-requisites for parent-child contact. Consider therapy for child. Monitor family's progress.	There is substantiated child neglect; emotional, physical, or sexual abuse; or exposure to intimate-partner violence, or abduction by parent. OR Parent has untreated substance abuse, mental illness, or psychotic delusions or sociopathic beliefs and behaviors about the other parent or child (e.g., threat of harm or abduction). OR Child is emotionally and behaviorally disturbed, has conduct problems, or engages in risky behaviors without either parent's intervention.
2. Protect parent's right of access to childs SOME MEASURES TO ACHIEVE GOAL 2. Parent-child contact may be restricted, monitored, or conditional upon participation in educational, counselling, or treatments programs, and continued evidence of problem parent's behaviour change. Sole authority for and care of the children remain with the non-problematic parent.	There is no prior abuse or exposure as described above. OR Parent is being held accountable for above abuse or exposure and has demonstrated some capacity for repair and reform at a pace tolerable to the child. OR Parent has had no prior relationship with the child.
3. Promote and protect autonomy of parent–child relationship. SOME MEASURES TO ACHIEVE GOAL 3. Appoint a coparenting co-ordinator; or consider a parallel parenting plan with a fixed time-sharing schedule and structured rules that limit the need for coparental communication. Each parent cares for their children as they see fit, without interference from restricted access or mandated treatment	In addition to above: Parent demonstrates capacity for warm-authoritative parent–child relationship or has demonstrated insight into and capacity for change. AND Parent respects other parent's rights and appropriately promotes and refrains from interference in child's relationship with other parent.

4. Protect autonomy of family as a group.

SOME MEASURES TO ACHIEVE
   GOAL 4.
Allow self-determination in parenting
   arrangements. Shared parenting,
   treatments and interventions are
   voluntary and require the consent
   of the parties.

In addition to all above: Both parents
demonstrate capacity to communicate and
cooperate with each other regarding the
children.

Ethical principle: "Do no harm"

Current treatment/intervention/custody
and visit order is ineffective or appears
iatrogenic; problem is worsening (e.g.
persistent or increased child distress and
cost); unresolved differences exist within
team of service providers.

The rationale for unwanted treatment and intrusive intervention with families where children refuse or resist contact with one parent can be derived from a prioritized list of four explicit intervention goals:

Highest Priority #1: Protect the safety and well-being of the child
Priority #2. Protect a parent's right of access to the child.
Priority #3. Protect and promote the autonomy of parent–child relationships,
Lowest Priority #4. Protect the autonomy of the family as a group.

These goals can be shared with all family members, together with the following decision-making rules that resolve conflicting goals in predictable ways. Begin with the plan of achieving all four goals. When this is not possible, relinquish the lower-priority goal(s) after providing reasonable opportunities for each parent to demonstrate his or her ability to meet the criteria. Helping parents meet the criteria for a prioritized goal becomes the therapeutic task for the family in question. Note that in Table 14.1 the responsibility to "do no harm" is an overarching ethical principle, to be checked at every level when imposing an intervention.

6.2. Honoring Parents' Voices

The decision-making rules outlined in Table 14.1 imply that until a parent is accountable for his or her abuse, interventions will not protect his or her right of access to the child. Access to the child *and* autonomy within the child–parent relationship will be provided by the intervention only when the parent demonstrates a history of warm-authoritative parenting skills *and* actively respects and promotes the other parent's appropriate role in the child's life. Thus the parent who is rated more highly on these criteria is provided more access opportunities and autonomy within the parent–child relationship. If both parents are able to achieve this level, then a parallel-parenting plan is optimal. When there are large discrepancies in the extent to which the parents have met criteria, sole custody is a more obvious choice. Coparenting plans are appropriate when both parents have met the criteria for all four goals—in which case no unwanted interventions are needed.

6.3. Hearing the Child's Voice

Whereas law defines parents' rights and responsibilities relative to those of their offspring, the age at which youngsters will actually be given significant choice about matters that involve their participation varies with custom, culture, and fam ily values. Parental disagreement creates a power vacuum that the child's voice can fill prematurely. Although this is obviously problematic for younger children, it is not necessarily so for older teenagers who are approaching the age of majority. The following decision-making principle can reward mature and responsible behavior:

> *Interventions should take minors' opinions and preference into account to the extent they are approaching the age of majority; are cognitively mature; and demonstrate accurate interpersonal perceptions, good judgment, and coping skills. Additional criteria include the absence of social, emotional, or behavioral difficulties or conduct problems and expectable school and work performance.*

7. SUMMARY

This book has addressed what to do about one of the most vexing problems in family law—children who resist and refuse contact with one parent—by bringing to bear the accumulated wisdom and experience of clinicians and the best available social science research. The product is a promising, innovative, and powerful new model of intervention. Even so, the interventions described herein represent work in progress. Development, refinement, and change are fully expected. In this concluding chapter, a set of prioritized goals and principles have been proposed to guide ethical and informed decision-making with respect to mandated treatment interventions until more definitive direction from the law and accumulated social science research becomes available. In this endeavor, what will best protect the safety and promote the well-being of the child is the goal of highest priority and one that will never be abandoned.

REFERENCES

Saini, Michael; Johnston, Janet; Fidler, Barbara, & Bala, Nicholas. (2016). Empirical studies of alienation: An update. In Leslie Drozd & Michael Saini (Editors) Second Edition. *Parenting Plan Evaluations: Applied Research for the Family Court*. New York: Oxford University Press.

Abduction risk, 7, 36b, 83, 113
Absolute, dichotomous thinking, 66
Active alienators, 18
Active listening, 184
Activere behandlugen, 153
Active therapy, 4
Adultification, 33, 175
Aerobic exercise, 95
Affinity, 16–17, 32, 277
Affirmation box, 141, 142
Aftercare, 6, 22–23
    East Group and, 188–89
    limited options for, 147
    referral challenges, 139–40
    referral process, 237–38
    West Group and, 203–5
Ainsworth, Mary, 67
Albertson-Kelly, J., 74
Alcohol abuse, 19, 228
Alienation, 1–2, 4, 13–14, 15–16, 307–13
    active alienators, 18
    affinity and alignment as risk factors
        for, 17–18
    behavioral manifestations, by level of
        severity, 29–32b
    behaviors and perceptions associated
        with, 58–62
    case illustration of, 308–9
    characteristics of, 18–20
    conceptual formulation of the
        problem, 308–10
    definition of alienated child, 18
    expert testimony about, 64
    features of the clinical
        formulation, 310–13

gender of the alienating parent, 173, 279
interventions for mild and moderate
    cases of, 40b
interventions for severe and moderate
    cases of, 37–39
justified rejection differentiated from,
    17–18, 21–22
in mixed/hybrid cases, 21
motivations for attitudes and
    beliefs, 311
naive alienators, 18
narcissism and, 114
obsessed alienators, 18
parental alienating behaviors, 66, 67, 78
parental strategies used in, 176
parent responsible for in OBFC
    evaluation, 279
principles for ethical interventions,
    320–24, 322–23t
research on, 318–20
screening tools for, 42n8
significant others' influence on, 313
source, type, and veracity of
    beliefs, 310–11
transmission of attitudes and beliefs, 312
whole-family approach to, 32
Alignment, 16–17, 277
All-or-nothing thinking, 66, 181–82
American Camp Association, 154
American Therapeutic Recreation
    Association (ATRA), 94
Anger, 214
Animal-assisted therapies, 83, 102, 254.
    See also Equine-assisted therapy
Anticipatory anxiety, 19

Antisocial personality disorder, 113, 114–15
Anxiety, 214–15, 256, 257
    anticipatory, 19
    five factors maintaining, 214
    justified rejection and, 18
Apologies, 7, 138, 228
Arbitrators, 33
Association of Family and Conciliation Courts (AFCC), 119–20, 143
Attachment-based reunification therapy, 78–81, 81t
Attachment history, 67–68
Attitudinal dimension of conflict, 116
Attorneys, 24, 26, 116–17, 132, 143, 148, 187, 287, 321
Authoritarian parenting style, 6, 65, 98, 111, 213, 219

Bailey, Rebecca, 3, 83, 253
Baker, A., 66, 77–78, 114, 176, 279–80
Baker Alienation Questionnaire (BAQ), 279–80
Bala, N., 28, 69, 176, 277
Behavior therapy, 243
"Best interests of children" standard, 321
Bias blind spot, 14
"Big Show" at OBFC, 141, 166, 209–10n3
Birnbaum, R., 69
Black, D. A., 120
Black-and-white, polarized thinking, 4, 17, 35b, 97, 107, 115, 174, 181–82
Blaming, 182
Blane, Carole, 4, 94, 254
"Blind taste test" exercise, 101–2
Borderline personality traits/disorder, 78, 80, 107, 118, 174
    defined, 113
    MMPI profile and, 110
Bottinelli, J., 173
Bottom-up processing, 93
Boundaries, 21, 134, 184–86
Bowlby, John, 67
Breach-and-repair sequences, 80
Bronfenbrenner, U., 215
Burkard, B., 74
Burnette, M., 113

CAGE, 42n8
Campbell, L. E. G., 107
Camp director at OBFC, 157–58
Case management, coordinated, 259–62
Child abuse or neglect, 7, 13, 15, 35b, 37, 228. See also Unsubstantiated allegations of abuse
    justified rejection and, 17–18
    OCB-based outpatient approach and, 255
    research findings on, 318–19
Child custody. See Custody
Child protection agencies, 23, 26, 35b, 38, 253
Children. See also Common Ground Center Family Camp
    ages of at OBFC, 137, 215
    attachment-based therapy for, 81t
    behavioral manifestations of alienation, by level of severity, 29–32b
    behaviors and perceptions associated with alienation, 58–59
    characteristics of at OBFC, 134
    cognitive-behavioral techniques for, 79t
    definition of alienated, 18
    equine-assisted therapy and, 100
    experiences at OBFC, 291–93
    family therapy goals and interventions for, 75–76t
    hearing the voices of, 324
    inappropriate empowerment of, 100, 227
Children's Hope Scale, 155
Childress, Craig, 78–80
Circle at OBFC, 166, 198
Client-centered therapy, 92
Clinical decision-making, 2–3, 13–62
    based on nature and severity of the problem, 28–39
    billing practices in, 26
    clinical intake in (see Clinical intake)
    differentiation of contact problems in, 14–22
    possible hypotheses in, 14
    preliminary screening in, 23–26, 25b
Clinical intake, 26–28
    areas of inquiry, 27–28b

in OCB-based outpatient approach, 244–46
in OCB program, 136–37, 141–42, 223
parties involved in, 26
process of, 26–27
Clinical intake questionnaire, 47–57
Clinicians. *See also* Countertransference/therapeutic relationship
experience and training required for, 317–18
intergroup tensions between, 225–26
tool and resource kit of, 251–52
Closing circle at OBFC, 140
Cluster A personality disorders, 112–13
Cluster B personality disorders, 112, 113–15
Cluster C personality disorders, 112, 115
Coaching, 72, 73, 227, 245, 250
Coercive controlling violence, 40–41n2
Cognitive-behavioral therapy (CBT), 4, 73, 181, 263, 315
goals and techniques, 77–78, 79t
OCB approach and, 133, 243
Cognitive biases, 14, 66–67, 174, 214
Cognitive distortions, 35b, 66–67, 100, 120, 133, 214
in Common Ground members, 217, 218
in East Group members, 181–82
Cognitive level, 66–67
Cognitive restructuring, 72, 73, 77
Common Ground Center Family Camp, 6–7, 132, 160, 197, 211–21, 253
children's dilemmas at, 212–15
described, 156
goals of, 138, 215, 216b
objectives for children in, 216b
stages of the group process, 216–19
structure of, 138
Communication skills, 3, 4, 38, 184
Compartmentalizing, 199
Confidentiality, 187, 197
Confirmatory bias, 14
Conflict-instigated violence, 41n2
Cooking and culinary activities, 91, 100–102. *See also* Nourishment/food at OBFC
Coordinated case management, 259–62

Coparenting, 6, 7, 316. *See also* Parallel parenting
East Group work with, 186–87
enabling parental re-engagement, 231–33
interventions for, 231–37
litigation contrasted with, 203t
outpatient therapy for, 74
West Group work with, 197–98, 202, 205–6
Cost analysis (OBFC program), 287
Countertransference/therapeutic relationship, 318. *See also* Clinicians
common patterns in, 119
definitions of, 108–10
high-conflict divorce and, 115–16
litigation, court involvement, and, 116–17, 120
managing among teams, 121–23
peer consultation and, 121
personality disorders and, 112–15
self-examination and, 121
Court orders, 33–34, 82, 223, 246–49, 261
checklist for, 248b
terms to be included in, 34
ultimate sanctions for violation of, 1
Court system involvement
as a risk factor for contact problems, 70
split alliances resulting from, 97
the therapeutic relationship and, 116–17, 120
Criminal charges, outstanding, 36b
Custody, shared, 193, 209n1, 233
Custody evaluations, 195, 245
Custody evaluators, 23, 26, 223, 253
Custody litigation. *See* Litigation
Custody reversal, 1–2, 37–38, 83

Darnall, D., 18, 66
Debriefings, 122, 141, 257–58
Decision Tree to Assess Alienating Parental Behaviors, 42n8
Defense mechanisms, 65, 68, 97, 110, 111, 114, 120, 173
Demandingness, 6, 213, 219
Denial, 68, 110, 114

Dependent personality disorder, 115
Depression, 18
Desensitization. *See* Systematic
 desensitization
Deutsch, Robin M., 3, 4, 6, 7, 8, 77, 84, 102,
 134, 243
*Diagnostic and Statistical Manual of Mental
 Disorders*, 112
Didactic training, 143
Disengaged parents, 6, 213
Doi Fick, L., 213
Domain (conflict dimension), 116
Domestic violence. *See* Intimate partner/
 domestic violence
Drawing exercises, 180–81
Drozd, Leslie, 74, 121
Drug abuse. *See* Substance abuse

East Group, 5, 137, 171–92, 197, 253
 adult-child boundaries addressed
  in, 184–86
 aftercare for, 188–89
 cognitive distortions addressed
  in, 181–82
 coparenting work in, 186–87
 dealing with thoughts, feelings, and
  beliefs in, 183–84
 defining and reframing objectives
  for, 180
 description of parents in, 173–77
 family narratives of, 180–81
 goals for, 179–80
 group closure for, 189
 identifying alternatives to litigation
  for, 187–88
 improving coping skills in, 183
 intergroup tensions between
  clinicians, 225–26
 learning listening and communication
  skills in, 184
 model limitations and future
  directions, 189–90
 psychoeducation for, 183
 resistance to OBFC program in, 171–72
 structure and format of, 178–79
 West Group and, 194
Emotional reasoning, 182
Empathy, 4, 114, 218

Enmeshment, 6, 21, 33, 73, 98, 164, 212,
 213, 219, 312
Equine-assisted therapy (EAT), 83, 91,
 94, 96–100
 education, interpersonal learning,
  and, 98–100
 engagement in, 97–98
 research on, 96
 selection of the horse in, 96–97
Ethics of intervention, 320–24
Evaluation of OBFC. *See also* Research
 cost analysis planning, 287
 design choice, 285–86
 developing a roadmap for, 281–83
 evaluation matrix, 299–300
 logic model in (*see* Logic model)
 measuring strained parent-child
  relationships, 283–85
 need for a common approach to, 281–87
 non-OCB interventions compared
  with, 278–80
 outcome, 282, 283, 284*t*
 previous, 280
 process, 282
 program fidelity assessment,
  286–87, 304–6
 results of, 287–93
 review of studies, 278–81
 summary of current evidence, 280–81
Evidence-based interventions, 319, 320
Evidence-informed interventions, 319–20
Existential therapy, 92
Experiential therapies, 3, 8, 91–106.
  See also Cooking and culinary
  activities; Equine-assisted therapy;
  Nature; Play; Recreational activities
 in family therapy, 92–102
 in OCB-based outpatient
  approach, 253–59
 in outpatient settings, 102
 theoretical influences on, 92
Expert testimony, 64
Exposure therapy, 19, 77, 95, 133, 256, 257

"Faking good" on psychological tests, 111
Families Moving Forward, 40*b*
Family-based interventions, 13–127.
  See also Clinical decision-making;

Experiential therapies; Outpatient
approaches; Perfect storm
Family Bridges, 38, 245
evaluation of, 82–83, 84–85, 279
goals of, 82
Family camp model, 155
Family narratives
East Group, 180–81
West Group, 200–202
Family play. *See* Play
Family Reflections Reunification Program,
38, 83–85, 280
Family systems theory/therapy, 3–4, 32, 93,
133, 145
Family therapy, 24, 243, 244
differing terminology used for,
41–42n7, 263n1
experiential therapies in, 92–102
goals and modalities of, 72–74, 75–76*t*
integrative, 120
options for less severe cases, 40*b*
whole-family approach (*see* Whole-
family approach)
Family therapy intervention
agreement, 269–76
Fathers
as alienating parents, 279
as rejected parents, 194–95
Favored parents, 1–2, 6, 7, 19, 20, 22, 32,
37–39, 71, 307, 314
attachment-based therapy for, 81*t*
behaviors and perceptions associated
with alienation, 59–61
cognitive-behavioral techniques
for, 79*t*
dyadic work with child and, 74, 185
equine-assisted therapy and, 97–99
family therapy goals and interventions
for, 73, 74, 75–76*t*
in high-conflict situations, 69–70
justified rejection and, 18
at OBFC, 134–35, 140, 141, 164, 166–67,
226–27, 232, 233, 234–35 (*see also*
East Group)
OCB-based outpatient approach for,
255–56, 257–58
parenting styles and skills of, 65–66
personality disorders in, 115, 173

Fidelity assessment (OBFC program),
286–87, 304–6
Fidler, Barbara J., 2, 6, 8, 28, 102, 176, 277
Final circle at OBFC, 141
Flexible thinking, 3, 38
Forging Families' Futures, 84
Freud, Sigmund, 109
Fried, C., 287
Friedlander, S., 77, 81
Friedman, M., 116

Garber, B. D., 67, 77, 80–81, 174–75
Gardner, Richard, 14, 29*b*, 30*b*, 31*b*, 63,
173, 278
Gatekeeping, 134
facilitative, 41n5
protective, 131
restrictive, 17, 41n5, 131, 173, 176,
195, 255
Gendered narratives, 13
Gestalt therapy, 92
Gil, E., 92
Gordon, R. M., 111, 173
Greenberg, L. R., 213
Green Shirts, 161, 164, 165, 166, 167, 168,
224, 235
constant supervision provided by,
163, 291
qualities and roles of, 158–59
"Groove, The" (OBFC camp area), 164
Group cohesion, 179
Guardians ad litem, 23, 223, 253

Hierarchical Decision Tree for
Alienation, 42n8
High-conflict family dynamics
OBFC therapeutic milieu and,
155–56, 167–68
outpatient approaches to, 69–70
the therapeutic relationship and, 115–16
typical presentation of, 131
Hiking, 95
Histrionic personality traits/disorder, 107,
113, 174
Holding environment, 95
Hope, 154–55
Humanistic therapy, 92
Hybrid cases. *See* Mixed or hybrid cases

"I Don't Want to Choose" program, 77–78
Immersion training, 143
Inability to disconfirm, 182
Infantilization, 33
Informed-consent service agreements,
        32, 246–49
Insabella, G., 68
Intake. *See* Clinical intake
Integrated problem-focused therapy, 244
Integrative family therapy, 120
Intensive immersion programs,
        144–46, 147
Intensive interventions, 32, 40*b*, 244
    OCB approach to, 144–46, 147
    programs for, 82–85
Internal working models (IWMs), 67
Intimate-partner/domestic violence, 7,
        13, 15, 36, 117, 228, 232. *See also*
        Unsubstantiated allegations of abuse
    alienating parent as perpetrator of, 19
    as a contraindication for OCB,
        141, 148n1
    justified rejection and, 17–18
    research findings on, 318–19
    screening tools for, 42n8
    typology of, 40–41n2

Johnston, Janet R., 15, 18, 63–64, 65, 68,
        107, 110, 115–16
Judge, Abigail M., 3, 4, 6, 253, 254
Justified rejection
    alienation differentiated from,
        17–18, 21–22
    characteristics of, 17–18
    as a contraindication for OCB, 148n1
    interventions for mild and moderate
        cases of, 40*b*
    interventions for severe and moderate
        cases of, 36–37
    in mixed/hybrid cases, 21
    whole-family approach to, 32

Kelly, Joan, 15, 18, 63–64, 122
Kumar, S., 278–79

Labeling, 182
Lawyers. *See* Attorneys
Learning theory, 19

Lebow, J. L., 120
Letter-writing exercise, 138, 206–7, 217–18
Liebman, R. E., 113
Listening, active, 184
Litigation
    chronic, 15
    coparenting contrasted with, 203*t*
    identifying alternatives to, 187–88
    personality disorders in sample
        population, 110–11
    the therapeutic relationship and,
        116–17, 120
Little, T. D., 68
Logic model, 283, 285, 298
"Lost in a Shopping Mall" example, 183

Magnification, 66
Mandatory child protection reports, 23
Media-based interventions, 236–37
Mediator's Assessment of Safety Issues and
        Concerns (MASIC), 42n8
Meditation, 93, 263
Memory, 100–101, 174, 183, 218, 316
Mental illness, 7, 19, 37, 38, 141,
        148n1, 173
Mild alienation
    behavioral manifestations of, 29–30*b*
    interventions for, 40*b*
Mild contact resistance, interventions
        for, 32–34
Mild justified rejection, interventions
        for, 40*b*
Milieu therapy. *See* Therapeutic milieu
Mindfulness, 93, 95, 263
Minnesota Multiphasic Personality
        Inventory (MMPI-2), 68, 110–11
Mirror neurons, 217
Mixed or hybrid cases
    characteristics of, 20–22
    interventions for, 32, 40*b*
    OBFC and, 135
MMPI. *See* Minnesota Multiphasic
        Personality Inventory
Moderate alienation
    behavioral manifestations of, 30–31*b*
    interventions for, 37–39, 40*b*
Moderate contact resistance, interventions
        for, 32–34

Moderate justified rejection, interventions
    for, 36–37, 40*b*
Moral treatment, 153
Moran, John, 3
Mothers
    as alienating parents, 279
    as favored parents, 173
    as rejected parents, 195
Multifactorial model of contact problems,
    15, 15*f*, 63–64

Naive alienators, 18
Narcissistic personality traits/disorder, 68,
    78, 80, 107, 111, 118, 311
    in favored parents, 65, 173
    MMPI profile and, 110
    therapeutic relationship and, 113–14
Narrative therapy, 244, 263
Nature, 94–95, 254
Neural exercises, play as, 93
Nourishment/food at OBFC, 162. *See also*
    Cooking and culinary activities
Nurse at OBFC, 159

OBFC. *See* Overcoming Barriers
    Family Camp
Obsessed alienators, 18
Obsessive-compulsive personality
    disorder, 115
OCB approach. *See* Overcoming Barriers
    approach
OCB-based outpatient approach, 8,
    102, 243–76
    case examples of, 258–59, 261–62
    case management and team approach
        in, 259–62
    contracting in, 246–49
    experiential and recreational activities
        in, 253–59
    goals, treatment plan, and clinician's
        tools, 250–52
    initial interviews in, 249–50
    rule-out criteria for, 246*b*
    screening and intake in, 244–46
    whole-family approach in, 252–53
Olesen, N. W., 121
One-way mirror technique, 256–57
Outcome evaluation, 282, 283, 284*t*

Outpatient approaches, 3, 4, 63–81
    definitions and practice
        standards, 70–71
    experiential therapies and, 102
    goals of therapy, 71–72, 72*t*
    for mild and moderate contact
        resistance, 32
    OCB model for (*see* OCB-based
        outpatient approach)
    treatment modalities, 72–81
Output performance, 282
Overcoming Barriers (OCB) approach,
    2, 3–9, 83, 91, 99, 131–334. *See also*
    OCB-based outpatient approach;
    Overcoming Barriers Family Camp
    affordability of, 317
    clinical experience/training required
        for, 317–18
    conceptualization of, 132
    contraindications for participation in,
        141, 148n1, 173
    conundrums of clinical practice, 317–18
    essence of, 146
    goals of, 135–37
    important components of, 313–18
    for intensive interventions, 144–46, 147
    key elements of, 132–33
    limitations of, 146–47
    parenting skills guide, 244
    scholar-advocacy bias risk in, 320
    sustaining long-term change and, 317
    theoretical influences on, 133
Overcoming Barriers Family Camp
    (OBFC), 3–6, 32, 40*b*, 84, 95, 122,
    136, 152–242, 277–306. *See also*
    Common Ground Center Family
    Camp; East Group; Evaluation
    of OBFC; Therapeutic milieu;
    West Group
    accommodations and cabin assignments
        at, 163–64
    balancing activities and connection
        in, 161
    characteristics of families at, 134–35
    children's experiences at, 291–93
    clinical work with children, 229–31
    closing the clinical work, 237–38
    coparenting interventions, 231–37

Overcoming Barriers Family Camp
    (OBFC) (*Cont.*)
  cost of, 4
  didactic and immersion training in, 143
  director of, 157–58
  evolution of, 141–46
  hypotheses guiding
    interventions, 223–24
  key questions remaining about, 9
  nourishment at, 162
  nurse at, 159
  origins of, 132–33
  parent-child reconnection
    interventions, 234–37
  parents' experiences at, 288–91
  parent survey, 301–3
  photographer at, 160
  physical space of, 160–61
  planning and support for
    interventions, 224–26
  preparation for parent-child
    interventions, 226–29
  psychological benefits of the
    experience, 153–56
  removal from family's typical
    environment, 161–62
  roles at, 157–60
  rules and expectations at, 162–63, 177
  safety at, 161
  staff of (*see* Green Shirts)
  structure of the program, 137–41
  summary of interventions and
    agreements, 240–42
  a typical day at, 164–67
Overgeneralization, 66, 182

Parallel parenting, 6, 7–8, 202, 203,
    233–34, 316. *See also* Coparenting
Parallel play, 236
Paranoid personality disorder, 112–13, 311
Parentification, 33, 174–75
Parenting coordination, 8, 203–5
Parenting coordinators, 6, 23, 33, 238, 253,
    260, 261
Parents. *See also* Coparenting; Fathers;
    Favored parents; Mothers; Parallel
    parenting; Rejected parents
  honoring the voices of, 323–24

OBFC experiences of, 288–91
OBFC survey of, 301–3
parenting styles and skills of, 65–66
Perfect storm, 3, 15, 107–27, 308
  components of, 111–19
  defined, 108
  strategies for managing, 119–23
  vignette illustrating, 118
Personality disorders, 36*b*, 111–15. *See also*
    specific disorders
  alienation and, 19, 37, 38
  in custody-litigating samples, 110–11
  in East Group, 173
  impact of presence and level of, 311–12
  as a risk factor for contact problems, 68
  the therapeutic relationship and, 112–15
Phobia-like responses, 19, 77, 95, 256
Photographer at OBFC, 160
Play, 92–94, 236
Polak, Shely, 3
Polarized thinking. *See* Black-and-white,
    polarized thinking
Post-traumatic stress disorder
    (PTSD), 18, 37
Preferred parents. *See* Favored parents
Prevalence
  of contact resistance, 63, 131
  of personality disorders, 112
Primitive defense mechanisms. *See*
    Defense mechanisms
Problem-solving skills, 3, 38, 218–19, 229
Process evaluation, 282
Projection, 68, 110, 111, 114
Proust phenomenon, 101
Pruett, M. K., 68
Psychoeducation, 72, 73, 243, 263
  for Common Ground members, 6, 218
  for East Group, 183
Psychopathology, 68
PTSD. *See* Post-traumatic stress disorder

Rand, Deidre, 82, 279
Rand, Randy, 82
Randomized controlled trials (RCTs), 285
Realistic estrangement. *See* Justified
    rejection
Reality-testing, 316
Reay, K. M., 83, 84–85, 280

Recency bias, 14
Recreational activities, 4, 8, 140
    in OCB-based outpatient
        approach, 253–59
    types and benefits of, 94–95
"Red light, green light" game, 94
Reflexive thought, 17
Reframing, 3, 72, 100, 180
Rejected parents, 4, 6, 7, 21, 22, 32, 37–39,
        68, 71, 307, 314–15
    attachment-based therapy for, 81t
    behaviors and perceptions associated
        with alienation, 61–62
    childrens' reasons for resisting contact
        with, 227–29
    cognitive-behavioral techniques for, 79t
    dyadic work with child and, 74
    equine-assisted therapy and, 97–99
    Family Reflections program for, 83–84
    family therapy goals and interventions
        for, 73, 74, 75–76t
    in high-conflict situations, 69–70
    MMPI profiles of, 110–11
    at OBFC, 134–35, 140, 141, 164, 166–67,
        227–29, 232, 233, 234–37 (see also
        West Group)
    OCB-based outpatient approach for,
        245, 255–57
    parenting styles and skills of, 65–66
    personality disorders in, 115
Relaxation techniques, 77, 256
Repetition bias, 14
Research. See also Evaluation of OBFC
    on alienation, 318–20
    on equine-assisted therapy, 96
Research-informed interventions, 319–20
Responsiveness, 6, 213, 219
Restraining orders, 36b, 232
Risk factors for contact problems, 65–70
    attachment history and prior
        relationship, 67–68
    cognitive level and distortions, 66–67
    court system involvement, 70
    interparental conflict, 69–70
    parental alienating behaviors, 66, 67
    parenting styles and skills, 65–66
    personality disorders and
        psychopathology, 68

Role corruption, 33, 164
Role play, 84, 182, 184, 185, 217, 218
Role reversal, 21, 98, 134, 175, 312
Role switching, 84
Rorschach test, 111, 114
Roseby, V. R., 107
Rossberg, J. I., 109
Rules at OBFC, 162–63, 177

Safety at OBFC, 161
Saini, Michael, 28, 135, 176, 318
Satir, Virginia, 155
Satir Family Camp, 155
Schizoid personality disorder, 112
Schizotypal personality disorder, 112
Schnider, R., 213
Scholar-advocacy bias, 14, 320
Selective abstraction, 66
Selective attention, 217, 218
Sensorimotor therapy, 93
Separation anxiety, 16
Separation-instigated violence, 41n2
Severe alienation
    behavioral manifestations of, 31–32b
    interventions for, 37–39
Severe justified rejection, interventions
        for, 36–37
Shared custody, 193, 209n1, 233
Significant others
    family therapy goals and interventions
        for, 75–76t
    influence of, 313
Single-family outpatient model, 32
Situational couple violence, 41n2
Situation room at OBFC, 224
Smart Parenting, 278–79
Sobol, B., 92
Sociopathic personality disorder, 311
Socratic questioning, 77
Solution-focused therapy, 244, 263
Somatic interventions, 93
Source bias, 14
Split alliances, 97, 120
Splitting, 68, 110, 111, 113, 114
Stable Paths, 38, 40b, 245
Stepparents, 26, 32, 70, 139, 195
Stoffey, R., 173
String-holding exercise, 93

Substance abuse, 7, 19, 36b, 141,
    148n1, 228
Suggestibility, 183
Sullivan, Matthew J., 3, 4, 5, 7, 122,
    134, 280
Sullivan, Tyler, 4, 94, 254
Systematic desensitization, 7, 19, 77, 95,
    133, 152, 167, 185, 256, 257, 263,
    263n4, 315

Tactics (conflict dimension), 116
"Tattoo" booth, 218
Team approach, 3, 8
    aftercare referrals and, 139–40
    countertransference management
        and, 121–23
    importance and value of, 140, 145, 315
    in OCB-based outpatient
        programs, 259–62
"Tender years doctrine," 173
Therapeutic alliance, 97, 120–21, 222
Therapeutic milieu, 4–5, 94, 152–68, 314
    defined, 152
    fostering healthy connections in, 167–68
    history of and relevance to OBFC, 153
    key components of, 160–67
    structure, principles, and goals
        of, 156–57
Therapist reactions. See
    Countertransference/therapeutic
    relationship
Toren, P., 280
Transitioning Families, 38, 40b, 83, 91, 95,
    96, 100, 245
Trauma, 18, 255
"Tribal warfare," 15, 142

Unsubstantiated allegations of abuse,
    35b, 109, 120–21, 190, 201, 239n2,
    255–56, 258

Walking, 95
Walters, M. G., 77, 81
Ward, Peggie, 2, 3, 4, 5, 7, 8, 84, 102,
    134, 243
Warshak, Richard, 18, 82, 83, 84–85,
    173, 279
Weitzman, J., 77, 256, 257
West Group, 5–6, 137, 193–210,
    217–18, 253
    aftercare for, 203–5
    characteristics of members, 194–97
    coparenting work in, 197–98,
        202, 205–6
    description of intervention, 197–99
    essential components of intervention,
        199–209
    expectations of, 193, 196
    family narratives of, 200–202
    group closure for, 208–9
    intergroup tensions between
        clinicians, 225–26
    parent-child relationship focus
        in, 206–8
    reconnection work in, 208
    support for members' goals in, 205–9
"What ifs," 182
Whole-family approach, 8, 39
    goals, indications, and contraindications
        for, 34–36b
    for mild and moderate contact
        resistance, 32–34
    in OCB-based outpatient
        approach, 252–53
    in OCB program, 135
Wilderness therapy, 95
Williams, T. Y., 68
Wishful thinking bias, 14
Wolfson, Daniel, 4, 254

Yoga, 165

CPSIA information can be obtained
at www.ICGtesting.com
Printed in the USA
BVOW03s1551240817
492979BV00003B/7/P

9 780190 235208